GARIBALDI AND THE MAKING OF ITALY

Liberta non tradisce i Volenti

G. Garibaldi

"LIBERTY DOES NOT FAIL THOSE WHO ARE DETERMINED TO HAVE IT"

GARIBALDI

AND

THE MAKING OF ITALY

JUNE—NOVEMBER, 1860

BY

GEORGE MACAULAY TREVELYAN

REGIUS PROFESSOR OF MODERN HISTORY IN THE
UNIVERSITY OF CAMBRIDGE

WITH FOUR MAPS AND NUMEROUS ILLUSTRATIONS

NEW IMPRESSION

LONGMANS, GREEN AND CO. LTD.

39 PATERNOSTER ROW, LONDON, E.C. 4
NEW YORK, TORONTO
CALCUTTA, BOMBAY AND MADRAS

1928

BIBLIOGRAPHICAL NOTE.

First Edition August 1911.
Reprinted October 1911, November 1911,
January 1912, December 1913,
April 1919, April 1926.
New and Cheaper Impression May 1928.

Made in Great Britain

TO

C. P. T. AND M. K. T.

PREFACE

A PREVIOUS volume entitled 'Garibaldi and the Thousand' described the landing at Marsala and the capture of Palermo by that handful of men in May, 1860. The present volume traces the course of larger military, diplomatic, and political events by which the original achievement of the Thousand led in six months to the formation of the Italian Kingdom.

I have once more endeavoured, in footnotes and appendices connected with a full bibliography, to indicate to the curious my authority for any statement made in the text. But in this as in previous volumes, considerations of time and space have made it impossible to explain the nature, limit, and degree of the value to be attached in each case to each of the authorities cited in a given note. And if any student ever has enough enthusiasm to visit various public and private libraries, and so verify all the references which I have given for any one important event—*e.g.* the Battle of Milazzo, or Garibaldi's entry into Naples—he will find that the authorities which I have cited contradict each other on minor points. Volumes would be required to explain in every case why I have preferred one authority on one small point, and another on another. In a few important cases I have given my reasons for preferring one authority to another (*e.g.* Appendix G), but more often I have merely given a list of the authorities the collation of which has led me to the conclusions recorded in the text.

As regards the estimates of the number of troops engaged or losses suffered in a campaign or battle, they are based on reports or calculations made by officers in command of the troops enumerated, never on the impressions of the opposite side which are always worthless as evidence—except, indeed, in the case of the capture of prisoners, for it is possible to count the enemy's forces when you have captured them, though not before.

I have used the Neapolitan military sources, particularly the documents printed in *Franci* for the Volturno campaign, more than has hitherto been customary with historians. In the light of the reports by Von Mechel, Ruiz, and the Swiss officers, material modification is necessary in the accounts usually given of the operations round Maddaloni and Castel Morrone on October 1. Otherwise the commonly received story of the campaign of 1860 appears to me to stand the test of careful scrutiny.

It has been a particular pleasure to me to unfold for the first time the most intimate workings of British diplomacy at the decisive crisis of the Italian question. I have been able to do this, partly owing to the kindness of the Foreign Office in opening to me the papers in the Record Office, and the Consular papers in Italy, and still more owing to the kindness of Lady Agatha and Mr. Rollo Russell in placing the private papers of their father Lord John at my disposal. The letters from which selections are printed in Appendix A show us 'the very pulse of the machine,' which is not always visible in the official dispatches. And it is particularly gratifying to have been able to establish beyond all question at the mouth of two or three witnesses, the most sensational details of the story, told hitherto on Lacaita's authority alone, of his strange commission from Cavour to speak to Lord John Russell on the subject of Garibaldi's passage of the Straits (pp. 104-105 and p. 315 below).

Again, as in the case of the former volumes, any success of mine in collecting material has been very largely due to the kindness and activity of scores of people in England and in Italy, on whom I had in the first instance no claim except as a would-be historian of Garibaldi, though many of them are now my friends.

In Italy, my original debt to Mr. Nelson Gay and his *risorgimento* library has been again increased. Like so many other English students in Rome I have benefited in many different ways by the indefatigable kindness of Dr. Ashby of the British School, and as illustrations in this volume show, I finally lured him far afield in the tracks of Garibaldi. Sir Rennell Rodd has found time, among his many more important activities, to take an interest in my work and to find me new material. The fact is that British students at Rome are just now in clover, not only on account of their compatriots resident out there, but also on account of the kindness of the Italians. How much I have experienced this, from how many people, and in how many ways it is impossible for me to recount. But I must here record a special word of thanks to some of those who have made my work in Rome so pleasant and so profitable to me—Count Ugo Balzani, Signor Carlo Segré, Count and Countess Pasolini, Sindaco Nathan, Signor Menghini, and the authorities of the Biblioteca Vitt. Emmanuele, Senator Cadolini, the authorities of the Ufficio Storico of the Stato Maggiore, and various officers of the regular army.

The same kindness has been extended to me outside Rome, at Milan by Signor G. Gallavresi and Signor Gualtiero Castellini, and the authorities in charge of the archives in the Castello ; at Bologna by the authorities of the Museum and by the Casa Zanichelli ; at Genoa by Avv. Pier Giulio Breschi, by Col. Sclavo and the whole Municipio ; at Cremona by Professor Manacorda ; at Mantua by Cav. Alessandro Luzio ; at Naples by the Società Storia Patria, and by our Consul, Mr. Churchill ; at Monteleone, Calabria, by Marchese Gagliardi and Signor E. Scalfari ; and at Staletti by my kind host the late Achille Fazzari and his whole family ; at Salò and London by the Countess Martinengo Cesaresco. Of Sicily and the kind help I received there, I wrote at length in the preface to the last volume.

Both in England and Italy I have had the advantage of conversation with many of the actors in the drama of 1860. Some, like Türr, Canzio, Missori, and Fazzari, have quite recently passed away ; others are with us still. Their names appear in the Bibliography under the heading, *Notes of Conversations*, but I wish here to thank them collectively for their patience under interrogation. Above all I must thank my friends Mr. Dolmage and Mr. Patterson for their continuous efforts to enrich my knowledge by their memory.

I have during the last two years been constantly in receipt of letters from Italy, America, and England, from persons who saw or did things in Italy in 1860. Some of this correspondence I have utilised, noting it in the Bibliography among the *MSS. belonging to private persons.* I heartily thank all those who volunteered to send me information in this way.

In England those who have most assisted me by placing documents or illustrations at my disposal are—

next after Lady Agatha and Mr. Rollo Russell—Mr. Chas. Lacaita, Hon. W. W. Vernon, Miss Peard, Lady Lockwood, Mrs. Osler and Mr. Malleson, Mr. Ingram of the *Illustrated London News*, and the late Dr. Nelson of Belfast.

I am indebted for valuable advice and assistance to Mr. Thayer of Harvard, whose life of Cavour will be a landmark in *risorgimento* history.

Three persons have been at the pains to read this book in MS. or in proof: Mr. Hilton Young; my wife; and Count Balzani.

One who did much to make me in love with the task which I am now bringing to a conclusion has recently passed away—the late Lord Carlisle, who had indeed a natural right to that title which I have heard him arrogate to himself—the title of '*italianissimo*.'

June, 1911.

CONTENTS

CONTENTS

LIST OF PLATES

LIST OF PLATES

LIST OF MAPS

N.B.—Maps II, III, IV are folding maps at end of book, p. 374. Map IV will be of assistance to the reader throughout the whole book. Places in Italy mentioned in the text, but not marked in the other maps, will be found there.

'Seldom do we find that a whole people can be said to have any Faith at all; except in things that it can eat and handle. Whensoever it gets any Faith, its history becomes spirit-stirring, noteworthy.'—CARLYLE, *French Revolution.*

GARIBALDI AND THE
MAKING OF ITALY

INTRODUCTION

THE choice of this title for a volume of which the principal theme is Garibaldi's part in the events of June to November 1860 requires, not apology, but comment. It is true that the 'making of Italy' had begun two generations before, when General Buonaparte crossed the Alps with his hungry French Republicans, and was completed in 1870 when Victor Emmanuel entered Rome after the news of Sedan : but 1860 was the decisive year in that long process, the year when Italy was made. After considering whether I should call the book *Garibaldi and the Fall of the Neapolitan Kingdom*, I have rejected any such title, not only because it would fail to cover some of the most important events described—the battle of Castelfidardo and the liberation of the greater part of the Papal provinces—but also because the motive that inspired Garibaldi from the first to the last moment of his great campaign in the South was less the desire to destroy the Kingdom of Naples than the desire to make the Kingdom of Italy. The reader's mind should not be diverted from the national and constructive character of the Italian revolution by the interesting but subsidiary fact that the Bourbon system of government in South Italy collapsed in 1860 for the fourth and last time. The revolution of that year differs from those of the Napoleonic epoch and from those of 1820 and 1848, in that it created a free State stretching from the Alps to Sicily, which has since maintained its place in the family of nations as securely as France, Spain, or the German Empire.   Although at the end of 1860 the Austrian was still in possession of his Venetian territories and the Pope of the small province that contained the city of Rome, the union effected between the other parts of Italy rendered the absorption of Rome and Venice merely a question of time.

This volume, starting from the accomplished fact of the capture of Palermo by Garibaldi and the Thousand described in a previous volume, narrates the events of the following half-year which brought this new State into being.   The story has variety and scope enough. It is a complicated tale of war, regular and irregular, of diplomacy open and secret, of politics high and low.   It carries us into palaces and peasants' huts from one end of Italy to the other and into half the capitals of Europe. And it has all the interest of long protracted suspense. For even after the taking of Palermo in June, it was by no means certain that, when the winter snows descended again on Aspromonte, four-fifths of Italy would be united and free.   The turn of complicated events brought this result about, but in June it was no more a foregone conclusion than the break-up of Austria-Hungary or the reconstruction of Poland, events which were confidently expected in Garibaldi's camp, and of which at least the former entered as a probable contingency into the schemes of Cavour.

In the following pages the reader will see by how narrow a margin Italy in her great year escaped another disaster like that of 1848; with what skill and fortune she avoided foreign interference while she achieved her union against the will of all the great European Powers except England; what gross political and military mistakes stultified the powerful resistance which the Pope and the King of Naples might have set up; how Garibaldi's luck and genius and the psychological atmosphere of a triumphant revolution again and again produced military results contradictory to the known science of war; how the bullet that might, in any one of a hundred scuffles, have reversed in a moment the fortunes of the campaign, never passed nearer than through his poncho or his felt hat; how the first check to his career northwards, when Capua held out against him in September, occurred at the very moment when the wiser friends of Italy were beginning to pray that he might get no nearer to the walls of Rome; how in the contest waged for six months between Cavour from his chamber at Turin and Garibaldi from his shifting bivouacs on the Southern Apennines, the divergent views of the two patriots as to the utmost pace at which the redemption could be pushed on were finally compromised exactly at the right point, so as to secure the essential union of Italy without the immediate attack on Rome and Venice which must have imperilled all.

The mass of the nation supported both Cavour and Garibaldi, and it was this that saved the situation. But many of the principal actors were naturally forced to group themselves behind one or other of the two chiefs. If either party had completely got the upper hand, if Cavour had succeeded in annexing Sicily in June, and if he had been relieved from the competition of the revolutionary bands, the great Powers would not have permitted him to attack either Naples or the Papal territory. If on the other hand the Garibaldini had succeeded in attacking Rome, Napoleon III would have been forced to undo all that they had accomplished for Italy. The principle of audacity and the principle of guidance, both essential for successful revolutions, had each in 1860 an almost perfect representative. But the death of Cavour in 1861, and the subsequent deterioration of Garibaldi, deprived both parties of the splendid leadership of the great year, so that the last stages of the Italian *risorgimento* were shorn of their meed of glory. Venice and Rome were

ultimately acquired, but in a back-handed manner
Between 1861 and 1870 the ship of Italy's fortunes drifted
and whirled amid shallow eddies, but was swept at last
safe into port, because in 1860, when bold and skilful
hands were still on board, the great flood tide had lifted
her over the breakers at the bar.

CHAPTER I

THE CONSEQUENCES OF THE CAPTURE OF PALERMO IN NAPLES, PARIS, TURIN, AND LONDON

'You've seen the telegram?
Palermo's taken, we believe.'

MRS. BROWNING. *Garibaldi.*

IN the first days of June 1860, the news spread throughout Europe that the capital of Sicily, guarded by 20,000 regular troops, by forts and artillery, and by the Neapolitan fleet in the harbour, had been taken after three days' fighting by Garibaldi and a thousand North-Italian volunteers in plain clothes, aided by a mob of half-armed Sicilians. How soon, men asked, and how far would the revolution advance?

When last Palermo had expelled its garrison in January 1848, half Europe had followed suit. To the excited hopes of patriots and exiles, to the indignant fears of kings and their chancellors, Palermo seemed but the first point fired in a train of gunpowder laid through Messina and Reggio to Naples, through Naples and Rome to Venice, through Venice and Pesth to Vienna, through Vienna perhaps to Warsaw and back to the Tuileries. It was in the interest of every monarch who was not, like Victor Emmanuel, out for revolution, to check by force or by diplomacy the progress of the red-shirted portent. The 'filibuster,' having failed to be shot in the authorised manner,[1] seemed an incarnation of the

[1] '*Le Flibustive* [*sic*] movement at Naples is very shameful. . . . Col. Walker [the Nicaraguan filibuster] has been shot, and Garibaldi, who comes out of that self-same school, is divinised.' *The King of the Belgians to Queen Victoria.* Nov. 2, 1860, *Queen's Letters*, Vol. III.

improbable, and for a while aroused hopes and fears, of which some were wildly extravagant.

> ' A Caesar he, ere long, to Gaul,
> To Italy an Hannibal,
> And to all States not free
> Shall climacteric be.'

It was a case for a Holy Alliance of sovereigns to restore order in Sicily, or, if that were no longer possible, at least for a Concert of Europe to prevent the further spread of mischief. The first person to invoke the protection of the Powers by an appeal to the common interest of all established governments, was the unfortunate King Francis II of Naples, whose house was already on fire at one end, and was packed from roof to floor with combustible matter.[1]

The Neapolitan appeal for protection might take one of two forms. Either it might be addressed primarily to the powers of reaction, Russia and Austria, and would in that case be accompanied by vigorous conduct of the war in Sicily and by continued repression on the mainland; or else, as actually occurred, it might be addressed primarily to the more Liberal powers, to England and France, in which case efforts must be made to patch up a truce with Garibaldi, and a constitution must be granted on the mainland. As the latter course was the actual path by which King Francis descended so rapidly to his doom, it is easy to say now that the bolder policy would have had a better chance of success. But the House of Bourbon had twice before weathered the revolutionary storms of the Bay of Naples by granting a charter, to be set aside when the danger had passed by; and no one in

---

[1] On June 7 Odo Russell, the British Representative at Rome, wrote to his uncle, Lord John: 'The other day the young King of Naples was seized with such a panic that he telegraphed five times in twenty-four hours for the Pope's blessing. Cardinal Antonelli, through whom the application had to be made, telegraphed the three last blessings without reference to his Holiness, saying that he was duly authorised to do so. The Convents are awfully scandalised at this proceeding.' *Russell*, ii. 323.

the Neapolitan Camarilla had the nerve of a Strafford or a Bismarck openly to continue in the reactionary course with Garibaldi in Palermo. The only man among all Francis II's counsellors was his Bavarian Queen, Maria Sophia, and she, though ready, as she afterwards proved, to fight for her crown behind the cannon of Gaeta, honestly desired a constitution and a complete change of system.[1]

Besides this, Russia and Austria, though more willing, were less able to afford protection than either France or England. Russia, who had dominated the European situation in 1849, when she had invaded rebellious Hungary on behalf of Austria, had since then had a fall on the ramparts of Sebastopol. In whatever light the Crimean war may be viewed from the standpoint of British or near-Eastern interests, there is no doubt that from the point of view of Continental Liberalism and the freedom of action of independent States, it had done much to secure the 'liberties of Europe,' the phrase inscribed at Macaulay's suggestion on the monument to our soldiers at Scutari. The great power of darkness had been disabled and discredited in pan-European affairs, and the new Czar had even begun the work of liberation at home. Austria, too, who had the most immediate reason to support the old governments in Italy, and to check Garibaldi's advance, was in like manner recovering from her Crimea, the Lombard war of 1859. She dreaded that if she again moved to interfere in Italy the Hungarian rebels would rise behind her, this time without fear of the Russian armies, for the ingratitude shown by Austria to Russia during the Crimean War had dissolved the political friendship of the two Powers. Napoleon III and Cavour were both in constant communication

---

[1] For Maria Sophia see *Garibaldi and the Thousand*, pp. 126, 130. The queen in Daudet's *Rois en exil* is admittedly based on Maria Sophia, but while Daudet's queen was an ultra-royalist, Maria Sophia had Liberal inclinations, at least while on the throne. Also the king in the *Rois en exil* has positive vices which were wanting to the real Francis II.

with Kossuth, and Cavour had a Hungarian rising ready
primed to fire in case of an Austrian war.[1]

Partly for these reasons, and partly because the
Sicilian and Neapolitan situation was more easily commanded from the sea, it was necessary for Francis II to
appeal not so much to the Eastern as to the Western and
naval powers.   In spite of the constant bickering between
France and England, the deepest line of diplomatic division lay between East and West.   The idea of an alliance
with the principles of Russian despotism, even for the
purpose of scoring a point against a near neighbour, was
abhorrent to Napoleon III on one side of the Channel,
and to Palmerston and Lord John Russell on the other.
In fact when Russia early in July proposed to join with
France in policing the Mediterranean against Garibaldi's
transports, the offer coming from that quarter was
promptly rejected.[2]   If Napoleon interfered on behalf of
Naples, it would be in concert with Great Britain, and,
if possible, with Piedmont, and only on behalf of a reformed constitutional Kingdom.

The decision of the young King of Naples to adopt a
Liberal policy, to abandon the friendship with Austria
and Russia so long traditional in his family, to appeal to
Napoleon III for help, and to conciliate France, England,
and his own subjects by the grant of a constitution, was
taken in principle at Councils held on May 30 and June 1,
1860.   They were the first-fruits of Garibaldi's success.
On June 1 the King also sanctioned General Lanza's
proposal to retreat with 20,000 royal troops from the
Palace to the suburbs of Palermo, and on June 4 he
sanctioned his further proposal to capitulate with Gari-

[1] See *Chiala's Pol. Seg. passim.*   In the *Russell MSS.* Hudson writes on
May 1, 1860 : ' Pulsky is in communication with Cavour, and yesterday in a fit of
enthusiasm he let out that Cavour and Kossuth are in correspondence, that the
revolution has commenced in Hungary, and Austria is on her last legs.'

[2] *F. O. Sard. Hudson*, No. 299, July 8, 1860, and *F. O. France, Cowley*, No.
860, July 9, 1860.   *Br. Parl. Papers*, vii. p. 27, Russell to Hudson, July 7.

baldi and to ship the whole royal army back from Palermo to Naples.[1]

The chief promoter in the Council of these important decisions was General Filangieri, the veteran Prince of Satriano, who had served with equal fidelity the Napoleonic Kings of Naples, and the restored House of Bourbon, who had reconquered Sicily for the Crown in 1849, and ruled it with wise moderation until recalled by his reactionary enemies at Court. He had often and in vain advised *Bomba* and his son after him to break with Austria and the reaction, and to come to an understanding with France abroad and with the Constitutionalists at home.[2] His advice, rejected year after year so long as it would have saved the throne, was now adopted a month too late, and was with his own full concurrence coupled with the fatal policy of military surrender at Palermo, at a moment when a renewed attack on Garibaldi and the rebel town, headed by General Nunziante or by the King in person, would not improbably have turned the tide of war.

It might have been expected that Filangieri, having at length completely overborne his reactionary enemies at the Council-board, would have helped to carry out the hard task, which he had himself set to his royal master, of changing horses in the bed of a roaring torrent which had already swept them all off their feet. But he preferred to retire to his country-house near Sorrento, whence at his ease he could watch the troubled city of Naples across the full breadth of the Bay. When the King sent General Nunziante to beg him to return to the head of affairs and to revive the body politic by a constitutional regimen, he replied with brutal frankness : ' Would you have me repeat the miracle of Lazarus ? I am not Christ, but a miserable mortal.' His interlocutor,

---

[1] *De Cesare*, ii. 275-278. *Filangieri*, 317. Readers of *Garibaldi and the Thousand* will observe that the last pages of that book and the first pages of this one overlap chronologically.

[2] For Filangieri see *Garibaldi and the Thousand*, pp. 131, 146-147, 265-266.

Nunziante, hitherto a staunch reactionary, who had been loaded with honours and emoluments by the late King, and was esteemed and trusted by Francis II as the ablest man in the Neapolitan service after Filangieri himself, had recently consented to take up the command against Garibaldi, and had drawn up plans for the reconquest of Palermo, but he was so deeply impressed by these words of Filangieri that he at once determined not to go to Sicily, and then and there began to calculate how best to desert the falling House of Bourbon, and to carry over the army intact to the service of the House of Piedmont and United Italy.[1]

Before the end of June the King himself crossed the Bay of Naples to try his own powers of persuasion on the recluse of Sorrento. When the royal yacht was unexpectedly seen approaching the landing-place below the villa, Filangieri fled to his bedroom and jumped into bed. Not having time to take off his clothes, he drew the blankets over him up to his chin, and received his royal visitor so. Was ever monarch before or since received in such fashion by the first subject in his kingdom ?

Francis II held an hour's private conversation by the bedside of the malingerer, and then returned to Naples. Filangieri, perhaps a little ashamed of himself, never disclosed even to his nearest and dearest what had passed in that strange interview, but no one doubted that he had again been pressed to form a constitutional Ministry, and that, pleading his feigned illness, he had again refused.[2]

Early in August, Filangieri went into voluntary exile at Marseilles. After the revolution was accomplished he returned to Italy, and till his death in 1867 resided as a loyal subject of Victor Emmanuel, refusing office and honours from the new Government, but never regretting the old. The ideal of his life had been an independent

---

[1] *Nisco*, p. 48. *Franci*, i. 63, 188-191. *De Cesare*, ii. 307.

[2] *De Cesare*, ii. 280-281. *Filangieri*, 319. In the latter work, the filial biographer does not relate that part of the incident referring to the bed, but the evidence given in *De Cesare* seems convincing.

South Italy, with a progressive and civilised Government of its own, such as that which in his youth he had helped Murat to conduct. After Waterloo the restored Bourbons and their subjects had left that path, and had since failed in numerous attempts to return to it again, in spite of the efforts of men like Poerio and Filangieri. Poerio, convinced after 1848 that South Italy was by itself incapable of maintaining a tolerable Government, had quickly come to believe in the Union of all Italy as a positive good ; and even Filangieri was at last forced to admit, after the event, that Union was the least bad of all practicable solutions.

Discouraged but not deterred by Filangieri's refusal to lend a hand in carrying out his own policy, Francis II continued in the prescribed course. In the first days of June he had frankly thrown himself on the protection of France. De Martino had been sent as the bearer of an autograph letter of the King of Naples to the Emperor. Accompanied by Antonini, the regular Neapolitan Minister at Paris, he went out to Fontainebleau on June 12 to interview Napoleon.[1] The envoys met with a chilling reception from the French courtiers. Even Thouvenel, the Foreign Minister, though no friend to Italian aspirations, was brutally rude to the representatives of the falling cause, and before the conference began was overheard by them saying in a loud voice in the antechamber, 'Now I must go and hear what lies the two Neapolitan orators will tell the Emperor.' Napoleon himself, though courteous and humane, held out no hope that he would actively interfere. He explained the difference between the claims of the King of Naples on his protection and those of the Pope. 'The French flag,' he said, 'is actually waving on the Pope's territory, and then there is the question of

[1] For this interview, reported by Antonini himself in two dispatches of June 13, see *Bianchi*, viii. 297-301, and *Bianchi's Cavour*, 78, 105-107, and *Liborio Romano*, 144-150.

religion. The Italians understand that if they attacked Rome I should have to act.' But in the case of Naples he declared that as the victor of Solferino and the liberator of Lombardy, he was bound not to stultify his own past by using his troops on behalf of an opposite principle in South Italy. '*Les Italiens sont fins*,' he said; 'the Italians are shrewd; they clearly perceive that since I have shed the blood of my people for the cause of nationality, I can never fire a cannon against it. And this conviction, the key to the recent revolution, when Tuscany was annexed against my wishes and interests, will have the same effect in your case.' The King of Naples' concessions, the offer of the constitution, failed to impress him. 'It is too late,' he said. 'A month ago these concessions might have prevented everything. To-day they are too late.'

It was now June 12. On April 15 Victor Emmanuel had written to his 'dear cousin' of Naples, suggesting a mutual alliance on the principle of Italian nationality and freedom, and ending with the words : 'If you allow some months to pass without attending to my friendly suggestion, your Majesty will perhaps experience the bitterness of the terrible words—*too late*.'[1] Eight weeks had sufficed to fulfil the prophecy, and the 'terrible words' were now on the lips of Napoleon himself.

But there was still, said the Emperor to the Neapolitan envoys, one chance for their master. Let him humbly ask for the Piedmontese alliance, which he had himself rejected earlier in the year when Victor Emmanuel had made the advances. 'Piedmont alone,' said Napoleon, 'can stop the course of the revolution. You must apply not to me but to Victor Emmanuel.' 'We French do not wish,' he added, 'for the annexation of South Italy to the Kingdom of Piedmont, because we think it contrary to our interests, and it is for this reason that we advise you to adopt the only expedient which can prevent or at least retard that annexation.' For the rest, he would

[1] *Garibaldi and the Thousand*, pp. 185-186.

be delighted if the Neapolitan Royalists proved able to
defeat Garibaldi and the revolution with the force of
their own arms, but he could not help them himself,
partly for the reasons which he had already given, and
partly because he was determined to do nothing con
trary to the wishes of England.[1]

His advice therefore to the Neapolitan envoys at
Fontainebleau was nothing more than a reasoned repetition of the programme which his representative
Brenier had several days before urged upon the Court
at Naples,[2] namely :—

First, a scheme of Sicilian Home Rule under a Prince
   of the Royal House of Naples.
Secondly, a Constitution for the mainland.
Thirdly, an alliance with Piedmont.

This triple programme was perforce adopted by the
Neapolitan Court, but the first item depended for its fulfilment on Garibaldi and the Sicilians, and the third on
Cavour and the Piedmontese. The Constitution, indeed,
could be published by the King without the consent of
any other party, but whether it would at this twelfth
hour conciliate the population of the Neapolitan provinces still remained to be seen.

The question was soon put to the proof. A Council
of Ministers sat on June 21, and after Antonini's report
of the interview at Fontainebleau had been read to them
decided by eleven votes to three to adopt the triple programme laid down by the French Emperor. A short
while back the same men would have voted by an equally
large majority against any concession, but in these weeks
life-long opinions were changing with a rapidity peculiar
to the crisis of a great revolution. Since the taking of
Palermo most of the reactionary party, headed by the

[1] *Bianchi*, viii. 664 top, Antonini's letter of June 16. This sentiment of the
Emperor's with regard to England as the tether of his range in Italian policy
this summer, is repeated in his letter to Persigny, July 27, printed in *Mem.
Stor. Mil.* ii. 186-187 and elsewhere.
[2] *F. O. Sicily, Elliot*, June 8, 1860, No. 256.

B

King's uncle, the Count of Aquila, had become ardent
Constitutionalists ; while the Constitutional party of
former years, headed by the Duke of Syracuse, another
uncle of the King (the Philippe Egalité of the Neapolitan
revolution) had turned against the dynasty, and were
working to bring in Victor Emmanuel. 'A year ago,'
wrote Elliot, the British Minister, 'there was hardly an
annexationist to be found in this part of Italy, and now
pretty nearly the whole country is so for the moment.'[1]

But even after the Council of June 21 the feeble King
still hesitated. Although he would not go to Sicily and
lead on his troops against Garibaldi, he was almost
equally unwilling to publish the Constitution and to
declare for the Piedmontese alliance. All the pieties and
instincts of his dumb nature were averse to the change,
and he was upheld in his passive resistance by the
clamours of his stepmother Maria Theresa, 'the Austrian woman,' whom he had been accustomed since boyhood to obey. But on the other side was his wife, Maria
Sophia, whose influence upon him was constantly growing throughout his brief reign, corresponding to a per-
ceptible increase of manliness on his part. For some
days after the Council of June 21 a final struggle was
waged between the two Marias, ending in the victory of
the younger. Her demand for constitutional reform was
urgently supported by the King's uncle, the Count of
Aquila, and by the French Minister, Brenier, who were
now in close partnership.[2] De Martino, meanwhile, had
been sent to Rome to obtain the Pope's leave for the
change of policy, which was grudgingly given on condition that any alliance with Piedmont was not to be
made at the expense of the Papal territories or the privileges of the Church. The Pope's consent turned the
scale in the King's mind, and on June 25 the Sovereign
Act was published recalling to vigour the Constitution of

[1] *Elliot*, 37, July 8.
[2] *Russell MSS. Elliot*, letters of June 11, July 23, Aug. 2. *Liborio Romano*,
6-8. *De Cesare*, ii. 283-289.

1848, granting Home Rule to Sicily under a Prince of the
Royal House, and announcing that an alliance would
be made with Piedmont—the complete triple programme
advised by Napoleon.   The tricolour flag, symbolic of
Italian nationality, was hauled up on all the public buildings and on the ships of the fleet ;[1] the political prisoners
were let loose throughout the Kingdom ; the exiles returned amid processions and rejoicings; pending the
elections to Parliament, a Ministry of moderate Liberals
took over the authority of the State.   As far as the
Government was concerned, everything was done in the
most approved manner according to the pattern of one
of those joyous Constitution-givings of the spring of 1848,
when monarchs and peoples had wept in each other's
arms.   But on this occasion it was only the monarch who
opened his arms and embraced the empty air.   When on
June 26 the King and Queen drove out in an open carriage to receive the ovations of liberated Naples, hats
were respectfully raised, but hardly a cheer was heard
in the whole length of the Toledo.[2]

The Constitution was still-born.   In some upland
villages, especially in the district between Naples and
the Roman border, it was regarded as a Jacobinical
betrayal of religion ; while the great mass of the King's
subjects in the capital and in the provinces south of the
capital regarded it merely as a first step in the direction
of Italian unity, a means of freeing themselves from the
police and the censorship, so as to be better able to
welcome ' him ' when he came.   ' He ' was at Palermo,
he would soon be at the Straits, and it was in that direction and not to the Palace of Naples that all men's
thoughts were turned.   The newly granted liberties
were used to destroy the Government that had conceded
them.   Newspapers sprang up by the score ; books,

---

[1] Victor Emmanuel's flag, used by Garibaldi, was the tricolour *with the cross
of Savoy upon it;* that is now the flag of all Italy.   There was no cross on the
tricolour of the short-lived ' Constitutional ' Kingdom of Francis II of Naples.

[2] *Liborio Romano,* 8.   *De Cesare,* ii. 289-291.

pamphlets, and proclamations appeared everywhere, and nearly the whole output of the liberated press was anti-dynastic. Its only disputes turned on the rival merits of Cavour and Mazzini, of Federation and Annexation and whether or not to await Garibaldi's coming before beginning the revolution.

The new Ministry formed by Spinelli, with De Martino in charge of Foreign affairs, consisted chiefly of mediocre but honest men, desirous of working the Constitution and saving the dynasty. But with one exception they had neither influence nor popularity, at a time when the mere possession of office lent but little authority to the opinions of its holder. Yet even the Ministers, without intending to do so, further undermined the stability of the throne. For they busied themselves, as indeed it was their duty to do if the Constitution was to be a reality, in turning out reactionaries and putting in old constitutionalists as prefects, magistrates, and police, regardless of the fact that the old constitutionalists were now for Garibaldi almost to a man. The expulsion of genuine royalists from the public service alienated the enthusiasm of the King's friends, without reconciling his enemies, to whom it gave the civil power in every Province from Calabria to Abruzzi. The bishops, more reactionary than their clergy, were the only persons in authority who could not be summarily dismissed, but they were watched by spies who reported their sayings and movements to the Minister of the Interior : some of the prelates fled from their dioceses in real or affected fear for their personal safety. In every town the new authorities formed and armed the National Guard, chosen out of the middle class, which became in effect a military force prepared to support the coming revolution.

The army alone was loyal to the King, but as it still consisted of about 100,000 well-armed and well-drilled men, it might still defeat Garibaldi, and if it could once drive the red-shirts in rout no one doubted that the Constitution, the National Guard, the Ministry, the press, and the tricolour flags would all be huddled away in twenty-four hours. After all, there had been a Constitutional Ministry in 1848, and shortly afterwards the principal Ministers were serving their time in irons. It was this supreme consideration which made real loyalty impossible for any man, however much he cared for the dynasty, if he also cared for the Constitution. No one except the reactionaries really wished to hear of a victory over the man who was in name the national enemy, and in reality the national deliverer. It was for this reason that the new Ministers were so unwilling to take the offensive against him in Sicily. For no Cabinet can be expected to conduct a war with vigour, when a decisive victory would mean twenty years' penal servitude for each of its members. General Pianell, the new War Minister, was a faithful and honest man, but he erred in accepting a post of which he could not, by the nature of the case, heartily fulfil the duties.[1]

Don Liborio Romano, the new Prefect of Police, was the sole exception to the rule that the Ministers had neither popularity nor influence; and he was also the exception to the rule that they were passively loyal to the King. 'Don Liborio,' as he was called in these days, was a native of lower Apulia, skilled in the insinuating manners and arts of political intrigue which the inhabitants of the region between Taranto and Brindisi are said to have inherited from their Greek ancestors. He had been an active Liberal as early as 1820, and had often suffered as such at the hands of the police. But he belonged essentially to the world of Levantine intrigue, rather than to the world of European revolution. For this reason he was able from June to September, 1860, to preserve the confidence of the inhabitants of the capital by a kind of masonic mutual understanding or sympathy of character, which a more straightforward man would have failed to establish with the Neapolitans. After his retire-

[1] *De Cesare*, ii. 292-322. *Elliot*, 34-42. *Nisco*, 50-54, 59-62. *Salazaro*, 47-52.

ment he always asserted that he had taken office, not in order to save the dynasty, which he believed to be already lost, but in order to preserve his fellow-countrymen from anarchy and civil war.[1]   This account of his motives, if a considerable allowance be also made for his vanity and ambition, is accepted by the most competent and un-biassed authorities who knew the Naples of that day well, and they are also of opinion that at the moment of entering office he did actually achieve his purpose and save the city and perhaps the whole Kingdom from a terrible disaster.[2]

The circumstances were as follows.   On June 27, two days after the proclamation of the Sovereign Act, when all the authorities of the old *régime* had lost their power, but before the new Ministry was well in the saddle, and before the National Guard or the new police had been formed, disorders broke out in Naples.   The police of the old Government were hunted down, and their archives burnt.   Unless the mob was checked, anarchy would soon prevail in its most hideous form.   But there was at the moment no armed force deriving its authority from the Constitution, and if the regular army, aflame with reactionary passions, had been called out to shoot the mob, civil war would have begun at once.   In the cir-cumstances Liborio Romano was entreated to become Prefect of Police, on the ground that no one else could save Naples.   He accepted the post on June 27, and on the next day the Prefecture of Police, till then execrated by every one, became the resort of the leading Liberals. But the Liberals alone could not control the vicious and non-political criminal class of Naples.   The *camorra*, hitherto in tacit league with the old Royal Government,[3] had now turned against all government.   Don Liborio, to avoid the imminent social catastrophe, struck a bargain with this secret association of criminals, in the name

---

[1] *Liborio Romano*, 14, 26.   *Trinity*, 232-233.
[2] *Trinity*, 233.   *De Cesare*, ii. 294-295.   *Nisco*, 53-54.
[3] *Garibaldi and the Thousand*, p. 132.

of the new Government, or at any rate of its Prefect of Police. The chiefs of the *camorra* were given places in the new police force, along with other more respectable members of society. The consequence was that there were no more disturbances in Naples during the next three months of turmoil, panic, and revolution, except on occasions when the reactionary soldiers broke loose from their barracks. In this ignominious manner Naples was saved. The price paid by the Italian Government in later years was high, but possibly not too high for the escape of society from promiscuous bloodshed and rapine.

Having thus tided over the immediate danger, Don Liborio formed the National Guard from among his own adherents in the respectable middle class. The National Guard, the police, and the *camorra* were now at his disposal, not only in Naples but throughout the provinces. He was master of the situation and held the stakes until either the King or Garibaldi had conquered. Throughout July and August he was the real ruler of the country for all domestic purposes except the command of the army. Francis II hated and distrusted Don Liborio, but dared not dismiss him.[1]

While the House of Bourbon was thus engaged at home in clothing its enemies with authority and its friends with confusion, the Piedmontese alliance, to obtain which all these sacrifices were being made, was eagerly solicited at Turin. Twice during the last twelve months Piedmont had asked for an alliance and been rebuffed by the counsellors of Francis II; it was now their turn to sue for the settlement which they had so recently refused. The House of Bourbon was on its knees, clad in the Constitution and the Tricolour for a garb of penitence. But the record of its perjuries prevented all confidence, and the record of its cruelties all

[1] *Liborio Romano*, 3, 8-21, 26. *Nisco*, 52-55. *De Cesare*, ii. 293-295, 301-303, 305-307. *Trinity*, 219-224, 230-233.

forgiveness. The 'Neapolitan prisoners,'[1] whose woes
Mr. Gladstone had made famous, the victims of *Bomba's*
dungeons, were now many of them residing in Turin,
several as Deputies in the North Italian Parliament
which was then in full session. Others, like Braico, had
gone to Sicily with the Thousand. When the news of
the fall of Palermo arrived, the Neapolitan exiles in
Turin met at the house of Mancini, one of their number,
and at the instance of Carlo Poerio declared for the
deposition of the Bourbons.[2] When, some three weeks
later, there arose the question of the alliance of Piedmont
with Naples, the uncompromising attitude of these men
strengthened Cavour's hands to resist the proposal.
Poerio, the Conservative Minister of the late King during the Parliamentary *régime* of 1848, had been rewarded
for his undisputed loyalty to Crown and Constitution
by a sentence of twenty-four years in irons obtained by
notoriously false witness, at the instance of *Bomba* himself. He had served eight years of that sentence, and
had come out of prison in 1859 converted to the programme of Italian Unity. He and his friends now put
themselves at the head of the popular agitation in North
Italy, which made it impossible for Cavour, even if he
had so wished, to accept the alliance and to protect the
Neapolitan State from further invasion by Garibaldi.
On June 29 Poerio, from the tribune of the North Italian
Chamber, uttered sentiments which, coming from the
mouth of one so moderate, so reticent, and so just, carried
the full weight of their literal meaning.

'The Neapolitan Government,' he said, ' has the tradition
of perjury, handed down from father to son. That is why it
now offers to swear to the Constitution, because it is clear that
in order to be perjured it is necessary first to swear. I trust
that the Ministers of Victor Emmanuel will not stretch out
their hands to a Government which certainly is the most declared of the enemies of Italian independence.'

The roar of applause that followed him as he returned

---

[1] *Garibaldi and the Thousand*, chap. iii.   [2] *Mancini*, 135-136.

to his seat showed that the North Italian Deputies had already made up their minds about the proposed alliance.[1]

The Neapolitan exiles, while they held this language in public, expressed themselves with no less vigour and decision in their private correspondence. Writing to Panizzi, the Librarian of the British Museum, and one of the chief unofficial agents of the Italian cause in our country, Poerio and his fellow-martyr Settembrini urged that the hour had struck to weld Italy into one State, and that if a truce were now patched up, when the trumpets should be sounding the final charge, ' enthusiasm would cool with time ' and the principle of ' dualism with all its terrible consequences ' would for ever divide the Italian Peninsula.[2]

Cavour was from the first aware that it was impossible to accept the alliance. On the very day of Poerio's speech in the Chamber, he telegraphed to Villamarina, the Piedmontese Minister at Naples : ' Take care to render impossible an agreement between the King of Naples and the national party. We must not allow Italy to believe that by complaisance or weakness we are ready to fraternize with the King of Naples.' [3] To accept the Neapolitan alliance would, as he knew, mean schism and possibly civil war in North Italy. And yet he dared not at once close the door on a proposal initiated by France, regarded by Austria, Russia, and Prussia as only too liberal, and at present supported officially by England herself. As soon as Hudson had finished persuading Lord John Russell to accept frankly the idea of annexation and united Italy, a task upon which he was busily engaged in a private and unofficial correspondence,[4] Cavour might take a bolder course. But ' even if

---

[1] *F. O. Sard. Hudson*, July 2, 1860, No. 292. See also *Manebrini*, 46.

[2] *Panizzi*, 428-433.

[3] *Chiala*, iii. 277, June 29. That it was the real intention of Cavour and Farini to refuse the alliance is borne out by Farini's words to Spaventa on July 11 (*Spaventa*, 295).

[4] *Russell MSS. Hudson*. Letters of May 31, July 16, 27, 31 ; see Appendix A. below.

we were helped by England,' he wrote to Ricasoli on July 8, 'we could not fight both on the Mincio and on the Alps,' against both Austria and France. So he could not 'reject scornfully a proposed settlement presented under French auspices and by French advice.'[1] He determined, therefore, to entertain the Neapolitan envoys, Manna and Winspeare, and to treat about the alliance on such terms as were certain to be refused by King Francis, making demands tantamount to the cession of Sicily and the further partition of the Pope's territory for the benefit of Piedmont.[2]

But the fear that the Italian people would suppose even these negotiations to be serious constantly haunted him. ' If we consent to the alliance we are lost. If we reject it, what will Europe say ? In my life I was never more embarrassed.'[3] To retain the confidence of the patriotic party Cavour more and more openly hastened the equipment and departure of the expeditions of volunteers to join Garibaldi, and that portion of the press which he inspired was observed to be scornfully hostile to the Neapolitan alliance.[4] At the same time he tried to cut the knot of his difficulties by engineering an immediate revolution in Naples. The Piedmontese diplomatic representative, Villamarina, was the centre of this movement and the Piedmontese Legation its house of call. Even in April, under the old *régime* of repression, Villamarina's house, with its immunities against police search, had been used for the meetings of conspirators, and the forwarding of their letters to North Italy.[5] And now in July he was instructed to act with Piedmontese agents of high character like Emilio Visconti-Venosta, and with the best of the Neapolitan exiles like Spaventa and Nisco, who openly came into Naples, some

[1] *Chiala*, iii. 282.

[2] *Ibid.*, iii. 273, June 27. *Bianchi*, viii. 305-312. *Bianchi's Cavour*, 108-114. *Spaventa*, 295.

[3] *Chiala*, iii. 284, July 12.

[4] *Chiala's Dina*, 311-314, *Opinione* of June 29 quoted. [5] *Mancini*, 134.

as naturalised Piedmontese subjects, others trusting to
the civil rights enjoyed under the new Constitution.
Some came with money supplied by Cavour and Farini to
start newspapers ; all came to talk to their old friends in
the army and elsewhere, and to stir up an annexationist
movement.[1]   Within a few days of his arrival in Naples,
Venosta wrote home to report that the army was Bour-
bonist in sympathy, and that the people only understood
the idea of revolution as connected with Garibaldi, for
whom they were waiting as for a second St. Januarius.[2]
But it was not until the end of August that Cavour could
be persuaded by his agents that a revolution without
Garibaldi was impossible.

It was indeed, neither a dignified nor an honest policy
to pretend to treat for alliance with the Government of
a country while arming bands of volunteers to invade
its provinces, and sending emissaries to excite a revolution in its capital.   But that was the system pursued by
Cavour during July and August, because he believed the
alternative to be the Austrian bayonets in Milan and the
French in Turin.   Danton once thundered out for all
the world to hear, *Que mon nom soit flétri, que la France
soit libre.*   Cavour's intellectually aristocratic temper had
no such unsafe confidences for the people at large, but
he said quietly to his friends one day : ' If we had done
for ourselves the things which we are doing for Italy,
we should be great rascals.'[3]   The magnificent integrity
of Cavour's private character and the entire disin-
terestedness of his public conduct, lends peculiar force
to this saying.   It must indeed be confessed that he
bequeathed to the statesmanship of the new Italy the
old traditions of duplicity, which have sometimes become
low cunning in the hands of successors with neither his
virtues, his abilities, nor his dire necessities for their

---

[1] *Spaventa*, 292-298.   *De Cesare*, ii. 364-365.   *Nisco*, 70-73.   *Mezzacapo*,
123-129.

[2] *Conv. Venosta.*

[3] Related in M. D'Azeglio's letter about the ethics of 1860-1, *Persano*, 463.

excuse. But before we condemn Cavour we must decide whether without a large degree of duplicity he could, supported by England alone, have made Italy against the will of a hostile Europe—against the destroyers of Poland, 'the man of December,' the Pope, and the perjured dynasty of Naples. This question I am unable to answer, and I believe that no answer, however confidently given, can be anything better than a reasoned guess.

There were not wanting at the time well-informed observers who believed that Cavour could have avoided all this chicanery, that even in June he could have carried out the bold and straightforward policy on which he finally embarked in September. 'I wish,' wrote Elliot to Lord John Russell on June 25, 'Victor Emmanuel would throw off the mask like a man and go to war. It would certainly be a very easy matter for him to roll down this rickety dynasty, and he would be received with enthusiasm by the nation.'[1] It was natural for the British Minister at Naples to write in this confident manner, for what Elliot had close under his own eyes was the rottenness of the Government to which he was accredited. But it was not any fear of resistance at Naples that withheld Cavour ; it was the fear of counter-attack from Vienna and Paris. There were many riddles in the complicated problem which Cavour had to solve, but the chief one was to guess the true colour of the chameleon of the Tuileries, the Liberal protector of the Pope, the friendly foe of Italian unity. If Cavour let loose the nation straining at the leash, if he made legal war on Naples and invaded the Papal Marches and Umbria, would Napoleon merely protest, or would he actively interfere ? Or if Austria attacked Piedmont when she was engaged in liberating the South, on what terms, if any, would Napoleon lend his protection ?

On this, the supreme problem of that summer, Cavour obtained a decided opinion from the Emperor's cousin,

[1] *Russell MSS. Elliot*, June 25.

Jerome.[1] This prince, a whole-hearted friend of Italian
unity, deserves more credit than he has got for his successful efforts in 1859-60 on behalf of that policy, which
for ever cut him off from all hope of an Italian kingdom
in Tuscany or elsewhere.   On June 30 he wrote to
Cavour that the time had come when he could attack
South Italy without fear of the Emperor's veto.   The
letter is one of the most important in the history of
Italy, for it foreshadows the course which Cavour
adopted two months later.

'Italy,' wrote Prince Jerome, 'is in a supreme crisis.   She
must emerge from it united under the sceptre of my father-
in-law [Victor Emmanuel] with Rome as her capital, or else
she will slide back under the oppression of priests and
Austrians, at Turin as well as at Naples and everywhere else
The die is cast. . . . Daring alone can save you to-day.   Be
strong.   Don't trust to yourself, no illusions, no vanity, you
have need of France and you can get her by means of
the Emperor.   (*Il vous faut la France par l'Empereur.*)   Be
then completely open with him.   No more *finesse ;* that served
your turn for Tuscany ; it will not serve your turn with Sicily,
Naples, and Rome.   Explain to him your views of the future,
not only your end but your means and your conduct.' [2]

Cavour did not at once adopt the course here prescribed for him by the Prince, but he did so before two
months were out, when he opened his innermost counsels
to Napoleon, and mobilised the Italian army to invade
the territories of the Pope and of the King of Naples.
The question is whether he could safely have ventured
upon this policy in the first days of July, on receipt of
the Prince's letter, or whether in fact it was necessary,
as he judged, to wait until the unofficial revolution under
Garibaldi had spread from Palermo to the gates of Naples.
Perhaps Prince Jerome ante-dated the readiness of his
Imperial cousin to condone the making of Italy.   It is
true that Napoleon at the end of August accepted it as
the only alternative to anarchy, but it was by no means

[1] On Prince Jerome see *Garibaldi and the Thousand*, p. 75 and note.
[2] *Principe Nap.* p. 54.

the only alternative prior to Garibaldi's victory at Milazzo and march through Calabria. Would Napoleon at the beginning of July have consented to throw over, at Cavour's request, all the proposals which he himself had just made for a reformed Neapolitan kingdom allied to Piedmont? It may be doubted—although the Emperor's gloomy words to the Neapolitan envoys at Fontainebleau perhaps imply a weakening of his resistance to Cavour.[1] But on July 6 Brenier, the French Minister at Naples, declared strongly against annexation.[2] And at Turin the French Minister, M. de Talleyrand, was pressing Cavour hard to grant the Neapolitan alliance, claiming first and foremost that Victor Emmanuel should at once write to Garibaldi to bid him make a truce. Talleyrand found that Cavour 'sheltered himself behind England,' and put off his demands with fair words and excuses to gain time. Victor Emmanuel was conveniently away hunting in his beloved Alps, and his return must be awaited.[3]

Meanwhile, in the better world up there, in the pine woods and beneath the moraines, the descendant of twenty generations of hunting rulers of Savoy unbosomed himself to his companions of the chase, the men to whom he could talk gruffly and freely, to ease his rugged nature of its weight of simple emotions. 'He talked much about Sicily,' wrote one of these after their return to the plains. 'He said he envied Garibaldi, and would like to be able to lay about him, like the Nizzard general. Victor Emmanuel really loves Garibaldi.'[4]

The affection for Garibaldi which the Italian King could only express to his confidants in the depths of the Alpine forest, was being proclaimed aloud in the streets by all classes in Great Britain. In the uncertain diplo-

[1] See p. 12 above.
[2] *Elliot*, 35, July 6. 'Brenier . . . blurted out . . . " You shall not have annexation." This was plain speaking.'
[3] *La Gorce*, iii. 391. De Talleyrand's dispatch of July 9.
[4] *Amari*, ii. 108.

matic situation, England's decided attitude became the governing factor. If at the beginning of July, when France asked for her support in forcing a truce on Garibaldi in Palermo, England had supported the other Powers in such a programme of interference, it is difficult to see how Sicily could have been annexed to Piedmont.[1] But England refused, and without her concurrence Napoleon, who at this time highly valued her friendship was unwilling to proceed to definite action.[2] And again at the end of July, as will be told in a later chapter, she refused to participate in Napoleon's scheme to prevent Garibaldi from crossing the straits, and thereby enabled the red-shirts to invade the mainland. This policy of Lord John's was not that of intervention in Italian affairs, but of non-intervention with an implied veto on the intervention of others.

The action of Great Britain in this summer, without which Italy could not have been made, was due partly to the steady pressure of public opinion, press, and Parliament on the Cabinet,[3] and partly to the personal attachment of the Minister for Foreign Affairs to the cause of Italian freedom. Lord John Russell had been brought up in boyhood and youth among the friends of Fox, that small group of Liberal aristocrats who, no fair-weather friends of freedom, had sacrificed their popularity and their chance of influence and power for forty years, on behalf of the principles of civil and religious liberty. Russell had inherited their traditions, had in early manhood led the great attack that re-established freedom in Great Britain in 1832, and now in old age was prepared to do all that in him lay to overturn on Italian soil worse

[1] *Chiala*, iii. 281, telegram of July 7. *F. O. France, Cowley*, July 9, 1860, No. 859.

[2] 'As to Southern Italy I am free from engagements and I ask nothing better than to concert matters with England on this point as on others' (*e.g.* Syria). 'Since the peace of Villafranca my only thought has been to inaugurate a new era of peace and to live on a good understanding with all my neighbours, particularly with England.' Napoleon III to Persigny, July 27, 1860. *Mem. Stor. Mil.* ii. 186-187.

[3] *F. O. France, Cowley*, July 9, 1860, No. 859.

tyrannies than had ever been known in England. In this task Lord John was opposed by the Court, but he was supported by the public, by the press, by the petitions of great municipalities, and by his two chief colleagues, Palmerston and Gladstone, both converts, at different dates and for different reasons, from those authoritarian principles in Church and State to which he himself had sworn eternal hatred while he was still a boy.

The British Minister for Foreign Affairs was therefore ready to take any step consonant with British interests that would assist Italian freedom, and fortunately he had for his advisers, at Naples and at Turin respectively, two men of marked ability who sympathised with these aims. Elliot and Hudson conducted a private correspondence with Lord John behind their official dispatches, and so enabled the British Minister to keep abreast of the rapid development of the Italian situation in 1859-60. It was for this reason that British policy never fell seriously behind the ever-increasing requirements of Cavour.

Before the middle of July 1860 both Hudson and Elliot had become converts to the idea of Italian unity. And both of them began to write private letters to prepare Lord John's mind to accept the annexation of the whole Peninsula by Victor Emmanuel. But their support of this programme was due only to the Garibaldian conquests. Union had not previously been favoured even by Hudson himself.

On May 18, while Garibaldi with his Thousand were still in the mountains overlooking Palermo, Hudson had argued in a long private letter to Russell that the fusion of North and South Italy in one State was difficult because of the intervening Papal territories, and not desirable because of the moral corruption of the South. He had recommended as a compromise the possession of the throne of Naples and Sicily by a cadet of the Royal House of Piedmont.[1] But the fall of Palermo at the end

---

[1] See Appendix A, below, for the important letters referred to in the remaining paragraphs of this chapter.

of May converted him to the idea of complete Italian unity.[1]

Meanwhile Lord John had not taken up with any warmth his suggestion of placing a cadet of the House of Piedmont on the throne of Naples, and 'the tidal wave of unity which the victory of Palermo set in motion carried that idea to the frozen sea of diplomatic nostrums,' as its author cheerfully acknowledged. Therefore on July 16 Hudson wrote to Lord John again, declaring himself this time 'cordially and entirely' in favour of Italian unity under Victor Emmanuel, 'because now that the notion of a Prince of the House of Savoy has been set aside by the force of circumstances,' he saw 'very great danger to the Balance of Power in the Mediterranean if France should in the midst of the Neapolitan confusion find means to place a creature of her own on that throne.' On July 27 he again wrote in favour of annexation 'as less prejudicial to British interests (of which you remind me) than the anarchy of Sicily and Naples, and the discontent of North Italy.' Finally on July 31 he wrote a long reasoned letter to Lord John to prove that Italian unity was in accordance with British interests. In this important letter Hudson uses two main arguments. First that annexation had now become the only possible form of stable government for South Italy : 'are the respectable classes of Naples to be subjected to the inconvenience of being shot, plundered, burnt, and violated because the Foreign Powers dislike Unity?' Secondly, when the whole Peninsula was united in one State, it would be strong enough to be independent of France, and would naturally gravitate to friendship with England and the German Powers. A good understanding between Austria, Prussia, Italy, and England, argued Hudson, would rid Europe of the nightmare of French domination which then oppressed her. 'It is my duty,' he concluded, 'under my instructions to support Duality, and I have

[1] 'I was then a dualist. I continued to be so till the capture of Palermo.' Hudson's letter of July 31, *Russell MSS*.

done so. But I should greatly fail in my duty if I did not point out to your Lordship the difficulties (I may say the impossibility) which prevent its accomplishment.'

These arguments, in which, as will be seen, the fear of French predominance was the chief, sufficed to persuade the British statesmen of 1860 that their earnest desire to help Italian freedom was compatible with the material interests of Great Britain, and that it was not only their pleasure but their duty to bring about the union of the whole Peninsula under Victor Emmanuel. Side by side with the love of Italy, the fear of France then dominated Englishmen, and not least among them Lord John Russell. He was in constant anxiety at this period lest Cavour should purchase from Napoleon the right to annex the rest of Italy by ceding the island of Sardinia and the Genoese Riviera to France. The rumour was in fact baseless. But although Cavour and Farini hastened to deny it with the utmost solemnity, Russell could not feel easy, remembering the protestations of innocence that had preceded the barter of Nice and Savoy. Hudson endeavoured to relieve his chief's fears, pointing out that Genoa was a vital part of Italy, whereas Nice had been a mere outpost. At the same time, with admirable skill, he turned Lord John's remaining fears on this head into an argument that England herself should support the Italian claims unconditionally, and so outbid the French by doing the work for nothing. 'I perceive,' he wrote on May 31, replying to Lord John's fears about the alleged cession of Genoa, 'that the more you hang back the more easy do you make the propagation of French notions in Italy.' It is difficult to see where Lord John had been guilty of 'hanging back.' In any case he was never seriously open to the charge again, but made himself thenceforth a willing auxiliary to the plans of Hudson and Cavour.[1]

[1] See Appendix A, below, the Russell Papers.

CHAPTER II

> ' Oh giornate del nostro riscatto !
> Oh dolente per sempre colui
> Che da lunge, dal labbro d' altrui
> Come un uomo straniero, le udrà !
> Che a' suoi figli narrandole un giorno,
> Dovrà dir sospirando : io non c'era ;
> Che la santa vittrice bandiera
> Salutata quel dì non avrà.'
>
> ALESSANDRO MANZONI.[1]

' Oh days of our country's ransoming !   Unhappy for ever shall he be who shall like a stranger hear of it from afar, from the lips of others ; who when he tells the tale to his children on a time, must say sighing, " I was not there ; " who shall not have hailed on that day of days our holy, conquering banner.'

A NEW nation cannot be made solely by the skill of a great statesman playing on the mutual jealousies of Foreign Powers.   The making of nations requires the self-sacrifice of thousands of obscure men and women who care more for the idea of their country than for their own comfort or interest, their own lives or the lives of those whom they love.   Cavour, with the help of England's attitude of ' non-intervention,' could, at best, only keep the ring while the revolutionaries struck down the Neapolitan Kingdom.   It remained to be seen whether volunteers would go out in sufficient numbers to enable Garibaldi to defeat the 100,000 Bourbon troops

---

[1] From Manzoni's Ode ' Marzo, 1821,' dedicated ' To the illustrious memory of Theodore Koerner, poet and soldier of German independence, killed at Leipsig, 1813.   A name dear to all the peoples who fight to defend or to recover a fatherland.'   This ode was published by Manzoni first in 1848, and again in 1860.   The verse printed above was frequently quoted by Italians in reference to 1860.

who, even after the fall of Palermo, refused to embrace the national cause.   The Italian revolution had produced martyrs by the hundred; could it now produce effective soldiers by the thousand?   The active patriots came from among all classes of the town population, and from the leaders of the rural districts, but the common peasantry of the North, though most of them had now been converted to the National cause, did not cross the sea to join Garibaldi.   A severe strain was therefore put on the cities of North Italy, not at that date as wealthy as they have since become, to supply at a few weeks' notice, out of the civil population, a complete army of volunteers.   The strain was the more severe because so large a portion of the patriotic youth of the Peninsula had already enlisted in the regular army of Piedmont, which, so long as Garibaldi was on the war-path, was urgently required for home defence against a possible attack from Austria.   Yet within three months of the capture of Palermo more than 20,000 volunteers were shipped off south from Genoa and Leghorn.[1]

The great majority of these Northerners proved in the battle of the Volturno that they could fight bravely. And it is reasonable to suppose that nine-tenths of them went to the war mainly from patriotic motives, for there was no compulsion to enlist except public opinion, no reward except mental satisfaction.   The pay offered was insufficient to supply their daily needs on a campaign where the plunder even of food was punished by death, and where the improvised commissariat was always insufficient, and often non-existent.   When Garibaldi at Palermo heard complaints of the irregularity of the pay, he said to Bandi: 'What do you want with pay?   When a patriot has eaten his bowl of soup and when the affairs of the country are going well, what more can any one want?'   However, he agreed to fix a scale, and thenceforward officers received two francs a day, and privates one franc or less.   The Intendant General calculated two

---

[1] See Appendix B, below, *Expeditions of Volunteers who joined Garibaldi.*

GIULIO ADAMOLI.
Piedmontese, student of Pavia.

GIUSEPPE MARGARITA, OF THE THOUSAND.
(Milanese.)

TWO NORTH-ITALIAN RED-SHIRTS, 1860

THE CAIROLI FAMILY, END OF 1860

Benedetto, of the Thousand,   Giovanni, mortally wounded   The mother   Enrico, of the Thousand,
eldest, survived.   at Villa Glori, 1867.   Adelaide.   killed Villa Glori, 1867.

Absent from the group, Ernesto killed at Varese 1859, and Luigi died in Calabrian campaign 1860.

francs per man as the average for pay and maintenance combined, including both officers and privates in the estimate.[1]

Neither was there any prospect that at the end of the war the spoils would be divided among the actual victors. For the South was to be liberated, not conquered ; and furthermore the Garibaldini well knew that they were fighting to win a kingdom for a Royal Government suspicious of them if not of their leader, and fully equipped with place-hunters of its own. Financially, far more was given up than was gained by the Garibaldino—though exceptions could be named. Physically, the campaign was no holiday ; in the mountains of Sicily and Calabria these town-bred youths of an unathletic community were exposed to the utmost hardships of hunger and thirst, heat, cold, and rain, and to the thousand petty miseries of campaigning in a half-barbarous country, all of which, as privileges of a patriot's life, the old South-American guerilla expected his followers to enjoy as much as he did himself. All this they endured, and the tortures of wounds treated in ill-provided field hospitals, with an uncomplaining courage which aroused the wonder of their British companions in arms.

The difficulty of raising at a moment's notice a purely volunteer army, and of leading it to victory over regular troops, is one on which modern military authorities lay ever-increasing stress. In the light of these doctrines it will be seen that the improvised campaign narrated in this volume, even when full allowance has been made for the inferior quality of the Bourbon troops, remains a remarkable feat. It proves that fine elements of character were widely spread in the cities and market-towns of North Italy, and were brought out and fused together by the patriotic ardour of that year, when the best men

[1] *Bandi*, 210-211. *Forbes*, 163. *Conv. Dolmage. Milan MSS. Bruzzesi*, Notebook, August 1-2, and printed table of scale of pay, September 30, 1860. *Risorg.* anno iii. fasc. 1-2, p. 88.

of a race too intermittent in its activities, and too uncertain in its emotions, were wrought up to six months
of steady heroism by the appeal of the great simple
passions of liberty and country.

The work of raising and equipping these 20,000 volunteers was carried out equally by the Cavourian and by
the more advanced parties. Their rivalry for the affections of the people, and their quarrel for the right to
direct the revolution, had the effect of stirring each side
to greater activity on Garibaldi's behalf. Since the
friends of Mazzini and of Cavour could not have sat side
by side in one office, there were three or more separate
organisations engaged in the work. First, there was
Bertani's *Central Committee in Aid of Garibaldi*, seated at
Genoa, conducted in the interest of the advanced groups ;
secondly, the more moderate *National Society*, seated at
Turin, of which Cavour's agent La Farina was now
President, in place of Garibaldi resigned ;[1] thirdly, the
Million Rifles Fund, with its armoury at Milan, founded
by Garibaldi but conducted from first to last under the
control of the Government.[2] The Million Rifles Fund
did not, like Bertani's Committee and the National
Society, actually enlist and equip men, but it supplied
the National Society with a great part of its arms and
money, and was itself secretly supplied, to this end, with
large sums from the Royal treasury, which in this
roundabout manner helped to finance Garibaldi's operations in June and July.[3]

One or both of the rival organisations, Cavour's
National Society and Bertani's Committee, had local
branches and agents collecting money and enlisting men
in every chief town of free Italy, from Turin to Rimini,
from Brescia to Leghorn.[4]

[1] For the previous history of the National Society, see *Garibaldi and the
Thousand*, pp. 65, 165, and index under heading Italy.

[2] For the previous history of the Million Rifles Fund, see *Garibaldi and the
Thousand*, p. 165 and index.

[3] *Luzio, Giorn. d' It.* 5 May, 1907. *Chiala*, iv. p. clxiii, note.

[4] See Appendix C, i. below.

In the enslaved provinces there was more secrecy but scarcely less activity; the conspirators of the Papal States were in constant correspondence with Mazzini and Bertani, who urged them not to send their young men to Sicily but to hold them in readiness for a rising which Bertani pledged himself to assist with an invasion of volunteers from the North.[1] But from Austrian Venetia, the liberation of which was not immediately contemplated, several thousands of young men escaped over the Lombard frontier by help of a committee that sat for the purpose at Milan and sent them on by way of Genoa to join Garibaldi.[2]

An English engineer named Denton who was travelling on business through North Italy that summer, described the excitement he found in every town and village; the patriotic newspapers read aloud at the street corner to satisfy a 'rapacity' for news 'astonishing to an Englishman;' Garibaldi's name overheard every moment; Garibaldi's photograph seen in every size and shape, from the shirt-stud to the 'big poster on the town's walls'; the volunteers openly departing by the light of day in their red shirts and képis. When Mr. Denton crossed into Austrian Venetia he found the flame burning not the less intensely for being forced to smoulder. He was able to see below the surface, because every patriot thought it safe to open his heart to him, when no stranger was by, on no other security than the fact that he was an Englishman. One Venetian merchant, leaving his home because the Austrian spies and police had at length rendered his life unbearable, said to him : 'That is my nephew, and he is going to join the ranks of the future liberator of Venetia. He will make the fifth nephew I shall have serving Garibaldi, and out of sixteen young men I had in my counting-house ten have left me' for Sicily. 'So it will be,' he said, 'throughout

[1] *Milan MSS. A. B.* Plico B, sec. G. *Bertani*, ii. 141-147. *Rome MSS. Mazzini letters, V.E.* 2366, secret agent's report from Northern Umbria.
[2] *Bertani Comp.* 4.

Venetia ; there will not be a young man of spirit left at home.'[1]

No class and no party and no district in North Italy was behindhand in the offering of lives or of money. Rich and poor sent their private offerings from all over the country, in sums which to our English standards are not immense, but which represented the widow's mite in many straitened Italian households.[2] The Cavourian municipal bodies of great towns like Milan voted large sums out of rates to the Million Rifles fund. Cremona alone, a town well below thirty thousand inhabitants, sent nearly a thousand volunteers and gave over 130,000 *lire*, partly by subscription, partly by a loan which the municipality raised in order to aid Garibaldi's expedition.[3]

But Bergamo, Brescia, and Pavia were the chief Garibaldian cities, next to Genoa herself. In Pavia the Cairoli exercised a supreme influence, based upon nothing more material than the respect of their fellow-citizens for their integrity and their leadership in patriotic endeavour. The father, Carlo Cairoli, Professor of Surgery, had been made Podestà of his native city in 1848, and had died soon after its re-occupation by the Austrians, leaving his five boys to the influence of his widow Adelaide. ' The mother of the Cairoli' had first lost Ernesto at Garibaldi's battle of Varese in 1859. In 1860 Benedetto and Enrico had gone with the Thousand and were both lying wounded in Palermo, when Luigi, aged twenty-two, threw up his commission in the regular army and followed them to Sicily. In September he died of typhus, the result of the hardships of the march through Calabria. During the days when he was contracting his fatal illness, he wrote a long and cheerful letter to his mother and to his betrothed, from the remote Calabrian village of Spezzano Albanese. ' Mama,' so the letter ended, ' I must tell you one thing, which I have tried to be silent about so as not to alarm your modesty,

[1] *Times*, August 31, 1860, p. 7, Mr. Denton's letter.
[2] See Appendix C, ii. below.   [3] *Cremona*, 10.

but which I can no longer leave untold. Yesterday evening my hosts asked me my name. You should have seen the effect which it had on them to hear that I was a Cairoli, or rather a son of the Cairoli mother, of Pavia. And this is not the first time that it has happened to me. Garibaldi's proclamation to the women of Sicily,' [in which Adelaide's patriotic sacrifices were held up for their imitation,] ' was greedily read in all Sicily and the Neapolitan continent, and so your name is already venerated by every good Italian of the South. . . . Good-bye, Mama, good-bye, Adriana.' [1] Luigi died a fortnight after writing this letter, but Benedetto and Enrico recovered of their wounds. Seven years later Enrico, and Giovanni the youngest of the five, received their death-wounds from the Papal troops at Villa Glori, while attempting at the head of a small band of men to force their way into Rome. Benedetto, the eldest, and the mother Adelaide alone survived the wars of liberation. The story of the Cairoli, all bound together by ties of the strongest affection, all devoted wholly to their country's cause, all free from any taint of self-interest, of bombast, or of violence, was revered by Garibaldi and his contemporaries, and has become traditional with posterity as the most perfect example of that family life which fostered the purest qualities of the Italian *risorgimento*.

The papers of Bertani's Central Committee in Aid of Garibaldi have been preserved. The historian can turn over voluminous masses of accounts, bills, purchases of steamers, lists of arms, uniforms, and stores acquired and despatched, besides many documents more poignantly human. There are hundreds of letters for May, June, and July offering service, or rather imploring to be allowed to serve under Garibaldi.[2] In many cases the writer offers to throw up for life some well-paid civil or military post under Government, the Italian idea of bliss, in order to be able to serve Garibaldi for six

---

[1] *Cairoli*, 89-92, 349.   [2] *Milan MSS. A. B.* Plichi xiii. xiv. xv.

months. Frequently the aspirant states his age to be seventeen, apparently as the ideal age for a soldier. Sometimes the letter speaks for a group of persons preparing to come. Sometimes it serves to introduce a would-be volunteer who brings it by hand. We can imagine Bertani, his emaciated body propped up on the pillows of his sick-bed, working night and day with the light of fever, almost of madness, in his eyes ; his hand shakes as he tears open one after another of these letters, and dashes off a line of answer to each in an almost indecipherable scrawl. Racked by an incessant cough, unable to speak articulately, unable to swallow his food, he had not in the middle of June the strength to leave or return to bed except by his friends' help ; when they told him he would die if he continued to work, he replied, 'What does it matter ?'[1] To their surprise he recovered as the summer drew on.

The misery of some who met with Bertani's point-blank refusal to accept them as volunteers is depicted in their piteous second appeals, refusing to be denied.[2] Meanwhile Genoa was crammed full of volunteers who had been duly forwarded by their local committees or who had paid for their own journey thither on the chance of getting a passage to Sicily ; all these complained bitterly if they were not shipped south by the very next steamer.

One important group of letters[3] proves that Bertani faithfully carried out Garibaldi's instructions that officers of the regular army should be restrained from sending in their papers, and men from deserting the ranks in order to join him. Garibaldi, when he sailed for Sicily, had left behind him a proclamation exhorting Italian

---

[1] *Bertani*, ii. 76-77.

[2] A girl of the Genoese working class writes to him confidentially on July 4 : 'Genoa and the world weary me, so far from the heroes of Italy. . . . My parents may perhaps be adverse to my decision to go to Sicily, but you who are, like Garibaldi, the incarnation of the Italian mind and heart, can find means to persuade them.' *Milan MSS. A. B.* Plico xv. No. 180. Teresa Penco's letter.

[3] *Milan MSS. A. B.* Plico xii. No. 13.

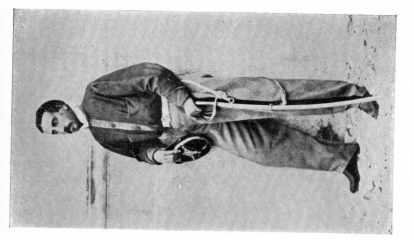

GIUSEPPE MISSORI, 1869

DR. AGOSTINO BERTANI.

COLONEL DUNNE, 1860

soldiers to remain at their posts, and Bertani, as we find, had a formula ready drawn out to the same effect, copies of which were stacked in his office. When, as often happened, he received an application from some officer in the royal army, desirous of joining Garibaldi, it was his custom to sign a copy of this formula and send it off to stop him. He made some exceptions, but this was his usual policy. In spite of it many royal officers, sergeants, and corporals appeared in Sicily, not a few having been sent out by the Cavourian agencies. Some had the tacit consent of Victor Emmanuel or of the military authorities, who knew that Garibaldi stood in need of drill masters ;[1] but others risked and in many cases lost their careers.[2] Without such a stiffening of regulars, it is doubtful whether the volunteers could have conquered. But if Garibaldi and Bertani had not done their best to keep the movement within limits, the discipline and numbers of the royal army might have been dangerously weakened.

Meanwhile Mazzini was lying hidden in Genoa, secretly exerting through Bertani and others an important influence on events.

The great exile, who in the 'thirties and 'forties had raised the Italian movement into a religion by which thousands lived and died, had since 1848 remained behind in his old position, while the national cause to which he had given the first vital impulse rallied under other leaders and moved forward to final victory. He was out of touch with the new age. Even this year 1860, which saw Italy united in fulfilment of his dream dreamt thirty years ago, seemed to him merely another chapter of national shame and weakness. Since the sacrifice of personal happiness was the soul of Mazzini's teaching and character, there is artistic fitness in his life-long

---

[1] *E.g. Bandi*, 60. *Adamoli*, 71-73, 78.
[2] *Conv. Dolmage.* Mr. Dolmage talked with many of them and heard their stories. These stories are indeed scattered thickly up and down Garibaldian literature.

disappointment; and his old age, though sad, is far above our pity. He would have been wiser as a statesman, but less great as a prophet, if he had reconciled himself to the monarchy and settled down to die content in the country which he had made a nation. But, as he wrote to Bertani at this time, 'after I have helped to make Italy one under the King, I shall go back to London and write to tell the Italians that they are idiots.' [1] He clung to his Republicanism, to his hatred for Cavour's methods and of royal officialdom. Politically he erred, but spiritually he thus found a means of telling himself the truth that the Italians of the new monarchy were not the regenerated mankind whose immediate advent he had prophesied with Shelley-like ardour in the great days of his youth. 'I shall have no more joy in Italy,' he wrote, 'I shall have none, even if to-morrow the Unity were to be proclaimed from Rome. The country, with its contempt for all ideals, has killed the soul within me.' [2] If he deceived himself, it was never to gain soul's ease. If it was delusion in him to believe that by calling their State a Republic his countrymen could materially increase their own chance of being great and good, yet there was Spartan courage in his acknowledgment of the fact that the Third Italy was not the Kingdom of God which he had set out to establish on earth. He saw the Kingdom of Italy established instead, and it pleased him not. But if the reformation of human nature had failed, the making of Italy was a sufficiently remarkable feat, as Carlyle was driven to confess for all his scorn of Mazzini's doctrines. It showed that the pre-scientific idealists, of whom Mazzini and Garibaldi were the survivors from an earlier age, had a power over the springs of human action which the politics of materialism may despise or explain, but can never imitate.

At the beginning of May, Mazzini had left London for Genoa. He came out intending to sail with Garibaldi and the Thousand, but finding that they had left Genoa

---

[1] *Mazzini*, xi. p. xcvii.   [2] *Ibid.*, xi. p. ciii.   Letter of June 19, 186c

two or three days before his arrival, he determined not to follow.[1] 'I am tired,' he wrote, 'of being misunderstood. If I was to go to Sicily now, every one would say that I had gone to undermine Garibaldi, or God knows what. Besides, as far as Sicily is concerned, it would be too late. And for what we intend to try on the mainland, I cannot hope to change Garibaldi, who loves me not.'[2]

Mazzini's presence in his native city was a secret kept by a few friends. He had to escape detection by the police, for Cavour would have been glad to deport or imprison him during the crisis. He strolled about, often by night and sometimes even by day, through the deep, narrow alleys of old Genoa, the scenes of his childhood and of his brooding student youth. He had no disguise beyond a shaven chin and a low felt hat pulled well over his tell-tale forehead and eyes. Thus attired he amused himself by stopping Cavour's spies and asking them to lend him a light for his cigar, or to tell him the way up some familar street.[3] By day he wrote notes to Bertani ; by night he came to visit his sick-bed. It was a delicate situation : for Bertani, being now Garibaldi's agent, wondered how far he ought, in that capacity, to connect himself again with his old master.[4] His evident hesitation grieved Mazzini, who was already suffering from a political difference with Aurelio Saffi, his fellow-exile in England, once his fellow-triumvir of the Roman Republic : Saffi, dearly as he loved Mazzini, did not feel justified in entrusting to him the expenditure of the money raised for Garibaldi's expedition in Great Britain.[5]

Bertani, however, in spite of occasional misgivings, fell once more under the spell of *l'amico*—'the friend'— as Mazzini was called by the whole subterranean world

[1] *Rome MSS. Mazz. letters V. E.* 2429, May 8 to Grillenzoni ; 2330, May 9 to Bertani. *Fam. Crauford*, 207-208.

[2] *Mazzini*, xi. p. ci. June 19, to Nicotera, Mosto, and Savi in Sicily.

[3] *Mario Supp.* 325-326.

[4] *Mazzini*, xi. pp. xcvi-vii. *Fam. Crauford*, 211-214.

[5] *Fam. Crauford*, 213-214.

of Italian conspiracy. Indeed, from 'the friend's' first arrival in Genoa early in May, Bertani entered with him into the great plan for invading the Papal States.[1]

It was the intention of Bertani's Committee in Aid of Garibaldi to send the volunteers whom they enlisted for his service, not to join him at once in Sicily, but to meet him at Naples, going by the land route, and liberating Umbria and the Marches from the Pope on their way south. The city and district of Rome, being garrisoned by French troops, was to be avoided for the present, but it was hoped that when Garibaldi from the south and Medici from the north had met in triumph at Naples, the enthusiasm for unity would overcome all obstacles, and they would be able before the year was out to proclaim Victor Emmanuel King of Italy from the Capitol. This plan had not been entirely foreign to Garibaldi's own intentions when he sailed for Sicily with the Thousand. He had then assigned to Medici the task of leading the next expedition, instructing him to send reinforcements both to Sicily and also to the Papal Marches and Umbria, where a rising was, said Garibaldi, about to take place.[2] Whether Medici in person was to go with the reinforcements to Sicily or with the invaders of the Pope's territories, was left undecided in Garibaldi's letter.[3]

---

[1] *Mario's Mazzini*, 406 (chap. xxiii.). *Fam. Crauford*, 210, letter of May 13. *Taylor MSS.* letters xciii., clxvi.

[2] Presumably to be stirred up by Zambianchi.

[3] Garibaldi's letter (see *Garibaldi and the Thousand*, p. 204, and *Medici*, 5), reads as follows :—

'GENOA, *May* 5, 1860.

'DEAR MEDICI,—It is better that you should remain behind, and you can be more useful so. Bertani, La Farina, the Directors [of the Million Rifles Fund] at Milan will furnish you, on the presentation of this letter, with all the means you will require. You must not only make every effort to send reinforcements of men and arms into Sicily, but to do the same for the Marches and Umbria where there will soon be a rising and where soon it will be necessary to support it to the utmost. Tell the Italians to follow you in entire confidence, and that the time has come to make the Italy that we all yearn for.' In the orders which Garibaldi gave to Zambianchi, he speaks of Medici going to the Papal States as a possibility, but not as a certainty. See *Garibaldi and the Thousand*, p. 216, *Mario's Mazzini*, 404.

Such were the vague instructions which he left behind, obviously requiring a good deal of interpretation. Bertani, under the influence of Mazzini, decided to divert practically the whole of the reinforcements to the Papal States. Neither of them military men, they were both under the delusion that Garibaldi could overrun Sicily and cross the Straits with his Thousand alone, aided by the islanders. 'Sicily is safe,' said Mazzini, 'let us think of the rest. . . . You do not know the genius of Garibaldi and the indomitable determination of the Sicilians to be rid of Bourbon rule. Henceforth we must help Sicily from Central Italy by way of the Abruzzi. Garibaldi has with him a body of good officers,' who would suffice to drill and lead the Sicilians. 'To the Centre every one: Umbria and the Marches liberated, we will reach Garibaldi across the Abruzzi.'[1]

The supposition that Garibaldi could have advanced from Palermo without strong reinforcements from North Italy was perhaps the crudest of the mistakes involved in this scheme, and was, moreover, the only point where the scheme deviated from Garibaldi's own instructions. But it may further be doubted whether a few thousand volunteers, under a chief other than Garibaldi himself, would have sufficed to liberate Umbria and the Marches. Mazzini told Bertani that all would go well because the Papal troops would join the liberators in the hour of battle.[2] But the Pope's fighting regiments, his newly levied Austrian, Irish, and French crusaders, were about as likely to join the red-shirts as the red-shirts were to join them. These Papal troops put up a gallant though hopeless fight against the superior force of the Piedmontese regular army in September, and there is no reason to think that they would not have opposed a very serious resistance to Medici's scanty volunteers in June.[3]

[1] *Mario's Mazzini*, 404-405. See also a letter of his to Bertani prior to the landing of Garibaldi: 'Collect money, but don't send it to Sicily. If Garibaldi does not get there it is not needed; if he gets there, it is equally not needed. His presence there will suffice.' *Rome MSS. Mazz. letters*, 2343.
[2] *Mazzini*, xi. p. xcix.   [3] Cadolini in *Mem. Stor. Mil.* ii. 176-180.

Even if victorious in the field, how could an army of irregulars without siege guns take Ancona? But if the plan to liberate the Marches and join Garibaldi at Naples was to succeed at all, it must succeed completely and at once.

For not only the Papal army but the Foreign Powers had to be considered. Austria, who until 1859 had herself garrisoned the Marches for the Pope, had since the beginning of 1860 been pouring into the port of Ancona thousands of Austrian subjects to be enlisted in the Papal army. Would Austria, then, have watched unmoved the capture of these districts by Revolutionary bands? And as to France, even if Medici had left Rome untouched, would Napoleon have allowed the red-shirts to do to Umbria in June what he allowed Cavour to do in September?

On May 7, the day after Garibaldi's departure, Medici still regarded the invasion of the Papal States as his own probable destiny;[1] but when all these grave considerations—the weakness of Garibaldi's military position in Sicily, the strength of the new Papal army and the old Papal fortresses, and the probable action of Austria and France—were laid before his cool judgment by Cavour's agents, La Farina, Amari, and Melenchini, he was not long in deciding for Sicily. As early as May 12, even before the news of Garibaldi's landing at Marsala had arrived, Medici had been won round to Cavour and common sense, and had declared that he would take his expedition by sea to join Garibaldi.[2]

The quarrel that divided Mazzini and Bertani's Com-

[1] 'I have remained behind to support the bold enterprise by a second expedition, or better still *by a powerful diversion elsewhere.*' Medici's letter to Panizzi, May 7, *Panizzi*, 425.

[2] *La Farina*, ii. 319, letter of May 12. *Amari*, ii. 83, letter of May 13. Chiala, iv, p. cclxii. *Bertani Comp.* 6. After having helped before May 12 to persuade Medici to take his men to Sicily, La Farina a few days later was foolish enough to advise that no men but only money should be sent to Sicily—the men apparently to go to Naples. See La Farina's letter of May 17, in *Medici*, 14-15. Fortunately no one listened to him.

mittee on the one side, from Cavour, Medici, and the National Society on the other, arose on this question of the destination of the volunteers, not on the question of Republic or Monarchy. On the latter point even Mazzini had, for the time being, surrendered.[1] But on the former the quarrel was in full vigour even before the fall of Palermo.[2] It first arose on the question whether Medici should go to Sicily or to the Papal States, and it was revived in the same form over the departure of every large consignment of volunteers that left Genoa in June, July, and August.

If Bertani's plan of invading the Papal States had been carried out, Garibaldi would have been left locked up at Palermo for want of men, and Italy would probably have met with a great disaster in the Centre. And yet Bertani's policy, though it would have been fatal if put into practice, proved invaluable as a stimulus to Cavour. The constant threat of the advanced party to send their own men into the Papal States, coupled with Garibaldi's success in the South, finally drove Cavour to invade the Papal States himself when the time was ripe. Mazzini and Bertani, wrong in detail, were right in their two general principles—first, that the Pope and the King of Naples ought to be attacked this year while the revolutionary enthusiasm created by Garibaldi's success was at its height ;[3] and secondly, that they ought to be attacked from both north and south at once.

[1] In one of his almost daily notes to Bertani, written in June, he says :—

'I have no republican intentions. I strive for nothing but the Unity. The cry *Viva la Repubblica* would seem to me a real mistake at this moment.' *Mazzini*, xi. p. xcvii.

Again in his letter to his republican friends, Nicotera, Mosto, and Savi, June 19 (*ditto*, p. cii), he writes that he would prefer the 'neutral banner' and the single cry 'Italy,' leaving the form of government to be settled by the nation later. But if the leaders of the volunteer movement insist on Garibaldi's cry, 'Italy and Victor Emmanuel,' Mazzini will make no protest even against that, and 'will follow the column in silence.'

[2] *Amari*, ii. 87-90. *Risorg.* anno i. fasc. 5-6, p. 993. *Dallolio*, 97-115, on some fruitless attempts to heal the breach, made in the last half of May.

[3] *Mazzini*, xi. p. xcviii. 'Enthusiasm cannot go on increasing indefinitely.'

At present Cavour was content to help Garibaldi. Having won over Medici to abandon the Papal States and to go direct to Sicily in Bertani's despite, the Government was bound to fit him out and send him with all possible speed. Medici's expedition, and the expedition of Cosenz a few weeks later, were armed, clothed, and shipped at the expense of the Cavourian National Society and the Million Rifles Fund.[1] Since these organisations had no offices in Genoa, the port of departure, it was necessary for Medici and Cosenz to set up there a *Military Office* of their own, as they did not wish to be dependent on Bertani's Committee.[2] Dr. Bertani did, however, fit out the ambulance for their expeditions, and both of them, when they respectively sailed, parted from him on speaking terms.[3]

The Bertani Committee also supplied the Military Office of Medici and Cosenz with a good many of its best recruits, in addition to the men whom the Cavourians raised for themselves in Milan and elsewhere.[4] But the steamers, the arms, and the money for the expeditions of June and July came almost entirely from the Cavourian agencies. It was only in August that Bertani and his friends sent out the great expeditions which they themselves had paid for and equipped. In June and July hundreds of thousands of *lire* were secretly supplied by the King's Government to purchase the steamers and equip the men for Medici and Cosenz.[5] Over 6000 firearms were obtained for them by Cavour from the armoury of the Million Rifles Fund at Milan, which had been closed to Garibaldi himself a month before by the inconvenient scruples of Massimo D'Azeglio, the Governor of the city.[6] Cavour now eased D'Azeglio's conscience by purchasing the weapons with the alleged

---

[1] See references in Appendices B (p. 320) and C, below, and *Bertani Comp.* 7-8 in particular.

[2] *Bertani Comp.* 3-4.   [3] *Bertani*, ii. 76-77, 91.   [4] *Bertani Comp.* 4, 9.

[5] *Luzio, Giorn. d' It.* May 5, 1907, Finzi's correspondence. See Appendices B and C, below.

[6] *Garibaldi and the Thousand*, 182-183.

intention of arming the National Guard,—and then sent them to Medici at Genoa.[1]

In the course of the summer D'Azeglio gradually discovered that he was being fooled. When in obedience to the ostensible orders of Government he tried to put difficulties in the way of recruiting volunteers in Milan, he found that all the neighbouring Governors gave him the cold shoulder. Finally a private letter from a highly placed official to one of D'Azeglio's subordinates served to open the Governor's eyes : ' It seems,' said the letter, ' that at Milan you are not much in touch with the real intentions of the Government.' Finally D'Azeglio retired, alleging the ground of ill-health. To the end of his life he would never allow that Cavour's underhand methods had been right.[2]

[1] *Luzio, Corr. della Sera*, Dec. 8, 1909, letter of Farini to D'Azeglio, May 29. *Bertani Comp.* 7.

[2] *D'Azeglio*, 306-308. *Persano*, 463-465.

CHAPTER III

' Addio, mia bell' addio
L'armata se ne va ;
Se non partissi anch' io
Sarebbe una viltà.'[1]

' Farewell, farewell, my true love,
The army's on the move ;
And if I stayed with you, love
A coward I should prove.'

THE three steamers which were to carry Medici and his men to Sicily had been purchased from a French company nominally on behalf of De Rohan, a Yankee devotee of the Italian cause. They had been hastily rechristened the *Washington*, *Oregon*, and *Franklin*, and the United States Consul at Genoa, accompanied by 'Garibaldi's Englishman,' Peard, who was starting with the expedition, went on board the *Washington* and hauled up on it the stars and stripes.[2] A little before dawn on June 10 Medici sailed with the *Washington* and *Oregon* from a spot a few miles west of Genoa, where a midnight embarkation had taken place, and on the same day the *Franklin* sailed from the shore between Pisa and Leghorn, where she had taken on board the Tuscan volunteers.[3] These two parts of Medici's expedition met

[1] There is always some popular song that is being sung, whistled, and hummed *ad nauseam*. In the Italian armies of 1860 it was ' Addio, mia bell' addio.'

[2] *Peard*, 813. *D. News*, June 26, 1860, p. 4. (The latter, signed ' A. J. M.,' is clearly by Alberto and Jessie Mario, who were in the *Washington*.) *F. O. Sard. Hudson*, June 9-10, Nos. 271, 277.

[3] *Peard*, 813. *F. O. Sard. Hudson*, June 10-11, 15, Nos. 271, 273, 277, 281. *Mariotti*, 417-419.

safely at Cagliari, the port in Southern Sardinia which became henceforth an important place of call for successive ship-loads of Garibaldini. But two other vessels, the small *Utile* and the American clipper *Charles and Jane*, which were also expected at Cagliari with another thousand men, were captured on the way by Neapolitan cruisers, and taken into the harbour of Gaeta. Medici, after awaiting them for some time in vain, left Cagliari with the *Washington*, *Oregon*, and *Franklin*, containing 2500 men, 6000 or 8000 rifles and muskets, and an immense store of ammunition. This was the first aid despatched to Garibaldi from the mainland, with the exception of sixty men and a stock of arms and powder which the *Utile*, since captured by the Neapolitans, had run through to Palermo by way of Marsala on an earlier and more fortunate voyage.[1]

Medici's three vessels left Cagliari early on the afternoon of June 16. Shortly before nightfall of the following day, when they were nearing the Sicilian coast and entering the zone of greatest danger from the Neapolitan cruisers, they saw a Piedmontese war-vessel steering towards them. When she came alongside she turned out to be the *Gulnara*, whose commander came aboard the *Washington* to speak with Medici. He had orders from his admiral, Persano, to conduct the expedition safely to Castellamare,[2] the landing-place agreed on between Persano and Garibaldi. The commander of the *Gulnara* also made in Persano's name a strange request for the instant surrender of Mazzini. Medici was able to assure him that, although the Republican Alberto Mario and his English wife, Jessie White Mario, were on board, Mazzini himself had not accompanied the ex-

---

[1] See Appendices B and C, below. Medici actually arrived with 2500 men, though he told Garibaldi that he was bringing 3500 at a time when he still believed Corte's 1000 men would be able to join him. *Persano*, 41 note. This led me to give the numbers wrongly in early editions of *Garibaldi and the Thousand*, p. 325.

[2] Twenty-five miles west of Palermo : it must not be confused with the Castellamare fortress at Palermo.

pedition.[1] A few hours later they reached Castellamare and began to disembark before midnight. Garibaldi came to meet them, and they marched in high spirits to Palermo, arriving there on the 19th and the two following days, just as the last of the Neapolitan garrison took their departure under the terms of the capitulation.[2] The new era in Garibaldi's enterprise had now fairly begun.

The demand made by the commander of the *Gulnara* for the surrender of Mazzini out at sea was the end of a curious story. Cavour, who after the fall of Palermo had adopted the policy of aiding Garibaldi—upon terms —instructed Admiral Persano to lend him what covert help he could, but at the same time sent out a confidential agent of his own to represent to the Dictator of Sicily the wishes of the Government of Turin.[3] Cavour's choice for this purpose had fallen on the Sicilian, La Farina, President of the National Society, who like Bertani, had done much to bring Cavour and Garibaldi together in old days, and like Bertani seemed now to aim at undoing his own work. He was already an object of dislike in Garibaldian circles when Cavour unwisely chose him for this delicate task. Those of Cavour's friends who knew Garibaldi foresaw inevitable disaster.[4] La Farina arrived in Palermo during the first week of June, and began almost at once to quarrel with the new masters of the city. He turned his reports to Cavour into a series of bitter attacks on the Dictator and his administration, some just and some unjust, but all calculated to alienate the two men on whose alliance the welfare of Italy depended.[5]

---

[1] *Persano*, 34-48. *Caraguel*, 25-27. *Peard*, 815. *Bianchi's Cavour*, 98 note. *Chiala*, vi. 564.

[2] *Garibaldi and the Thousand*, 325-327. *Peard*, 815-817. *Cremona*, 39.

[3] *Chiala*, iii. 257. *La F. Biundi*, ii. 78.

[4] Valerio wrote to Castelli on June 3, ' For heaven's sake don't send La Farina. Garibaldi and his friends detest him.' *Castelli Cart.* i. 305.

[5] The degree to which La Farina's letters must be discounted, may be judged from the fact that in November he wrote to Cavour from Naples that

On June 12 Cavour, misinformed by his spies at Genoa as to Mazzini's movements, sent the following message to Admiral Persano :—

'We are assured that Mazzini and Miss White [Jessie Mario] have embarked on board the *Washington* that is taking volunteers to Palermo.   Send La Farina to Garibaldi to invite him in the King's name to arrest Mazzini, and to give him into your hands.   He must tell him that Mazzini's presence in Sicily would necessitate the recall of the squadron and ruin the national cause in Europe.   You will send Mazzini to Genoa on board the *Carlo Alberto*. . . . Should Garibaldi refuse to have Mazzini arrested you will immediately prepare to depart with the fleet and will send the *Authion* to Cagliari to receive instructions.' [1]

This letter proves that there were limits to Cavour's understanding of Garibaldi, though it was large compared with Garibaldi's understanding of Cavour.   It was an error to expect Garibaldi to hand over to prison his former master and honoured rival, now in the decline of years and prosperity, and a folly to enforce the demand by a threat to the liberator of Palermo in his hour of triumph.   Cavour had never had the chance of studying Garibaldi and his friends at close quarters ; otherwise he would have known that Garibaldi himself was above all things a gentleman, and that Mazzini was regarded by the whole world of exiles and advanced patriots, even when they most differed from him, with a reverence which to Cavour was foolishness.

La Farina flatly refused to carry out the mission, saying that he had no influence with the Dictator, and compelled the Admiral to take the message himself.   Persano, who was at this time popular with all parties, was not ordered out of the room as La Farina would probably have been, but Garibaldi replied that he would not arrest Mazzini unless he began to intrigue against

Mazzini was speculating for his private gain under cover of collecting money to liberate Rome and Venice.   For this vile charge and for its refutation see *La Farina*, ii. 443.   *Ire Pol.* 98-101.
    [1] *Chiala*, iii. 263.

the monarchy of Victor Emmanuel. Persano, fully realising Cavour's mistake in tactics, determined, instead
of making preparations to leave Palermo, to effect the
arrest of Mazzini before he landed in Sicily. That was
why he commissioned the commander of the *Gulnara*,
when he went to meet Medici, to make the arrest out at
sea. But since Mazzini was all the while in Genoa the
incident ended in *fiasco*.[1]

The main object of La Farina's mission to Sicily was
to secure the immediate annexation of the island to
Piedmont. Cavour was unwilling to allow Garibaldi,
by prolonging his Dictatorship, to acquire a civil and
military establishment of his own, independent of the
Royal Government. It was necessary to send out arms
and men to Garibaldi, but it was impossible not to dread
some of the uses to which he might turn those arms and
his own immense popularity. Surrounded as he was in
great measure by the friends of Mazzini and Bertani, by
the Marios, by Crispi, by Nicotera, it was probable that,
while continuing loyal as ever to the monarchy, he might
grow less and less amenable to the advice of the King's
Ministers. Cavour was struggling to keep his feet in a
flood of diplomatic troubles which Garibaldi thought it
unpatriotic even to consider, and yet the Dictator's independent actions were the prime factor in the diplomatic situation of which he ignored the very existence.
There were also grave political dangers of an internal
character in a prolonged Dictatorship : Cavour was endeavouring to build up the unity of Italy on the only
possible basis, that of a constitutional monarchy, and if
the advanced parties were to get all the credit of the
revolution in South Italy and enjoy an indefinite tenure
of power in the Provinces which they liberated, it would
be a bad beginning for the principle of authority in the
new State as represented by the King's Parliamentary
Cabinet at Turin. Therefore Cavour desired as soon
as possible to dominate the revolution, and like the

[1] *Persano*, 36-48, 53.

falconer to lure his hawk back after it had struck the prey.

These motives, and these principles of action, were sound in themselves, but there remains always the question of particular application. If indeed the enemies of Italy had already been struck down by Garibaldi, or if Cavour had been prepared to strike them down himself in open war, then no date would have been too early for the annexation of Sicily. But the House of Bourbon still reigned on the mainland, and could be overturned by Garibaldi alone. When Cavour attempted to obtain the annexation of Sicily in June and early July, he was acting on the mistaken belief that an annexationist revolution could be engineered by his own agents in Naples.[1] He imagined that the rank and file of the Neapolitan army was prepared to come over to the Italian cause, and that a civil and military *pronunciamento* would speedily bring the Bourbon dynasty to an end by the act of the Neapolitans themselves. If such a revolution had been possible, it would no doubt have been safer to dispense with Garibaldi's further service as an independent chieftain, and to bring him back to the place which he had occupied in the war of 1859, as the leader of volunteers fighting in front of the royal armies of Italy, whenever they should next be led against Pope or Austrian. But Cavour had yet to learn by experience that the Neapolitans would effect no revolution for themselves, and that as he was not himself prepared to declare war on Francis II, Garibaldi must be allowed to cross the Straits of Messina if Italy was to be free.

If in June the Dictator had yielded to the cry for immediate annexation which La Farina stirred up among the Sicilians, the island would have passed officially into

---

[1] For these agents and their mission, see pp. 22-23 above. On July 14 Cavour wrote to Admiral Persano :—

'On the one hand, we must at all costs prevent Garibalda from passing on to the continent, and on the other, we must provoke a revolution in Naples. If this succeeds, the government of Victor Emmanuel would be proclaimed without delay.' *Persano*, 88.

the hands of Piedmont, and before Garibaldi had marched onward from Palermo, Victor Emmanuel would have found himself completely responsible to the Powers for every act of every red-shirt in Sicily. In that case Garibaldi, who even as it was came very near to being stopped at the Straits of Messina by the Powers, would most certainly have been prevented from crossing to the mainland, since Cavour could no longer have pleaded inability to control his action. Then, when the Neapolitan revolution had missed fire, the great statesman would have discovered too late the flaw in his plans, and the Pope and the King of Naples would have continued to govern Central and Southern Italy.

All this was clearly foreseen at the time by not a few Cavourians, including Michele Amari, the wise and learned historian of the Sicilian Vespers, who was just returning from exile to his own Palermo to work there for Italian unity. Amari was certain that the Dictator did right to refuse annexation in June, because annexation would have confined him to the island ; but he was equally certain that he was wrong to refuse annexation when once he had crossed the Straits.[1]

For nearly a month La Farina laid siege to Garibaldi. At his instigation, petitions were sent up by Sicilian ministers and municipalities, and demonstrations were held in the streets of Palermo, which showed a genuine popular desire for immediate annexation. The attitude of the islanders was neither that of Cavour nor that of Garibaldi. They desired annexation at the earliest possible moment, because they saw in it the best security against reconquest by the Neapolitans and the quickest way to a settled government. They cried *Italia Una* with no

[1] See Amari's letter of 1862, quoted in *R. S. del R.* anno 1897, vol. ii. p. 136. See *Mario Mac.* 248 for Garibaldi's own views in June. Emilio Visconti Venosta, an out-and-out Cavourian, sent by Cavour to Naples in 1860 to stir up the revolution there, told me in 1910 that in his opinion Cavour made a mistake in desiring the annexation of Sicily before Garibaldi had crossed the Straits. Cadolini himself, politically the wisest and the most Cavourian of the red-shirts of 1860, expressed to me the same opinion.

feigned zeal when they saw their protectors, the red-shirts, and hoped for the Bersaglieri to follow, as averters of Bourbon reconquest; but they cared little whether the hated Neapolitans were or were not brought into the Union, and only the more enlightened individuals among them strongly supported Garibaldi's project of crossing the Straits.[1]   But while, from these selfish motives, they favoured Cavour's plan of immediate annexation, on the other hand, their devotion to *Garibardi*, who had come to their rescue like a Paladin of old, was so powerful a compound of superstition with pure human gratitude and love that no difference of political opinion could wear it away.   As late as the middle of September, when Garibaldi was clearly wrong in delaying the annexation any longer, he had only to come to show himself in Palermo, and although he was standing in the way of the popular desire, all opposition was silenced in heart-felt shouts of welcome and applause.[2]   When, therefore, in June, La Farina represented the island to Cavour as being already on the point of 'a terrible explosion' of popular wrath against the Dictatorship, he was writing nonsense such as only an angry man can write.[3]   Garibaldi said in effect to the people of Palermo and to his Sicilian ministers : ' I know you desire to vote the annexation at once, but I desire to free the rest of Italy first.   I have freed you, and in return I ask you to wait while I free your brothers.   Fight first and vote afterwards.'   They consented to wait, less for the sake of their brothers than for the sake of the man who asked of them this slight return for all that he and his Thousand had done.

La Farina, in his letters to Cavour, not only represented the Sicilians as more hostile to Garibaldi than they really were, but he also represented the island as falling into a state of anarchy, whereas in fact the disturbance was merely such as war and revolution must necessarily

[1] *Bertani*, ii. 86.   *Guarneri.   La Farina*, ii. 341-350.   *Castellini*, 48. *Bandi*, 206.
[2] See p. 230 below.   [3] *La Farina*, ii. 347.

bring in their train among a population unaccustomed to self-government. Bitter personal animosity to Crispi, Garibaldi's factotum in the island, goaded on La Farina to these exaggerations. The two Sicilians were deadly rivals for the affections of their countrymen. La Farina was so far right that Garibaldi was utterly unfitted to cope with any purely political or administrative situation, or to bring order out of the chaos of revolution ; but the chaos was not of the kind which destroys society. La Farina was right in saying that annexation was desirable at the earliest date possible in the interests of administration in Sicily, and, as Amari pointed out, the gendarmerie of North Italy were the only force capable of restoring complete order in the island. Yet Sicily continued under the Garibaldian rule for nearly six months without any positive catastrophe. Nor, when Victor Emmanuel's Government took over the administration, did the Cavourians find it an easy task. For ten years the island was in a continual state of unrest.[1]

The 'hermit of Caprera' was the last man likely to succeed as administrator or politician. Beyond the life of the sailor, the poet, the farmer, and the soldier in active service, he understood nothing of the ways of men. His friend and biographer has justly said :—

'Finance, police, taxation, law courts, bureaucratic machinery were to him artificial and oppressive additions to the life of nature, invented by the wickedness or craft of man ; if he could, he would have swept them all away. As he could not, he resigned himself to submit to them, but in his heart despised and abhorred them. Now for one holding these ideas, it is not easy to govern States well, or even to choose the best men to govern them, and so it was with Garibaldi. . . . One thing he saw with unerring vision during his Dictatorship, from his landing at Marsala till his arrival in Naples, and that was that he must put off the annexation of the Kingdom to the Monarchy of Victor Emmanuel until the revolution, which was to lay the foundations of Italian Unity, had become an accomplished fact.'[2]

[1] See Appendix D, below. The state of Sicily.   [2] *Guerzoni*, ii. 124-125.

Garibaldi endured La Farina for a month, and then his patience gave way. He had always held high ideas of the Dictatorial Power in times of crisis, when the freedom of the country was at stake. He was determined to advance on Naples and make Italy, and if Cavour's agent strove to lock him up in Sicily by arousing there a movement for premature annexation, the man must take the consequences. He decided to send him back to his master.

On July 7 La Farina's house was surrounded by the police ; he was made prisoner, taken on board the Piedmontese flagship and handed over to Admiral Persano, from whom La Farina's captors had the impudence to demand a 'receipt' for his person. Nor was this all. A notice of his expulsion from the island was inserted in the official paper of Sicily in terms of malignant insult. La Farina was spoken of as expelled with two other men, Griscelli and Totti. 'The three men thus deported,' said the official journal, ' were in Palermo conspiring against the existing order of things.' Now Griscelli and Totti were two of the meanest of mankind, who had narrowly escaped execution on a charge of plotting to assassinate the Dictator,[1] and La Farina had no more to do with them than he had with the beggars on the steps of the Cathedral.[2]

For the decision to deport La Farina there was much to be said. It restored political peace at Palermo, and

[1] They asserted that they had actually been paid and sent by the Bourbon Government for this purpose. Griscelli, the 'first murderer,' was primarily a police spy in the pay of Piedmont, and only secondarily a Bourbon agent, so he revealed the alleged plot to his real masters, Cavour and Villamarina, who warned Persano and Garibaldi. But the identity of Griscelli as a Piedmontese secret agent was left in doubt at Palermo for more than twenty-four hours, and he consequently had a very uncomfortable time before a Garibaldian council of war. The truth was revealed in time to save this innocent but exceedingly undesirable prisoner.

Since the complicity of the Bourbon Government in the assassination plot rests on the word of these double-lived police agents only, I do not regard it as proved. *Crispi*, 1911, p. 231. *Griscelli*, 23-29, 210-218. *Persano*, 68-71.

[2] *La F. (Biundi)*, ii. 87-97. *Persano*, 72-74. *Raffaele*, 270. *Bandi*, 206. For the La Farina incident see *Crispi*, 1911, pp. 211-235.

cut short a controversy which could not safely be conducted in the face of the enemy, who had still 20,000
troops in the island.   But the manner of his deportation
was most offensive and leaves a stain on the chivalrous
character of Garibaldi.   It is not known whether the
details were planned by him or by some ill-natured fol-
lower, but it is certain that he never punished or reproved
the gross insult offered to the emissary of the Royal
Government.

The expulsion of La Farina from Sicily, and still
more the manner of the expulsion, embittered the quarrel
of Cavourian and Garibaldian throughout the Italian
world.   But the nation as a whole, with a political in-
stinct inspired by the supreme nature of the crisis, continued to regard Cavour and Garibaldi as partners in
the great work.[1]   The Dictator had now cut the knot
of Sicilian politics and was free to advance and cross the
Straits if he had the military strength.   Indirectly he
had done Cavour a service, of which the latter was quick
to take advantage.   The incident could be used as a
proof to diplomatic Europe that the Royal Government
had no control over the Dictator's actions.   'Cavour,'
wrote Hudson to Lord John Russell, 'says that the Government have no influence with Garibaldi, who has
ordered La Farina to quit Sicily.'[2]

In spite of La Farina and the vexed question of
immediate annexation, June and July were full of happy
days for Garibaldi, for the Sicilians, and for the
volunteers who came pouring in by every steamer from
the North.   All classes of the population of Palermo,
with priests and monks conspicuous among them, trooped
down to the harbour to work at dismantling the Castellamare, the fortress whence the Bourbons had so long
held Palermo in awe.   The Church in Sicily lost none
of its enthusiasm for Garibaldi on nearer view.   The

---

[1] *Chiala*, iii. 283-290.   *Dallolio*, 123-145.   *La Farina*, ii. 355-383.
[2] *F. O. Sard. Hudson*, No. 300.

Archbishop was friendly, and even consented to bless the troops. In the nunneries of Palermo, where almost every noble family had a daughter shut up for life, the enthusiasm for 'Giuseppe' and his young followers, who had in several cases during the street fighting saved them and their churches from the brutality of the Neapolitan soldiers, was shown in many pretty and pathetic ways.[1] Garibaldi, writing to Ruggiero Settimo, the veteran statesman of Sicily's former revolutions, described the feelings which he shared so fully with the people. 'This brave people is free. Joy is written on every face, the country echoes with the glad cries of the liberated.'[2]

Garibaldi had good reason to be happy. He was fulfilling, by his own methods and with his own followers, the dream of his life which had seemed foolishness to the wise. The vision of all that he might some day do for Italy had first risen before his mind's eye more than twenty years before, as he rode over the Pampas leading a few dozen partisans to nameless skirmishes in long-forgotten wars. The vision had drawn near, only to vanish again like a mirage on the walls of Rome. Dim with fears of failure, it had yet given him strength to endure in the marshes of Ravenna and in the trading vessel on the far-away Pacific. It had cheered his farm life at Caprera with a steadier glow of hope. And now all Europe was watching this poet's daydream enact itself in the world of living men.

Bixio and many other volunteers, officers and privates, wounded and whole, lodged in the Trinacria, the famous hotel looking out upon the esplanade. Its host, Ragusa, a worthy Piedmontese, announced that for thirty days he would dine any of the Thousand for nothing, but next year he told an English guest that there had not been a man of them but had insisted upon paying his bill.[3]

---

[1] *Red Shirt*, 2-5. *Arrivabene*, ii. 62-63. *Nievo*, 360. *De Cesare*, ii. 354-355. *Conv. Dolmage.* *Bandi*, 202-203.

[2] *Ciàmpoli*, 161. June 21.   [3] *Forbes*, 76. *Conv. Dolmage.*

The Dictator and his aides-de-camp lived at the other end of the town, in the so-called 'Observatory' of the Palace over the Porta Nuova.[1] It had two balconies, one looking eastward down the mile-long Toledo to the sea, the other westward across the *Conca d'oro* to the mountains above Monreale. Its interior consisted of a modest hall of audience with the beds of the four officers on duty concealed behind screens in the four corners, and two little bedrooms beyond for Garibaldi and his secretary. The manners and way of life of the Dictator in the Palace at Palermo, as afterwards in Naples and Caserta, were in no way different from those on his Caprera farm. Formality there was none. Important visitors were sent to him to have audience whatever he was doing. Not infrequently they found him combing out his hair, to which he still gave long and careful attention, although the thick, flowing locks which had adorned the defender of Rome no longer fell over his shoulders. On another occasion, with more dispatch, he evacuated his red shirt and grey flannels and retired into bed, still discussing the business in hand with his astonished visitor.[2]

The terrace roof, connecting the Observatory, where the General lived, with the main part of the Palace, was a *rendezvous*, in the summer evenings, for the principal Garibaldini, for the ladies of Palermo, and for the officers of the Piedmontese and British navies. Eager questionings and endless stories about the battles and adventures which had led them thither so far, were mingled with confident prophecies of the coming campaign. All were agreed that they would enter both Rome and Venice before the winter. The perfumes rising from the gardens of the plain, the sun setting behind the distant mountains where the Thousand had suffered and fought, 'the place, the time, the events produced a sort of delicious ecstasy

---

[1] There is a photograph of it opposite p. 326 of *Garibaldi and the Thousand*.

[2] *Red Shirt*, 8. *Menghini*, 153. *Ashley Nat. Rev.* 495. *Elliot*, 120-121. *Miller MS.*

which annihilated distances and transfigured facts. Nor
was this a mere effect of the southern temperature, for
English officers shared those emotions, those illusions,
those errors of enthusiasm.'[1]

Among this happy crowd on the terrace appeared
one evening, like death at the feast, a group of young
men, prematurely aged and bent, looking about them
with eyes that seemed to gaze without seeing. They
were the eight remaining followers of Pisacane, who
had started with him three years before from Genoa on
his rash attempt to overthrow the Bourbon power.[2]
Since their defeat and the death of their leader and companions, they had lain in the dungeons of the island of
Favignana, whence, only six weeks ago, they had seen
through the prison bars the *Piemonte* and *Lombardo* sail
past with the Thousand to Marsala.[3] The revolution had
now reached Favignana and set them free, and they had
come straight to Palermo to demand places in the fore-
front of Garibaldi's battles. The first person whom they
met on the terrace was the long-bearded Antonio Mosto,
leader of the Genoese Carabineers. As soon as he had
recognized his friends beneath the changes that misery
had wrought in them, he granted them the privilege,
sought by many in vain, of enlisting as privates in his
little company that fought in the van of the army and
bore the highest proportion of the losses. They were
then taken into the Observatory to see the General. He
was deeply moved. 'This,' he said, 'is a type of human
life. We, whom fortune favoured with victory, lodge in
royal palaces. These brave fellows, because conquered,
are buried in the vaults of Favignana. Yet the cause,
the undertaking, the audacity was the same. . . . The
first honours are due to Pisacane. He led the way and
these brave fellows were our pioneers.' Their leader,
Nicotera, who had been Pisacane's lieutenant, was sent

[1] *Red Shirt*, 9.
[2] The Sapri expedition. See *Garibaldi and the Thousand*, pp. 68-70.
[3] *Garibaldi and the Thousand*, pp. 229-230.

to organize the new expedition of volunteers preparing in Tuscany, where his incorrigible Republicanism soon caused trouble. The others marched with Garibaldi, and a few weeks later five out of the seven fell dead or wounded on the field of Milazzo.[1]

But the terrace and Observatory were sometimes besieged by less disinterested visitors. Even before the capture of Palermo was complete, even before the Bourbon troops had signed the capitulation, no less than 3000 petitions for employment had been sent in, each petitioner setting forth his own claims on the State in terms of fulsome panegyric. If Garibaldi had placed Northerners in the governorships and magistracies, these duties might have been more effectively fulfilled, but in so disposing of patronage he would have alienated the Sicilians. This must be remembered by those who criticise the undoubted maladministration under the Dictatorship.[2] Many of the better sort of Sicilians, especially the returning exiles, retired into private life, disdaining to advance their real claims on the State, but the worst class of petitioners set upon him like yelping hounds. He was utterly unfitted to choose among the pack: 'The Dictator says *yes* to every one and leaves me to disentangle matters,' complained Nievo the poet of the Thousand, now Vice-intendant of the National forces in Sicily. 'Every one makes court to me,' he wrote in disgust, 'Princes and Princesses, Dukes and Duchesses by shovelfuls, coveting salaries of twenty ducats a month.'[3] On the civil side Crispi made selection among his fellow-islanders, for better, for worse. Garibaldi's only way of dealing with this foul Levantine disease of State-sycophancy was to apply the ineffectual remedy of his own example. The Dictator took ten francs a day for his civil list, and did not add to it by any indirect means.

[1] *Red Shirt*, 9-14, 39. *Mario Mac.* 248-249. *Nicotera*, 43-44. *Ricasoli*, v. 206-207. *Bandi*, 205.
[2] *Times*, July 26, 1860, p. 10, c. 2. See Appendix D, 5, below.
[3] *Nievo*, 253, 256. *Castellini*, 48.

Once when he burnt a hole in his clothes he was hard
put to it for a change.   To Alexandre Dumas, who had
come over in his yacht to see historical romance in the
living reality, Garibaldi said one day : ' If I were rich I
would do like you, I would have a yacht.'   Dumas was
much moved, for he had just seen him sign a cheque for
half a million francs of public money.[1]

It was fortunate for Garibaldi that North Italy was
so generous with the purse, and that by one of his usual
pieces of luck he had captured from the Neapolitan
Government an immense sum of ready money which had
been called in for re-coinage and lay in the mint at
Palermo.[2]   For by the middle of July the Sicilians had
subscribed voluntarily no more than £5000 : the British
Consul, who had seen them win and lose their freedom in
1848-1849, observed the same characteristics once more,
passion wreaked on the statues of the Bourbons and the
stones of the Castellamare, flags, shoutings, bombastic
processions, but no foresight, no fruitful fear of reconquest, no general and public self-sacrifice.[3]   Since on this
occasion they had North Italy to protect them, their sense
of security was less ill founded.   But Garibaldi's edict
of conscription remained a dead letter, and he was soon
induced by deputations from the upland communes to
suspend it ' until the agricultural work of the year was
over,' that is, until the Greek Calends.[4]   Most of the
squadre, or irregular bands of peasants, went back to
their homes before or after the capitulation of Palermo.
But several thousands of Sicilians volunteering for more
regular service were formed into regiments and drilled
by native, by North Italian, and by English officers.
They proved far more efficient than 'the *squadre*, and
although the degrees of courage which they displayed

[1] *Monnier*, 208-209.
[2] *Forbes*, 59.   *Conv. Dolmage.*   Appendix C, ii. below.
[3] *F. O. Sicily, Elliot, Consul Goodwin's Political Journal*, July 19-24.
Forbes, 78.
[4] *Türr's Risposta*, 13.   *Crispi*, 1911, pp. 172-175.

in the coming campaign varied from time to time, on the whole they did credit, both in their own island and on the mainland, to the officers who had in a few weeks knocked them into soldiers.

Some of the upper class of the island behaved poorly, refusing to serve unless they were at once given commissions, although scores of the noble and wealthy families of North Italy had sons doing the meanest duties of the camp, and thinking a red shirt better wear than epaulettes.[1] There were indeed many of the Sicilian upper class who did their duty well,[2] but the island regiments consisted of the lower orders of the population to a greater degree than did the regiments from the North.

Dunne's ' English regiment,'[3] in particular, was largely recruited from the corner-boys of Palermo, who under discipline and good influences behaved with marked courage in Milazzo fight.   Many of these lads had passed a fortnight or three weeks in the 'Garibaldi Foundling Hospital,' established and conducted on excellent military lines by Alberto Mario.   Happy as they were in this institution, they deserted from it fast to join Dunne's regiment, because they were told that under ' *milordo* ' they would go sooner to the wars with *Garibardi*.[4]   *Milordo* himself was one of the most romantic figures in the Garibaldian camp.   Dunne had a share of the mysterious power of Nicholson or Gordon to inspire confidence, discipline, and courage into untrained races.   He had commanded Turkish levies for the British Government in the Crimea. Shortly before the capture of Palermo he accepted, at Hudson's suggestion, a dangerous mission from Cavour and La Farina to carry a political message through to

---

[1] *Adamoli*, 107-108.   *Forbes*, 78-79.

[2] *E.g. Brancaccio*, 261.   *De Cesare*, ii. 357-358.   *Whitaker*, 277-278 and *passim*.

[3] Though it was so-called, only a part of the officers were English and the men were Sicilian.   It must not be confused with the British Legion that only appeared at Naples in October.

[4] *Red Shirt*, 15-39.   *Fazio*, 55-56.   *Conv. Patterson*.

Garibaldi and to smuggle into Sicily the Cavourian agent, Scelzi, disguised as his servant. Scelzi and Dunne had landed in North Sicily, raised several hundred *squadre* on their own account, skirmished with the Bourbon troops, and entered Palermo at the head of their men a few days before the capitulation was signed. Dunne then discarded his *squadre* and set to work to make a real regiment out of apparently unpromising material. Aided by Wyndham, an Englishman, formerly of the Austrian army, by a dozen civilians just come from Great Britain and Ireland for love of Garibaldi, and some ex-sergeants of the Piedmontese army, he soon manufactured a force of 600 young Sicilians whom the Dictator could have ill spared in the coming battle.[1]

Whatever his political errors, Garibaldi had a firm hold of the military situation, and did not waste a day. On June 20, twenty-four hours after the departure of the last Neapolitan troops, and while Medici's men were still arriving in Palermo, a column under Türr started for the centre of the island with orders to march by way of Caltanisetta to Catania on the eastern sea. The force, when it left the capital, numbered little more than 500 men, consisting chiefly of members of the original Thousand, together with a small company of foreign deserters from the Bourbon army, and a dozen Sicilian gentlemen. This 'brigade,' as it was called, was the more formidable in report because of two obsolete cannon retrieved from the ignominious position of posts in the streets of Palermo, remounted and dragged across the island as 'artillery'. The foreign company had good Enfield rifles, but the majority of the force, the remnant of the Thousand, still had their old bad muskets. Ammunition was procured on the way in the sulphur district of Caltanisetta.

Being the first column to leave Palermo for the front,

[1] *Dunne MSS.*, Scelzi's letter, etc.　*Conv. Patterson.*　*Conv. Dolmage Dumas*, 120-121.　*Crispi*, 1911, p. 168.

Türr's ' brigade ' created great interest. It was accompanied by some of the best war-correspondents in Europe, and by Alexandre Dumas with a female midshipman in tow. The vain, good-natured, luxurious giant, liked by some, disliked by others, and laughed at by all of his companions on the march, left them half-way and returned to head-quarters at Palermo. The expedition, though romantic and picturesque, was uneventful. At Misilmeri the population, which had shown fierce enthusiasm and sent its *squadre* for the attack on Palermo when Garibaldi passed that way three weeks before, was found to be sullenly hostile because of the edict of conscription. When they learnt that it was to be inoperative, they recovered their cheerfulness, and enjoyed the eloquence of Garibaldi's friar, Father Pantaleo,[1]— which produced two volunteer recruits. Here Türr fell dangerously ill and was forced to return to the continent for a few weeks to recover his health. The command of the column devolved on his fellow-Hungarian Eber, who did not on that account give over his functions as *Times* correspondent. Eber was a reserved and quiet gentleman, known and respected in the English Lake district, where he had passed many years of exile, and in the best London society. He had neither Türr's military experience and vigour nor his popularity with the troops, but he had an easy part to play and fell into no capital errors. Passing through the heart of the island by Enna and the rock citadel of Castrogiovanni, which commands the finest view in Sicily, Eber and his men skirted Aetna on the South and entered Catania unopposed on July 15. After Misilmeri they had been well received, in most places with real enthusiasm, and they had put down some incipient brigandage; but they did not pick up many recruits in the course of their march from sea to sea.[2]

[1] See *Garibaldi and the Thousand*, pp. 249-250, 268.
[2] See Map IV, below. *Türr's Div.* 79-102. *Zasio*, 66-67. *Adamoli*, 104-131. *Abba Not.* 160-190. *Brancaccio*, 261-276. *Türr's Risposta*, 13. *Dumas*, 142-

FATHER PANTALEO, 1860
The red-shirt friar of Sicily.

FRANCIS II.

On June 25, less than a week after the departure of
Türr's and Eber's column, Bixio left the capital with
another ' brigade ' of about 1200 men, consisting partly
of Sicilians and partly of Northerners under Caldesi, who
had come out in Medici's expedition.[1] Passing through
Piana dei Greci, where he enlisted sixty of the warlike
Albanians, through Corleone and by the temples of
Girgenti, Bixio reached the southern coast, sailed along
it from Licata to Terranova, and marched thence straight
across country to Catania, where he joined Eber's column
in the latter half of July.[2]

Meanwhile, as will be recounted in the next chapter,
Medici with a far better organised, better armed, and
better disciplined force was moving along the north
coast towards Milazzo.   This Northern detachment
could be most quickly supported by Garibaldi himself
with the reserves which he was busily forming in
Palermo.   The columns of Eber in the centre and of
Bixio in the South were to a large extent stage armies,
not therefore the less effective in paralyzing the Bourbon
generals at Messina.   Garibaldi justly relied on the inactivity of those veteran warriors, or else he would not
have sent two weak columns to roam at large through
the island, and finally to unite at Catania, not far from
Messina, where lay fifteen to twenty thousand Bourbon
troops.   Judged by the rules of ordinary war, the division
of the Dictator's slender forces into three appears an
absurd error.   But under the actual conditions he was
justified in making the division, because, while the force
with which he intended to strike home on the north
coast was immensely the strongest and proved sufficient

182. *Morning Post* and *Times*, July, 1860 (*passim*).   *Notes and Memories*,
James Cropper, for Eber in England, and *Atkins' Life of W. H. Russell*, i. 167-
168, for Eber in the Crimea.   *Conv. Dolmage* (Mr. Dolmage was with the column;
he does not think they got nearly as many as 1000 recruits during the march to
Catania, as stated by *Adamoli*, 107).

[1] *Medici (Pasini)*, 17.
[2] See Map IV, below.   *Türr's Div.* 81, 94, 97, 103.   *Bixio*, 209.   *Menghini*,
144.

for its purpose, the other two flying columns served to alarm the Bourbon generals and to render them less willing to advance from Messina and attack his real force in front of Milazzo with the requisite vigour.[1] But the chief purpose of the columns of Eber and Bixio was not military but political. They established the authority of the Dictator in three-quarters of the island, they nipped in the bud the beginning of anarchy and brigandage, they obtained several thousand recruits, mostly after their arrival on the east coast,[2] and they set up before Europe the claim of Garibaldi to the real possession of the island.[3]

But that claim had still to be made good in the battle of Milazzo.

[1] The presence of Eber on the east coast was not the only reason why Clary did not send more troops to Milazzo, but it was one of the reasons. See p. 93 below.

[2] *Adamoli*, 125, 133.

[3] Cf. *Medici (Pasini)*, 15-16, and *Türr's Div.* 103, to *Cuniberti*, 94-95.

CHAPTER IV

THE BATTLE OF MILAZZO

' Who is the happy warrior ?   Who is he
Whom every man in arms should wish to be ?
—It is the generous spirit, who, when brought
Among the tasks of real life, hath wrought
Upon the plan that pleased his childish thought :
Whose high endeavours are an inward light
That make the path before him always bright.

.   .   .   .

Whose powers shed round him in the common strife
Or mild concerns of ordinary life
A constant influence, a peculiar grace ;
But who, if he be call'd upon to face
Some awful moment to which heaven has join'd
Great issues, good or bad for human kind,
Is happy as a lover; and attired
With sudden brightness, like a man inspired ;
And through the heat of conflict, keeps the law
In calmness made, and sees what he foresaw.'

WORDSWORTH.

By June 19 Palermo and most of the other garrison
towns in Sicily had been completely evacuated, but
there still remained 18,000 effective Bourbon troops in
Messina, 2000 in Syracuse, over 1000 in Milazzo, and 500
in Augusta.[1] On the mainland were some 80,000 more,
of whom large numbers could be shipped to the island
from Naples in a few hours.   In these circumstances two
rational courses were open to the Royalists.   Either
a vigorous counter-attack might be made, first on the
columns which Garibaldi was sending out from Palermo,
and then upon that city itself, before the three thousand
North-Italian volunteers had grown to ten, fifteen, and

---

[1] *Nove Mesi*, 2.   *Palmieri*, 38-48.   Of the 18,000 in Messina, 3000 or more
were sent under Bosco to Milazzo on July 14.

twenty thousand. Or else the opposite course might be chosen, a course less ambitious indeed but more consistent with the grant of the Constitution and the new diplomatic attitude adopted towards France, England, and Piedmont : Sicily might be written off as lost, and the troops in it confined to garrison work within the sea-fortresses of Messina, Syracuse, Milazzo, and Augusta. These places, if supplied and assisted by the fleet, could not be taken by the means at Garibaldi's disposal. Further fighting would thus be avoided in the island, and a claim would thereby be established on the good offices of England and France. The sea powers, pleased at such moderation in the Court of Naples, might not improbably vse their fleets to stop Garibaldi at the Straits of Messina. With or without such aid, the military defence of the new constitutional kingdom could be reorganized on the Calabrian shore of the Straits, with the citadel of Messina as a hostage effectively held on the enemy's ground.[1]

If logically executed, either the offensive or the defensive plan had a good chance of success, but since they were mutually inconsistent, a clear choice had to be made between the two systems. Any compromise between them might easily lead to disaster.

The offensive system was favoured by General Clary in command at Messina and by most of his subordinate officers, by the King at Naples, and by those of his advisers who were still reactionary at heart. But the new Liberal Ministry, and above all the new War Minister, General Pianell, wished to suspend operations in Sicily and organize a diplomatic and military defence behind the Straits. The Ministers had good reason to deprecate further hostilities, for while a victory of Garibaldi would overthrow the dynasty, a defeat of Garibaldi would overthrow the Constitution, and their own position depended on the maintenance of dynasty and Constitution together.

While the Ministers remained inactive and sought the

[1] *Pianell*, 12, gives a clear statement of this defensive plan by its principal advocate.

ways of peace, neither the King at Naples nor the General
at Messina had the nerve to wage a vigorous offensive
war in their despite. But the reactionary party was not
entirely without influence on events in June and July.
It had sufficient power in Court and camp to sow distrust
between the Ministers and the Crown, and to initiate in
Sicily a feeble and partial offensive movement under
Colonel Bosco, of which Garibaldi took advantage to
escape the danger of an armistice, to win the battle of
Milazzo, and thereby to create the panic among the
Bourbon troops on the Straits which enabled him to
march almost unresisted to Naples. Such, in brief, is the
significance of the events narrated in this chapter.

General Clary had distinguished himself on May 31
in suppressing an attempt of some local *squadre* to occupy
Catania. When, immediately after this little victory, he
was ordered to abandon Catania and retire to head-
quarters at Messina, he obeyed under protest. As one
of the very few Generals who had shown any spirit
during the operations in May, Clary was in June pro-
moted Marshal, and placed in command of the Royal
forces at Messina. A strong reactionary, he at once drew
up schemes for the reconquest first of Catania and then
of Palermo, and applied to Naples for approval. On
June 25 King Francis sent him orders to take the offensive in accordance with his own proposals. But the new
Marshal, on whose brave words the reactionaries had for
some weeks been building their hopes, proved after all
to be of much the same calibre as the other Generals.
For as soon as he was ordered to advance, the tone of
Clary's reports changed wonderfully; he began to write
of the unfitness and unwillingness of his troops, of the
necessity of remaining on the defensive, of the probability that if he left Messina with a part of his force,
Garibaldi would slip in behind his back, as he had slipped
into Palermo behind the back of Von Mechel. But again,
as soon as the Ministry countermanded the advance and

bade him remain on the defensive, Clary recovered his courage and complained bitterly that such orders damped the spirits of his men.[1]

Meanwhile King Francis was consulting his Generals and Ministers at Naples on a proposal to send strong reinforcements from the mainland to reconquer Sicily. In a council held on July 13 the Ministers opposed it, giving their voices in favour of armistice and diplomatic action, and their arguments were supported by Generals Nunziante and Pianell, the two best soldiers in the service since Filangieri's retirement.[2] The plan was therefore abandoned, and next day Pianell, in an evil hour for his own reputation and peace of mind, was induced to become Minister of War. An honest, cultivated, and high-minded man, true to the dynasty and to the Constitution, he failed to see that the one could now be saved only at the expense of the other. He was fully persuaded that Sicily could not be reconquered—perhaps he did not dare to ask himself whether he wished it to be reconquered. He maintained that the island had been lost because of the demoralised condition of the army, and that it would be his chief duty as War Minister, while passively defending the Straits, to revive the discipline and military spirit of the Royal forces. A critic might have urged that the only way to revive their spirit would be to discard tricolour and Constitution, and bid them march forward under the white flag of the Bourbons, with the King in their midst, as was afterwards done with some success at Capua a few months too late. No troops could feel enthusiasm for the Constitution and at the same time fight loyally against the man who was the cause of the Constitution's existence.

But whatever Pianell's plan was worth, it never had a fair trial, for on July 14 Marshal Clary sent Colonel Bosco with 3000 picked troops along the north coast

[1] *Cronaca*, 170-171, 175, 182-186 (June 19-22, 25), Clary's messages of June 27-28, 30, July 4, 6, 9, 13. *Franci*, i. 60-63. *De C.* ii. 360-362.

[2] *Pianell*, 12-13, 179. *Liborio Romano*, 35.

from Messina, with orders to occupy the open country between Milazzo and Barcellona. This half-hearted measure, taken without the knowledge of Pianell, had all the faults and none of the merits of the defensive plan decreed by the Ministers, and of the offensive desired by the King.[1]

Bosco was the fighting man of the army,[2] and the news that he had been sent into the open field with a force of his own was regarded by every one as a bid for the reconquest of Sicily. Yet the actual orders given by Clary to the Colonel on the day before he left Messina reflect the divided counsels of the Royalist camp. In this document Bosco is reminded that the Ministry has forbidden any fresh attack to be made ; he must therefore leave it to the enemy to begin the fighting, but when attacked himself he has the right to make a counter-attack and dislodge the Garibaldini from their positions ; the object of the expedition is defined as being to guard the threatened garrison of Milazzo from a blockade—though in fact this end could have been far more simply effected by the use of the fleet ; for this purpose Clary advises Bosco to occupy Archi and certain other places some miles outside Milazzo ; he is not to proceed farther westward than Barcellona, even if victorious, but is to await orders there.[3] These instructions, which might be interpreted in many different ways, when thus placed in the hands of a spirited officer, were certain to lead to a pitched battle, for when Bosco left Messina, Medici, in command of 2000 Garibaldini, had already for a week made Barcellona his head-quarters, and had been scouting with his friends on the mountains that tower above the plain of Milazzo.[4]

Giacomo Medici, who had held the Vascello for four

[1] *Pianell*, 12-18, 23, 180. *Cronaca*, 189. *Nove Mesi*, 10-13. *Liborio Romano*, 35.
[2] *Garibaldi and the Thousand*, pp. 315-318.
[3] *Palmieri*, 47-50, doc. 1, or *Nove Mesi*, 10-12.
[4] *Peard's Journal MS.* July 7-14.

weeks against the French army on the Janiculum,[1] was the friendly rival of Bixio for the first place among Garibaldi's lieutenants. To him the General had entrusted the leadership of the most important of the three columns now advancing through the island on Messina, that one which was to keep the north coast and be supported in case of need by Garibaldi himself and the reserves from Palermo. Medici left the capital with 1800 of the well-armed volunteers whom he had brought from North Italy, Simonetta's Lombards and Malenchini's Tuscans.[2] The General's orders were that he should occupy Castroreale (*see Map II at end of book*), a strong position in the mountains above Barcellona, and there await orders. But when he found the coast towns enthusiastic in the national cause, when he was joined by several hundred local volunteers and bands from eastern Sicily, he felt unwilling to retire into the mountains on Bosco's approach, leaving his hosts at Barcellona to the Bourbon vengeance. Such a retreat would inflict a wound on the growing prestige of the Garibaldian armies, which stood to them in the place of cavalry, artillery, and big battalions. In order, therefore, to protect Barcellona, Medici moved his head-quarters to Meri and there awaited the enemy's attack, drawn up behind the broad *fiumara*, or torrent bed of white stones, that passes in front of the village on its way from the neighbouring mountain gorge to the sea.[3] (*See henceforth Map I p. 81 below.*)

On July 15 Bosco and his three thousand approached by the high road from Messina to within a short distance of the *fiumara*, where Medici's men lay eagerly awaiting them; the Royalists, however, wheeled off sharply to the right, and marched across the plain to Milazzo.[4] It is possible that Bosco declined battle on account of his

---

[1] *Garibaldi's Defence of Rome*, 199-200.

[2] The remaining 700 of those whom Medici had brought to Sicily, namely Caldesi's battalion, had gone south in Bixio's column. *Medici (Pasini)*, 17-18.

[3] *Medici (Pasini)*, 17-19. *Peard's Journal MS.* July 7-15.

[4] *Peard*, 819 (or *Journal MS.*), July, 15. *Medici (Pasini)*, 19.

instructions from Clary not to initiate hostilities. On his arrival in the town, beneath the precipice on which the mediaeval fortress is perched, the inhabitants fled for refuge into the thick olive groves that cover the hills of the peninsula beyond, where they remained hidden during the events of the following week.[1] Bosco and his army occupied the deserted town and put themselves into communication with the garrison on the castled rock overhead.

Medici, encouraged by Bosco's refusal of battle, sent out detachments across the *fiumara* of Meri to occupy Coriolo and Archi, hamlets sheltered among the olives of the last foot-hills that overlook the plain of Milazzo. Now one part of Bosco's instructions had been to occupy Archi, and therefore, in spite of that other part of his orders which forbade him to be the first to attack, he felt justified in recapturing Archi now that a Garibaldian outpost had occupied it and thereby cut off his connection with Messina. He had passed through the village on the 15th on his way to Milazzo, but had neglected to leave any guard behind. And so, early in the morning of July 17, he sent back across the plain four companies,[2] with cavalry and artillery, under Major Maringh, with orders to retake Archi. The hamlet and surrounding hills were defended by 300 Lombards under Simonetta and about seventy Sicilians. Maringh skirmished for some time, used his cavalry well, captured a score of prisoners, and then unaccountably returned to Milazzo. Bosco placed him under arrest and sent out in the afternoon six companies under Lieutenant-Colonel Marra, who assailed Coriolo, and brought their artillery into

[1] *Forbice*, July 23 and 24, 1860, letters from seat of war. *Zirilli*, 18-22, 35-42, docs. 2-5. *Piaggia*, 54-55. In view of these documents it is clear that the charges against the inhabitants of Milazzo of sympathizing with the Bourbon troops were mainly false. But the Milazzesi were not as helpful to the Garibaldini as the people of Barcellona.

[2] A company in the Neapolitan army was supposed to be 160 men; a battalion was about 1000 men, and Bosco had three battalions of infantry. *De Sivo*, iii. 121-122.

action. Medici sent up more men from Meri, including Malenchini's Tuscans, and fierce fighting took place
in the street of Coriolo and along the *fiumara* above
which it stands. The street was taken by the Bourbon
troops and retaken at the point of the bayonet. Marra's
men tried to turn Medici's flank by penetrating up into
the mountains towards Sta. Lucia, but they were headed
off near S. Filippo. At the end of an arduous day
Coriolo remained in Medici's hands, and Archi in those
of the Royalists. But at midnight Bosco, who had come
out when the fighting was over to review the situation,
ordered a retreat to the town. He had been persuaded
that Medici had 7000 men, whereas in reality he had
scarcely more than 2000 all told.[1]

Although Bosco's deserved reputation for courage
saved him from wholly losing the confidence of his men,
his conduct on this day had been neither spirited nor
wise. He should have come earlier to direct the action
himself, and he should not have sent out such small
detachments if he seriously intended to occupy the slopes
of the mountains, and so debar the further advance of
the Garibaldini along the north coast. He had allowed
Medici to out-manœuvre him, to drive him down off the
hills, to get between him and Messina, and to lock him
into the plain of Milazzo with his back to the sea. The
Garibaldini were elated at their success, and rejoiced over
an intercepted letter of Bosco's to Clary, written in the
usual querulous style of Neapolitan despatches : ' Maringh
basely betrayed me. I have him under lock and key.
I can't do more. I am left to do everything, everything,
everything (*tutto, tutto, tutto*). The officers are so many
nullities.' But if he were reinforced from Messina either

---

[1] *Cronaca*, 193-196, 200, 218-219, *Nove Mesi*, 13-15, 20-22, *Palmieri*, 30-40,
50-51, docs. 2-3, and *De Sivo*, iii. 310-311, contain Bosco's reports and other
matter on the Neapolitan side. *Medici* (*Pasini*), 20 ; *Piaggia*, 21-29 ; *Mistrali's
da N.* 611-614 (identical with *Mattignana*, 382-386) ; *Times*, August 4, p. 10,
cols. 1-2 ; *Conv. Cadolini; Da Forio* 619-620 ; *Fonvielle*, 110-119 ; *Forbice*,
July 23, letters of July 17-18 ; *Veritas*, 32-36 ; *Pozzi*, 22 ; *Menghini*, 180, 196-199 ;
Peard, 820 ; *Milazzo* (*G.B.Z.*) 8, 9 ; *Pungolo, Milano*, July 27, letter of July 19.

by sea or by land, he boasted that he would enter Palermo
'on Medici's horse.'[1]   Those of his dispatches which
reached Messina, being signalled by semaphore, were
conceived in the same tone of complaint against his subordinates, and demanded fresh men and fresh officers,
although in fact he had in the *cacciatori* the best regiments
of the army.[2]   The feeling of the 15,000 officers and men
left idle in Messina was that they ought at once to be led
to the rescue of the gallant Bosco, who was far more
popular than Clary.   But the Marshal, who had already
quarrelled with his subordinates at Messina as well as
with Bosco himself, sent him, not the reinforcements
which he demanded, but a Captain Fonsecca to make
excuses and to explain that there were not enough horses,
carts, or ships to carry an army by sea or by land to
Milazzo.[3]   Clary's inactivity was in part due to the
telegrams which he received from the Minister of War
ordering him to remain on the defensive, and denouncing
Bosco in the strongest language for having resumed
hostilities.[4]

But although Medici had drawn a cordon round
Milazzo, it was a very thin line, and if Bosco discovered
that he was being contained not by 7000 but by 2000 men,
he might attack once more.   In the telegram reporting
to the Dictator his success of July 17, Medici begged for
reinforcements.[5]   Nor had he long to wait.   Some troops
were already on the way.   On the 18th there marched
into Meri Dunne's regiment of 600 Sicilians with its
English officers, and Cosenz with a first detachment of
the excellent troops whom he had just brought to Palermo
from Genoa.[6]

The Dictator, on receiving Medici's telegram in the

[1] *Milazzo (G.B.Z.)*, 9.   *Piaggia*, 30.   *Forbice*, July 23.   *Brancaccio*, 299.
[2] *Nove Mesi*, 14-15.   *Palmieri*, 50-51, docs. 2-3.   *Bandi*, 229.
[3] *Nove Mesi*, 15-16, 31.   *Cronaca*, 219.
[4] *Cronaca*, 192, 196.   [5] *Guerzoni*, ii. 137.
[6] *Da Forio*, 620.   *Forbice*, July 23.   *Medici (Pasini)*, 21.   *Nelson MS.*
Peard's Journal MS.   For Cosenz' expedition see p. 46 above, and Appendices
B and F, ii. note below.

small hours of the morning of the 18th, made one of those sudden resolves, quick as the flash of a sword, that with him always marked the end of a long period of suspense. Breaking through all his engagements in Palermo, and not even announcing his departure, he went on board an old Scottish cattle-steamer called the *City of Aberdeen* that had brought volunteers from Genoa a few days before and happened still to be in the harbour. At four in the morning he made arrangements for her use with her Scottish crew and captain, who were passionately devoted to his cause and person. He instantly put on board the Carabineers of the Thousand, and those of his *aides-de-camp* whom he could muster at a moment's notice. Just as they were about to weigh anchor, there happened to enter the port the steamer *Amazon* from Genoa bearing Corte and his volunteers, captured a month before in the *Charles and Jane*, and now released from their captivity at Gaeta by the Constitutional Ministers of King Francis, as part of the policy of friendship with Piedmont. They had been sent back to Genoa, but had instantly sailed again for Sicily in another ship ; on account of this adventure they were henceforth known as the 'Gaeta battalion.'[1] Garibaldi ordered them not to land, but to come on board the *City of Aberdeen*. The transfer of men, arms, and ammunition was effected in half an hour, and about eight in the morning the cattle-steamer left Palermo with the whole expedition on board. She was accompanied by the Piedmontese war-vessel *Carlo Alberto*, under orders from Persano to see them safely landed.[2] They disembarked at Patti before dawn on July 19. Leaving his men to march after him, the General drove at a gallop towards Barcellona and Meri.[3]

[1] See p. 49 above and Appendix B, below. For Corte's capture and release see *Castellini*, 26-29. *Baroni. Menghini*, 434-440. *F. O. Sard. Hudson*, June 30, Nos. 291, 301.

[2] *Persano*, 89.

[3] For the departure and voyage from Palermo see *Miller MS. Milazzo* (*G.B.Z.*), 6, 9-10. *Rome MS. Savi. Red Shirt*, 41. *Times*, August 4, p. 10, col. 2.

At Barcellona the principal church was employed as a hospital for Medici's wounded. As Garibaldi passed through the town, the noise of his reception in the street penetrated into the quiet of that gloomy hall, where a gigantic crucifix looked down upon the sufferers. In an instant they were struggling off their couches and crawling to the door on hands and knees. As they lay crowded on the steps of the church, he waved his gentle salutations and thanks to them, and passed on towards Meri. One young Lombard who had been shot through the lungs crawled to his bed again, fell back on it, and died.[1]

When Palermo discovered that the Dictator had gone, the streets were filled with angry and inquiring crowds. His departure was a complete surprise. The Palermitans felt only half safe in his absence, and many of his old followers and friends were aggrieved because he had left them behind in the hurry of his departure. Such was the eagerness to follow him that in a few hours nearly all the North Italians in the Sicilian capital had thrown up the civil or military posts which kept them from the front. In many of these cases substitutes were found among the wounded, who were unwilling to remain in hospital at such a time. Those who could, set out post-haste for Milazzo, and quiet was restored.[2]

There was little doing at Meri on July 19. Medici and Cosenz were away scouting, and their men were eating their dinners in the filthy houses of the village, or beside the white stones of the *fiumara*, glowing in the midday heat, when an open carriage was noticed coming along the high-road from Barcellona. As it drew near they saw whom it contained. In an instant all the camp was in an uproar. The uneaten dinners were left smoking, and the volunteers rushed to seize him as he stepped from the carriage. It was his official birthday, being celebrated at that hour in Palermo with flags and speeches,[3] but he had come to spend it among friends in

---

[1] *Veritas*, 36-39.   [2] *Red Shirt*, 32-37, 41.
[3] His real birthday was July 7, but they celebrated it on the 19th. *Forbice; Giorn. di Sic.*

the field.   Confidence and joy were in his looks, and were reflected in the faces of the soldiers who pressed round him.   They now knew that on the morrow they would fight and conquer.   He did not linger in Meri but took horse to find his old companions in arms, Medici and Cosenz, and to spend the rest of the day riding with them over the mountains of Sta. Lucia, surveying through his spy-glass the plain below, where Bosco was in the act of taking up a new and formidable position to cover the approaches to Milazzo.[1]

The plain of Milazzo is enclosed to north and west by the two sea-beaches, that converge on the town and castle at the neck of the peninsula.   To the south and east the plain is bounded by the white *fiumare* of Meri and of Coriolo and by the low hills covered with olives that lie between the mountains and the plains.   The ground on which the battle was fought, confined within a radius of a mile and a half from the southern gate of the town, was perfectly flat and almost on a level with the neighbouring beach.   On this seaward plain stood farms, mills, and small hamlets, scattered about in a manner foreign to the interior of the island, where the whole population was housed at nightfall in hill-towns of several thousand inhabitants each.   These isolated houses strengthened the Royalist position on the plain. The ground was occupied by cornfields and vineyards, or near the sea by brakes of canes, seven feet high, used by the peasants for training their vines.   The vineyards and cane brakes were enclosed by thick hedges of cactus, or by high white walls, which had been loopholed by the Bourbon troops.   These were formidable barriers against an army of irregulars without artillery.   The only way by which Garibaldi's men could pierce the enemy's line without scaling the loopholed walls and

[1] *Milazzo* (G.B.Z.), 10.   *Fonvielle*, 128-129.   *Da Forio*, 620.   *Piaggia*, 32.   *Mistrali's da N.* 616.   *Peard*, 820-821.   *Menghini*, 199-200.   *Pozzi*, 23. *Mariotti*, 423.   *Castellini*, 35, 37.

hewing through the cactus hedges was to charge along
the two beaches and along the various roads converging
on Milazzo. But the roads, and the beach on either side
of the town, were remarkably straight and were swept
by the cannon of the Royalists. Against their eight
excellently served pieces the Garibaldini had nothing to
oppose except two useless carronades, dragged about by
hand, which were brought into action only to be withdrawn after a few minutes.[1] The one road that was not
straight enough to be swept by the Bourbon artillery
was a sunk lane that wound through the vineyards,
hollowed out by a water-course that finally entered the
side of the S. Palino road as a culvert, and issued into
the sea under the main road, beneath a little bridge 500
yards from the town gate.[2] This bridge was chosen by
Bosco to be the scene of the final stand outside the town,
in case his more advanced positions were forced, and
here two of the cannon were placed. Two more stood
a mile in front near the 'angle' of the high-road to
Messina. Beyond this 'angle' the Bourbon left wing
occupied the Mills near the seashore, thus forming an
advanced post which could enfilade Garibaldi's advance
against their centre near S. Palino. Their right was
supported by the other four guns, which were placed at
Casazza and on the western beach.[3]

These formidable positions in front of the castle were
held, according to Bosco's own report, by 2500 excellent
Neapolitan *cacciatori*, the flower of the army, aided by
the eight guns and a squadron of cavalry. In the castle
on the rock overhead was the garrison, about 1000
infantry of the line, and over forty cannon of different
sorts, some of which were able to fire with effect towards

[1] Appendix F, ii. below.
[2] This water-course, dry in spring and summer, is called a *fiumara* in
Bosco's report and by some of the inhabitants to-day. But it is not a typical
fiumara as it is of brown earth only, not of white stones.
[3] *Mem.* 369. *Palmieri*, 44-45 (Bosco's report). *Piaggia*, 36-38, 40-41,
which shows among other things that when Bosco speaks of Casa Unazzo he
refers to the place usually called Casazza.

the close of the day.   In the peninsula behind the castle
Bosco had stationed another 400 *cacciatori* to prevent a
landing from taking place in his rear.   The total of all
arms defending these positions was reckoned by the
Neapolitan staff at 4636 men and officers.[1]

Against this series of concentric lines of defence,
culminating in the precipice and castle, Garibaldi was
leading a force perhaps slightly larger in numbers than
that of Bosco,[2] but altogether inferior if judged by the
normal military standards.   He had no cavalry and until
late in the day no artillery.   The infantry consisted of
North Italian and Sicilian volunteers, hastily raised
and regimented in so-called 'battalions' of 300 to 900
each, many of which, like Corte's newly landed 'Gaeta
battalion,' had handled fire-arms only during the last
forty-eight hours and did not know the elements of
drill ;[3] while even Medici's and Dunne's men, who had
had a few weeks' drill, did not know how to use the
sights of their Enfield rifles.[4]   But in most of the 'battalions' there was a large proportion of veterans of '48
and '59 ; of sergeants who had deserted, collusively or
otherwise, from the regular army ; and of officers of old
experience and in some cases of remarkable talent in revolutionary war.   Above all, the whole force was inspired
by an ardour for their cause and for their leader which
did much to take the place of discipline, and made them
ready to endure the very heavy losses without which
even the first positions could not possibly have been
stormed.

Shortly after dawn on July 20 the Garibaldini moved
down to the attack off the hills of Olivarella and Coriolo.
In the centre, S. Pietro was occupied without opposition ;
on the east, Simonetta and his Lombards began their
attack on the enemy's advanced post at the Mills ; while
on the other flank Malenchini and his Tuscans, marching

---

[1] Appendix F, ii. below.   [2] *Ibid.*
[3] *Baroni.*   [4] Appendix E, 2, 5, below.

through S. Marco and S. Marina, developed the attack on Casazza and along the western beach.[1]

The day began with a disaster. Malenchini carelessly led his men up to the mouth of the Bourbon rifles and batteries, which opened on them with terrible effect and fairly drove them off the field. Garibaldi, who was watching the first stages of the fight from the roof of a wine-store on the edge of the plain, sent Cosenz with fresh troops to rally the fugitives and to take over the command of the left wing. Nevertheless the Royalists, supported by cavalry and artillery operating on the broad beach, advanced and drove back the Garibaldian left and left-centre for nearly a mile. Although Malenchini and many of his Tuscans returned to the fight, it was all that Cosenz could do to hold the Zirilli farm and the western approaches to S. Pietro.

The General himself, rightly confiding in the calmness, authority, and military talent of Cosenz, had not gone to rally the defeated left wing, but had bent all his personal energies to effect an advance along the other shore, at the head of the right wing under Medici. If he could penetrate by way of the Mills and the 'angle' of the road as far as the bridge, he would be able to threaten the rear of the victorious advance of the Royalists on the west, which was in fact a dangerous move on their part at so early a stage in the battle.

Garibaldi's method of sending his troops into action on this day was to stand well exposed to the fire at some spot by which the next detachment would have to enter the battle, and to speak, almost in a whisper, some word of encouragement to the young soldiers, of whom many were then hearing the bullets for the first time in their lives. In a small army of volunteers depending more on individual courage than on discipline, the General's exercise of his strange powers of fascination considerably increased the chances of victory. As one section of

[1] Hitherto Malenchini's men had been part of Medici's force, but on the 20th they fought, first independently, then under Cosenz' orders.

Dunne's Sicilians with their English officers and cadets
filed by him into action up the ride of a cane-brake, he
kept repeating in a low voice *Avanti ! Coraggio, uomini !* [1]
When the veteran company of Genoese Carabineers,
destined to lose nearly half their number before nightfall,
were brought about ten in the morning to the place where
they were to enter the battle, they found the General there
before them, standing almost alone in the middle of the
road, a conspicuous mark at which the enemy were
directing their fire. [2]

The first success of the day was the capture of the
Mills by the Northerners of Simonetta's and of Specchi's
'battalions.'   It cost a severe struggle, for Bosco was
there in person encouraging his men, and he had skil-
fully placed two guns near the 'angle,' one on the high-
road, the other in the Mill Lane.   The latter, after doing
great execution, was captured through the devotion of a
volunteer named Alessandro Pizzoli, who, leaving his
comrades in ambush behind a wall flanking the Mill
Lane, himself sprang down a few yards in front of the
cannon's mouth in order to draw its fire.   He was blown
limb from limb, and the next moment his comrades leapt
down after him and captured the piece. [3]

Thus the Royalists were slowly pushed back on the
east flank from one vineyard and farm to another.   But
the few positions gained by the red-shirts seemed to many
but little compensation for the long train of wounded continually passing to the rear, for the suffocating heat, the
thirst, the hunger, and, as the day wore on, the sheer
fatigue.   Those who had no stomach for eight hours of
such work went off with the wounded and forgot to return.   The better sort of men, getting together in groups
often irrespective of their proper 'battalions,' followed
any officer with a turn for leadership whom the chance

[1] *MS. Nelson.*

[2] *Rome MS. Savi.*   For a similar experience of the 'Gaeta battalion' see
Baroni.

[3] *Piaggia,* 43-47.   *Palmieri,* 43-44.

of battle brought their way. Scarcely ever seeing the enemy through the cane-brakes and behind the loopholed walls, but always exposed to his shots, firing only at close quarters, making headway by rushes and rallies, by dashes down the sunk lane, here leaping over a wall and there tearing through a cactus hedge into the flank or rear of the enemy, they carried on the battle, which had now become a mere test of individual prowess. And more and more as the day went on the General himself appeared, now here, now there, heading charges which behind him never failed of success. One of our countrymen, a lad of seventeen, who had left his home a few weeks before for love of Garibaldi, found himself with a few of his comrades from Dunne's, and a number of men from other battalions, standing at the end of a cane-brake through which the Royalists were firing at them from behind a wall. The bullets were crashing through the tall canes which snapped under the shower, the men were falling fast, the position was untenable. Suddenly the Englishman was aware of Garibaldi galloping up to them, leaping off his horse, and without a word or a look dashing up the narrow ride between the canes, straight at a small opening in the wall lined by the enemy's rifles. He did not once look round to see if his men were following, for he knew that none who saw him would linger. The Bourbons stood to it to the last, and the bayonet was used before the wall was cleared.[1]

By a series of such charges Bosco's *cacciatori* were pushed back, well after midday, to their last position outside the town. This was the bridge over the culvert, where stood the two reserve guns commanding the straight roads that converged on that spot. Close by, on the shore, was a large factory for pickling tunny-fish. Here the crisis of the battle took place. The General sent Missori to fetch up a detachment of Dunne's Sicilians which had not yet lost its identity in the mêlée. With

---

[1] *Conv. Patterson.* Mr. Patterson was later in the day wounded at the bridge, and Garibaldi made him lieutenant for his services that day.

these and some North Italians under Pilade Bronzetti, he passed through a garden, climbed a wall, and dropped down upon the two guns. One was captured, the other limbered up and escaped into Milazzo. Bosco ordered a handful of cavalry, who were standing near the town gate, to rescue the lost piece. A score of them made a spirited charge over the bridge, and Dunne's men scrambled out of the road to let them pass. If Bosco had followed up the charge with a body of fresh infantry he might have won the battle, but his last reserves on this side of the castle had been used by Colonel Marra to support the advance of his right centre. As the cavalry rode back from running the gauntlet through the Garibaldian lines, Dunne's Sicilians emptied half a dozen saddles, firing from behind the cactus hedge that lined the road. But two men, who had not taken refuge behind the hedge when the cavalry first charged by, were still standing alone in the roadway, on the line of their retreat. Of these two one was Garibaldi and the other was his aide-de-camp, Missori, a handsome young Lombard of noted gallantry. Both were on foot, and the horsemen, unable to avenge their fallen comrades on any one else, swarmed round, eager to cut them down. Missori shot the horse of the Bourbon captain, who rose in the stirrups as it fell and slashed at the Dictator. Garibaldi parried the blow, and laying his hand on the bridle of the kneeling animal struck the captain in the neck with his sabre and killed him on the spot. Missori with his revolver shot two more of the cavalry, and the half-dozen who were still left alive galloped back through the gates of the town.[1]

[1] For a portrait of Missori see illustration, p. 38 above. I have given this incident, including the details about Dunne's men and the guns, as it was told me by Missori himself, about a year before his death. The story is confirmed by many other authorities (see below). From Bosco's report we may deduce that the name of the unfortunate Bourbon captain was Giuliani, and that his lieutenant, Faraone, got back to the town with seven shot wounds. The only question is whether the cavalry charged up the main road or the sunk lane or up both. On this there are various opinions given. *Piaggia*, 50-51. *Mem.* 371.

GIACOMO MEDICI, 1860

MILAZZO HARBOUR, TOWN, CASTLE AND PENINSULA, FROM NEAR THE
TUNNY FACTORY

MILAZZO CASTLE, SHOWING OUTER WORKS AND KEEP

The Garibaldini, having now occupied the bridge, had turned Bosco's left flank and were threatening his rear. The rash advance of his right wing would have to be turned into a hasty retreat if the red-shirts could maintain their newly won position. That was indeed no easy task, for the cannon of the fortress, firing over the roofs of the town, played full upon the bridge, while the *cacciatori* below fired on it at close quarters from the town gate and from the houses along the side of the port. Garibaldi's men fell fast. One of his best and most popular lieutenants, Migliavacca, was killed, and Corte was wounded. An attempt to bring the two carronades, the only artillery of the force, into action on the bridge proved that they were perfectly useless, and in a few minutes the General ordered them to be withdrawn.[1] Seeing that an immediate advance on the town was impossible, he put most of the men for rest and shelter into the tunny-factory and some wood stores near by, while others kept up a fire against the walls of Milazzo from the bridge and neighbouring gardens, and from behind the fishing-boats on the beach. In particular, Peard, Garibaldi's Englishman, whose long beard and fine head reminded his comrades of King Lear, kept his company of thirty men at the bridge, suffering severe losses, and demonstrating that Colt's five-chambered revolving rifle, with which they were armed, leaked fire at the breech, woefully scorching the hand that used it, and had therefore no future in the history of modern armaments.[2] During two hours in the early afternoon the affair continued in this state, the Garibaldini losing men, but holding the position they had taken, and resting after the fatigues of the morning's attack.

Villari Cosp. 701. *Times*, August 4, p. 10, col. 3. *Menghini*, 239-241. *Palmieri*, 45. *Durand-Brager*, 107. *Conv. Patterson. Conv. Sclavo.*

[1] Appendix F, ii.

[2] *Garibaldi and the Thousand*, 88, 96 for Peard. *Peard*, 821-822 and Appendix E, 1, below for Peard's company at the bridge and for the rifles. Mr. Patterson, of Dunne's, who was wounded on the bridge, tells me the same about Peard's rifles, which he saw being used there.

Having thus established his men on the bridge, Garibaldi left them under Medici's command and rode off to deal with Bosco's victorious right wing, which was still pressing Cosenz near the Zirilli farm and S. Pietro. For this purpose he made his way down with a few staff officers to the western beach, found a small boat, and rowed out to the *Tüköry*, a paddle-steamer of 400 horse-power carrying ten guns [1] which had arrived on the scene that very afternoon from Patti. This vessel, formerly the *Veloce* of the Bourbon service, had recently deserted to him at Palermo, and now composed his whole fighting navy, over and above his transports and such help in convoy work as was afforded him by the Piedmontese warships. His aides-de-camp watching from the shore soon saw him swarm up the mast of the *Tüköry* to view the field. Taking her close inshore under fire from the guns of the castle, he proceeded to bombard the enemy's cavalry on the western beach. The victorious right wing of the Royalists, feeling the fire of the *Tüköry* from the west, and learning that their rear had been turned on the east, at length hastened to retreat. This incident calls to mind the obvious truth that if the Neapolitans had sent a part of the fleet to protect Milazzo, their fire would have rendered it impossible for Garibaldi to occupy or even to attack the town. [2]

Cosenz and his men, thus relieved by the retreat of their assailants, followed up, and joining with Medici on the bridge, stretched a line across the neck of the Peninsula, and invested the walls of Milazzo. Next after Garibaldi, Cosenz had borne the burden of the day. He came of a French-Neapolitan family, whose military and patriotic traditions dated from the days of the Partheno-pean Republic, of Marengo, and of Murat. But his friends said that Enrico Cosenz seemed rather to belong to some northern race, for his manners were imperturbable in their calm. He was modest and retiring almost to a

[1] *F. O. Sicily, Elliot,* September 30, No. 541.
[2] This is pointed out in the *Forbice* of July 26, 1860.

fault.   He has been well called Garibaldi's good angel
in politics and war.[1]   This thin, quiet man in spectacles
had restored the courage of Malenchini's routed troops
and held them to their post all day.   Now in the late
afternoon he was standing close under the walls of
Milazzo, in the hottest fire from the fortress, wiping his
spectacles with the deliberation of Mr. Pickwick, while a
breathless aide-de-camp from Garibaldi, waiting for his
reply to a message, wished that he would either make up
his mind more quickly, or continue his meditations in a
more secluded spot.[2]

Bosco might still have held out in the town with some
likelihood of success.   By his own account he had lost
not more than 150 men, a fifth part of the loss confessed
by the victors.[3]   But his troops were overcome with
exhaustion and discouragement at the end of their brave
but unsuccessful fight of eight hours under an almost
tropical sun, and the fear of Garibaldi, which Bosco alone
of the Bourbon officers had for a while conjured away,
returned upon them like a fate.   He therefore marched
his *cacciatori* up into the castle to join the garrison there,
leaving only a few soldiers to keep up a fire from the
town walls.[4]   When about four o'clock the Garibaldini
began to make their way into Milazzo, creeping in first
along the port-side where the walls no longer existed,[5]
they found to their surprise that the streets were empty.
Even when they advanced into the upper part of the
town, no enemy was there, although marksmen in the
fortress overhead opened fire upon them and wounded
Cosenz.   Before sunset the whole city was occupied, and
the entrances of the streets were barricaded against the

---

[1] *Cosenz*, 10-13.

[2] *Conv. Tedaldi* (Tedaldi was the aide-de-camp in question).

[3] Appendix F, iii. below.

[4] *Zirilli*, 41, Neapolitan officer's letter.

[5] The walls of the town have now disappeared altogether, but in 1860 they
existed along the west side and at the gate facing the bridge.   *Piaggia*, 34 ;
Zirilli, 10 ; there is a sketch of the walls in the *l'Illustration*, reproduced in
Menghini, 234.

castle. Garibaldi chose for his head-quarters the steps of a small church beside the sea ; there he sat giving his orders, propped up against his South-American saddle, which he always took off his horse with his own hands. For a few hours at midnight he slept, as he liked best to sleep, with his head upon that soldier's pillow, which had served him when youth and love were still his, in lands where man needed only sword and saddle for the free rover's life upon the uplands.[1]

[1] For the authorities on which this account of the battle is based see Appendix F, i. below.

CHAPTER V

'Garibaldi a une grande puissance morale, il exerce un immense prestige
non seulement en Italie mais surtout en Europe. . . . Si demain j'entrais en
lutte avec Garibaldi, il est probable que j'eusse pour moi la majorité des vieux
diplomates, mais l'opinion publique Européenne serait contre moi.   Et l'opinion
publique aurait raison, car Garibaldi a rendu à l'Italie les plus grands services
qu'un homme pût lui rendre.   Il a donné aux Italiens confiance en eux-mêmes :
il a prouvé a l'Europe que les Italiens savaient se battre et mourir sur le champ
de bataille pour reconquérir une patrie. . . . Cela n'empêche pas qu'il ne soit
éminemment désirable que la révolution de Naples s'accomplisse sans lui.'
Cavour to an intimate friend, August 9, 1860 [*Chiala*, iii. 321.]

THE castle of Milazzo, which Garibaldi had yet to take,
rose between the two seas on a granite precipice more
than three hundred feet high.   Founded by the Saracens,
improved by Norman and Angevin, it had been finally
enlarged and beautified by the Emperor Charles V.   A
place of importance throughout the Middle Ages, it had
in the war of the Vespers been occupied by Sicilians and
French in turn.   In 1675 it had successfully sustained
a regular siege, and in the wars of the early eighteenth
century and again in the struggle with Napoleon, it had
been occupied by the British and their allies.   The
English cavalry barracks of fifty years back could be seen
on the shore below.   When Bosco held it against Garibaldi, it was, as it still is to-day, a spacious and pleasant
place, unlike some of the featureless castle-prisons of the
Neapolitan mainland, of which the very style of architecture seems to symbolize cruelty and crime.   Below the
fine mediaeval keep lay grass plateaus a quarter of a mile
broad and long, enclosed by the outer works of Charles
V.   Thence the defenders could view the Calabrian

coast ; the Lipari islands and the eternal smoke of Stromboli ; the gulf of Milazzo where Duilius with his grap-
pling-irons destroyed the fleets of Carthage and made Rome
mistress even of the sea ; the plain where Garibaldi had
just triumphed in conflict man against man ; the bare
mountain ridges stretching away towards hidden Messina ; and near at hand a profusion of cactus, fig-trees, and
shrubs clinging to the precipices of the castle rock. In the
silent midday heat the stronghold gives the impression,
not of decay, but of long unbroken peace. Its defences,
if antiquated, were in good repair, and could only be
breached by siege cannon, which Garibaldi did not
possess.[1]

To defend such a place against irregular troops would
have been an easy and even a pleasant task, if Bosco had
taken care to lay in provisions while his communications
were still open. But there was little food and that bad,
the water stank, and the dirty habits of more than 4000
soldiers, who would not even take the trouble to bury
the corpses of man or beast, soon rendered the whole of
that large area insanitary.[2] The Royalists had fought
well in the battle, but defeat had destroyed their discipline, and when they were put on half-rations they
muttered threats about opening the gate. At the first
sound of mutiny the fighting Colonel himself lost his
nerve and began signalling to Messina the tale of his
distresses in messages on the semaphore which Garibaldi
and his officers read with delight.[3] He enlarged on the
state of the provisions and water ; he complained that
the enemy had in the last twenty-four hours shot one
man dead on the ramparts besides wounding eight men
and three mules ; he declared that a breach for a storm-

---

[1] *Symth*, 103. *Piaggia*, 34. *Conv. Sclavo. Zirilli*, 22. *Amari, G. del
Vesp. Sic.* Personal observation.

[2] *Forbes*, 107-108. *Medici (Pasini)*, 28. *M. Post.* August 9, p. 6. *Cronaca*,
208-209, 212-214. These reports, the first three by Garibaldini, the last by Bosco,
seem to me to outweigh the statement of *Zirilli*, 22, that the place was provisioned for 5000 men for more than a month.

[3] *Forbes*, 104. *Times*, August 4, p. 10, col. 4. *Conv. Dolmage.*

ing party could be made in a few days. The latter proposition was undeniable as a piece of abstract military
theory, for the Windmill Hill, whence the Garibaldini
were sniping, was only 500 yards away, and was on a
level with the lower parts of the castle. But the practical inference was *nil*, because the assailants had no breach-
ing cannon, and the fortress was defended by forty pieces.
'The morale of the troops,' so ended Bosco's tale of woe,
'is destroyed.' And so, he might have added, was that
of their commander, who could no longer distinguish
between a real danger of starvation and imaginary
dangers of storm and battery.[1]

On July 21 Marshal Clary held a council of war at
Messina. His subordinates hated him and one another,
and the prevailing sentiment at the council was each
man's desire to throw upon his neighbour the responsibility for disasters present and to come. The sense of
the council of war appears to have been that they were
bound in honour to march at once to relieve Bosco, but
that there were not enough horses and carts for the
transport service, and that a column of Garibaldini advancing northwards from Catania would step into Messina if any part of its garrison of 15,000 were rashly sent
to Milazzo. This fear was somewhat out of place, since
Eber's column at Catania as yet barely numbered 1000
men, and only two or three hundred had been sent as
far north as Taormina ; but this trivial reconnaissance,
as Clary's own dispatches show, seriously affected his
decision not to move to the help of Bosco.[2]

Once indeed, on July 22, Clary ordered three regiments to embark, and signalled to Bosco that they had
already sailed to his relief. But in a few hours he
countermanded the movement, either from fear of the
Garibaldini at Taormina, or else in obedience to orders
from the War Minister, Pianell.[3]

[1] *Cronaca*, 208-209, 212-214.
[2] See p. 68 above. *Palmieri*, 19-28. *Cronaca*, 212, 219. *Türr's Div.* 113.
Adamoli, 133-136. *Conv. Dolmage*.
[3] *Cronaca*, 214, 219-220. *Nove Mesi*, 28.

When first the news reached Naples that Bosco's force was shut up in Milazzo, Pianell, much as he wished to suspend all hostilities, felt that he must extricate the rash Colonel before resuming the defensive. He therefore ordered a large expedition to be put on board the fleet in the bay of Naples, to sail to the relief of Milazzo. But the fleet, more liberal in political sentiment than the army, refused to take the troops on board, and the mutiny was encouraged by the Admiral, Count D'Aquila, the King's uncle. The case was brought up for discussion before the Ministers, into whose willing ears D'Aquila poured such effective arguments against a resumption of hostilities in Sicily, that they decided to send, instead of a relieving fleet and army, empty transports to fetch away Bosco and his men. Following the transports they dispatched a large part of the fleet, with a Colonel Anzani on board, whose instructions from Pianell were to negotiate the capitulation both of Milazzo and of the garrison of Messina. But Clary, as soon as he was assured that the Ministry did not require him to relieve Milazzo, again assumed the part of aggrieved hero, and refused to evacuate Messina on any account.[1]

On July 23 the approach of the Neapolitan war-vessels to the port of Milazzo caused some anxiety among the volunteers. If the town were bombarded from the sea, it would be necessary for them to retire and to lose the fruits of the victory which they had so dearly bought. Garibaldi, as usual, showed a bold face and fitted up a battery on the mole with cannon landed off the *Tüköry*. The new-comers, however, proved to be intent on more charitable thoughts. Colonel Anzani and the Dictator soon signed a treaty of capitulation by which the troops in the castle were to march out with their arms and half the battery mules. The cannon and ammunition of the

[1] *Liborio Romano*, 35-36. *Pianell*, 23-24, 182. *Türr's Div.* 398-399, doc. 32. *Cronaca*, 220. *Pianell* (23) says that on July 20 he ordered Clary to march to the relief of Bosco. Clary does not say so and implies the opposite. In any case such orders were countermanded when Anzani was sent to make the capitulation.

castle, the rest of the mules and all the horses were to be left behind for the conquerors. Bosco had boasted that he would enter Palermo on Medici's horse, so Garibaldi had determined that Medici should enter Messina on Bosco's horse, as shortly afterwards took place.[1]

On the morning of July 25, when the Bourbon troops were to march out of the castle, the Piedmontese fleet appeared in the offing. Admiral Persano, seeing Neapolitan war-ships lying off Milazzo, ordered his decks to be cleared for action, presumably intending to save Garibaldi from bombardment even at the cost of a rupture with Naples. When he found how peacefully matters had been settled, he contented himself with embracing the Dictator, and congratulating him in the name of Victor Emmanuel on his fresh victory for the common cause.[2]

The Bourbon troops filed down to the point of embarkation, with the honours of war, between two lines of ragged volunteers. Although they had full opportunity to desert, and were loudly invited to fraternize and to join the army of true Italians, few except among the artillery answered the appeal.[3] At the tail of the column walked Bosco, guarded as a prisoner, fuming and pulling at his moustache. He was hissed by the townspeople, who were beginning to return to their houses from their hiding-places in the peninsula. It was an unpleasant scene and moved the Garibaldini to sympathy for Bosco in spite of his hectoring manner, which did not desert him in this dramatic exit from before the footlights of history.[4]

It soon became known why Garibaldi had caused Bosco to be placed under arrest during the embarkation.

---

[1] *Türr's Div.* 399-400, doc. 33. *Re* Bosco's horse see *Cronaca*, 214, Anzani's report to Clary; *Brancaccio*, 299; *M. Post*, August 9, p. 6; *Conv. Missori*; *Medici (Pasini)*, 28-29; *Guerzoni*, ii. 145-146; *Conv. Sclavo*; *Durand-Brager*, 117; *Castellini*, 41-42; *Risorg.* anno ii. fasc. 1, p. 18.

[2] *Persano*, 94-97.   [3] *Times*, August 4, p. 10, col. 5.

[4] *Forbes*, 107. *M. Post*, August 9, p. 6. *Brancaccio*, 302. *Milan MSS.*, *Bruzzesi, Evac. di Milazzo. Conv. Sclavo.*

When Peard with a few of his fellow-countrymen and others went to take possession of the abandoned castle, they found the mules which had been surrendered under the capitulation lying about dead on the turf, and many of the guns spiked. They luckily detected, before they had trodden upon it, a train of gunpowder hidden under straw, thickly strewn with detonators and running under the door of a magazine, which was intended to blow the citadel and its new occupants sky-high.[1]

When Garibaldi, accompanied by Admiral Persano and the Marios, came up into the castle, they found Bosco's horses, abandoned and frightened, running round and round the grass plateaus of the outer enclosure. The Dictator took his lasso, and amused himself and his companions by a display of the skill which he had acquired in South America more than twenty years before.[2]

Alberto Mario and his English wife Jessie had arrived from Palermo in pursuit of the army. They found a number of truants from their 'Garibaldi Foundling Hospital' enlisted in Dunne's ranks, half a dozen of them badly wounded. Although they had run away from the institute they had not run away from the rifles of the *cacciatori*. One little wounded Sicilian apologised to Mario, stroking his hand as he said : 'Are you angry with us, Signor Commandante ? So many of our brigade are wounded and killed : *Milordo* the Colonel says that after the battle of Milazzo no one can say again that the Sicilians never fight.' Another boy of twelve suffered amputation sitting in the lap of Jessie Mario, who said that she cried more than he did.[3] These young scamps

[1] Mr. Dolmage, who was present at this discovery, writes to me (July 8, 1910) describing the incident, and adds : ' We afterwards heard that Garibaldi had known of the slaughter of the animals and the spiking of the guns early in the day, and that the disgrace of Bosco was the consequence. The gunpowder train was our little find. But we never suspected that Bosco had to do with the stupid act. It must have been the work of some understrapper. The Neapolitans did not always play the game properly, and some of them were brutal enough.' For other eye-witnesses see *Peard*, 823. *Times*, August 4, p. 10, col. 5. *I.L.N.* August 11, pp. 136, 138.

[2] *Mario Mac.* 249.   [3] *Red Shirt*, 38-40.

off the streets of Palermo were not the only class who behaved admirably in hospital. Throughout the campaign,
in the ill-equipped ambulances, without chloroform or
proper dressings, the silent endurance of pain by Italians
of sensitive and cultivated natures aroused the admiration
of British military men. The terrible, and partly unnecessary sufferings to which the patriots were exposed
by the absence of proper provision never moved them to
indignation or even to complaint; they would bear anything for Italy and for the General. In Milazzo, where
lay half the men wounded in the recent battle, there was
no straw to fill the bed-ticks which the Marios had
brought from Palermo. At Barcellona, which took in
the remaining 300, the inhabitants were more active and
things went better.[1]

Both here and later on at Naples and Caserta 'that
excellent creature of the Lord, Jessie White Mario'[2] as
one of her patients called her, did her best to be the
Florence Nightingale of the campaign, though she had no
staff of trained nurses. Fanatical in her republicanism,
lacking in toleration and in charm of manner, she had the
Spartan virtues of her creed and a power of complete
self-sacrifice which she had learnt perhaps from her friend
and master, Mazzini. She was equally the friend of
Garibaldi, who knew well how much he owed to 'Jessie,'
and how many of his best followers were saved by her
ceaseless exertions. Superficially at least there was little
in common between this lady of fixed and fiery faith and
the comfortable citizens of her native island. But they
too were ready to praise her when they heard how she
attended the wretched pallets of hundreds of wounded
Italians, who blessed her in their pain and her country
for her sake.[3]

---

[1] *Conv. Dolmage. Caraguel*, 68. *Bertani*, ii. 106. *Piaggia*, 56 note.
Red Shirt, 38. *Menghini*, 290-293, 225. *F. O. Sicily, Elliot, Goodwin's Pol.
Journal*, August 3.

[2] '*Quella eccellente creatura del Signore che si chiama Jessie Mario
White.*' *Menghini*, 293.

[3] *M. Post*, August 9, p. 6.

Desiring to take advantage of the enthusiasm for his cause prevailing in England, Garibaldi, while still quartered in the castle of Milazzo, consulted his British companions in arms, who had borne themselves so well in the battle, as to the possibility of raising more of their compatriots to come out and join him on the Neapolitan mainland. The idea was suggested to him by Hugh Forbes, the gentleman who, wearing a white top-hat, had shared the perils of his retreat from Rome to the Adriatic in 1849.[1] In the interval between the two Italian revolutions, Forbes had been in the United States, where he had had some peculiar dealings with old John Brown previous to the Virginia raid. He now appeared at Milazzo. Garibaldi fell in with Forbes' proposal that a British Legion should be raised, but refused to give him the command, and left him behind as Governor of Milazzo Castle. The scheme aroused little enthusiasm among those who would have been best qualified to carry it out. Mr. Dolmage, who was a British officer on leave from Malta, refused to touch it, and Dunne himself, who had quarrelled with his countrymen when he left the Queen's service, angrily declared that he did not want any more of them out there. He prophesied that a whole regiment raised at a few days' notice among a civilian population and shipped to a strange land would contain good elements, but that, for disciplinary reasons, it would be more trouble than it was worth during the short period that the war was likely to last. But Garibaldi, though he knew that the British Legion would not come in time to be of much assistance in the Neapolitan kingdom, looked forward to a campaign in the Papal States, and to the capture of Rome. He therefore sent to England as agent for the raising of the Legion, a certain Styles, who had behaved well in the battle of Milazzo, but who

---

[1] See *Garibaldi's Defence of the Roman Republic.* Hugh Forbes must not be confused with Captain C. S. Forbes, R.N., Peard's friend, who in 1860 went in the van of the advancing army as a non-combatant, and whose book is often cited in this volume.

turned out no better than he should be, and soon fell out with the disinterested committee who took up the project in London.[1]

It was now evident that there would be no further fighting in Sicily. Since Marshal Clary and his 15,000 at Messina had not moved to the relief of Milazzo, they certainly would not take the field on their own account now that it had fallen. Garibaldi's way lay open down to the shore of the Straits. Medici, duly mounted on Bosco's horse, led the vanguard into the streets of Messina, and on July 28 he signed a treaty with Clary, by which the citadel was to be held by the Royalist garrison and the town by the Garibaldini. Hostilities between them were to be suspended by sea as by land, so that the citadel, which completely dominated the entrance of the harbour, might not fire a shot at the Dictator's vessels, even when they sailed out under the muzzles of the King's cannon to invade his Calabrian provinces. Such a treaty, extorted without bloodshed from 15,000 men in an impregnable fortress, was a great advantage for the inferior forces of the volunteers, who would have had much difficulty in entering the streets of Messina if Clary had resisted their approach on the mountain ridges above the town, and in the forts designed for its protection. Nor could they have remained in Messina if the citadel had been free to open fire. The terms of this treaty are a measure of the panic struck into the heart of the Royalist troops by the defeat of Bosco, and a measure also of the ardour with which the Neapolitan Ministers desired to avoid further

[1] *Convs. Dolmage* and *Patterson. Russell MSS. Misc. It.*, containing Hugh Forbes' report dated November 28, 1860; Forbes rightly says that Dunne, although he signed the papers with which Styles returned to England, ' did so unwillingly, objecting to any English coming there.' This is borne out by Mr. Dolmage, to whom Dunne spoke freely. *Holyoake*, i. 243-256, for the London end of the story. In *Schwabe MS.* 2, is a letter of De Rohan which says that Garibaldi at Milazzo only intended individual volunteers to come out to him from England, and that the idea of equipping a Legion was invented by the London Committee; but Hugh Forbes (*Forbes MS.*) writes: ' In Milazzo I proposed to General Garibaldi the creation of an English Legion,' and Mr. Dolmage bears this out.

fighting in the island. The greater part of the garrison were now withdrawn from the citadel of Messina to the mainland.[1]

During the anxious month that followed the battle of Milazzo, the politics of Europe turned on the question whether Garibaldi could succeed in crossing the Straits. Would the naval Powers interfere to prevent him? And even if they did not, could he cross in the face of the Neapolitan army and fleet?

The diplomatic part of the question was destined to be settled in a few days by the secret activities of Cavour. He was now fully determined to acquire the Neapolitan kingdom for Victor Emmanuel, if possible without, but if necessary with further aid from Garibaldi. On July 14 he had still believed that he would be able, before Garibaldi could leave Sicily, to engineer a revolution in Naples by means of the agents whom he had sent there; at the critical moment the Piedmontese fleet was to appear in the bay. Sanguine of success, he had written to Admiral Persano:[2] 'We must at all costs, on the one hand prevent Garibaldi from crossing the Straits, and on the other excite a revolution in Naples. If this were to succeed, the government of Victor Emmanuel would at once be proclaimed there. In that case you would immediately sail with your whole squadron for Naples.' The plan presupposed some active disloyalty in the army, and some power of initiative in the inhabitants of Naples. Neither were forthcoming. A week after he had written this letter to Persano, Cavour had become so far doubtful of his ability to provoke an internal revolution, that he decided to clear the way for Garibaldi's passage of the Straits. His earnest wish to forestall the Dictator at Naples no longer blinded him to the fact that the advance of the red-shirts might prove after all the only means of deposing the House of Bourbon. He continued, indeed,

---

[1] *Rüstow*, 223-225. *Cuniberti*, 102-105. *Franci*, i. 79-80, 213-215. *Castellini*, 43-44. *Forbes*, 120-122, 125.
[2] July 14. *Persano*, 88.

until after the middle of August to work and hope for a wholesale desertion of the Neapolitan army to the national cause, which would remove the need for Garibaldi to cross the Straits, and would place all authority at both ends of the peninsula in the hands of the Ministry at Turin.[1]

But meanwhile, not allowing himself to be duped by these golden hopes, Cavour entered into a conspiracy with Victor Emmanuel to open Garibaldi's way before him, in spite of the threats of European diplomacy, to which it was necessary all the while to appear subservient. The King and his Minister, while publicly requesting the Dictator to halt, secretly urged him to advance. And while not daring to dispute, through regular diplomatic channels, the proposition that he ought to be stopped at the Straits, they dissolved by a hint to England the concert of naval Powers that was being formed for that purpose. These two pieces of secret service, Count Litta's mission to Garibaldi, and Sir James Lacaita's mission to Lord John Russell, have only recently been established as certain historical facts. Their importance in the history of the crisis that made Italy is very great.

At four o'clock on the evening of July 22, Count Litta Modignani came by appointment to the Palace at Turin to receive from the King's hands a written message which he was to take to Garibaldi. Victor Emmanuel first gave him a letter requesting the Dictator not to cross the Straits—the ostensible royal message published to the world to allay the threatenings of France. But here, said the King to Count Litta, is a second note which you will at once administer to Garibaldi 'to neutralize the effect of the first.' So saying Victor Emmanuel handed over a letter containing the following words in his own handwriting :—

---

[1] See Cavour's letters of these weeks. *Ricasoli,* v. 196. *Persano,* 101, 123, 127, 134-135. *Chiala,* iii. 322.

'To the Dictator General Garibaldi.

'Now, having written as King, Victor Emmanuel suggests to you to reply in this sense, which I know is what you feel. Reply that you are full of devotion and reverence for your King, that you would like to obey his counsels, but that your duty to Italy forbids you to promise not to help the Neapolitans, when they appeal to you to free them from a Government which true men and good Italians cannot trust: that you cannot therefore obey the wishes of the King, but must reserve full freedom of action.'

With these two missives in his pocket, Count Litta left the royal presence. The same day he saw Cavour and Farini, who chaffed him on the 'Garibaldian part' he was about to play. He sailed to Palermo and thence to Milazzo, where he arrived on the morning of July 27, just in time to catch Garibaldi before he started to over- take Medici and the vanguard at Messina. As soon as they were closeted together, the King's messenger pro- duced the two letters in their order. At the second, delivered by Litta with sly excuses for the first, Garibaldi burst out laughing. He rose at once and went into his bedroom, where Sirtori, Trecchi, and others were talking so loudly that he was forced to say, 'Gentlemen, I have got to write a letter, please don't make so much noise.' So saying he sat down and wrote his answer to the King, which thrilled the heart of Italy in the ensuing weeks.

'Sire,' he wrote, 'Your Majesty knows the high esteem and love I bear you. But the present state of things in Italy does not allow me to obey you, as I should have wished. Called by the peoples (*chiamato dai popoli*) I refrained as long as I could. But if now, in spite of all the calls that reach me, I were longer to delay, I should fail in my duty and imperil the sacred cause of Italy. Allow me then, Sire, this time to dis- obey you. As soon as I shall have fulfilled what I have undertaken, by freeing the peoples from a hated yoke, I will lay down my sword at your feet and obey you for the rest of my life.'

Litta hastened back to Turin, the public bearer of this

famous reply.   But the world knew nothing of the other
document which he safely carried back, the King's original draft, of which the Dictator's answer was but a
paraphrase adorned with a few Garibaldian touches.
That most compromising of documents has just come to
light after a discreet interval of fifty years.[1]

It was easy thus, while saving appearances, to make
sure that Garibaldi would obey the law of his being and
go forward as fast and as far as he was able.   But to
prevent the maritime Powers from stopping him at the
Straits was a harder task.

For the moment little was to be feared from Austria,
alienated as she was from the Government of Naples by
the nature of its appeal to England, France, and Piedmont.
The diplomatic representatives of Naples did not hesitate
to allege that if the western Powers would force a six
months' truce upon Garibaldi, their country would be able
to hold the elections to her new Parliament, and would
lend her regular army as soon as it was required for the
'inevitable' war against Austria in Venice.   Though
such promises were only the result of abject fear
and were unlikely to be fulfilled, they caused irritation,
if not alarm, at Vienna,[2] and postponed the season of
Austrian intervention.

Napoleon, on the other hand, at that moment desired
to preserve the Bourbon dynasty on the mainland as a
constitutional State under French direction far more
ardently than he desired a month later to preserve the
Pope's Adriatic dominions.   He was therefore most
anxious to stop Garibaldi at the Straits; but he was no
less anxious to preserve good relations with England.[3]
Both these objects could be achieved by a naval combina-

[1] *Risorg.* anno ii. fasc. 1, pp. 1-48, Litta's diary, and photograph of the
secret letter. *Risorg.* anno ii. fasc. 3-4, pp. 651-662, in no way impairs the
truth of the story. *Arrivabene*, ii. 71-73, bears out some minor details of Litta's
diary.

[2] *Vitzthum*, i. 95-96.

[3] See his letter of July 27 to Persigny, *Mem. Stor. Mil.* ii. 186-187.

tion of France and England to hold the Straits of Messina against the passage of the Garibaldini, and this was proposed by the French Ministers to Palmerston and Russell. Lord John, in his English simplicity, supposed that Victor Emmanuel and Cavour meant what they said when they declared against Garibaldi's invasion of Calabria, and no doubt felt that he could best serve Italy by acting in accordance with the publicly expressed wishes of Cavour.[1]

The British Ministers, therefore, were not indisposed to listen to the arguments of Napoleon when he proposed that England and France should send the two greatest fleets in the world to protect the Calabrian coast against the red-shirts. Details as to the number of ships to be employed were actually arranged at Naples between King Francis' Ministers, Brenier, and the French Admiral.[2] The final consent of the British Cabinet had yet to be received, but if Palmerston and Russell fathered the scheme it would meet with no resistance from their colleagues, who, except Gladstone, were less enthusiastic than they in the Italian cause.

It was a moment full of danger, but Cavour was warned just in time of the blow which the extreme subtleness of his policy was preparing for him in the house of his friends. The warning came, it is said, through an indiscretion of one of his worst enemies. The story goes that the French Empress in conversation with Nigra, the Piedmontese representative at Paris, let drop a hint of the negotiations with England, that Nigra extracted the whole truth from her by pretending to sympathise with the project, and sent on the news to Turin.[3]

Cavour, gravely alarmed, went straight to the British

[1] *Russell MSS.* Lord John to Hudson, July 23. ' I am told that the only man who has influence with Garibaldi is the King. If he likes to send a message to Sicily to desire Garibaldi to stay where he is and not to go to Calabria he will have our full concurrence. Pray ask to see the King and tell him so, first warning Cavour of the purpose of your audience.'

[2] *Liborio Romano*, 37.

[3] Villari's story, as he obtained it from Lacaita; it is, of course, not first-hand evidence. *Villari Pasq.*

Legation and asked Hudson point-blank how to prevent
Russell from being made an unconscious agent in the
ruin of Italy's best hopes. Hudson, happily inspired,
advised Cavour to send Sir James Lacaita, the intimate
friend of the Russell family, to explain the real situation
to Lord John.[1]

Giacomo Lacaita, a gentleman of Apulia and a lawyer
of Naples, had in 1850 been Mr. Gladstone's political
mentor during his famous visit.[2] Driven into exile for
this, he became naturalised in England and was knighted
as Sir James Lacaita for public services rendered to his

---

[1] Sir James Hudson's autograph letter to Lacaita written in 1885 to bear
witness to this event is in possession of Mr. Charles Lacaita, who has given me
a photograph of it. The letter, which runs as follows, at length puts the story
beyond all possible doubt :—

                                          ' FLORENCE,
                                            ' 9 May, 1885.

   ' MY DEAR LACAITA,

      ' I have a clear recollection of the circumstances connected with your
visit to Earl Russell in 1860, and as far as the action of Count Cavour was concerned I can declare, that he called upon me at the Queen's Legation at Turin,
and pointing out the dangerous complications which must arise if a stop was
not put to the negotiations then in progress between France and Naples, into
which it was hoped to induce England to enter (i.e. to exercise a direct armed
pressure upon Garibaldi), begged me to take such steps as I might deem practicable to prevent this mischief to the Cause of Italy.
      ' I told the Count that the only thing which occurred to me would be to
address you upon the subject desiring you to go immediately to Lord Russell and
explain to him the real bearings of the case—that I proposed yourself because
you were intimately known to the family of Lord Russell as a man of honour
and a Neapolitan Gentleman having a perfect knowledge of the whole case and
its deplorable consequences if not promptly checked : and, moreover, because
this was not a case where a Regular Diplomatic Agent could be of use, who, if
he acted at all, could only do so under Protest ; to which if no attention was
paid at the instant, would render the " agreement " between the Powers concerned an " accomplished fact ".
      ' Therefore the success must lie entirely in the personal qualifications of the
gentleman employed in so delicate a conjuncture.
      ' Count Cavour agreed in this view of the case, and said he would telegraph
to the King's Minister in London to concert with you the steps to take.
      ' Your success on that occasion added one more to the many services you
had already rendered to Italy.'

                                          ' Yours sincerely,
                                            ' JAMES HUDSON.'

[2] Garibaldi and the Thousand, pp. 48-49.

adopted country. In July, 1860, he was engaged in examining the candidates for our Indian Civil Service. On
the 23rd, the rain of an English summer's day gave him
a severe cold, and further to his distress, as he noted in
his diary, he heard that a special Neapolitan envoy, the
Marquis La Greca, had arrived in London and had been
closeted with Lord John. On the next day, Tuesday
July 24, he spent another chilly morning examining the
young men *vivâ voce*, came home exceedingly ill, and took
to his bed. He was called up by an unexpected visit
from Emmanuel D'Azeglio, the Piedmontese Minister in
England, who, in obedience to Cavour's message, came
to request Lacaita to go at once to Lord John ' and put
him on his guard against an application he would receive
for intervention to force an armistice on Sicily '.[1] In
spite of his illness, Lacaita dressed again, and disregard-
ing the protests of his family dragged himself into the
streets to obey the orders of Cavour, and, as it chanced,
to bring about the making of Italy.

Arriving at the Russells' town house [2] he rang the
bell. The servant who appeared knew him well as a
friend of the family. The conversation that followed
was to this effect :—

' Is Lord John at home ? '

' Not at home, Sir James.'

' Is he out or only busy ? '

' He's engaged, most particular, Sir James, with the
French Ambassador ; I've turned away the Turkish Ambassador, and I've strict orders to let in no one except
the Minister for Naples.'

' There's no time to lose,' thought Lacaita, and then
inquired :—

' Is Lady John at home, then ? '

' She's in bed, Sir James, ill.'

Then Lacaita took out a card and wrote upon it,

[1] *Lacaita's Journal*, MS.

[2] Lady Agatha Russell writes to me : ' I think my parents were probably at
Chesham Place : they came to Pembroke Lodge Saturdays to Mondays.'

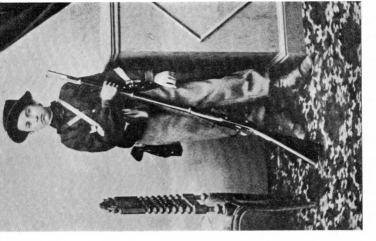

TWO SICILIAN RED-SHIRTS, 1860

Pietro San Martino, Sicilian nobleman, distinguished himself at Palermo and at Milazzo.

Pollacie, son of a respectable glover in the Toledo, Palermo, æt. 12. Behaved with admirable courage at Milazzo, where Garibaldi made him a sergeant on the field. Mr. Dolmage, who says he was "a quiet modest child," had this photograph of him taken in Palermo in the following year.

LORD JOHN RUSSELL

'For the love you bear the memory of your father [1] see me this instant,' and sent up this strange message to the lady of the house. In a few minutes he was by her bedside. He persuaded her to send down to her husband the simple message, 'Come up at once.' Thinking to find his wife suddenly taken worse, Lord John left Persigny, the French Ambassador, sitting there, rushed upstairs, opened the door of the bedroom, and found himself face to face with Lacaita. It was no time for apologies or explanations. In a flood of impassioned words the Apulian poured forth his soul to his English friend. Was 1848 to be repeated? Then Sicily had revolted, then England and France had helped to prevent the Sicilians from invading Naples, and then Sicily had been reconquered. If Garibaldi crossed now Italy would be made. If he was stopped, division, reaction and disaster would ensue as before. Did Lord John wish to be for ever loved or for ever hated by Liberal Europe? A violent paroxysm of coughing shortened his eloquence. But he had said enough to show Lord John what Cavour wanted England to do. 'Go to bed,' he said to Lacaita, 'and don't be so sure that I am going to sign the treaty yet.' [2]

Russell's mind was well prepared for these ideas, for during the summer his wife had received letters from her Neapolitan friend Poerio, urging that the Bourbon must be dethroned and Italy made, now or never [3]; and for a

---

[1] Gilbert Elliot, second Earl of Minto, a great friend to Italy in public and to Lacaita in private life.

[2] Such is the story told by Lacaita to Villari, printed in *Villari Pasq.* and elsewhere. The story was first published in 1880 in an imperfect form in *Fagan's Life of Panizzi* (ii. 207). Lacaita was annoyed at this, and Villari therefore asked Lacaita for the real details, which Lacaita furnished. Villari's story is Lacaita's authorised version. His son, Mr. Charles Lacaita, told me this. Sir James told the story not only to Villari but to his son, and to various other people. Lady Russell's journals for 1860 are lost, but see Appendix A, p. 315 below, for complete evidence from Mr. Vernon's diary that she and her husband acknowledged the truth of Lacaita's story. For the remarkable personality of Lady John Russell, see the *Memoir* of her by Mr. Desmond MacCarthy and Lady Agatha Russell (Methuen, 1910).

[3] *Lady Russell MS.*

fortnight past Hudson and Elliot, themselves new converts, had been preaching the doctrine of complete
Italian unity in their private letters to the Foreign
Minister. Going downstairs, Lord John presumably
put off Persigny with what excuse he could, for two
hours later he sent round a messenger to Lacaita to tell
him to be of good cheer.[1] And at the Cabinet held on
the afternoon of July 25 it was decided to reject the
French proposal with regard to coercing Garibaldi.[2]

Persigny was amazed at the *volte-face* of the British
Ministers, for, as he himself tells us, 'he had obtained
Lord Palmerston's promise' to join in stopping Garibaldi.[3] On July 26 Lord John wrote to our Ambassador
at Paris a dispatch suitable for publication, no reader
of which would ever guess that the majestic current of
British foreign policy had just been deflected from its
course by one of the Civil Service Examiners. 'I informed M. de Persigny,' writes Russell, 'that Her
Majesty's Government were of opinion that no case had
been made out for a departure on their part from their
general principle of non-intervention.' Her Majesty's
Government had only come to this conclusion within the
last forty-eight hours. 'That the force of Garibaldi was
not in itself sufficient to overthrow the Neapolitan Monarchy. If the navy, army, and people of Naples were attached to the King, Garibaldi would be defeated; if, on
the contrary, they were disposed to welcome Garibaldi,
our interference would be an intervention in the internal
affairs of the Neapolitan kingdom.' This was sound

[1] See Appendix A, p. 315 below.

[2] *Br. Parl. Papers*, vii. p. 40, No. 50. The Cabinet held on the afternoon of
the 25th (see *Times*) is the meeting referred to. The visit of Lacaita to Lord
John's house must have occurred some time between D'Azeglio's call on Lacaita
on the 24th, and this Cabinet on the 25th, *viz.* either in the afternoon of the 24th
or the morning of the 25th July.

[3] *Persigny*, 274-275. So also we read in *Elliot*, 48, under the date July 26,
' Brenier yesterday read me a dispatch from Thouvenel . . . saying that Lord
John, after having shown himself disposed to come to an understanding with
France with regard to Naples, had now announced the determination of the
English Government to abstain completely from all interference.'

doctrine. To come to the point : ' If France chose to interfere alone, we should merely disapprove her course and protest against it. In our opinion the Neapolitans ought to be masters either to reject or to receive Garibaldi.[1]

Napoleon was not prepared to take a course against which England would protest, and the project of foreign intervention fell dead.

Garibaldi had no longer anything to fear from the French and British fleets, but he still had before him a military operation of immense difficulty, to cross the Straits of Messina through the midst of the Neapolitan fleet and to land on the Calabrian coast in the face of the Neapolitan army. The modern Odysseus stood on the sandy cape of Charybdis, and gazing across at Scilla's now castled rock, bethought him of his many devices.[2] Other heroes had striven in vain to become masters of this event. Half a century before, the generals of the great Napoleon, including Murat himself, had been baffled by this same strip of sea, two miles wide at the narrowest point, which had guarded Sicily from the French as safely as twenty-one miles of northern ocean had guarded from them a more favoured island.[3]

---

[1] Br. Parl. Papers, vii. p. 40, No. 50.

[2] The currents in the Straits, which had given rise in the sea-ports of ancient Hellas to the fable of the Charybdis whirlpool, are so slight that they caused but little inconvenience to Garibaldi's transport operations from the Faro, although these were principally conducted in scores of row-boats, each one smaller than Odysseus' ship. Times, August 20, p. 9, c. 1.

[3] See Johnston (ii. 118-119, 239-242) for the two attempts of the French to invade Sicily, in 1806 and 1810. On the second occasion ' the King of Naples [Murat] arrived at Scilla on the 3rd of June, saluted by the ringing of bells and by salvos of artillery that were re-echoed, but with solid shot, by the British batteries on the further side. The Strait of Messina at this point appears little more than a river winding between hilly and picturesque banks. It gradually widens from about two miles across at the Faro to eight or nine miles at Messina. The troops of both armies were mostly encamped at the narrowest point, and so slight was the distance between them that from the lofty rock of Scilla, 550 feet above the sea, nearly all the British camps and intrenchments could be discovered. From the further side the view was no less remarkable and clear, and one English traveller claimed to have distinguished and recognised from the Faro through a

The lighthouse which gives its name of 'Faro' to the cape of Charybdis, and an old fort and battery by its side, stand at the end of the spit of sand where the north and east sides of the triangle of Sicily unite. On the sand dunes behind the lighthouse the greater part of the Garibaldian army was bivouacked during the first three weeks of August. The depth of the water round the cape, which enables the tunny-fishers to row their boats within a few yards of the pebbly shore, made it an excellent place for a great embarkation. Two salt-water lakes near at hand gave safe harbourage to the larger transports and to rafts which were being constructed to take across horses and cannon; while the flotilla of small boats which Garibaldi collected from Messina and the neighbouring fishing villages were drawn up along the beach of the sea. The mean houses of Faro village afforded useful shelter. It was on these sands that the British had been encamped fifty years before, and the remains of their trenches could still be seen. Garibaldi had three new earth-work batteries erected, where he mounted some indifferent cannon, taken from off his only war-ship, the *Tüköry*, and from the castle of Milazzo. With these and the three small cannon in the fort beside the lighthouse, he made pretence to command the Sicilian side of the narrow waters.[1]

On the roasting sand between the lighthouse and the lakes the volunteers lay encamped day after day, amid scenes of nature and of man very different from the rainy streets of London and the dim rooms in Chesham Place where their fate had just been decided. The crowded quarters soon became insanitary; the food and water were insufficient; on the open sands the sea mist soaked them by night and the sun scorched them by day, and

telescope the person of the King of Naples.' Garibaldi was now using his telescope from the spot where the 'British traveller' had used his fifty years before.

[1] *Morgan MS. Forbes*, 124-125. *Du Camp*, 62. *Milan MS. Bruzzesi's note-book*, August 9. *Türr's Div* 119-120. *Orsini*, 51-52. *Times*, August 20, p. 9.

GARIBALDI AT THE STRAITS OF MESSINA

(*Illustrated London News*, sketch on spot.)

Shows the earthworks and flotilla at Charyldis sands, and Calabrian mountains across the strait.

ALTIFIUMARA FORT (NOW ' FORTINO GARIBALDI ')

Left of Photograph on hill above coast road. View from the shore where Musolino's men landed.

BAGNARA

And coast to Scilla point. Sicily in right background.

there was little to relieve body or soul except constant bathing in the sea, drilling, and guessing how the General meant to carry them across.[1] Among Garibaldi's own retinue the gaiety of the days in Palermo Palace and Milazzo Castle had given place to a more serious mood. Their chief was silent for hours together, passing about between Messina and the Faro, sometimes mounting the lighthouse to watch the coming and going of the Bourbon ships, sometimes vanishing no one knew whither, concealing even from Medici the plans that engrossed him all day long, but keeping his telescope ever directed on the Calabrian shore.[2]

The eyes and thoughts of all men were fixed on the coast opposite, so near and yet so far, the ground whence one could march to Naples, to Rome, to Venice. The toe of Italy[3] has for its bone the enormous granite mass of Aspromonte, 'the rugged mountain,' of which the plateaus and spurs, clothed in forests of oak, pine, and chestnut, and cut by deep cañons each paved with a dry *fiumara* of stones washed white by flood, run down to the shores upon which the Garibaldini were so covetously gazing. Where the last steep precipices of Aspromonte overhang the Mediterranean, a road crawls beneath them along the narrow strip of shore, joining the crowded villages of Bagnara, Favazzina, Scilla, and Cannitello. Along that road the red-shirts could watch the enemy's columns moving to and fro.

The narrowest point of the Straits was commanded from the Calabrian side by two small forts of Torre Cavallo and Altifiumara, built on the hill-side about a hundred yards above the road and the sea. If Garibaldi could capture one of these forts, his guns would command the narrowest part of the Straits from side to side, for he would then have batteries on both shores. The Neapolitan fleet would therefore be compelled to stand out

[1] *Fonvielle*, 202-203.
[2] *Mario Mac.* 249. *Red Shirt*, 43. *Castellini*, 47, 51.
[3] See henceforth Map II, at end of book.

of the narrows, and he could pass his army across from the Faro to the captured fort. It was on this basis that he planned his first attempt.

On the night of August 8, a forlorn hope of 200 men, picked out to capture the fort of Altifiumara, embarked in row-boats at the Faro. Garibaldi himself, always to the fore in any maritime operation, arranged and guided the flotilla into mid-channel. He then returned to the Sicilian shore where the rest of the army was embarking in steamers and fishing-boats, ready to cross at dawn if a signal from the opposite shore announced the success of the enterprise. Meanwhile the 200, under cover of a cloudy night, rowed through the middle of the Neapolitan cruisers, and landed not far from the desired place. Their leader, Musolino, a Calabrian, had visited his native soil in disguise a few days before, and had arranged, as he believed, that the gates of the fort should be opened from the inside.[1] But the alarm was given, their night attack was repulsed, and they had no course left but to escape into the mountains of the interior. At first they ascended the *fiumara* that debouches beside the fort, guided through the night by the glint of its white stones ; later on they climbed the mountain walls in complete darkness, dragging each other up the steepest places by the muzzles of their guns.

During the next ten days these 200 men were the only invaders on Neapolitan soil. They wandered about the upper plains of Aspromonte at a height of over 3000 feet above the sea, suffering from intense cold by night and August sun by day, sometimes starving in the mountain desert, sometimes falling in with trains of mules bearing ample provisions sent up for them from the Liberal Committee of Reggio. Owing to the fact that

---

[1] The fort in question was that of Altifiumara, now called *fortino Garibaldi*, as is shown by the eye-witness, Alberto Mario, in his *Red Shirt*, 49, 54, and by *Arrivabene*, ii. 88. *Times*, September 4, p. 7, c. a. *Mem.* 373, and *Forbes*, 130. *Türr's Div.* 123 incorrectly says that it was the neighbouring fort of Torre Cavallo.

the new Intendant of Reggio appointed by Don Liborio
Romano was a 'constitutionalist' in tacit sympathy with
the invaders, this rebel Committee acted with singular
publicity, in spite of the presence of the royal troops in the
town. The old Royalist militia—the *guardie urbane*—had
just been disarmed by an order of Don Liborio from
Naples, and the new National Guard, Liberals to a man,
had been armed in their stead. The civil and local authorities, therefore, no longer gave any support to the
regular army camped in their midst.[1]

The pitiful numbers of the invading force in Aspromonte were increased by small bands of Calabrian
peasants, hardy mountaineers in goat-skin sandals, knee-
breeches, shirt-sleeves, and brimless sugar-loaf hats orna-
mented with streamers of black velvet—the romantic
Calabrian costume which the opera-house and the picture
gallery of that era had made as familiar to cultured Europe
as the kilt of Sir Walter Scott's Highlanders. Their
leader was Plutino, a local magnate jealous of the fame
which his fellow-Calabrian Musolino had acquired in the
province as leader of this expedition. Both Musolino
and Plutino were feudal chiefs and political leaders
rather than expert military men, and the command of the
expedition was made over by consent to Missori, the
Lombard who had saved Garibaldi's life at Milazzo.
Under his spirited leadership these few hundred men
kept the Neapolitan army perpetually on the *qui vive*.
Every night they lighted a blaze of bonfires along the
heights, to show their friends on the Sicilian shore that
the insurrection was alive in Calabria. Once they came
right down to the coast, captured Bagnara, and held it
until driven out by several thousand troops. The Calabrians behaved well in this first skirmish.

In mountain hamlets like Solano and Pedavoli the
invaders learnt something of Calabrian local politics, the
blood-feuds which under the form of Liberal and Bourbon

---

[1] See pp. 16-19 above. *Morisani*, 16-20. *Salazaro*, 49-51.

faction-fights had devastated the villages in '48.   Since
that year the course of events had so far alienated or
discouraged the Royalist party, that Missori's men were
almost everywhere assisted and were nowhere opposed
by the Calabrians themselves.   This was the more remarkable seeing that the country was still occupied by
the Neapolitan troops, and that for the ten days preced-
ing Garibaldi's crossing, Missori was being hunted like a
partridge in the mountains.   On August 15 General Ruiz
with two battalions was sent up after him from the coast,
and pursued him in vain through the forest gorges, of
which the fantastic magnificence had more than once attracted landscape-painters like Arthur Strutt and Edward
Lear to brave very real dangers of brigandage.   The
Garibaldini escaped over the upper plains of Aspromonte,
many miles across, where only a few huts and sheepfolds
broke the monotony of the desert, and where 'the only
point visible on the horizon was Etna's purple cone.   It
was impossible,' wrote Alberto Mario as he tramped
behind Missori through such scenes, 'even in the
hazardous project which absorbed us, not to be at times
subdued by a mighty awe.'[1]

After this first failure, Garibaldi was only the more
anxious to cross the Straits.   The 'call of the peoples'
for his presence among them, of which he had spoken in
his letter to Victor Emmanuel, was growing daily more
insistent.   Half Calabria, in anticipation of his coming,
was already in open revolt ; the liberty of the press, the
sympathies of the new 'constitutional' magistracy and
police, made rebellion easy in any town or village not
actually occupied by the regular troops ; and the lower
clergy, in contrast to the bishops, often took the popular
side.   In the toe of Italy the presence of 16,000 troops

---

[1] *Red Shirt*, 44-107.   *Menghini*, 446-450, 454-455.   *Fonvielle*, 207. *Zasio*,
71.   *Ruiz*, 9-10.   *Mem.* 373.   *Milan MS., Bronzetti's note-book*, August 9.
Türr's Div. 122-123.   *Arrivabene*, ii. 88-93.   *Forbes*, 130-131. *Strutt* and *Lear*,
passim.

prevented the insurrection from breaking out along the thickly populated coast-line, and confined the movement to the wanderings of Missori's bands in the heights of Aspromonte. But the province of Cosenza in Upper Calabria fell more or less into the hands of revolutionary committees in the first days of August, and the Basilicata followed suit on August 18. The movement in Calabria had been stirred up by the great local proprietors—the Plutino family, Stocco of the Thousand, and Pace of Medici's expedition, whom Garibaldi had sent on to their old homes to prepare the way before him. In the Basilicata a like part was played by Mignona, also commissioned by Garibaldi. The leaders of the insurrection in the provinces south of the capital showed both sense and courage, and succeeded in overawing the troops in their midst, such as the formidable garrison of Cosenza, who remained passive spectators of the rebellion. If the Northern provinces had been equally Liberal, and the inhabitants of Naples equally bold, Cavour would have got his revolution without need of further help from Garibaldi.[1]

As the moment for invading the mainland drew near, the recently enlisted Sicilian bands, considering their part in the affair completed, began to desert in hundreds from Messina and the Faro. Many of them had fought well for the deliverance of their own island, but few shared the enthusiasm of their Northern Liberators for the idea of Italian Unity. In so far as it meant protection by Piedmont against the return of the detested Neapolitans, Italian Unity was good; but in so far as it meant friendly dealings with the Neapolitans, it was nought. Now that their own island was safe, they returned to their homes.[2] Only Dunne's regiment of six hundred and a 'Sicilian brigade' of eight hundred *Cacciatori d' Etna*, led by real enthusiasts like La Masa, Corrao, and

[1] *De Cesare's F. di P.* cix.-cxxxviii., cxliii. *Mignona*, 198-214.
[2] *Milan MS., Bronzetti's note-book*, August 2-4. *Castellini*, 48. *Conv. Dolmage.*

La Porta, of whom the last two were good soldiers, shared
the fortunes of the army until the end of the Volturno
campaign.[1]

If the Dictator had any doubts as to the real wishes of
the Court of Turin, they were removed by another secret
message which reached him at the Faro through the
hands of Victor Emmanuel's aide-de-camp Trecchi, the
regular medium of royal communication with Garibaldi.
The King's positive orders to the Dictator were to occupy
Naples, and thence to invade the Pope's territory of
Umbria and the Marches.[2]

It is not easy to judge whether or not Cavour was a
party to this message.   On the one hand it was a habit
of Victor Emmanuel to carry on a policy of his own
through secret agents acting behind the back of his
Ministers.   And certainly Cavour was on principle opposed to a red-shirt invasion of the Papal States.   He
wished to keep the liberation of the Marches and Umbria
as a royal prerogative, and not to allow it to become a
new source of strength to the advanced parties, who, he
feared, would then dictate terms to the Monarchy and
attack the city of Rome at the risk of a war with France.

On the other hand, the King's message, though in
apparent contradiction to Cavour's policy, was perhaps
one of the subtlest moves in the Minister's game.   In
order to interpret the royal words of encouragement to
Garibaldi, dictated on August 5, it is necessary to understand that Cavour had already, four days earlier, deter-

[1] *Paolucci's Corrao*, 144-145.

[2] Like the secret letter carried by Count Litta (pp. 101-103 above), it has only
just been made known to the world after fifty years (*Nuova Antologia*, June 1,
1910, *Trecchi* papers).   The text of the message in Trecchi's handwriting,
dictated apparently on August 5, runs thus:—

'Words dictated by Victor Emmanuel to be conveyed to Garibaldi. Gari-
baldi in Naples. Will regulate himself according to opportunity, either occupying
Umbria and the Marches with his troops, or allowing bands of volunteers to
go. As soon as Garibaldi is in Naples he will proclaim its union to the rest of
Italy as in Sicily. Prevent disorders which would harm our cause. Keep the
Neapolitan army in being, for Austria will soon declare war. Let the King of
Naples escape, and if he is taken by the people, save him and let him escape.'

mined in his own mind to invade the Papal States from the north with the regular army of Piedmont. On August 1 he had written to Nigra in Paris and to Emmanuel D'Azeglio in London disclosing to them this secret, the key to all his subsequent policy, in 'ultra confidential' letters which were to be destroyed as soon as read.[1] The grounds on which he adopted this decision, the greatest and boldest of his whole life, will be discussed in a future chapter. The policy did not take effect until September, and till then was not foreseen by the world at large. It is, therefore, enough at this stage to point out that by August 1 Cavour had secretly determined to invade the Papal States himself. He had, therefore, the less objection to the further advance of Garibaldi, because he now knew that the King would be able at once to assist and to control the red-shirts, by meeting them with the regular army either at Naples or on the southern border of the Papal States. He was not yet prepared to disclose this plan to Garibaldi, but he was perhaps not sorry that the King should keep the Dictator in good humour by talking about a Garibaldian invasion of the Papal States from Naples, which would now never really take place, since the royal troops would forestall him in the Pope's territories. It was the more necessary to tell Garibaldi that he might invade the Papal States from Naples, because Cavour was at this moment putting his veto on Mazzini's plan to invade the Papal States direct from Genoa with Bertani's private army.

Bertani's Committee in Aid of Garibaldi had not yet sent out to him any large body of men. Throughout June and July the expeditions despatched to Sicily had been organised chiefly by the moderates and by the supporters of Cavour.[2] Although Bertani had been levying and equipping volunteers ever since Garibaldi sailed in May, he had hitherto held them in reserve for a blow at

[1] *Bianchi, Polit. de Cavour*, p. 378 and note.   [2] See p. 46 above.

the Papal States. Garibaldi had all along favoured such a design, while at the same time demanding reinforcements for himself in Sicily. On July 30 he wrote from the Faro to Bertani : ' As to the operations in the Papal and Neapolitan territories, push them on with all possible vigour.'[1] The time had now come to strike the blow. In the first days of August Bertani had at his disposal 8940 volunteers, who, unlike the men of the earlier expeditions, were ready armed, uniformed, and organised for immediate service in the field.[2] Six thousand of them were at Genoa, but some were at Florence under Nicotera, and a few more in the Romagna. The detachments at Florence and in the Romagna were to invade Umbria and the Marches respectively, while the main body were to sail from Genoa, land in the Papal territories at a point north of Civita Vecchia, and march by way of Viterbo to join Nicotera and the others in the east. Rome and Civita Vecchia, the only places occupied by French garrisons, were to be spared for the present.[3]

There were grave objections to this plan. First, Lamoricière's newly levied army of Papal crusaders, being superior in numbers[4] and not wholly inferior in enthusiasm to Bertani's volunteers, could not be destroyed with the rapidity which was essential if French and Austrian interference was to be forestalled. Nine thousand Italian volunteers under the command of Pianciani, whom Mazzini and Bertani had chosen for his politics

---

[1] *Ciàmpoli*, 168. The letter was delayed in transmission for a fortnight, so it was of no use, except as a proof to the historian of Garibaldi's wishes at the end of July. *Mario Supp.* 313. On July 30 he also wrote to Ricasoli asking him to let the Tuscan volunteers cross the Papal frontier. *Ricasoli*, v. 171.

[2] *F. O. Sard.* Brown to Hudson, from Genoa, August 11, 1860, No. 317. ' The men are already formed into companies and regiments, and unlike the previous volunteers are already equipped with uniforms. They are chiefly Lombards, and are a fine, soldier-like body of men.' Bertani had paid for their equipment, etc., chiefly out of the five million *lire* which he had received from the Government of Sicily, through Garibaldi, see Appendix C, ii. below.

[3] *Rüstow Brig. Mil.* 6. *Guerzoni*, ii. 155. *Pittaluga*, 126-120. *Bertani*, ii. 143-144. Appendix B, below.

[4] Appendix K, ii. a. below.

rather than for his military capacity, would not be worth
half the number under Garibaldi.[1]   Further, Garibaldi
was beginning to find, as August advanced and the
Sicilians dispersed to their homes, that he could not cross
the Straits in face of the Neapolitan armies on the Calabrian shore until he received strong reinforcements from
the North.   On August 11 he was expecting shortly to
be joined at the Straits by the volunteers whom Bertani
had organised at Genoa.[2]   But Pianciani was preparing
to lead them off to a wholly different part of the Italian
Peninsula, under the delusion that Garibaldi would have
6000 Sicilian soldiers to take with him across the Straits,
in addition to his Northern followers.[3]

Cavour, however, prevented this fatal mistake from
being made.   He could not allow revolutionary armies,
organised by Mazzini and Bertani, to start from Genoa
direct for the Papal States.   An invasion made under
such conditions must inevitably provoke French interference.   He therefore sent to Genoa his principal
colleague Farini, to negotiate with Bertani about the
destination of Pianciani's force.   Saffi, ex-triumvir of
Rome, was present at the interview.   Farini told Bertani
that the King's Government intended itself to invade the
Papal States : 'before many days,' he said, 'our own
bugles will be sounding.'   In any case the time was not
quite ripe, and therefore the Government must insist that
Pianciani and his volunteers should sail first to the Golfo
degli Aranci in Sardinia, and thence to Sicily, where they
would necessarily become subject to Garibaldi's orders.
After touching at Sicily they might go to whatever part
their leaders wished, not excluding the Papal States, provided that they did not re-enter Piedmontese territory as
a base from which to attack the Pope.   This compromise

---

[1] *Mem. Stor. Mil.* ii. 177-178, Cadolini's opinion.   See pp. 43-44 above.

[2] *Ciàmpoli*, 175, Garibaldi's letter to Musolino.   But he expected Nicotera's
men to invade the Papal States from Tuscany, see *Ricasoli*, v. 171, and *Bertani*,
ii. 170.

[3] *Pianciani*, 204.

was agreed upon by Farini for the Government, and by Bertani for the volunteers.[1]

The clear intention of the authorities to use force rather than permit the invasion of the Papal States direct from the port of Genoa had compelled Bertani to temporise. But he had no real thought of fulfilling his part of the bargain by sending Pianciani's men to Sicily. The Government had promised to let his volunteers sail for the Golfo degli Aranci : he intended to persuade Garibaldi to come to meet them at the Sardinian port and himself to lead them thence, not to Sicily, but to the Papal States. With this object in view, he sailed to the Faro, landed there at dawn on August 12 and laid his proposal before the Dictator. Garibaldi took ship with Bertani that very evening for the Golfo degli Aranci, stealing away from the camp beside the Straits so secretly that no one knew whither he had gone nor why. But all felt that great events were in the air, and that when next they saw him there would be an end of this wearisome delay.

It is hard to know what were Garibaldi's intentions on board the *Washington*, as it carried him and Bertani on their hazardous voyage to Sardinia through the midst of the Neapolitan cruisers. Bertani was under the erroneous belief that the General would consent to lead the volunteers straight from the Golfo degli Aranci to the Papal States.[2] But until the moment of Bertani's arrival at the Faro, Garibaldi had intended to use the greater number of them to assist his passage of the Straits of Messina,[3] and he himself tells us that he rejected Bertani's proposal to go to the Papal States, and was considering instead whether he might not attempt a direct *coup-de-main* on Naples.[4]

[1] *Risorg.* anno ii. fasc. 1, pp. 29-30. *Mazzini*, xi. p. cxxx note (Saffis' evidence). *Bertani*, ii. 151-153. *Mario's Mazzini*, 408.

[2] *Bertani*, ii. 168. *Ire Pol.* 66-67. *Pianciani*, 211-213. Pianciani never shared this delusion of Bertani's as to Garibaldi's intentions.

[3] *Ciàmpoli*, 175, Letter of August 11.

[4] *Mem.* 374. In *I Mille*, 150-152, he does not even allow this, and is unfair on Bertani. In these autobiographical works of a later day Garibaldi speaks

But the vigilance of the Piedmontese Government had settled the matter beforehand.   When at dawn of August 14 the *Washington*, bearing Garibaldi and Bertani, steamed into the Golfo degli Aranci, only one part of the fleet that had transported the volunteers from Genoa was to be found in the bay.   The rest had already been compelled by Piedmontese war-ships to go on to Sicily, in accordance with the agreement which Bertani had made with the Government and was now plotting to evade.[1] He was wild with fury when he saw that he had been frustrated.   Garibaldi, on the other hand, fell back without any serious loss of temper on the plan which he had entertained three days before of using Pianciani's men to force the passage of the Straits of Messina.[2]

Since he had chanced to come so near to his island home of Caprera,[3] he went to pass a few hours there in repose.   With the poignant affection and delight of a boy at home on his day's *exeat* in the middle of term, the Dictator wandered amid the sweet-smelling shrubs and the chaos of granite rocks, called his favourite cows up to him by name and fed them from his hand.[4]   Then he took ship again for Palermo, where all Pianciani's expedition was soon assembled, 6000 strong.

with hostility of Bertani and the Mazzinians as ' these gentlemen ' who ' perhaps felt repugnance to submitting themselves to obey the Dictatorship.'   He may have felt these suspicions of Bertani at the Golfo degli Aranci, or he may have conceived them retrospectively in later years.   In any case he was far indeed from being the tool or dupe of the Mazzinian party : if anything he made ' these gentlemen ' his dupes by using the troops they had raised for his purposes and not for theirs.

[1] *Maison*, 6-27.   Madame Mario's suggestion (*Bertani*, ii. 168) that Bertani meant Garibaldi and the volunteers to touch at Sicily first and thence sail for the Roman States is not admissible.   There is nothing about this in Bertani's own words as published by Madame Mario, or in *Ire Pol*. 65-67, or in *Pianciani*, 211.   If that was Bertani's plan, why was he so angry at the volunteers being sent to Palermo, and why did he drag Garibaldi to the Golfo degli Aranci at the risk of being caught by the Neapolitan cruisers ?

[2] *Mem*. 374.   *Ciàmpoli*, 175.

[3] The need to coal took them from the Golfo degli Aranci to Maddalena. *Mem*. 374.

[4] *Guerzoni*, ii. 159.   *Du Camp*. 19-20.   *Bertani*, ii. 169-170.   *Durand Brager*, 164-165.

Even at Palermo, Bertani again implored him to lead the men to the Papal States, but his mind was now once more intent on the problem of the Straits of Messina. Pianciani therefore resigned his commission and went home, but Bertani remained at the seat of war, hoping to use his influence upon Garibaldi in opposition to the more moderate counsels of the soldiers, Medici, Türr, Bixio, and Cosenz, who were well aware of the necessity of avoiding a breach with Cavour.[1]

There still remained some 2000 volunteers in Tuscany under Nicotera, who had not been specifically mentioned in the terms of agreement between Bertani and Farini at Genoa. Garibaldi, though requiring Pianciani's men in order to effect the passage of the Straits, was still willing that Nicotera should invade the Pope's territory by land, and wrote to him to that effect.[2] But Cavour instructed Ricasoli, as Governor of Tuscany, not to permit any such movement. After an embittered quarrel, in which Ricasoli and Nicotera behaved each with small consideration for the other, the Governor had his way, and the last of the volunteers were forcibly shipped to Sicily.[3] Thus the whole army which Bertani had prepared against the Pope, more than 8000 in number, finally swelled Garibaldi's force in the South, and was of indispensable service to him in his occupation and subsequent defence of Naples. They were almost the last volunteers who joined him from North Italy. For Cavour, alarmed by the constant threat of the advanced parties to invade the Papal territory, and now fully determined to invade it himself, prohibited on August 13 the further levy or dispatch of volunteers under any pretext, and this time, to the surprise of diplomatic Europe, actually enforced his proclamation. There were no more departures *en masse* from Genoa, though some hundreds of private

[1] *Pianciani*, 212-213. *Mem. Stor. Mil.* ii. 182. *Türr's Risposta*, 15-16.
[2] *Bertani*, ii. 170.
[3] *Pianciani*, 313 *et seq.* (documenti M, N). *Ricasoli*, v. 171-224 *passim.* *Nicotera*, 44-47. Nicotera was more republican in his expressions than even Mazzini liked, see *Mignona*, 193. Appendix B, p. 319 below.

individuals went south with Government passports.[1]   In all, Garibaldi had about 20,000 Northerners under him in the course of the year,[2] and at the Straits he already had, at the time of his crossing, much the greater part of this total, besides Sicilians.   He was a match, even in numbers, for the troops in the toe of Italy, provided his transports could escape the enemy's fleet.   But by all ordinary calculation that was impossible.

[1] *Pittaluga,* 159-161.   *Mem. Stor. Mil.* ii. 179.   *F. O. Sard.* No. 332. Brown to Hudson, August 27, 1860.
[2] Appendix B, below.

CHAPTER VI

THE CROSSING OF THE STRAITS

'Che volete, Signorini; io sono un vecchio soldato, e perciò m'attendeva
che Garibaldi m'attaccasse di fronte, ed invece m'è capitato alle spalle!'
'What do you expect, gentlemen; I am an old soldier, and so of course I
expected Garibaldi to attack me in front, and he came from behind instead!'
General Gallotti's explanation of his defeat overheard by Arrivabene (ii. 112).

'Lu curaggio è nu donu di Dio, ed io nu l'aggiu.'
'Courage is a gift of God, and I have it not.' *Saying attributed to a
Neapolitan soldier by the Garibaldini. Whitaker, 283.*

BETWEEN the working of one great action and the
next, Nino Bixio was heard of chiefly through his deeds
of insane violence. After the taking of Palermo, 'the
second of the Thousand' had distinguished himself in
the Sicilian capital by his quarrel with a brother in arms,
the self-sacrificing Agnetta, whom he struck in the face
for an imaginary insult. Since Garibaldi would allow no
duel on campaign, they did not fight it out until late in
the following year, in Switzerland. Bixio came tardily
and unwillingly on to the 'field of honour,' because he
of all men had scruples against duelling. Agnetta shot
him in the hand, crippling it for the rest of his life,
whereupon Bixio said, 'I am punished in the hand that
gave the offence.' He subsequently earned Agnetta's
gratitude by services of real friendship.[1]

Bixio was not present at the battle of Milazzo, for he
was leading his command through the south of the
island. When at the end of July all the Garibaldian
columns met near the Straits, he was sent by the Dictator

[1] *Busetto*, 23, 42. *Whitaker*, 292. *Bandi*, 191-192. *Adamoli*, 91-93.
Abba's Bixio, 102-105. *Bixio*, 206-207, 463. *Bixio MSS.* contain Agnetta's
letter of gratitude.

to suppress a predatory and murderous anarchist rising under the western slopes of Ætna.   There, at Randazzo and on Nelson's old estate of Bronte, his summary methods and manners soon terrified the wrongdoers into submission at the cost of only a few actual executions.[1] Bixio's own soldiers were always complaining of him. 'He is mad, he is intolerable.'   'Very well, under whom do you wish to serve then?'   'What? Eh? Oh, under Bixio, of course.'[2]   At Bronte one morning some volunteers recently arrived from North Italy, and not accustomed to his ways, were late in turning out of bed. He went into the houses after them with a horse-whip. The older troops, who had marched under him and learnt to love him, with difficulty saved his life from the fury of the new men, who had come out to fight under Garibaldi, not to be whipped-in like hounds.[3]

But now an action was in hand on which his rage to be up and doing for his country could be spent to better purpose.

The Dictator had been away in Sardinia and Palermo for nearly six days, and no one at the Straits knew when or whether he would return.   The suspense on both shores was terrible.   On the morning of August 18 he suddenly reappeared in the Faro camp, gave his orders, left for Messina, and an hour afterwards was seen driving through its streets in a three-horse carriage along the southern road.   His movements were still as mysterious as ever, for he was again travelling away from the scene of active operations at the Faro.[4]   But in fact the camp and flotilla beneath the lighthouse were to serve during the next twenty-four hours only as a decoy to fix the attention of the enemy's ships and regiments on the narrow waters of Scilla and Charybdis, while the real

---

[1] *Bixio*, 215-224.   *Bixio Sclavo*, 22-25.   *Fonvielle*, 215-216.
[2] *Abba Not.* 213.   [3] *Conv. Capurro.*
[4] *Peard MS. Journal*, August 18.   *Forbice*, August 26, letter from Messina August 19 *re* passage of Garibaldi 18th.   *Forbes*, 135, 147.   *Mem.* 374.

crossing took place at the broader part of the Straits, thirty miles to the south.

On the afternoon of August 18 Garibaldi's carriage reached the hamlet of Giardini, which stretches along the beach between the wall of mountains and the sea, at the southern foot of Taormina rock.   Here Bixio's men from Bronte and Catania had been secretly collected during the last two days.   Here the *Torino* and *Franklin* had safely arrived, after steaming round the whole island from the Faro in order to avoid the Neapolitan cruisers in the Straits.   The captain of the *Torino*, a man of peace, who objected to the use of his transport vessel for an enterprise so hazardous as an attack on the Calabrian coast, had been silenced and placed under arrest by Bixio.   The troops, 3360 in number, were already on board the two steamers when Garibaldi drove up.   When all was ready, it was found that the *Franklin* had sprung a leak.   The hole could not be found, and Bixio proposed that they should start with the *Torino* alone, but, when Garibaldi took the matter in hand, the hole was soon found and stopped.   To judge by the space which he allots to this operation in his Memoirs, the Dictator recalled it with more interest than all his historic achievements during the next fortnight.   That he should cause 15,000 soldiers of tyranny to lay down their arms seemed to him no more than an inevitable fate, now that Italy's hour had struck; but to find and calk a hole in a ship which had baffled the other seamen, was an action of which a man had good right to be proud.[1]

At nightfall the two vessels steamed out from below the rock of Taormina.   The distance to Melito, the point chosen for the landing in Calabria, is thirty miles, and, if at any point in the crossing the unarmed transports had fallen in with a Neapolitan war-ship they could have been sunk to the bottom.   But the enemy were all away at the narrows, watching the camp and flotilla at the Faro.

[1] *Mem.* 374-375.   *Menghini*, 451.   *Times*, August 25, p. 9, c. 5.   *Arrivabene* ii. 100-101.   *Tosi*, 91.   *Bixio*, 232.   *Forbes*, 147.

NINO BIXIO
(Civilian Costume.)

SHORE NEAR MELITO WHERE GARIBALDI LANDED IN CALABRIA
Chapel of S. Maria di porto Salvo.

FAVAZZINA, WHERE COSENZ LANDED

The night voyage was unbroken by anything more terrifying than the voice of Bixio from the *Torino* continually shouting through his megaphone to the silent Garibaldi in the *Franklin*.[1]

When dawn revealed Ætna's cone and the long ranges of subject Sicilian mountains at her feet, the Calabrian coast lay close ahead. Again, as at Marsala, Bixio ran his vessel aground on the shallows. But the men of both the steamers were taken off in the ships' boats and landed on the desolate beach called Porto Salvo, a mile from Melito village. There were no houses near, but an old chapel with a cupola rose amid the cactuses and aloes at the edge of the sea sand. The flat country behind, though it bore olive groves and scraps of cultivation, was arid for the most part, stripped and scarred each winter by the torrents from Aspromonte. The mountains themselves here stand back a mile or two from the coast, but the Garibaldini as they landed saw the pillar rock of Pentedatilo raising its five grotesque fingers against the dawn.[2]

Garibaldi spent the whole morning of the 19th in a vain attempt to salve the *Torino*. He was waiting also for Missori's men to come down from the mountains near San Lorenzo, whither he had sent them a message to announce his landing. In the afternoon Neapolitan war-vessels appeared from the direction of Messina, destroyed the grounded and derelict *Torino*, and fired, not without some effect, into the red-shirts on shore. The *Franklin* had returned safely to Sicily. Towards evening the vanguard of Missori's men appeared on the neighbouring mountains, and the night of August 19-20 was spent in bivouac not far from Melito.[3] For thirty-six hours

[1] *Tosi*, 91.

[2] Pentedatilo had been a favourite place of Edward Lear's during his painting tour in Calabria which was cut short by the revolution of 1848. Very few others have visited Pentedatilo before or since ; Calabria is out of fashion now even with painters, though safer and no less magnificent than of old.

[3] See Appendix G, i. below. *Mem.* 376. *Menghini*, 451-452. *Bixio*, 233 234. *Tosi*, 92. *Red Shirt*, 108.

many of the troops had neither food nor drink; some of them who were inland-bred dug holes in the sea-shore and lapped the water that oozed up, in the desperate hope that Neptune would lose his salt by filtering through the sand.[1]

On August 19 the telegraphs and semaphores in the Neapolitan kingdom had been wagging all day with ominous rumours from the south, and before midnight the Ministers at Naples knew that there had been a landing in force a dozen miles beyond Reggio.[2] There were now some 16,000 Royalist troops in Lower Calabria.[3] General Vial, their commander-in-chief, had his headquarters at Monteleone, too far removed from the scene of operations. His regiments were scattered along fifty miles of the road between Monteleone and Reggio. His lieutenants, Melendez and Briganti, were guarding the supposed points of danger opposite the Faro, but at the moment of Garibaldi's landing there were no troops south of Reggio, and in Reggio itself only some 1000 men, chiefly of the 14th line. When, forty-eight hours later, Garibaldi fell upon the city, the numbers of its garrison had not been increased by a single man. The news of the landing at Melito ought to have caused an instantaneous move in that direction on the part of each of the columns scattered along the coast road, but neither Vial, Melendez, nor Briganti stirred until it was too late to save Reggio, in spite of a stream of indignant telegrams from Pianell at Naples. The War Minister had been anxious to avoid fighting in Sicily, and had perhaps not sent enough troops to guard the Straits, but his telegrams show that he did his best to make the generals fight Garibaldi when once he had landed.

Old General Gallotti, in command at Reggio, was the

---

[1] *Conv. Tedaldi.*   [2] *Pianell*, 45-46.

[3] They are sometimes estimated at 12,000; but Garibaldi *took* 14,000 [1000 at Reggio, over 3000 at Piale and San Giovanni, and 10,000 at Soveria, pp. 131, 137, 148 below]. Besides these 14,000, we know that 1000 disbanded from Monteleone and Pizzo, and 1000 more returned thence with Vial to Naples, see p. 141 below.

most complete dotard of them all.   When informed of
the landing at Melito, he said that Garibaldi had taken
to the mountains and that Reggio could not be attacked
from that side, but only in front from the sea.   He therefore made no preparations to defend the city.   He forbade
the energetic Colonel Dusmet to take up a good position
near the castle, and compelled him instead to bivouac in
the middle of the Cathedral Square, a mere trap for those
who occupied it unless the entrances to the city were
strongly guarded.   These, however, were confided to
the National Guard of Liberal *bourgeoisie*, whose loyalty
was more than doubtful.   Gallotti himself remained in
the castle with a garrison.   The castle of Reggio is a tall,
grim building, flanked by round towers, somewhat similar
in strength and appearance to the Bastille of old Paris,
though on a smaller scale.   But unlike the Bastille it
does not rise clear above all possible assailants.   For
Reggio is [1] built on the side of a hill, and since the castle
is only half-way up the hill, its battlements can be commanded by sharpshooters at the top of the town.

On the 20th the invaders marched from Melito, passing over the top of the sandstone cliff of Capo dell' Armi
—*Leucopetra*, whose 'white rock' had been a famous
sea-mark to the sailors of the ancient world.   The General
walked with his sabre over his shoulder, talking and
singing with the men.   All were hungry but in high
spirits.   Near Reggio they rested again, and at midnight
advanced to the attack.   Garibaldi with Missori's men
entered the upper town by way of the hills, through
Spirito Santo.   Bixio with the main column kept the high
road through Sbarre, and came in by the principal streets
below the castle.   His men stumbled upon outposts at
the entrance of the city.

' *Chi va là ?* '
' Garibaldi.'
' *Avanti !* '

[1] Or rather ' was.'   *Fuit Ilion*.   But the castle has withstood the earthquake.

It was the National Guard standing aside to let them pass. They hurried on through the sleeping streets. In the middle of the town they came upon other sentries.

'*Chi va là ?*'

' Garibaldi.'

Bang !

They had come upon the loyal troops at last.[1]

A fierce struggle raged in the great Cathedral Square until the morning. Colonel Dusmet and his son, not yet of age, fell gallantly fighting in front of the Royalists. Bixio's horses received nineteen wounds, and their rider two in the arm to which he paid no attention till Garibaldi sent him to bed the next night, saying, ' I suppose the balls that reach you are made of puff-paste.'[2]

The odds were all against the 14th line, and Garibaldi's column was pouring in upon their rear from the upper town. As day broke the red-shirts possessed themselves of all Reggio except the castle, which was provisioned for a month and could easily be defended against its present assailants.

Later in the same day (August 21) Briganti approached Reggio from Villa San Giovanni with about 2000 men. Garibaldi led his troops out into the country just beyond the northern suburbs and took up a position to cover the town. After the exchange of a few shots in a feeble reconnaissance, Briganti fell back, leaving Reggio to its fate. Garibaldi afterwards wrote that if the attack had been pressed, the Royalists might very possibly, with the help of the garrison in the castle, have recovered the town, and that in that case his own position would have been desperate. Indeed the troops in the castle had clamoured to be led out to attack him in the rear and

---

[1] *Conv. Tedaldi*, his account of his own experience.

[2] Bixio himself wrote afterwards to a friend : ' My horses received ten bullets at Rome (1849), nineteen at Reggio in Calabria, three at Maddaloni (Volturno). My own carcase was honoured by three bullets at Rome, one at Palermo, two at Reggio, and a fracture of the leg at the passage of the Volturno.' *Bixio*, 229, note. *Busetto*, 49. *Red Shirt*, 110-111. *Bologna MSS. Bixio*, Letter of August 24.

join hands with the relieving force.   But Gallotti had
refused to allow a sally.   Hitherto the Royalist garrison
in Reggio with the exception of Gallotti himself had
behaved well, but after Briganti's retreat they felt themselves deserted and began to lose courage.   When sharp-
shooters placed by Garibaldi in the upper part of the
town commenced picking off the men on the battlements,
panic set in, and the castle, which might have held out
for weeks, was surrendered within twenty-four hours.
The taking of Reggio had cost the victors about 150 in
killed and wounded.[1]

On the same day another important event took place
to the north of the Straits.   Garibaldi had left Cosenz
in command at the Faro with instructions that he was to
carry his troops across the water at the moment when
the Dictator himself attacked Reggio.   There was a good
chance that Cosenz would be able to cross in safety
because the Neapolitan war-vessels had now, too late,
left the narrow waters and gone south to attend to
Garibaldi after his landing at Melito.   Before sunrise
on August 21,[2] to the sound of the distant firing
from Reggio, the flotilla of row-boats put out from
Faro, carrying between 1000 and 1500 volunteers; they
struggled successfully against the currents of Charybdis,
made a wide detour to avoid the cannon-balls from the
fort of Scilla, and landed the same morning on the strip
of flat shore beneath the wall of wooded mountains at
Favazzina.   The Neapolitan war-ships, hastily summoned
back from Reggio, sank and captured a large number of
the boats as the fishermen were taking them back empty
to the Faro.
    A few minutes after Cosenz and his men had landed

---

[1] *Morisani*, 65-98.   *Pianell*, 45-55.   *Franci*, i. 90-96.   *Mem.* 378-379.   *De
Sivo*, iii. 365-369.   *De Cesare*, ii. 390.   *Bixio*, 229-231.   *Arrivabene*, ii. 108-112.
Red Shirt, 109-111.   *Zasio*, 76.   *Türr's Div.* 133.   *Menghini*, 453-454.   The
date of the surrender of Reggio Castle was the evening of the 21st, and not the
22nd as some have stated: see on this *Ruiz*, 32 ; *Franci*, i. 225-226, doc. 55.
    [2] See Appendix G, ii.

at Favazzina, they were attacked while crossing the coast road by Neapolitan troops from Scilla on one side and from Bagnara on the other. The enemy were repulsed chiefly by the Genoese carabineers, the pick of Garibaldi's original 'Thousand,' and the whole force proceeded straight up the sides of Aspromonte by precipitous tracks through the brushwood. At noontide the greater part had reached the hamlet of Solano, 2000 feet above the sea. Overcome by heat, thirst, and fatigue they took their siesta in the houses, believing that all the Royalist forces were far below them on the level of the shore. From the precipice edge of Solano they looked back down the gulf of an enormous ravine below, but the village is itself closely overshadowed by other heights, covered with chestnut woods, and in these a few hundred Neapolitan troops were lying concealed. They were a detachment of Ruiz' men who had not yet gone down off Aspromonte from their vain pursuit of Missori's column.[1] Though inferior in numbers to Cosenz, the Royalists seized their advantage, surprised the sentinels and burst into the village. The Garibaldini had an hour's hard fighting before they could drive them out. Two little companies of French and English volunteers distinguished themselves in the scuffle under the leadership of De Flotte and of Goodall.[2] De Flotte was killed in the street at the head of his men. He was a French Republican exile, who had played a part in Paris in '48, and narrowly escaped Cayenne after Napoleon III.'s *coup d'état.* He had been loved by all his companions in arms, English, Italians, and French ; and Garibaldi, when he heard of his death, mourned for him as a true soldier of liberty. They buried him where he fell, high up among the granite gorges and the chestnut woods, far from his fierce, gay city and the Boulevard lights.

After repulsing this attack, Cosenz' column mounted

---

[1] *Morisani*, 108-109. See p. 114 above.

[2] *Arrivabene*, ii. 123, says: ' After De Flotte's death they were led by Captain Goodall, a dashing young Englishman.' *Menghini*, 278.

another 1500 feet to Forestali on the higher plains of Aspromonte. There they received a message from the Dictator bidding them march westward and join him above Villa San Giovanni. Their sufferings on the plateaus of Aspromonte were severe. Starved and sun-baked all day, at night they were soaked with the dew and chilled with the intense cold of the mountain, so that Goodall and other useful soldiers were put out of action.[1]

The movements of Garibaldi and Cosenz are a model of combined action from two separate bases. Each had enabled the other to succeed, by distracting the attention of the enemy's naval and military force. And now they were about to join hands at a spot above and in rear of the enemy's main line of defence.

On August 22, the morning after the fall of Reggio, the Dictator and Bixio moved northward to attack the forts and regiments commanding the narrowest part of the Straits. Again Bixio kept the coast road and Garibaldi the hills. On the evening of that day the Dictator joined forces with Cosenz above Piale and Villa San Giovanni. After this junction he had with him about 5000 men, and was for a while superior to the enemy both in numbers and position. Down below, between him and the sea, lay rather more than 3000 troops under Generals Melendez and Briganti.[2] The greater part of this force was in Villa San Giovanni on the coast road, under the command of Briganti; but Melendez with 1200 men occupied Piale village, a mile up the hill-side. Garibaldi was above them both at Campo Calabrese, where Murat had pitched his tents when he threatened Sicily with invasion. These seaward heights now oc-

[1] For Cosenz' crossing and Solano fight, *Conv. Goodall, Conv. Patterson. Pianell*, 56. *Caraguel*, 115-132. *Times*, September 4, p. 7, c. 3. *Maison*, 44-50. *Red Shirt*, 130. *Menghini*, 276-279. *Magni*, 7-9. *Mem.* 379. *Morisani*, 105-109.

[2] There is no Neapolitan estimate of the numbers, though *De Sivo*, iii. 373, says Melendez had 1200 men at Piale. Briganti's force below was larger, as all agree. The *Times* and *Morning Post* correspondents, who were present at the surrender on the 23rd, respectively estimate the haul at 3800 and 3500.

cupied by the red-shirts bore no resemblance to the wooded and precipitous mountains below which Cosenz had landed. It is a tumble-down land of broken mud banks on which vineyards, fruit gardens, cactuses, and houses maintain an ever precarious existence. The landscape on this part of the Calabrian shore is more weird than beautiful, but the view thence of the Straits, of Sicily and of Ætna—*Mongibello*, 'the fair mountain,' as the Calabrians call it—filled the Garibaldini with delight as they waited for the surrender of their foes. An artillery duel between the Neapolitan ships and the batteries at the Faro was watched by both armies as from the seats of a theatre, of which the lower circles were occupied by the Royalists.

On the 22nd Melendez and Briganti might still have retreated to Scilla, for it was only during the following night that the Dictator cut off their retreat by pushing his advance guard down to the coast at Cannitello. But they let the hours slip by in the vain expectation of reinforcements from the north. Besides the men whom they had with them, there were more than 10,000 Royalist troops in Lower Calabria,[1] and they naturally supposed that Vial would lead these to their rescue. But the commander-in-chief had no advantage except in point of age over his dotard lieutenants. A pleasure-loving and idle young man, raised by personal influences at Court to a command for which he had no qualifications, Vial had too much of the heartless flippancy of the Neapolitan to be serious over even the gravest situation. He continued to linger and amuse himself at Monteleone, saying that he 'would give Joe a ducking'[2] if he tried to cross the Straits. When he heard that 'Joe' had crossed, and was taking Reggio, he still lingered with the greater part of the troops under his command fifty miles from the scene of action. At length, driven to the front by furious

---

[1] *Franci*, i. 97, places Vial's [= Ghio's] men at 10,000 for infantry alone.

[2] '*Avrebbe pescato Peppariello.*' (*Peppariello = Giuseppe* Garibaldi.) *De Cesare*, ii. 390-391.

telegrams from Pianell, the War Minister, he sailed from
Pizzo on the morning of August 22, taking with him one
of his best battalions. He landed alone at Villa San
Giovanni, interviewed Briganti and Melendez, and ordered
them to hold out while he set this battalion ashore at
Scilla and led it to their rescue. He then returned to
Scilla, but as a sea had arisen which made the landing
of troops momentarily difficult, he hailed the excuse to
sail back with the battalion to Pizzo and Monteleone,
leaving his lieutenants to their fate without even warning
them that he had changed his plan and run away.

Meanwhile, Melendez and Briganti were expecting
aid not only from Vial, but also from General Ruiz, who
had at length descended from Aspromonte to the coast
road, and was hurrying along it to their rescue. Like
Vial, Ruiz came on alone in front of his column to take
stock of the situation. He visited Melendez and Briganti
up at Piale and then went down to the main road again
to bring up his column from Altifiumara. But on his
way back through Villa San Giovanni he could not fail
to observe that Briganti's men were in a state of complete
demoralisation. Red-shirts were going about among
them with impunity in *cafés* and at street corners, exhorting them not to prolong a useless and fratricidal contest ;
and it was only too evident that the men were listening.
There was little of active disloyalty or of political Liberalism among the rank and file. But they had in August
small motive, or encouragement to fight. They were at
once terrified and fascinated by the name of Garibaldi,
and after the taking of Reggio regarded him as uncon-
querable. During the last two months, ever since the
grant of the Constitution, they had been forced to march
under the tricolour flag,—the flag, as it seemed to them,
of their enemies. They witnessed, in every street down
which they passed, the enthusiasm of the populace for
the revolution and the open disloyalty of the new civic
authorities, who had proclaimed 'Long live the King' as
a seditious cry. Their own officers were visibly shaking

with fear, muttering their doubts to each other, or preoccupied with private thoughts of which the character
was only too evident. Their General, Briganti, was
known to be in favour of negotiation. The enemy, it
appeared, was to be regarded as more than half a friend,
since no one prevented his emissaries from entering their
lines to talk sedition in the open street of Villa San
Giovanni.

As Ruiz rode through the town noting what he saw,
he judged that Briganti and his troops did not mean to
fight, and that he had best save his own men from shar-
ing in their surrender. A few miles further north, at
Altifiumara, he met his column hastening up, ordered it
to turn right about and before nightfall on the 22nd had
led it back to Bagnara. Like Vial, Ruiz was pursued by
indignant telegrams from the War Minister at Naples to
the effect that Melendez and Briganti were preparing to
die at their posts, while he basely deserted them. But
he knew better, and rather than face Garibaldi again, resigned his command. His successor, Morisani, on the
morning of the 23rd began to march back once more to
the relief of San Giovanni, but was met and turned back
for good and all by a messenger from Melendez himself,
who declared that it was now too late.[1]

In this fashion Melendez and Briganti, lured by false
hopes that Vial and Ruiz were marching to their relief,
had let slip the opportunity to escape out of their untenable positions on August 22. At daybreak on the 23rd
they saw that retreat was no longer possible. During
the night Garibaldi had drawn the net round them by
sending down detachments from Campo Calabrese to
Cannitello. They were completely surrounded with a
semicircle of sea on one side, and a semicircle of red-
shirts on the other. As the sun rose the Garibaldini
began to descend upon them from the hills. The Nea-

---

[1] *Ruiz*, 13, says that he had had only 1400 men in his column. But *Morisani*, 132-134, and *De Sivo*, iii. 373, say that Ruiz had 3000 (21 companies), at
any rate when he handed over the command to Morisani.

politan rifles and cannon opened fire, but the advancing host made no reply. The slow, ordered, noiseless approach of their enemies affected the nerves of the Royalists, as Garibaldi had intended that it should. They opened negotiations. A Garibaldian *parlementaire* with the white flag in his hand was shot dead, but General Briganti himself came out to apologise. He explained to the Dictator that he would have been a Liberal himself, but that he had two sons in the Neapolitan army and so felt gratitude to the Bourbons. 'Otherwise,' he said, 'I would join you.'[1] He asked to surrender with the honours of war. Garibaldi gave him and Melendez till three o'clock to surrender unconditionally, and allowed them to send out a messenger, who, as already related, stopped the further advance of Morisani to their rescue.

Meanwhile, the Garibaldian army halted on the hillside and watched the confusion growing hour by hour among their enemies below. When the appointed time had run out the advance was resumed. As the redshirts drew the circle close upon them, the Royalists threw away arms and knapsacks and fled in a mob along the northern road. They were turned back by a volley, and crowded together like driven sheep in the centre of their position. Garibaldi rode almost alone into their midst. 'Soldiers,' he said, 'you as well as my companions are the sons of Italy ; remember that. You are at liberty. Whoever wishes to remain with us may address himself to General Cosenz, your countryman, who is charged to enlist you. But whoever wishes may go home.' At these words they rushed at him with cries of joy and much to his disgust began kissing his hands, arms, and feet. Three thousand five hundred men, four field pieces, and the fort of Punto del Pezzo with its artillery were the prize of this bloodless victory. Very few of the men chose to enlist under Cosenz, but as they scattered to their homes they spread the news that Garibaldi's custom was to send off his prisoners free, and this knowledge

[1] *Conv. Sclavo* (eye-witness).

greatly increased the readiness of the troops under Vial
and Ruiz to follow the example set at Villa San Giovanni.

That example proved contagious along the whole
road to Naples. The next day, August 24, the fort of
Altifiumara, which had resisted Missori's attack a fortnight before, the neighbouring fort of Torre Cavallo, and
the more formidable castle on the rock of Scilla, armed
with twenty-two cannon, all opened their gates to the
outriders of the invading army, among whom Garibaldi
himself was one of the foremost. As soon as the batteries
of these forts had compelled the Neapolitan navy to sail
out of the Straits, Medici's regiments at Messina were
brought safely across to the mainland.

The race to Naples had now fairly begun. It was
led by Garibaldi and his staff, many hours ahead of the
van of their army, accompanied by Jessie and Alberto
Mario, and by some English gentlemen who liked fatigue
and had the luck and money to hire horses that could
keep the pace. There were more than 10,000 of the
enemy close ahead, but no one feared that they would
resist when overtaken. Basilicata and Upper Calabria
were already rising in arms. The Dictator and his companions set out to ride unchallenged along the great
trunk road that stretches for 250 miles through mountains
and forests and fever-stricken plains from the foot of
Aspromonte to the foot of Vesuvius.[1]

---

[1] *Pianell*, 48-81. *Morisani*, 120-139. *Ruiz*, 11-18. *Marra Oss.* 38-41.
Arrivabene, ii. 115-129. *Red Shirt*, 112-147. *Conv. Tedaldi*. *Forbes*, 167-177.
Peard Journal MS. *Conv. Goodall*. *Conv. Patterson*. *Menghini*, 455-457.
De Cesare, ii. 390-392. *Franci*, i. 93-95. *De Sivo*, iii. 372-377. *Times*, Sep-
tember 4, p. 7, c. 5. *M. Post*, September 6, p. 5. *Conv. Sclavo*. *Bologna MSS*.
Bixio, Letter of August 24.

CHAPTER VII

THE MARCH THROUGH CALABRIA

' O how comely it is, and how reviving
To the spirits of just men long oppressed,
When God into the hands of their deliverer
Puts invincible might,
To quell the mighty of the earth, the oppressor,
The brute and boisterous force of violent men,
Hardy and industrious to support
Tyrannic power, but raging to pursue
The righteous, and all such as honour truth !
He all their ammunition
And feats of war defeats,
With plain heroic magnitude of mind
And celestial vigour armed ;
Their armouries and magazines contemns,
Renders them useless, while
With winged expedition
Swift as the lightning glance he executes
His errand on the wicked, who, surprised,
Lose their defence, distracted and amazed.'

> MILTON. *Samson Agonistes.*

THE Calabrian Liberals were not altogether unworthy of such a deliverer. The Garibaldini, who had seen little to admire in the inhabitants of Eastern Sicily in spite of all the facile enthusiasm at Messina, declared that when they had crossed the Straits they soon found themselves among 'a staid, manly, and athletic population.'[1] Travellers who to-day visit those remote but magnificent regions notice with relief that the corruption of Naples has not infected the whole South of the Peninsula.

The Calabrians of those days were not unaccustomed

---

[1] *Forbes*, 158. *Du Camp*, 163-164. *Maison*, 61, 64. *Red Shirt*, 106-107. On September 3, Luigi Cairoli, after the march through Calabria, wrote to his mother : ' quanto è bello, quanto degno dell' uomo italiano è il carattere Calabrese.' *Cairoli*, 340.

to war. For sixty years past they had from time to
time conducted guerilla campaigns for and against the
Bourbons. Some towns had always been on the side
of reaction, like Pizzo, whose fishermen had arrested
Murat among their nets on the beach, and handed him
over to his death ; while others, like Monteleone on the
hill above, had no less constantly been Liberal. In the
period of those French and English wars, the prevailing
sentiment in Calabria had been reactionary, or at least
anti-French. But since Waterloo, forty years of obscurantist inquisition into every household by spies and
police officers had left the restored Bourbons but few
zealous adherents, and had made every man of spirit and
intelligence their active enemy. In 1848 the Calabrian
peasants had upheld the national cause with a valour
that distinguished them among the populations of
Southern Italy. In the reaction that followed, the
leaders of the movement—doctors, professors, and landed
proprietors—had gone into prison and into exile. Their
day was now come. Francesco Stocco of the Thousand,
the principal landlord of the Catanzaro district, reappeared among his own people, with the wound which he
had received at Calatafimi yet unhealed. In 1860 feudal
devotion was still strong in Calabria, and helped much
to make the rising effective.[1] Even in exile Stocco had
been regarded as the real leader of the country, like a
Highland chief living across the water after 1745. And
now that he was among his people once more, they
answered to his call as to that of a tribal king, who interpreted the will of Garibaldi the racial deity. Fortunately Stocco was a simple and disinterested man and
used his authority well.[2]

[1] *Conv. Fazzari.* Plutino at Reggio, Morelli at Cosenza, Pace at Castrovillari, played the same part as Stocco at Catanzaro.

[2] *Conv. Fazzari. Forbes*, 197, 201. *Stocco.* The late Achille Fazzari (ob.
1910) was another, younger Calabrian leader in 1860. A few months before he
died, he sent Dr. Ashby and me in a boat from his house at Capanello, near
Staletti, to visit the great sea-cave, a Cathedral choir of granite hollowed out in
the roots of Aspromonte, in which he had lain hid with a price on his head, under

On August 26 the citizens of Catanzaro proclaimed the Dictator's government, while the town was still occupied by the Bourbon garrison. When it marched out next day towards Nicastro, it was surrounded and disarmed by the people of that region two days before the arrival of the Garibaldian vanguard.[1] Meanwhile, the mountain shepherds of Aspromonte, and the farmers of the fruit-bearing hills that overlook the fever-stricken plain of Maida, gathered to a head under Francesco Stocco. They pitched their camp, several thousands strong,[2] on the plateau of Campo Lungo, above the bridge of Angitola, and prepared there to cut off the retreat of Vial and his 12,000 men. Vial still lay at Monteleone, while Stocco thus blocked his road to the north, and Garibaldi advanced upon him from the south. Pianell had at length ordered him to retreat on the capital, but the only path left open was by sea, and he had only one steamer lying off Pizzo. He used it to effect his own escape to Naples, taking on board with him a thousand of his men. The rest he bequeathed to General Ghio, with instructions that they should march back by land. A thousand more disbanded, leaving Ghio with 10,000, the last Royalists in Lower Calabria.

From the semaphore station on the heights of Monteleone, the grass-grown site of an ancient Greek city, Ghio could watch through his telescope the bivouac of Stocco's Calabrians on the table-land of Campo Lungo, close above the high-road by which alone he could hope to retreat. Seeing himself thus cut off he sent a flag of truce to the Dictator and begged for a free passage to Naples with the honours of war. On August 26 Ghio's

sentence of death, a month before Garibaldi's crossing. He then led his neighbours to join the army of liberation, fought well at Volturno, became a friend of Garibaldi, spent several years with him on Caprera, and received him as guest at Capanello in 1882, a few months before the hero's death.

[1] *F. O. Sicily, Elliot*, Catanzaro, Sept. 2, 1860, *H.M. Vice-Consul's report*.

[2] Fazzari, who was there, told me that Stocco never had 10,000 men, as is sometimes said; he never had more than 6000 in Calabria, and only managed to induce 2000 to come as far as Naples. *Conv. Fazzari*.

F

messenger found Garibaldi at Nicotera, a town perched
on the sea-cliff, some miles off the great trunk road along
which the armies were moving. The Dictator had made
his way thither with two or three companions alone, in
order to superintend the disembarkation of Medici's
troops from Messina. Taking a short cut from Gioja he
and his friends had left their horses and walked seven
miles through the deep sand and marshes of the plain,
wading through rivers above the knee. He thus arrived
in time to welcome Medici's men as they landed on the
beach below Nicotera. Thence he sent back Ghio's
officer to Monteleone with a demand for the unconditional
surrender of the ten thousand.[1]

At dawn on the 27th the Dictator posted over the
hills to Monteleone, by way of Mileto, where he rejoined
the vanguard of his army coming up from Rosarno by
the great trunk road. Mileto, situated half-way up the
long rise out of the plain to the heights of Monteleone,
was famed for the numbers of its clergy and of its brigands. The wealthy Bishop had fled, but the priests and
people welcomed Garibaldi and his men. In the middle
of the main street was to be seen a dried pool of blood
and the charred remnants of some large animal. On
that spot, two days before, the Bourbon troops had detected their general Briganti, attempting to ride through
Mileto in civilian disguise. It was he who had so recently surrendered at Villa San Giovanni. They fell
upon him with cries of '*Traditore*,' and emptied their
rifles into his body, which they stripped and mutilated in
beastly fashion, while others killed and burnt his horse.
All this took place in the open street of Mileto, beneath
the eyes of the regimental officers, who drank shame to
the dregs, looking on at the murder with pale cheeks

[1] *Red Shirt*, 148-151. *Pianell*, 81. *De Cesare's F. di P.* p. clxxvi
Menghini, 458-459. *Peard's Journal MS.* August 26. There is some difference among these authorities as to whether Ghio or Vial sent the messenger to
Garibaldi, but in any case when the messenger returned to Monteleone, Vial had
sailed and Ghio was in command. Mario, in the *Red Shirt*, gives the true
nature of Garibaldi's reply.

and ineffectual murmurs of remonstrance. Some of the soldiers boasted that they had killed the general because he was a Liberal and a traitor, others because he was a Royalist, others because they wanted his boots.[1]

Horrified, but encouraged by this evidence of the utter demoralisation of his enemies, Garibaldi, after a *siesta* in a garden at Mileto, drove on to Monteleone the same day, hoping to receive the surrender of these wretched men. On the afternoon of the 27th his carriage mounted to the edge of the green and prosperous table-land of Monteleone, whence the moral and material squalor of the towns down below seems to have been banished by decree of nature, ever since the ancient Greeks founded their city of Hipponium upon this pleasant sward. The Garibaldini, like other travellers before and since, were enchanted by the panorama of the Mediterranean, Stromboli, Sicily, and nearer at hand the long outline of Aspromonte; by the city with its hospitable inhabitants, its free and cheerful life, its unexpected treasures of statuary and architecture. Garibaldi himself, the first to arrive, was given a welcome that is remembered in Monteleone as the greatest event in its civic life. For sixty years its inhabitants had been true to the cause of freedom, and for more than forty of those years had been subject to cruel oppression; for weeks past their town had been the enemy's headquarters; the day before they had narrowly escaped massacre at the hands of the soldiery who had murdered Briganti, and they had been saved only by the wisdom and energy of the Marquis Gagliardi, the patriot leader of the town. But now Garibaldi was among them, standing in a balcony with arms crossed and head bowed, looking long and in silence at the crowd below. 'Unworded things and old' seemed passing between him and them by some mysterious sympathy of race. At length he spoke: 'When a people replies as you have

[1] *Times*, September 8, p. 8, cols. 1-2. *Du Camp*, 141-146. *Arrivabene*, ii, 149. *Forbes*, 187-188. *Peard's Journal MS.*, August 27.

done to the call of freedom, then freedom is its due. The
destinies of Italy are secure, and no power on earth can
alter them.' But it was the silence and not the words
that dwelt most in the memory of some present.[1]

There was, however, one cause for disappointment.
Ghio's ten thousand, who had marched out of the town
shortly before Garibaldi's arrival, were allowed by Stocco
to march past him unchallenged. It appears that Sirtori
had sent Stocco a message which he interpreted to mean
that the Neapolitan troops had joined the national cause
and were to be treated as brothers in arms. They were
therefore allowed to file across the long bridge of Angitola, and below the wooded precipice of Campo Lungo
under the eyes of Stocco's army, who stood at ease and
cheered them as they passed. But Ghio's men were, in
fact, still bearing arms against Garibaldi, and he had
declared for nothing short of their unconditional surrender.[2]

The mistake, whether due to Sirtori or to Stocco,
called for instant remedy. If Ghio's men recovered their
morale, or fell in with Caldarelli's troops in Upper
Calabria, they might yet occupy one of the thousand
strong mountain positions that barred the road to Naples
and seriously delay the Dictator's advance. In any case
he did not want 10,000 more added to the Royalist
troops collecting for the defence of the capital. He
therefore left Monteleone on the 28th at a hand gallop to
ride down the fugitive army. He was partly accompanied
and partly pursued by the mounted portion of his staff
and by some English ladies[3] and gentlemen in a carriage.

---

[1] *Monteleone, Peard's Journal MS.* and *Forbes,* 187-189. *Du Camp,* 148-
149. *Conversations* at Monteleone.

[2] *De Cesare's F. di P.* pp. clxxvii-clxxix. *Red Shirt,* 150-151, 162. Garibaldi afterwards told Fazzari that he never remembered giving any order more
favourable to Ghio's men than the demand for their surrender (*Conv. Fazzari*).
Du Camp, 159. *Forbes,* 196-197. *Arrivabene,* ii. 153. *Times,* September 8, p.
8, c. 2. Some of Stocco's men appear to have skirmished with Ghio's column
near the Grazia bridge long after it had got through the dangerous pass below
Campo Lungo (*Türr's Div.* 139, 415. *Franci,* i. 97).

[3] Jessie Mario and Corte's wife. *Bertani,* ii. 177. *Peard's Journal MS.*

THE ROCK AND FORT OF SCILLA

ANCIENT GREEK WALL AT MONTELEONE

CASTLE OF PIZZO WHERE MURAT WAS SHOT, 1815

Sea to left. The execution took place in the small court yard concealed by the lower part of the wall in this photograph.

BATTLE-FIELD OF MAIDA, 1806

As seen by Garibaldi in passing. Sea in centre background.

There were as yet no cavalry, so the rest of his men, with Stocco's bands well to the fore, were to come on behind as fast as their legs would carry them.

The country through which the race now ran, with its ever-changing views of mountain, plain, and sea, was rich in memories of the last sixty years of feud between revolution and reaction. First, they left behind them Pizzo, hanging on a cliff over the beach, with its squalid little castle where Murat had been shot, an eagle trapped in a filthy cage and torn to pieces by vermin. At the bridge of La Grazia they passed a battle-field of '48. Then the road wound among low, fruit-laden hills, skirting the *campagna* of Maida. On that seaward plain, half-covered with brushwood and cut by sandy streams and white *fiumare*, the British infantry, set ashore by our fleet in July, 1806, had in half an hour of volley-firing proved the superiority of the line-formation over the French column, which had carried all before it since the revolutionary wars began.[1] The grand mountains looking down on the battle-field from north and east had been the scene of the Calabrian rising against the French that followed on the British victory, when the methods of the reactionary bands so horrified our officers that many of them were glad to be driven back to Sicily and swore never again to let loose such devilry on the mainland.[2] Following up the valley of the Amato, Garibaldi turned into the heart of these mountains, where far other political sentiments now prevailed among the peasants,

[1] As Paul Louis Courier, who was in the battle, wrote: 'Avec nos bonnes troupes, et à forces égales, être défaits en si peu de minutes! Cela ne s'est point vu depuis la révolution.' *Courier*, ed. 1828, iv. 113. For the great effect of the lesson of Maida on our Peninsula tactics, see Mr. Oman's article, published by the British Academy.

[2] *Johnston*, i. 127-128, 136. Paul Louis Courier thus describes the character of the war between the French troops and the Calabrian peasants: 'Ceux que nous attrapons, nous les pendons aux arbres; quand ils nous prennent, ils nous brûlent le plus doucement qu'il peuvent. Moi qui vous parle, Monsieur, je suis tombé entre leur mains. Pour m'en tirer, il a fallu plusieurs miracles. J'assistai à une délibération, où il s'agissait de savoir si je serais pendu, brûlé ou fusillé. Je fus admis à opiner.' *Courier*, iv. 128.

and, under his influence, far other methods of warfare. Those blood-feuds of Bourbon and Jacobin, those marchings of foreign armies on the soil, belonged to an era that was passing away, as the flag of Italy and Victor Emmanuel brought the hope of an ordered freedom.

Garibaldi and the best-mounted officers in his staff were acting militarily as their own scouts, politically as their own heralds. The first-comers of all their army, they were enthusiastically welcomed by the peasants, who saw with special delight that the Dictator was wearing the conical hat of Calabria. He and his friends had no baggage and no change of clothes ; each had one travel-stained red shirt, which was sometimes washed at the midday *siesta*, and put on again to dry as they rode forward under the scorching sun. In this guise the small group of horsemen climbed the steep ascent out of the Amato valley to the ancient town of Tiriolo, that hangs on the edge of the mountain-wall, 2000 feet above the Tyrrhenian and Ionian seas. Besides this simultaneous view of the two parts of the Mediterranean, the riders admired the gorgeous Calabrian costumes of the women which, then as now, were seen at their best in the neighbourhood of Tiriolo. Thence the trunk road runs northwards for a two days' journey to Cosenza, at an average height of over 2000 feet, through an endless succession of oak and chestnut forests, above the flanks of deep, wooded gorges, down which even in August and September the clear water went leaping and gurgling to the sea. In these altitudes Garibaldi overtook Ghio's army. On the evening of August 29, five miles beyond Tiriolo, he suddenly came in sight of the tail of the enemy's column winding round the flank of the mountain a few hundred yards in front. Since he had only half a dozen companions with him, he turned aside for the night into the neighbouring village of S. Pietro, after sending to bid Stocco's Calabrians to come up with all possible speed. While the staff was at supper an earthquake shook the village, and

TIRIOLO

S. PIETRO
From the road by which Garibaldi approached it coming from Tiriolo.

THE SURRENDER AT SOVERIA

North end of the village. (*Illustrated London News*, from sketch on the spot.)

all rushed out into the street, except only Garibaldi, who remained seated as if he had felt nothing.[1]

At dawn he started on again to seize his prey. While the rising sun flooded the peaks and valleys with light, he followed the road along the crest of a wooded ridge, which opened out after six miles into the high cultivated table-land of Soveria. At the farther end of this plateau, close beneath still higher mountains to the north, lay the village of Soveria-Mannelli. In its long street and on the flat corn-land around, Garibaldi saw bivouacked the whole of Ghio's army of 10,000 men, packed like sheep in a fold, without rear-guard or advance-guard, without sentinels placed or out-posts occupying the surrounding heights. The men were disconsolately cooking some stolen lambs ; the officers were doing nothing ; there was no sign that they intended to proceed with their march.

Ghio had in fact abandoned the idea of further retreat, because he had learnt that the pass of Agrifoglio, five miles to the north, was blocked against him by the men of Upper Calabria. These bands from Cosenza and Castrovillari, led by their feudal chiefs, Pace and Morelli, had already on August 27 compelled 3000 troops under General Caldarelli at Cosenza to enter upon an agreement to retreat with arms in their hands to Naples. The rebels had next proceeded to occupy Agrifoglio pass, fearing that if Ghio crossed the water-shed and marched down into the district of Cosenza with 10,000 fresh troops from the south, Caldarelli would throw over his agreement and unite with the new-comers to strike another blow for the royal cause. On the summit of this forest pass, more than 3000 feet above the sea, were encamped the Calabrian mountaineers in their theatrical costume, armed with shot-guns, axes, pikes, and scythes. Among them, superintending the defences of the pass, rode the white-haired Altimare, with the medal of S. Helena and the Cross of the Legion of Honour upon his breast. He

---

[1] *Bertani*, ii. 177-178. *Menghini*, 459-460. *Forbes*, 195, 198-199. *Du Camp*, 171, 185-188. *Arrivabene*, ii. 154-155. *Red Shirt*, 156-157.

had known colder work than these August days and nights among the oak woods, for he had marched to Moscow and back ; he had been one of the half-million combatants in the Armageddon on the plains of Leipzig ; he had led his fellow-Calabrians in 1820 and in 1848, and now his eyes were to see the coming of Garibaldi. Under his direction trenches were dug and trees felled across the road up which Ghio would have to march. But Ghio, on being informed that Caldarelli had come to terms and that the summit of Agrifoglio pass was thus forti. fied against his own retreat, determined to proceed no farther, but supinely to await the arrival of Garibaldi at Soveria.

There, throughout the morning of August 30, band after band of Stocco's Calabrians came in from Tiriolo and the south, exhausted with their forced march but eager to be led into action. As fast as each arrived on the plateau, Garibaldi led them up into S. Tommaso village and the other hills to east and north of Soveria. Down below, the Bourbon troops still sat cooking their lambs, and watching Garibaldi's encircling movement with the fixed indifference of despair. In the course of the morning Mario, Peard, and the ex-priest Bianchi from the camp at Agrifoglio, severally entered the village and demanded the surrender of Ghio's army. They were received with courtesy by the General, and by some of the troops, while others were with difficulty restrained from shooting them. Soon after midday Garibaldi found himself at the head of 2000 of Stocco's Calabrians and a few of Cosenz' red-shirts ranged in a circle round the village below. He gave the word to advance, and the Garibaldini silently and slowly moved down upon Ghio's ten thousand as they had done upon Briganti's smaller force at Villa San Giovanni a week before. There was no resistance, and no formal capitulation. It was understood that the men were free to go each his own way, and that the officers were to be supplied with journey money They spontaneously gave up their 10,000 rifles and twelve

cannon, and without more ado disbanded, each to his
home or to a life of brigandage.

Several thousand of the rifles were distributed among
the Calabrian bands of Stocco, Pace, and Morelli,
many of whom, thus armed, came on to Naples and took
part in the Volturno campaign. The captured horses
enabled Garibaldi for the first time since he had crossed
the Straits to mount a hundred cavalry.   Hitherto his
Hungarian hussars had trudged all the way, trailing their
huge spurs and sabres through the dust.   But when the
enemy's horses were made over to them at Soveria, the
gallant gentlemen sprang into the saddles with the alac-
rity of a cavalier race reared on the Magyar plains to
horsemanship and war.   They seemed to the onlookers to
be suddenly transfigured from tired tramps into knights of
old romance galloping off joyfully into the forest in search
of dragons and giants and some glorious way to die.[1]

In the midst of these scenes of confusion and triumph
in the squalid street of Soveria a messenger arrived from
Naples and handed a letter to Garibaldi.   It was from
Alexandre Dumas, who had recently gone to the capital
in his yacht.   He wrote that he had obtained an interview with Liborio Romano, now the principal Minister
of the King and by far the most influential person in
Naples.[2]   'Liborio,' wrote Dumas, 'is at your disposition,
together with at least two of his fellow-Ministers, at the
first attempt at reaction on the King's part.   At this first
attempt, which will set him free from his oath of fidelity,
Liborio Romano offers to leave Naples with two of his
colleagues, to present himself to you, to proclaim the deposition of the King and to recognise you as Dictator.'

[1] *De Cesare F. di P.* clxvii-clxx, clxxvii-cxci, cxcix-ccii.   *Red Shirt,* 158-
169.   *Franci,* i. 97-99.   *Peard,* 824-826.   *Arrivabene,* ii. 154-156.   *Cairoli,* 340-
341.   *Forbes,* 199-201.   *Ciàmpoli,* 177.   *I.L.N.* October 13, 1860, pp. 331-332.
F. O. Sicily, Elliot (Catanzaro Consul), September 2, 1860.   *Adamoli,* 150-151.
Du Camp, 179-180.

[2] See pp. 17-19 above.

[3] *Dumas,* 285-288, 295, 308-311, 315.   The interview of Dumas and Liborio
had been held on August 23.

Garibaldi sped the messenger back to Naples to tell Liborio that the Neapolitans ought to be prepared to rise at any moment in case it should prove necessary, but that they were, if possible, to postpone the decisive event until he himself was at the gates. He set out to follow the messenger as fast as horses could carry him, again leaving his army days behind upon the road. Two fears drew him on to the capital at his topmost speed : the fear that anarchy, massacre, or civil war would break out before his arrival; and the fear that Cavour and Victor Emmanuel would seize the reins of power in Naples and so bring to an end his Dictatorship and with it his chance of invading the Papal States.

Meanwhile, the other detachments of his army, scattered along the road between Scilla and Tiriolo, were toiling after the vanguard by forced marches. It was the hottest period of the year, cooled by occasional thunder-storms. There was no proper commissariat, and the food of the country was scarce, especially for the rear-guard who followed where Ghio's 10,000 and their own main body had already swept the villages clean. Fruit was in season, and in some places on the route abundant; but few of Garibaldi's followers could, like their leader, be satisfied with a bunch of grapes, a cigar, and the thought of Italy as a substitute for a day's rations. Everything taken was paid for at a good price, and grape-thieves were liable to be shot. Once at least the corpse of a red-shirt, laid out between the vineyards and the road, warned the passing columns that the General's discipline was still as severe in his hour of triumph as it had been eleven years before during the disastrous retreat from Rome. 'When I remember the plundering propensities of my own countrymen,' wrote an English gentleman who had beheld this wayside portent, 'I shudder to think what may be the consequences should many join the army.'[1] His fears were well grounded,

[1] *Forbes*, 178-179.

for two months later five members of the British Legion
were condemned to be shot for plundering on the north
bank of the Volturno, where they had been left on the
usual Garibaldian short rations, an intolerable torture to
the hungrier Saxon race; but their sentence was com-
muted for imprisonment.[1]

The liberated populations were enthusiastic in their
welcome, and profuse of all the hospitality which they
had to offer; but in those days the material resources of
civilisation in Calabria and Basilicata were of the most
meagre kind.[2]   Hunger, exposure, and the ceaseless
forced march made the race to Naples one of the severest
physical tests of patriotic endurance.   It took away from
the mother of the Cairoli another of her boys, Luigi,[3]
who died of typhus contracted on the road; and many
stronger men were left behind disabled.   Both French
and English, who shared in the march, admired the endurance and self-restraint of the Italian volunteers.[4]

The Dictator, at first on horseback, later in an open
carriage, was forging on ahead with a few companions.
Five miles above Soveria, on the top of the water-shed
of Agrifoglio which divides Upper from Lower Calabria,
he was greeted with wild delight by the Calabrians
who had blocked the pass there against Ghio's army.
Thence he galloped along the well-engineered road
which leads down the side of a forest gorge of Alpine
proportions to Carpanzano and Rogliano, and thence he
pushed on again the same afternoon to Cosenza.   The
capital of Upper Calabria is built on the steep sides
of three separate hills above the meeting-place of two

[1] *A.Y.R.* 200-201. And I have other first-hand evidence.

[2] Those Garibaldini who had the fortune, good or ill, to be received into
the houses of the hospitable Calabrians, had to be prepared for an evil which I
will veil for the English reader in the decent obscurity of Luigi Cairoli's classical
Italian: ' Cimici affricani, piccoli e rossi, feroci divoratori di carne umana.'
Cairoli, 343.   Indeed it was ' the season of the year ' for more than grapes.

[3] See p. 37 above.

[4] *Du Camp,* 145-146. *Conv. Dolmage. Cremona MS. (Carasi). Uzielli,* 935-
937. *Tosi,* 94-96. *Adamoli,* 150-152. *Caraguel,* 152-153. *Mariotti,* 430-431.

mountain torrents, in one of which, the Busento, Alaric the Goth lies buried. At nightfall on the last evening of August, Garibaldi was welcomed into the streets of the city lit up in his honour.[1]

There were memories at Cosenza. Here, sixteen years before, one of Italy's forlorn hopes had perished : the attack of a handful of idealists, led by Ricciotti and the brothers Bandiera against the Bourbons in the pleni-tude of their power, had here come to its tragic, pre-meditated end, in order to teach Italians by example a lesson which many had since learnt, how to die for their country. Garibaldi well remembered how the news had reached his penurious household in Montevideo, and how Anita and he had named their second-born after Ric-ciotti.[2] The most sacred place in Cosenza was a nameless slab in an aisle of the Cathedral under which the bodies lay. The victors of 1860 all went to do it honour. Gari-baldi himself had not time to visit the other scene, four miles distant in the mountains, where the execution of the Bandieras had taken place. But after he had passed on his way, when, some days later, the main body of his followers began to arrive at Cosenza, nothing could re-strain them from marching out, regiment after regiment, to see the water-washed stones in the torrent bed below Rovito, where their forerunners had dropped one by one before the firing party, with the forbidden name of Italy upon their lips. There the regiments stood bareheaded, while Nino Bixio addressed his men in words of fire.[3]

During the short night that Garibaldi spent at Cosenza he made important military dispositions, in consequence of the arrival of Bertani, who had come up thither from Paola on the coast. Bertani announced that he had brought to Paola by sea 1500 men of that large and well-

---

[1] *De Cesare, F. di P.* cxc-cxciv.

[2] See *Garibaldi's Defence of Rome*, pp. 38-39. I am glad to say that evi-dence has come to hand that the Bandieras were *not* betrayed in any sense by the British Government, as I stated in an early edition of that work ; see *Times*, August 22, 1907, Lord Stanmore's letter.

[3] *Menghini*, 297-298. *Abba Not.* 232. *Bandi*, 272-274. *Nuvolari*, 307.

equipped force which he had organised to invade the Papal States, but which Cavour and Garibaldi had between them diverted to Sicily and the south.[1] When the Dictator learnt from Bertani that 1500 men lay ready to his hand at Paola, with transports at their disposal, he sent Türr down to the coast to take over the command and carry them forward by sea from Paola to Sapri. In this way a force that Bertani had raised in the interest of the advanced Mazzinian party passed under the control of Türr, the most Cavourian of Garibaldi's lieutenants. Bertani, concealing his chagrin, attached himself to the person of the Dictator, and began, after they had travelled together for a few days, to recover the influence which he seemed recently to have lost. Meanwhile Türr rode down from Cosenza to Paola, took command of the troops collected there and carried them by sea to Sapri, where they arrived on September 2, twenty-four hours before Garibaldi himself. In this way these 1500 men from the rear became the vanguard of the advance on Naples, owing to their good fortune in finding transports while the others had to march by land.[2]

At three in the morning of September 1, Garibaldi with Cosenz and Bertani left Cosenza in an open carriage, pursued and gradually overtaken by a second carriage containing Peard with an English party. All morning their wheels ploughed through twenty miles of sandy high road along the desolate banks of the Upper Crati. On each side the mountains shut in the long valley bottom, a flat surface two miles broad over which the muddy and rapid river spreads itself uncorrected in a hundred irregular channels, hidden from the eye by dense brushwood, trees, and reeds of the marsh. This *macchia*, as

---

[1] See pp. 120-122 above. They had crossed from Sicily to Tropea, marched thence to Pizzo, and thence come by sea to Paola. *Rüstow's Brig. Milano,* 11-16. *Rüstow,* 299.

[2] *Rüstow,* 299-300. *Rüstow's Brig. Milano,* 11-18. *Türr's Div.* 147-149. *Forbes,* 206. *Bertani,* ii. 179-184 (on p. 179, line 23, read Cosenza for Rotonda). *Peard MS. Journal.* Türr who had been invalided from Sicily (see p. 66 above) had recently returned more or less cured from Aix-la-Chapelle.

the watery jungle is called, unreclaimed by man since the beginning of time, seems fantastically out of place as the sole occupant of a broad and well-watered valley, that looks, when first seen from distant hills, to be another Val d'Arno or Upper Tiber. But the sandy soil has deterred Greek, Roman, and modern Italian alike from introducing civilisation or agriculture into the upper valley of the Crati. Even the hills around were thinly inhabited and notorious for brigands. At length, at noon, the trunk road led the travellers up out of this gigantic ditch on to the heights of Tarsia and thence to Spezzano Albanese, where the Albanian colonists, like their kins-men of Piana dei Greci, near Palermo,[1] greeted the Dictator even more warmly, if that were possible, than the Italian villages along the road. From the hill of Spezzano, Garibaldi—and his army, when it followed during the next week—gazed over the plain of Sybaris, bounded on three sides by peaked mountains, and on the fourth by the Gulf of Taranto. The view resembles that of the Campagna from Tivoli, save that there is no Rome. Like Anio and Tiber, the lower reaches of the ancient Crathis and its tributaries still wander through the vast plain to the sea ; but there is no city, no civilisa-tion, and no history save the knowledge that somewhere in that comfortless expanse, now breeding death at night, stood once Sybaris, mother of luxury. The site is un-known ; Sybaris has disappeared as completely as Sodom and Gomorrah, though not by any catastrophe of nature. Only her name is left as a proverb of degeneracy, but whether the Sybarites deserved such eternal censure more than their neighbours who destroyed them, and the civilisations that have succeeded them, remains a secret guarded for ever in the memory of that silent plain.

From Spezzano, Garibaldi descended into the western corner of the plain of Sybaris, and crossed it on a cause-way through a marsh, out of which grew forest trees, swarming with birds like an English park. Thence he

[1] See *Garibaldi and the Thousand*, p. 158.

mounted to Castrovillari, one of the pleasantest towns
south of Rome, a rival in importance to Cosenza, and a
great centre of revolution that year under the leadership
of Pace. Castrovillari stands in the midst of a fruitful
plateau, raised half-way between the plain of Sybaris
below and the limestone peaks of the Monte Pollino,
which tower above to a height of 7000 feet. The old
town with its mediaeval churches and palaces is built in
pleasing disorder round the edge of some precipitous
cañons which here cleave the plateau. But already in
1860 the old town was falling into disrepair in favour of the
more cheerful modern streets, long, straight, and spacious,
in which stood Pace's house, the centre of the insurrection, and on this night the head-quarters of Garibaldi.

Next morning (September 2) he passed on across the
luxuriant plain that lies close at the foot of Monte Pollino,
rivalling Tuscany in wealth of vegetation, and thence
passed at once into the regions of naked limestone, the
heart of the mountains which divide Calabria from Basilicata. At the top of the first pass he entered the Campo
Tenese, a meadow 3000 feet above the sea, and several
miles in extent, enclosed on all sides by mountains.
Here in a snowstorm in 1806 the French had put the
army of the Bourbons to rout. At the far end of the
Campo Tenese Garibaldi climbed another pass,[1] and
thence descended out of Calabria into the Basilicata. The
first place which he reached in the new province was
the hill-town of Rotonda, where he found the National
Guard and all the paraphernalia of revolutionary authority already in being, as if it had been Paris, or Cosenza
at the least.[2]

At Rotonda a change took place in Garibaldi's method
of travelling. Hitherto he had kept to the great trunk
road the whole way from the Straits of Messina. But
now, close in front of him on that road, were General

[1] *Not* by Mormanno, where the modern branch of the high-road from Campo
Tenese runs, but by the higher pass to the right.

[2] *Bertani*, ii. 183-184. *Peard's Journal MS.* September 1-2. *Forbes*, 207-
213. *Arrivabene*, ii. 158-162. *Cairoli*, 343-349. *Racioppi*, 198-199.

Caldarelli's troops, retreating on Naples with arms in their hands according to the agreement which they had made with the revolutionary committee of Cosenza. If he proceeded farther, he would find himself at Castelluccio in the midst of these demoralised Royalist troops. Their intentions were doubtful, perhaps even to themselves. At one moment Caldarelli sent a message to Garibaldi at Rotonda saying, 'This army of yours puts itself at your orders;'[1] at the next he was promising to his soldiers the victory of the Bourbon cause through the intervention of Austria.[2] The Dictator's friends wisely persuaded him not to trust himself defenceless among these men, who might shoot him as readily as one of their own generals, but to go round by the mountains and the sea to Sapri, where he would find Türr's 1500 men newly come from Paola. With them he could march up to Lagonegro, present himself there in force upon the line of Caldarelli's retreat, and negotiate with him under more favourable conditions.

So on the night of September 2, the General and six companions, including Bertani and Cosenz, left the high road at Rotonda and, mounted on mules, rode towards the coast through the western mountains. Near Laino they entered the trackless gorge of the Lao River and followed it down by the light of the moon for several miles. 'Here we are,' cried Bertani, 'seven of us on seven mules, going to conquer a kingdom.' Out of the Lao valley they climbed once more into the highest part of the mountains, and on the morning of September 3 struck the coast at some point not far from Tortora and Maratea. Thence a small boat took them on to Sapri. There is no finer part in the whole coast-line of Italy than this unvisited riviera, where the precipitous ridges run out one beyond another and sink into the waves.[3]   The

---

[1] *Bertani*, ii. 184. *Peard's Journal MS.* September 2.

[2] *Forbes*, 214.

[3] There is not, and never was, a coast road, but since 1860 a railway has been driven along this coast. But those who pass through its tunnels to Sicily have no idea under what magnificent scenery they are travelling.

MONTE POLLINO
From road near Morano along which Garibaldi passed.

CAMPO TENESE
Looking back south from the road by which Garibaldi crossed the pass to Rotonda. On the right is the road to Mormanno.

ROTONDA

SAPRI

The bay and town from a point just beyond the Roman villa.

rugged coast is best seen from a boat, but Garibaldi, exhausted by the night's ride, lay asleep in the prow, while his friends covered him with a sail to protect him from the rays of the noonday sun. Only as they entered the bay of Sapri, they all stood up to gaze on the beauty of the scene, and to honour the memory of Pisacane, who, in 1857, had run into this bay to raise the Italian flag upon the mountains.[1] On the beach where his fore-runner had landed under the shadow of doom, Garibaldi stepped ashore on the full tide of victory, welcomed as '*fratello Garibaldi*' by the people of Sapri, who three years before had frowned on Pisacane and his more questionable following. Here also the Dictator found Türr's troops, who had sailed in the day before from Paola.[2]

There is a fine beach, but no artificial landing-place at Sapri. Only there may be seen in the clear water the ruins of an ancient pier. It runs out from the foundations of a palace built long ago by some magnate of Imperial Rome, who discovered the beauty of the little bay, and carried thither the whole apparatus of ancient luxury, leaving less adventurous pleasure-seekers at Puteoli and Baiae. Some modern Lucullus will imitate him ere long. Meanwhile Garibaldi landed there and spent the night in a straw hut upon the beach.

Next day the Dictator and Türr's 1500 men, mostly Milanese, marched up all morning from Sapri by precipitous forest paths to a shoulder of Monte Cucuzzo, and thence descended on the Lagonegro high-road, along which Caldarelli and his men were retreating. The road here runs at an average level of over 2000 feet. The point where Garibaldi dropped down on it from the west was the wayside tavern of Il Fortino. Here, on September 4, he was overtaken by Piola, an officer of the Piedmontese navy, whom Depretis, his Pro-Dictator

---

[1] See *Garibaldi and the Thousand*, p. 69.
[2] *La Cava*, 702. *Bertani*, ii. 184-185. *Ire Pol.* 71-72. *Racioppi*, 200. *Maison*, 63-64. *Rüstow's Brig. Mil.* 18-19. *Türr's Div.* 149.

in Sicily, had sent on commission to persuade him to permit the immediate annexation of the island to the dominions of Victor Emmanuel. Türr and Cosenz, the soldiers in attendance on the General, eagerly seconded Piola, begging their chief to allow Sicily to be annexed on condition that Depretis should for the present continue to govern it as Victor Emmanuel's lieutenant, and that supplies of men and money should continue to be sent from Sicily to the Garibaldian camp.   Garibaldi yielded to their entreaties, and had actually dictated to his secretary the words, 'Dear Depretis, have the annexation made whenever you like,' when Bertani came in upon them from the other compartment of the tavern and caught his Cavourian rivals in the act.   'General,' said the agitator, 'you are abdicating;' and in spite of all that Türr and Cosenz could say, Bertani in a few minutes persuaded him to rely for the further liberation of Italy not on the co-operation of Cavour and the Piedmontese Government, but on the men and money which, so Bertani declared, would be supplied in unlimited quantities by Sicily and by the provinces of Naples as fast as they were liberated.   The half-written letter was torn up and another was sent, bidding Depretis delay the annexation yet awhile.[1]

Bertani's triumph at this unlucky pothouse of Il Fortino opened the way for the struggle between Garibaldi and the Government of Turin, which during the ensuing months marred with unseemly altercation the solemn act of the Making of Italy.   Depretis was right. The time had come to annex Sicily, if Garibaldi could but have seen it.   When in June he had refused to allow annexation because it would have prevented him from crossing the Straits, he had been right and Cavour wrong.[2]   But in September he could have no object in further delaying the annexation, except to keep himself

---

[1] *Rüstow's Brig. Mil.* 20-22.   *Türr's Div.,* 149-150.   *Ire Pol.* 72-77.   *Bertani,* ii. 185-186.   *Türr's Risposta,* 16.
[2] See p. 54 above.

free to attack the cities of Rome and Venice or otherwise to thwart and embroil the policy of Victor Emmanuel's Ministers.   It is possible that if at Il Fortino he had known that Cavour was on the point of invading the Papal territories himself, he might have rejected Bertani's advice and consented to work hand in hand with the Piedmontese Government.

Meanwhile, the military business in hand was to catch Caldarelli and his three thousand.[1]   On September 3, before leaving Lagonegro, Caldarelli had again assured Garibaldi's emissaries that he and all his men intended to desert to the side of the nation.[2]   He had, however, continued his retreat on Naples, and had passed through Il Fortino a few hours before Garibaldi struck into the road at that point.   On September 5 he was finally overtaken near Padula, where Pisacane had three years before been defeated by the Royalist troops under Ghio. There Caldarelli's column nominally came over to the Garibaldian army, but the transaction was really a disbandment rather than a desertion.   Indeed, some of the troops retained enough loyalty to attempt the murder of their general for having betrayed the cause, but the Garibaldini saved him out of their hands.[3]

At Casalnuovo, on September 5, Garibaldi was met by Mignona, Governor in his name of the Province of Basilicata, which had declared for him more than a fortnight before while he was engaged in crossing the Straits. The 'Lucanians,' as the men of Basilicata called themselves in memory of classical times, sent through Mignona a goodwill offering of 6000 ducats (25,500 francs), and raised a 'Lucanian brigade,' which followed Garibaldi to Naples.   Thence 900 returned home, but the remaining 1200 took part in the Volturno campaign.[4]

From Casalnuovo the Dictator raced on in an open

[1] See p. 156 above.   [2] *Forbes*, 215-216.
[3] *La Masa* (Sic), pp. lxxxv-lxxxvi, 204-206.   *Türr's Div.* 130.
[4] *Racioppi*, 217.   *Mignona*, 214-215.

carriage through the Province of Principato Citeriore.
As he drew nearer to the capital its corrupting influence
became ever more apparent in the moral degradation
of the people, and warlike volunteers were no longer
forthcoming. But south of Naples there were no signs
of reactionary feeling. All along the road the people
and the local authorities vied with each other in the
frenzy of their enthusiasm, which was compounded
of joy at deliverance from a cruel and inquisitorial
tyranny ; interested subservience to the rulers of the
hour ; and good human devotion, in which also superstition had a part, for the person of the almost mythical
Garibaldi.[1]

For several days, however, these semi-divine honours
were paid to the wrong person. Peard, 'Garibaldi's
Englishman,' as he posted along the road from Sala Consilina to Eboli, was universally taken for the Liberator
himself. He was accompanied during this strange adventure by Gallenga, one of the *Times* correspondents,
by Commander C. S. Forbes of the British Navy, and by
Fabrizi, who was commissioned by the Dictator to survey
the military positions in advance. These men, having in
the capacity of non-combatants passed through Caldarelli's
column prior to its disbandment, had kept the high-road
the whole way from Cosenza, and had thus gained fifty
miles on Garibaldi, who had been forced to go round by
the coast. In the afternoon of September 3, while the
Dictator was sailing into the bay of Sapri, Peard was
entering Auletta amid a scene of ' tremendous enthusiasm. The people,' he noted in his diary, ' thought I
was Garibaldi, and it was thought that it would do good
to yield to the delusion. It became a nuisance, for

[1] One Garibaldi legend, seriously told and believed a few years later, was to
this effect. Once when his army was in need of water, Garibaldi fired a cannon at
a rock and water gushed out. This adaptation of a Bible story to modern conditions is a curious example of the growth of hagiology. If Garibaldi and his
educated followers had been professional traders on popular superstition, it would
have been easy in the 'sixties to have set up a Garibaldian Lourdes in South
Italy, and to have worked profitable cures with red shirts.

deputations arrived from all the neighbourhood to kiss my excellency's hand, and I had to hold regular levées. The town was illuminated and *Te Deum* sung in honour of his arrival.

Next day, while the real Garibaldi was weaving and un-weaving the web of his uncertain policy in the tavern at Il Fortino, Peard and Fabrizi, accompanied by National Guard, brass bands, and people of Auletta, ascended to the hamlet of Postiglione, where they found every one 'mad with excitement. At the Syndic's, one of the priests (there were numbers of the fraternity present) went on his knees,' writes Peard, 'and called me a second Jesus Christ. I was not prepared for so excessive a bit of blasphemy.' Postiglione hangs on the side of Monte Alburno, commanding a view of the plain of Eboli with the gulf and mountains of Salerno beyond. Somewhere in that plain or in those mountains, as Fabrizi and Peard well knew, Francis II. must fight for Naples, or else abandon his capital without a blow. Twelve thousand of his soldiers lay in Salerno and on the pass of Cava behind it; the plain of Eboli in front, patrolled by his squadrons, had for several days past been considered as the ground where the regular army, strong in cavalry and artillery, would have the best chance of defeating the Garibaldini. There were, at the lowest computation, 40,000 infantry and 4000 cavalry ready to hand in Naples and its environs. The Dictator had with him only Türr's 1500 men, recently landed at Sapri, but if he could afford to wait for a fortnight, which was extremely doubtful, he might hope to collect his full force of some 20,000 infantry and 100 cavalry. If even on these terms a Royalist victory was not to be won in the plains of Eboli, the steep wall of mountains behind Salerno would still form a natural barrier, protecting the approaches to Naples.[1]

Peard and Fabrizi determined to take advantage of their strange situation to spread such reports as would

[1] *Franci*, i. 110. *Palmieri*, 85. *Liborio Romano*, 62, 66. *De Cesare*, ii. 395. *Pianell*, 82-87.

strike panic into the enemy's head-quarters and lead to the abandonment of these all-important positions. In pursuance of this design they hastened on to Eboli on the evening of September 4, at some risk of being caught there by the enemy's patrols or arrested by the local authorities, who had not yet come within the sphere of the advancing revolution. But the pseudo-Garibaldi brought the revolution with him wherever he appeared. 'Within half an hour of our arrival,' wrote Commander Forbes, Eboli 'was brilliantly illuminated, the entire population besieging the Syndic's, brass bands banging away in every direction, and the crowd roaring themselves hoarse and calling on the General to appear, reminding one more of an election than anything else, the National Guard being all this time severely engaged on the staircase in a vain endeavour to keep the inhabitants out of the house. Deputations arrived; first came the Church, headed by a Bishop.' Forbes at one moment tried to persuade some of the leading men that Peard was not Garibaldi. 'Oh! you're quite right to try and keep your secret,' they replied, 'but you know it won't do; we know.' The gigantic Englishman did not, in fact, resemble the Nizzard at all closely, but his greater height and longer beard in no way impaired the belief of the people that they had the hero among them.

Peard and his Italian companions of the jest decided to turn the absurd situation to serious account. Shortly before midnight they sent for the official in charge of the telegraph, who appeared trembling before the 'Dictator' between a file of the National Guard. He reported that the Neapolitan general commanding at Salerno had an hour before wired for information about Caldarelli's brigade and Garibaldi's movements. Peard dictated the reply, announcing Garibaldi's presence at Eboli and exaggerating to four or five thousand the number of troops that he had close at hand. Above all, he announced that Caldarelli's brigade had changed sides and was now marching with the national forces. All these statements were inaccurate, but they appear to have been believed both at Salerno and in the capital. Gallenga, who was with Peard, wired the same reports to private friends in Naples closely connected with the Court and Ministry. The belief, erroneous in fact, that Caldarelli's men had gone over of their own accord to the invaders, led every one to expect that the troops at Salerno would do the same, unless they were withdrawn before Garibaldi could reach them from Eboli. Thus the misleading reports circulated by Peard and Gallenga, and the presence of the supposed Garibaldi at so short a distance from Salerno, were among the influences which induced Francis II not to fight for his capital. This decision was taken beyond recall on the morning of September 5, when the commander-in-chief at Naples telegraphed to Marshal Afan de Rivera at Salerno, ordering all the troops at Salerno to retreat by way of Cava to Nocera.[1]

Meanwhile, the pseudo-Garibaldi and his party, not knowing that their bluff would succeed in scaring the enemy away, escaped unnoticed from Eboli in the small hours of the morning. Peard returned as far as Sala Consilina to meet the real Garibaldi, who heartily approved what he had done. When they heard that the Royalists had evacuated their positions, Peard hastened forward again at Garibaldi's request, and entered Salerno in triumph at five in the morning of September 6. The whole town turned out to welcome 'the Dictator,' who received deputations in public all the morning, detected by no one in authority or out of it, except by a single officer who whispered him in the ear.

In the course of the morning the Piedmontese vessel *Authion* appeared off Salerno and set ashore Evelyn Ashley, son of the good Lord Shaftesbury, and private secretary to Lord Palmerston. The young man, to the intense delight of his chief, had gone out to spend his holidays with Garibaldi instead of with the partridges.

---

[1] See Appendix H, below. *Immediate Causes of the Evacuation of Salerno.*

A few days before, Ashley had presented himself to Cavour in Turin, with a letter of introduction from the British Prime Minister, and had asked where he could find Garibaldi. 'Garibaldi! Who is he?' said Cavour, with a twinkle in his eye. 'I have nothing to do with him. . . . He is somewhere in the Kingdom of the Two Sicilies, I believe, but that is not, you know, at present under my King.' However, Cavour put Ashley on board the *Authion* and sent him to search for himself. He took with him Mr. Edwin James, Q.C., and at Naples fell in with others of his fellow-countrymen, with whom he continued to coast southwards. Off Salerno they saw flags and heard the shouting of a vast multitude in the town. On being informed that it betokened the arrival of Garibaldi, the Englishmen landed, only to find that it was in reality Peard, by this time exceedingly anxious to be relieved from his task of impersonation. He asked his compatriots to go and meet Garibaldi and hasten his coming. On the road the English party met hundreds of disbanded Royalist troops, unarmed, starving, and in the last state of misery, dragging themselves home along the road, or lying prostrate by the wayside. Garibaldi had shared with them all the money he had at hand, but their condition was pitiable. Arrived in Eboli, Ashley found the Dictator, who greeted him warmly as England's emissary, and allowed him to follow his staff as a non-combatant, on the sole condition that the new-comer should wear his simple livery, in order to be safe from maltreatment in the confusion of the times. And so our Premier's secretary donned the red shirt.

At five in the evening of September 6 the Dictator and his staff entered Salerno in a string of open carriages, two days' march in front of his nearest troops, the 1500 under Türr,[1] and many days in front of the rest of the army. Outside the town he was met by the Syndic, the National Guard, and his English precursor, now deposed. *Viva Garibaldi!* he cried, taking off his hat in mock hom-

[1] *Türr's Div.* 162. *Rüstow's Brig. Mil.*, 23-24.

age to Peard, and every one joined in the cry with shouts of laughter and applause.   Darkness fell as they forced their way one step at a time into Salerno, amid the delirium of 20,000 people, who seemed desirous to tear the real Garibaldi in pieces.   The town was illuminated, and all the heights far away towards Amalfi and Sorrento were ablaze with fires of joy.[1]

On the same evening the last of the Bourbons and his queen were leaving the Palace of Naples by the water-gate and taking ship for Gaeta.

[1] Appendix H below.   *Peard's Journal MS.* and *Cornhill*, June, 1908.   *Forbes,* 219-231.   *Arrivabene,* ii. 168-169.   *Ashley,* 492-496.   *Times,* September 13, p. 10, c. 4 (James's letter), September 15, p. 10, cols. 3-4.   *De Cesare,* ii. 422-424. *Revel's da Ancona,* 65.   *Elliot,* 96.   *Persano,* 206-207.   *Galton,* 22.

CHAPTER VIIı

Venu è Galubardo!
Venu è lu più bel!

Neapolitan Song of 1860.

THE flight of King Francis from Naples on September 6
was but the final catastrophe in a process of dissolution
which had set in with the news of the fall of Palermo
and the consequent proclamation of constitutional rights
in June.   Freedom of press and person had effectively
and instantly broken up the machinery of repression.
The police had, in Liborio Romano's conjuring hands,
been turned in a few days into an instrument of Liberalism.   The King had handed over the civil administration
to his enemies, and had gained nothing in return except
the diplomatic support of France that failed him at every
crisis.   At home the constitution won over to him a few
individuals, but no class or party.   The decadent nobility
of the capital, the peasants of certain districts in the
northern provinces, and the bulk of the army remained
loyal not because of the constitution, but in spite of it.
Every one else was looking to Piedmont.   The perfidy
of his ancestors divided King Francis from his people.
Remembering the fate of the constitutions of 1820 and
1848, the citizens refused to enroll themselves on the
electoral lists, because in case of reaction the appearance
of their names on the register might be used against them
as evidence of treason.[1]   And when Garibaldi in August
came marching up through the constituencies, all talk of
holding elections for Parliament ceased.

[1] *D'Ayala*, 286.

The King suspected his Ministers, though most of them were passively loyal. Above all and with good reason he hated Don Liborio Romano. But Don Liborio, like Lafayette in the autumn of 1789, was the man of the hour with whom neither Court nor people could dispense : he had at his beck and call the police, the National Guard of respectable burghers, and the *camorra* of criminals. So King Francis had to endure him throughout all July and August, first as Police Minister only and then as Minister of the Interior also. In the latter half of August, Don Liborio held confidential interviews on the subject of coming events with the Dictator's friends in Naples,[1] with the Piedmontese admiral, Persano, and with the King's uncle, the Count of Syracuse, who had already openly declared for a change of dynasty. Persano wrote to Cavour that Don Liborio was helping the cause of national unity 'so far as he was permitted by his very delicate situation' as Minister of Francis II.[2]

His object, however, was not actively to compass the destruction of his master, which he regarded as already certain, but to prevent the fall of the dynasty from involving in its ruin the public peace and safety. For this reason, as well as for the satisfaction of his own vanity, he had accepted office in June, and for this reason he determined to remain in power during the days or hours that must elapse between the fall of Francis II and the establishment of any new form of government. If he forced the King to accept his resignation, the *camorra* would, he believed, break loose in the great city, which contained a larger proportion of criminally disposed persons than any other in Europe, the Royal troops would begin to fight with the National Guard, and disasters of the most appalling character might occur. The respectable part of the citizens took the same view, begging Don Liborio and his colleagues to retain office under the Crown at any sacrifice to their own dignity or

[1] *Dumas*, 285-287, see p. 149 above.
[2] Persano's words to Cavour, *Persano*, 144-145, 175, 189.

honour.   And those who knew best the Naples of those
days were the least inclined to deny the claim afterwards
put forward by the discredited politician that he saved
the capital from destruction.[1]

Meanwhile, the Cavourian agents were striving in
vain to precipitate a revolution.[2]   Villamarina, the Piedmontese Minister at Naples, and Admiral Persano, who
arrived there with his fleet from Sicily at the beginning
of August, lent their aid to Finzi and Visconti Venosta,
to Nisco, D'Ayala, and Nunziante in their attempts to win
over the army and incite the civilians to resolute action.
But the army remained loyal, in spite of the propaganda
of the popular general, Nunziante, among his old companions in arms, and in spite of the blandishments of the
Piedmontese Bersaglieri.   Some companies of the latter
were allowed to land off Persano's ships and to show
themselves in the streets, partly in order to encourage
the population to revolt and partly in order to fraternize
with the Neapolitan troops, who replied by breaking
their heads.[3]

The citizens were more sympathetic but not more
active than the soldiers.   The Neapolitans did not see
the use of doing at the risk of their own skins what
Garibaldi was coming to do for them.   Moreover, the
Mazzinian 'Committee of Action,' which contained the
bolder and more energetic spirits, had resolved to wait
for the Dictator's arrival, fearing that if they rose before
he appeared on the scene, Naples would fall at once into
the hands of Cavour ; while the Cavourian 'Committee
of Order,' which would fain have seen a revolution
effected while Garibaldi was still on his way, consisted
of 'moderate men' unfitted by nature to initiate a revolt.[4]

[1] *Trinity*, 232-233.   *D'Ayala*, 319.   *Liborio Romano*, 26, 67.   *Dumas*, 367.
For Don Liborio and the *camorra* see pp. 18-19 above.

[2] See pp. 22-23 above.

[3] *Persano*, 143-145, 158.   F. O. Sicily, *Elliot*, No. 450, 459, August 20, 24.
Nisco, 70-74.   *Russell MS. Elliot*, August 20.   *D'Ayala*, 305-307.   *Mezzacapo*,
123-129.

[4] *Persano*, 185, 189.   *D'Ayala*, 310.

The motives of Cavour's policy throughout August are relatively clear to those who will read them in the light of two established facts : first, that he had, in the last days of July, persuaded Russell to permit Garibaldi's passage of the Straits ;[1] and secondly, that he had as early as August 1 made up his mind to invade the Papal provinces with the Piedmontese army.[2] His desire was, without more delay, to possess himself of Naples and so to forestall a Garibaldian Dictatorship ; while at the same time he would invade the Papal States and so link up the north and south of the Peninsula in one free monarchy. It was only because he feared that the revolution in Naples would perhaps miss fire without the help of the guerilla, that he had persuaded Russell to let him cross from Sicily to the mainland. Even after he had taken this step as a measure of insurance in case of his own failure, he continued to work for the overthrow of Francis II through his own agents, and since time was needed for this experiment, he was not sorry to see the Dictator kept waiting three weeks at the Straits. That is the reason why in the first days of August he wrote to Admiral Persano, ' Do not help the passage of General Garibaldi on to the continent, but rather try to delay him by indirect means as far as possible.'[3]

When the Dictator had safely crossed and was beginning his march through Calabria, Cavour caused arms to be landed at Salerno and distributed among the rebels of the south ' in order to open out the way for Garibaldi's advance.'[4] But at the same time he made a last effort to obtain possession of Naples for his own party, writing to Villamarina on August 27, ' Do all you can to avoid a Garibaldian Dictatorship, on which you count too much.' He instructed Persano to accept the Dictatorship if it was offered to him. Even now Cavour shrank from the one sure method of avoiding the Garibaldian regime in Naples, which he so much dreaded, namely, an open

[1] By Lacaita's mission, see p. 105 above.   [2] P. 117 above.
[3] *Persano*, 123.   [4] *Ibid.* 157, 159, August 21, 23.

declaration of war by Piedmont on King Francis, because, as he told Villamarina, that would 'compromise us altogether with Europe.'[1] By 'Europe' he meant most of all Napoleon, with whom he was at that moment secretly negotiating for leave to attack the Papal territory.

A few days later he saw that he had lost the race for Naples. On August 30, while the Dictator was receiving the surrender of Ghio's ten thousand at Soveria, Cavour wrote to Villamarina acknowledging defeat and bidding him abandon all thought of forming a Government at Naples independent of Garibaldi. 'You must act frankly in unison with him, trying only to get the fleet and the forts into our hands.'[2]

Although Cavour failed actually to overturn Francis II before the arrival of Garibaldi, the prestige of the Royal family and of the Royalist party was rapidly melting away throughout the whole of August. The National Guard, the police, the citizens, and the Piedmontese agents were all in a tacit conspiracy against the King and his soldiers, and whenever any of the latter gave vent to their feelings by rioting in the streets, their bad discipline was pointed to as proof that Francis II intended to destroy the constitution by military force.[3] A series of half-hearted reactionary plots were unearthed by Don Liborio's police and their details published to the further discomfiture of the King. In one of these conspiracies his uncle, the Count of Aquila, was supposed to be implicated. Aquila had been for a few weeks an ardent constitutionalist, but he had rejoined the ultra-Royalists in the hope, it was said, of displacing his incompetent nephew in their affections. On August 14 the Ministers succeeded in driving him into exile, under cover of sending him on a foreign mission.[4]

---

[1] *Chiala*, iii. 347. *Persano*, 182. *D'Ayala*, 310.
[2] *Chiala*, iii. 355-356. [3] *Elliot*, 41. *Nisco*, 54.
[4] 'What led at last to the decision to send him off was the arrival of three cases of revolvers and one case of pictures of him waving his hat, which have fallen into the hands of the Government.' *Elliot*, 73. The real seriousness of

On August 20 Don Liborio presented to the King his famous Memorandum, in which he tried to persuade his master to retire from the Kingdom 'for some time,' leaving as regent 'a Minister who would inspire public confidence.' In this way alone, wrote Don Liborio, could 'the horrors of civil war' be averted, seeing that mutual confidence between the people and their prince 'has become not only difficult but impossible.'[1] Four days after Francis had received this broad hint from his principal Minister of State, he was made the target of a public letter from his uncle of Syracuse, in which the Count exhorted his nephew to sacrifice his throne on behalf of the glorious idea of Italian unity. Such language from a prince of the blood produced a very general impression that all was now lost. Syracuse had shown the letter to Persano in his flag-ship five days before it appeared.[2]

The ever-shifting intentions and intrigues of the King and his many rival counsellors during the last fortnight of Bourbon rule in Naples are known to us at present chiefly through the narratives of Liborio Romano and of General Pianell and his wife. These represent the constitutional party alone, and even so are inconsistent with each other on several important points. Unless other documents come to light the historian will never be able to trace confidently and in detail the story of those days of cowardice, treachery, confusion, and panic. Only the main outline of events is clear.[3]

It was agreed by all parties in the Palace that the

the plot is doubted by *De Cesare*, ii. 338-340, but see *Liborio Romano*, 49-51. *Nisco*, 97-99. *Mundy*, 207-215.

[1] *Persano*, 152-156.   [2] *Ibid.* 148.

[3] Pianell's own narrative unfortunately stops at the end of the month. His wife's goes on longer and is a contemporary journal, but on the other hand she could only record what her husband told her each day. The Pianells are more trustworthy witnesses than Don Liborio (see *De Cesare*, ii. 409), yet modern histories have relied almost entirely on Don Liborio alone. Whitehouse's excellent book was written before the publication of the Pianell papers. What we most want is some analogous narrative by a member of the *camarilla* or reactionary Court Party.

presence of the King himself in the field was necessary
if the demoralised troops were ever to face Garibaldi
again.   It was also common ground that the Capital
should be spared and should not, like Palermo, be made
the scene of conflict.   The main division of opinion between constitutionalists and reactionaries arose on the
question whether the King should go south to defend
the Capital in the plains of Eboli and the mountains of
Salerno ; or whether he should abandon Naples and retire north with all the loyal troops in the Kingdom behind
the line of the Volturno.   In the latter case he could
base his new position on the strongly fortified towns of
Capua and Gaeta, which might prove for him what the
quadrilateral had been to Austria in 1848, a rock of refuge
on which the rebels would vainly waste their strength,
until the time was ripe for a Royalist counter-attack and
a triumphal return to the Capital.   Against Garibaldi,
who had no siege guns and no siege science, the plan
had a fair likelihood of success, as subsequent events
showed.   It was a political as well as a military move,
for the retreat northwards would mean the abandonment
of the tricolour in favour of the old white flag of the
Bourbons, the burying of the constitution and a frank
return to reaction on the *Bomba* model.   The removal
of the soldiers from the Capital northwards would enable
them to indulge their loyalist sentiments freely in a more
favourable atmosphere.   Don Liborio and his colleagues
would remain in Naples, while the Queen-Dowager and
her reactionary clique were already at Gaeta waiting for
the King.   The reactionary peasants of the Volturno
district were already threatening the lives of the local
Liberals.   The Papal border and the Papal army were
close in the rear of Gaeta.

It may therefore be supposed that the advice to retreat behind the Volturno originated from the King's
secret advisers of the ultra-Royalist party.[1]   As early
as August 27 his constitutional Ministers found that

[1] So Villamarina believed. *Persano*, 209-210.

he was meditating such a retreat.[1] But his purposes
wavered from day to day and from hour to hour, and
only the sound of the approaching footsteps of Garibaldi
could bring him to the point of a resolve.

On August 29 his Ministers for their part urged him
to go south and head the troops at Salerno in defence of
the Capital and the constitution, though it is difficult to
suppose that they wished him a complete victory.[2]

On the same day the reactionaries, headed by Count
Trapani, another of the King's uncles, were hatching a
plot to arrest the Ministers. The loyalist proclamation
which was to have been published as the watchword of
this *coup d'état* was seized overnight by Don Liborio's
police, and produced at the council-board by the indignant
men against whom it had been aimed. King Francis, red
with mingled anger and embarrassment, gasped out that
he agreed with much in the proclamation, and gave
his Ministers to understand that he was to some extent in
the confidence of the conspirators who had plotted their
arrest.[3] The Ministry, who had already attempted to
resign, now pressed with somewhat greater earnestness
for leave to be quit of the Royal service. But even now
the King refused to part with them, on the ground that
he could find no one else willing to form a Cabinet, and
when their friends of the National Guard warned them
that anarchy would break loose in the streets as
soon as their resignation became known, they consented,
all except Pianell, to continue awhile longer in office.[4]
Affairs remained in this suspended condition until the
night of September 4, when Peard's telegrams, the
supposed presence of Garibaldi at Eboli, and the reported
desertion of Caldarelli's troops[5] brought the King's ir-
resolution to an end, and gave him the requisite energy
to carry out his plan of retreat to Gaeta.

---

[1] *Pianell*, 91.   [2] *Liborio Romano*, 62-63.
[3] *Pianell*, 88-89, 588-589.   *Russell MS. Elliot*, September 1.   *Elliot*, 83-84.
[4] *Russell MS. Elliot*, September 1.   (Appendix A, below.)   *Pianell*, 90
193-195. *Liborio Romano*, 67. *F. O. Sicily Elliot*, No. 485, September 2, 1860.
[5] See p. 163 above and Appendix H, below.

Accordingly on September 5 Francis II announced his approaching departure to the Ministers, the Mayor, and the officers of the National Guard, to whom he committed the charge of keeping order in the Capital during his absence. He spoke without bitterness, of which there seems to have been singularly little in his mild and foolish nature. He excused himself for going : but 'your Joe, I mean our Joe, is at the gates,' he said to these men, whom he well knew to be preparing in their hearts an enthusiastic reception for Garibaldi.[1]

On the same day he and his brave Bavarian Queen went for their last drive in the streets of Naples. They sat in an open carriage, like simple private citizens, and the passers-by, who took off their hats to them in silence, observed that they were laughing and talking together as usual. The clumsy shyness of the King's demeanour to his wife, which had distressed her in the early months of their marriage, had now to a large extent passed away.[2] A few yards from the Palace, at the busy entrance of the Chiaja, their equipage was brought to a stand by a block in the traffic, and they were forced to wait some moments close to a gang of workmen who were taking down the Bourbon lilies from over the shop front of the Chemist to the Royal Family. Francis pointed out to Maria Sophia the too significant nature of the men's task, and husband and wife turned to each other and laughed.[3]

Next morning, September 6, the walls of Naples were placarded with the King's proclamation of farewell to his people. In restrained and dignified language he protested against the way in which he was being driven from his Capital, in spite of his constitutional concessions, and announced that he hoped to return if the luck of war and politics favoured his claims. In the course of the day the main part of the army marched out of the town by the Capua road, indignantly refusing D'Ayala's in-

---

[1] '*Il vostro—e nostro—don Peppino è alle porte.*' *De Cesare*, ii. 408-409.
[2] See *Garibaldi and the Thousand*, pp. 126-128. *De Cesare*, ii. 29-30.
[3] *De Cesare*, ii. 408.

vitation to fraternize with the National Guard and desert to the side of Italy.[1] A garrison of six or ten thousand [2] was left behind to guard the fortresses of the Capital, but their commanding officers were strictly ordered by Francis II to remain neutral and to shed no blood. Nothing was said to them about surrender or evacuation, although if they were attacked they could only hold the forts by shedding blood, which would transgress both the letter and the spirit of the King's commands.   It is probable that he had not clearly thought out what he wished them to do.[3] But it may fairly be said that he adhered in an honourable manner to his decision not to inflict the horrors of war on Naples, and the rumour that he ordered the castles to bombard the town, after he had gone, was pure fiction.

At four in the afternoon the constitutional Ministers were summoned to the Palace to take their leave of the King.   There was no party in the State that wished them to accompany him to Gaeta.   They found him courteous and cheerful, buoyed up by excitement at a great change and by relief after long tension. He said to Don Liborio, half in jest, half in earnest, 'Don Libò, look out for your head,' referring no doubt to his own prospective return.   'Sire,' was the unabashed reply, 'I will do my best to keep it on my shoulders.'   The Ministers were not invited to say farewell to the Queen.

Shortly before six in the evening Francis and Maria Sophia walked down arm-in-arm from the Palace to the dock which lay close under their windows.   Both were composed and cheerful.   The Queen left her wardrobe behind, saying to her maids, ' We shall come back again.' The hundreds of Neapolitan grandees and officials who had fattened on the Court for twenty years past were notable by their absence.   But the faithful Captain Cris-

---

[1] *J. des D.* September 15, 1860, Letter of September 6.   *D'Ayala*, 318.
[2] The list in *Franci*, i. 125-126, 244, reprinted in *Türr's Div.* doc. 52, makes 10,000.   But *De Cesare*, ii. 413, says 6000.
[3] *Marra Oss.* 45-50.   *Cava*, 109-110, are, I think, the only first-hand authorities on this subject.

cuolo received his sovereigns on board the *Messaggero*, a small ship of 160 horse-power and four guns. As she steamed through the crowded port of Naples, she ran up a signal for the rest of the fleet to follow, but not one vessel stirred. The captains were already in league with Persano, and the prevailing sentiment of the men and still more of the officers favoured United Italy.[1]

The little ship, shunned by all her fellows, carried the last of the Bourbons for ever out of sight of Vesuvius and the Bay. At dusk she passed the island of Nisida where Gladstone had visited *Bomba's* victims. A few minutes later, off Procida, she met another section of the fleet, signalled again, and was again disobeyed. All night she ploughed her solitary way under the stars, through a tranquil sea.[2]

The interregnum of twenty hours that followed the King's departure was outwardly the quietest, but inwardly the most anxious day that Naples had passed for several weeks. Knowing that Bourbon garrisons were still in the four great castles—Nuovo, S. Elmo, dell' Ovo, and Carmine—the population stayed indoors until something decisive occurred. Fortunately the authorities took the right steps. Liborio Romano still continued to act and to sign himself as 'Minister of Police and the Interior,' though under which King seemed uncertain. His continued presence at the head of affairs helped to preserve public confidence and peace. He sent at once for the Mayor, Prince d'Alessandria, and for De Sauget, the General of the National Guard, and agreed with them that Garibaldi must enter Naples as soon as fitting preparations had been made

---

[1] Some Spanish vessels escorted the *Messaggero* for a very short distance. Two other small vessels, the *Delfino* and *Saetta*, and the sailing frigate *Partenope* were the only ships of the Royal Navy which later on joined the *Messaggero* at Gaeta. The remaining thirty-five vessels of the fleet passed over to the National cause. *F. O. Sicily*, Elliot, September 30, 1860, full list. *De Cesare*, ii. 425. *Persano*, 207-215.

[2] *De Cesare*, ii. 413-426.

for his reception, and as soon as he had troops enough at his side to ensure his safety against the Bourbon garrison. Within an hour of the King's departure two officers of the National Guard were sent off to Salerno on what was then the only railroad south of the Capital; it ran along the coast past Vesuvius, turned inland by Pompeii and ended at Vietri two miles outside Salerno. On their way the two officers met a number of Bavarian mercenaries retreating northwards from the abandoned positions of Salerno and Cava. At Salerno, which they reached by ten at night, they found the streets lighted up, and groups of people still cheering 'disturbedly.' Garibaldi had made his entry,[1] and had gone to rest. The envoys reported to Cosenz the flight of the King and announced the intention of the Mayor and the commander of the National Guard to come from Naples early next morning.

Garibaldi, when he awoke on September 7, telegraphed to Don Liborio: 'As soon as the Mayor and commanding officer of the National Guard arrive from Naples, I will come to you: I am waiting for them first.'

Don Liborio wired back: 'To the invincible General Garibaldi, Dictator of the Two Sicilies—Liborio Romano, Minister of the Interior and Police.

'Naples awaits your arrival with the greatest impatience to salute you as the redeemer of Italy, and to place in your hands the power of the State and her own destinies. . . . I await your further orders and am, with unlimited respect for you, invincible Dictator,

'LIBORIO ROMANO.'

This exchange of telegrams barely preceded the arrival at Salerno of the Mayor and General, who were at once ushered into the presence of Garibaldi. He was surprised to hear from them that Naples did not expect him that day, and expressed annoyance at the suggestion of any need to erect triumphal arches and to make official pre-

[1] See p. 165 above.

parations for his entry. More serious arguments for delay were the presence of the Bavarians on the railway line between Salerno and the Capital, the garrisons in the four castles with cannon trained on the heart of the city, and the absence of Garibaldi's own army. His nearest force, Türr's 1500, were still forty-eight hours behind, and the rest of his 20,000 men were scattered along the roads of Basilicata and Calabria at distances varying from four to fourteen days' march. His staff officers, Bertani, and the emissaries from Naples, all besought him to wait at least till Türr's force came up, and till the departure of the Bavarians for Capua was completed. But Garibaldi, hearing some talk of difficulties and dangers in the Capital, swept all this aside. 'Naples is in danger,' he said, rising to put an end to the conference. 'We must go there to-day ; we must go this minute.' His friends were horror-struck, but they knew better than to resist. His decision was approved by the event, and indeed hesitation on his part might have dispelled the illusion of his invincible power and compromised his peaceful occupation of the city. And thus he was able to enter, as he wished, not like a conqueror surrounded by an army, but as a deliverer welcomed and protected by the people.

After despatching a telegram to the Capital announcing their arrival for midday, the Dictator and his party drove out of Salerno, at exactly half-past nine on the morning of Friday the 7th of September, amid another scene of frantic enthusiasm.[1] At the terminus station of Vietri they boarded a special train, which was soon packed to overflowing, first by Garibaldi, his staff, and personal friends, and then by a score of the so-called National

[1] 'At half-past nine we heard the roar of *vivas* in the street, and, coming to the window, saw Garibaldi himself passing in the direction of Vietri. One of the crowd, while cheering in the most frantic manner, suddenly fell in a kind of convulsive fit.   I asked our landlady, a vivacious, black-eyed Calabrese damsel, whether he had not been drinking the General's health. "No," she said, "it is joy. Ah," in a tone of reproach, "you English, who have always been free, cannot imagine the delight of deliverance."   And she made a gesture as if she were about to fly.' *Galton*, 23.

Guard of Salerno, and any one else who could wedge himself through a door or climb on to a carriage-roof. During the journey the Liberator was calm and quietly radiant; so was that other fine soldier, Cosenz, who smiled behind his spectacles at the thought that he would in a few hours see his mother, from whom he had been separated by twelve years of exile. The rest of the company in the train, which included Palmerston's secretary in his red shirt, W. G. Clark the Public Orator of Cambridge University, Captain Forbes, R.N., and Edwin James, Q.C., were for the most part in boisterous and noisy spirits. The Italians kept singing over and over again :—

> ' Siamo Italiani,
>   Giovani freschi,
>   Contro ai Tedeschi
> Vogliam pugnar.
> Viva l'Italia !
> Viva l'Unione !
> Viva Garibaldi !
>   E la libertà ! '

At Nocera the enemy's Bavarians, entrained for Capua, were shunted to let the victors pass. A little before they reached Pompeii, Garibaldi, who sat by the window on the side towards the mountain, said, 'Look out, we shall soon see Vesuvius.' When its cone and streamer hove in sight, Cosenz was visibly moved by the familiar form of the mountain of his boyhood.

It was a day of scorching Southern sun. Beyond Pompeii the train made slow progress even for an express south of Naples, for between Torre Annunziata and Portici the line was occupied by tens of thousands of the inhabitants of that densely populated coast. Fishermen who left their nets on the beach, swarthy fellows naked to the waist who had been winnowing corn on the flat roofs of the houses, priests and monks leading their flocks, men, women, and children in countless multitudes, rushed shouting on to the line, and swayed to and fro round the train in their attempts to see and touch Garibaldi.

In his carriage the Mayor of Naples and the staff officers were arranging the route which was to be taken in the streets of the Capital. It was decided to go by the centre of the town and not by the quay-side, lest they should needlessly provoke the Bourbon garrison by dragging the triumphal procession under the muzzles of the cannon at the Carmine and Castel Nuovo. Beyond Portici the train was stopped by a naval officer who forced his way into the carriage in a state of frenzy, crying out to the Dictator : ' Where are you going to ? The Bourbon troops have trained their cannon on the station of Naples.' Garibaldi replied unmoved : ' Bother the cannon ! When the people are receiving us like this, there are no cannon,'[1] and ordered the train to proceed. As .they went forward again the Commandant of the National Guard questioned the young officer, and it soon appeared that he was referring only to the cannon in the Carmine Castle close to the station, a danger which they had already taken into account.[2]

In 1860 there were only two short railways in the whole Neapolitan kingdom, connecting Capua and Vietri respectively with the Capital.[3] At that time both these

[1] ' Ma che cannoni ! quando il popolo accoglie in questo modo non vi son cannoni.'

[2] For this account of the journey from Salerno to Naples the best single authority is Rendina's narrative in the Lega del Bene, from which De Cesare's well-known account is drawn. It is wrong in two small points : Peard was not in the train, for he tells us in his MS. journal that he drove separately. Also the terminus station whence they started was at Vietri, no longer at Cava, whence it had been extended that very year; see Murray, 1862, p. xiii, and Galton, 23 ; Times, September 15, p. 10, c. 4 ; Bertani, ii. 193. The narratives of W. G. Clark in Galton, 23-25, of Lacava in Pungolo, September 8, 1904, of Edwin James in Times, September 18, p. 7, c. 3, of Ashley (497), of Zasio (86-87), of Bertani (ii. 193) and of Liborio Romano (73-79), and of Forbes, 232, should be collated for the story of the train journey.

[3] The first of these had a branch line from Cancello to Nola and Sarno and the second a still shorter branch to Castellamare. Murray, 1858, p. xlviii, and 1862, p. xiii.

lines terminated in a small junction some few hundred yards nearer to the sea than the present Central Station of Naples.[1] On the morning of September 7 the timid silence of the streets was broken by Count Ricciardi, who drove along the Toledo, standing up in his carriage with the Italian flag and shouting out to the citizens that they should assemble at the station to greet the Dictator, who would arrive there at midday. But most men preferred to wait and see if Ricciardi's prophecy would be fulfilled before they committed themselves in face of the garrison, and it was a crowd of relatively moderate proportions that assembled at the appointed hour and place. Don Liborio, however, and the National Guard were there to represent the official world. An hour and a half passed by, till at 1.30 the train was seen to approach, and the Liberator stepped out on to the platform.

As fast as the news that he had come spread through Naples, the whole city awoke as from sleep; myriads seemed to spring out of the ground, and before Don Liborio had finished reading an address of welcome to which no one even pretended to listen, an irresistible multitude stormed the station, swept aside every official barrier, swamped the lines of the National Guard, and took Garibaldi to itself. Don Liborio was whirled off on the flood and could not fight his way to the coveted seat in the Dictator's carriage. Cosenz, who had an equally good right to be next his chief, was borne down another eddy, but secured a horse and rode off to see his mother. After a few minutes' fierce battling, Garibaldi found refuge in an open carriage, into which Bertani and half a dozen of his old fighting companions managed to climb after him,[2] 'such fine old heads with whitened beards, and all with their red shirts covered with purple stains, like English hunting-coats which have been

[1] *Murray*, 1858 and 1862, maps.
[2] According to Zasio, who was one of them, the others were Bertani, Nullo, Gusmaroli, Manci, and Stagnetti, while Cosenz and Missori went on horseback. *Zasio*, 87.

through sundry squire-traps,' as a lady wrote who watched the simple procession pass.   At the back of the carriage clung a Neapolitan artist named Salazaro holding over their heads an enormous tricolour with the horse of Naples on one side and the lion of Venice on the other. In this fashion, without official escort or guard of any kind, 'did a son of the people,' to use Garibaldi's own words, 'accompanied by a few of his friends who called themselves his *aides-de-camp*, enter the proud Capital acclaimed by its 500,000 inhabitants, whose fierce and irresistible will paralysed an entire army.'

According to the official plan, Garibaldi was to have entered Naples by the centre of the city in order to avoid the forts.   But outside the station, in what is now the Corso Garibaldi, the mob turned to the left instead of to the right, and in another minute they were passing under the muzzles of the loaded cannon of the Carmine.   The soldiers were seen looking out at the carriage and its occupants, whom they could have blasted to pieces by moving a finger.   Garibaldi stood up, folded his arms, and looked them straight in the face.   Some of them saluted and no one fired a shot.   It is true that they were only acting in accordance with the pacific orders of the King, but it is a matter of deep congratulation that no one in that unscrupulous and ill-disciplined force was tempted loyally to disobey.

The mob had now reached the water's edge, and as the carriage turned to the right round the corner of the Carmine its occupants were greeted by the most amazing sight and sound.   For a mile long, the broad quay-side was packed by as many of the half-million inhabitants of Naples as could find standing room, and all at first sight of Garibaldi broke out in one protracted yell of welcome. Along the north side of the quay, lined by tall commercial buildings, every window was astir with faces and waving arms and fluttering handkerchiefs.   On the other side, where lay the great port crowded with shipping of all nations, every mast was loaded with sailors shouting or

singing songs of welcome in chorus.   In middle distance,
far overhead, the tyrant's castle of S. Elmo looked down
upon the scene.

When the procession first left the station, Garibaldi
had 'sat for the most part apparently unmoved, but from
time to time he lifted his hat, and smiled, as it were, with
the eyes rather than the lips.'   But as they began to pass
along the quay, he 'stood up,' writes Zasio of the Thousand, who was with him in the carriage ; 'his head was
uncovered, and his face in token of reverence (*in atto
riverente*) betrayed deep emotion.'   The carriage moved
at a foot's pace on the long, open quay, and before it
reached the shadow of the Castel Nuovo his bared
features seemed to his companions in the carriage to have
bronzed visibly under the scorching rays of the sun.
'Did you ever see such a triumph ?' asked Bertani of
Zasio.   'No, not *seen* it,' replied the veteran, 'but I have
often *dreamt* of it for the chief.'

At length they reached the Castel Nuovo, sinister of
aspect with its tall round towers of black tufa.   Here
again they might have been blown to pieces, but here
again the enemy's sentinels saluted, and the guard turned
out to do him honour.   Thence he was carried along the
side of the Palace, also occupied by a Bourbon regiment.

The Foresteria, an annexe of the Palace used for the
entertainment of Court guests, was the goal of the procession.   It stood on one side of the Largo San Francesco
di Paola, an immense open space which was packed tight
with spectators.[1]   From the windows of the Foresteria
Garibaldi looked out sideways on the front of the Palace
a few yards off with the enemy's soldiers in the gateway,
and straight below him on the heads of the vast multitude,
whom he addressed as follows : 'You have a right to
exult in this day, which is the beginning of a new epoch
not only for you but for all Italy, of which Naples forms
the fairest portion.   It is, indeed, a glorious day and

[1] The Foresteria is now (1911) the Prefettura, and the Largo San Francesco
di Paola is called Piazza del Plebiscito.

holy—that on which a people passes from the yoke of servitude to the rank of a free nation. I thank you for this welcome, not only for myself, but in the name of all Italy, which your aid will render free and united.'[1] His speech showed clearly that it was of the union of Italy that he was thinking as much as of the liberation of Naples.

From the Foresteria he was taken to the Cathedral, where he was again almost smothered by the embraces of men and women. His fighting friar, Sicilian Pantaleo, conducted the service, and the terrified canons showed him the relics of St. Januarius, on the virtues of which he maintained a judicious silence.[2]

Thence he was taken to the Palazzo d'Angri, now chosen as his permanent head-quarters. It is a fine private mansion, standing conspicuously, half-way up the mile-long Toledo at the debouchment of another important street, so that its balconies look down on both thoroughfares. The people filed in endless procession up and down the two streets, while Garibaldi showed himself to them on one of the highest balconies of the tall palace.

The inhabitants of Naples were now in full delirium, gyrating through the streets like the dance of all the devils on the witches' Sabbath. True joy at liberation from tyranny moved the greater part of them; the feverish desire for the excitement of an unexampled *festa* drove on the rest, many of whom had been Bourbonists a few months before, and would be Bourbonists again if the King returned. Men and women waved swords

---

[1] This is the version of W. G. Clark, an ear-witness (*Galton*, 26). There are various others, to much the same effect.

[2] Next day (Sept. 8) he attended the popular religious festival of Piedigrotta, which had always been attended by the Monarchs of Naples : he had said at the Straits that he would be at Naples in time for that feast, and he kept his word. On September 19 the Blood of St. Januarius duly liquefied for the benefit of the Dictator's Government, following precedent, since it had liquefied for the benefit of the atheist French Republicans in 1799. Garibaldi was not present at the performance. *Galton*, 29, 53-55. *Zasio*, 92.

which they would never wield in earnest, and brandished daggers which they were more accustomed to employ. As the night wore on, the various cries of *Viva Garibardo, Gallibar, Galliboard* were finally shortened into *Viva 'Board*. When the voice gave out, a single finger was held up in token of the union of Italy. Even after the first rage was spent, the Saturnalia continued intermittently for three days and nights in the thousand noisome alleys which composed the Naples of that era.

But in the Toledo, while the crowd on the first evening was shouting under the Palazzo d'Angri for the Dictator to reappear, a red-shirt stepped out on the balcony and laid his cheek on his hand in token that his chief was sleeping. '*Egli dorme*,' whispered the vast multitude and dispersed in silence. During the rest of that night's carnival the centre of the city was left as noiseless and deserted as the streets of Pompeii.[1]

[1] The following are the authorities on which my account of the entry is based. I consider the first seven of them the most important. *Zasio*, 87-91. *Galton*, 25-28 (Clark's narrative). *Lega del Bene*, December, 1888 (Rendina's narrative). *Pungolo*, September 8, 1904. *Trinity*, 236-242. *De Cesare*, ii. 430-433. *Times*, September 13, p. 10, c. 3 ; September 15, p. 10, c. 5 ; September 18, p. 7, c. 3. *Meuricoffre*, 51-52. *Nisco*, 122. *Dumas*, 367. *De Sivo*, iv. 67. *D'Ayala*, 320-326. *Cosenz*, 20. *Liborio Romano*, 79-80. *Conv. Missori. Mem.* 380. *Monnier*, 283. *Menghini*, 461. *Salazaro*, 54-55. *J. des D.* September 15, 1860. *Ashley*, 499. *Bertani*, ii. 194. *Colet*, iii. 12.

CHAPTER IX

GARIBALDI'S MISTAKES IN NAPLES. THE CHECK BEFORE CAPUA

'Tra qualche anno, di tutti questi piccoli guai, che ora ci preoccupano tanto, chi si ricorderà? D'una cosa sola ci ricorderemo tutti, e per sempre: ci ricorderemo che in questi due anni s'è fatta l'Italia!' *Manzoni's saying in the winter of* 1860. (*Venosta*, 607.)

'In a few years who will recollect all these little troubles which now obsess our minds? One thing only we shall all of us remember for ever: we shall remember that in these two years Italy was made.'

On September 8, the day after Garibaldi's entry, the Bourbon commandant of the castle of S. Elmo sent word that he could no longer restrain his men from bombarding the city at their feet. 'Very well,' said the Dictator, 'let them fire, and we will fire back.' He had on that day no military force in Naples except the National Guard, who were fit only for policing the streets, but his fearless tone quelled the enemy's soldiers. They did not open fire, and in the course of the next three days handed over all the four castles to the National Guard. None of the outgoing regiments would listen to the invitations to desert that were showered upon them, but marched off scowling at the people, full of zeal to join their King and comrades in the last stand behind the Volturno.[1] The loyalty of the army to the Bourbons, even stronger among the rank and file than among the officers, defeated the calculations alike of Garibaldi and of Cavour, who had each confidently expected that if the revolution succeeded at all, the army would come over wholesale to aid in the wars of liberation for the rest of the Peninsula.[2]

[1] *Türr's Div.* 161. *D'Ayala*, 328. *Mundy*, 245. *Forbes*, 239-240.
[2] *Spaventa*, 297-298. *Bandi*, 268-269. *Conv. Venosta.*

NAPLES, LAST PART OF GARIBALDI'S ROUTE ALONG THE QUAY

(St. Elmo in distance on hill; Castle Nuovo on left, middle distance.)

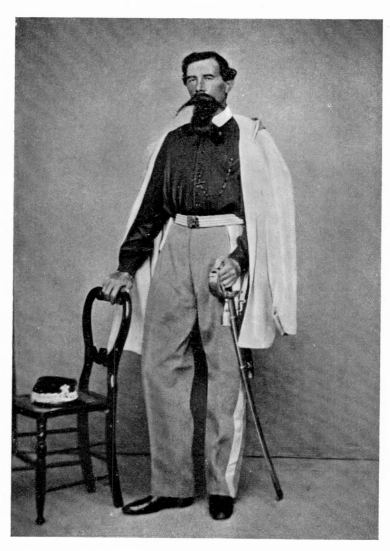

GENERAL TÜRR, 1860

The loyalty of the soldiers was a measure of their professional feeling and of their isolation from the community at large, to whom they had been related not as defenders of the fatherland or representatives of the national honour, but as the tyrant's body-guard kept to repress the citizens. Therefore they were left untouched by the tide of popular sentiment for United Italy, and while one-half of them rallied round Francis II at Capua and Gaeta, the other 50,000 disbanded and went sulkily to their homes or took to the hills as brigands.

In the north of the kingdom, where a part of the population itself was reactionary under clerical influence, there ensued a state of sporadic civil war of which the worst horrors had been spared to the southern provinces. On September 8 news reached the Dictator from the district of Ariano to the east of the capital that Generals Bonanno and Flores with 4000 Bourbon troops had there roused up the Royalist peasantry, who were robbing, massacring, and raping in the houses of the Liberals. The first 1500 of Garibaldi's army who arrived in Naples on the 9th were allowed only a few hours' rest before they were sent off again to quell the insurrection. Türr, who went in command, took them by train to Nola, there put them into carts and carriages and drove with the utmost speed to the scene of operations. Bonanno, in spite of his superior numbers, agreed without a blow to disband his force. It appears that conversations with comrades returning to their homes from Calabria had so much discouraged his men that he no longer dared rely upon them to fight.

Türr acted not only with vigour but with clemency. He shot two of the ring-leaders of the peasant massacre, though the local Liberals who had suffered begged him to shoot a round dozen, and disliked the practical application of his doctrine that a new era of liberty and brotherhood had dawned for all Italians. The repression of similar reactionary massacres in Molise and the

Abruzzi, as conducted by General Cialdini and the Piedmontese regulars in the later months of the year, was on a scale of vengeance more calculated to satisfy the local demand than anything that Garibaldi or his lieutenants were ever known to permit.[1]

The arrival in Naples of the rest of the army from Calabria and Basilicata was accelerated by the help of the newly acquired shipping of the port. Some of the regiments in the rear were brought by sea from Paola and some from Sapri, while others marched. The last division under Medici reached Naples on September 15 and the following days. In the course of a quarrel at Paola for the first passage on board a steamer, Nino Bixio had broken the heads of several of his companions in arms with the butt end of a musket; as usual he repented of his savage rage and made friends with the victim whom he had nearly killed.[2]

Cavour was agreeably surprised by the Dictator's first acts in Naples. On the evening of his entry, before he lay down to rest, he had issued a decree generously handing over the whole Neapolitan fleet to King Victor Emmanuel, and placing it forthwith under the orders of Admiral Persano, to the detriment of his own power and authority. Three days later he invited a battery of Piedmontese artillery and a battalion of Bersaglieri in the harbour to land and co-operate with him in garrisoning Naples. He also chose Moderates and Cavourians as his Ministers, among others, Liborio Romano, whom he continued in the offices which he had held under Francis II. These first steps, taken as Cavour knew on the advice of the sage Cosenz, proved to all the world that no thought lurked in Garibaldi's mind of any ultimate settlement for Sicily and Naples except union under the

[1] *Franci*, i. 103-104, 232-234. *Türr's Div.* 161-172. *Türr's Risposta*, 16-19. *Rüstow Brig. Mil.* 27-33. *Abba Not.* 234.
[2] *Türr's Div.* 178-180, 514-515, and map. *Castellini*, 61-64. *Bandi*, 279-282. *Adamoli*, 153-155.

monarchy of Victor Emmanuel.[1] But he intended to
postpone that union until he could proclaim the King of
Italy on the Capitol, and he publicly announced that he
would march on Rome over the last ruins of the Neapolitan army on the Volturno.

The desire to march to the deliverance of the Holy
City was inspired in his mind not by political calculation
but by poetic passion, by the memories of antiquity and
of his own defence of the Janiculum in '49. The romantic
element was the strongest in his nature and ruled him
for good or evil at all the great crises of his life. The
lover's passion for Rome was fostered in him by Bertani
and the other extremists, who saw in it a means towards
their own political ends. It was to them a method of
delaying annexation until it could be effected on terms
fatal to Cavour's continuance in office and dangerous to
the prestige of the monarchy, which would be reduced
to the position of accepting the crown of Italy as a
gift at the hands of the revolutionary leader.

Garibaldi and the Mazzinians were alike under a
delusion as to the practicability of taking the city of
Rome. They believed that the French people were on
the Italian side in this matter, and that the tyrant,
Napoleon III, when seriously challenged, would be
forced to withdraw his garrison from Rome for fear of
revolution in France. They were equally wrong about
prince and people : in reality the clerical and anti-Italian
feeling of the France of that day was the main reason
why Napoleon could not utterly desert the Pope, for
whom at heart he had little love.

Until, in the latter half of September, it became
apparent that the Bourbon forces rallied behind the
Volturno were strong enough to check Garibaldi's advance on Rome, Cavour was at his wits' end for ways
and means to prevent a complication which must involve
Italy either in civil war or in war with France. Know-

---

[1] *Persano*, 222, 239. *Savio*, i. 323. *Chiala*, vi. 594. *Cosenz, Guardione*, 55.
Elliot, 96, 102-103.

ing that he had lost all influence of his own with the Dictator, Cavour turned in every direction to find others who could remonstrate with better chance of success. At his instigation Kossuth wrote to Garibaldi, congratulating him on his triumphs in the cause of freedom, and imploring him not to embroil Italy with France in a quarrel under the walls of Rome, that could only redound to the advantage of Austria at the expense of Hungary and of Venice.[1]

Cavour even commandeered the services of the English to remonstrate with their favourite. Lord Shaftesbury wrote from London to tell Garibaldi that he gave thanks to God for his success, and to conjure him not to imperil it by attacking the Pope too soon.[2] Even Edwin James, the barrister on a holiday, had been set on to use his influence with the Dictator in favour of immediate annexation.[3] Persano implored Admiral Mundy, for whom Garibaldi had conceived a great affection since the events of Palermo,[4] to persuade his friend not to advance on Rome. Lord John Russell had instructed Elliot, the British Minister to the deposed King, to remain at Naples, and if possible to dissuade its new master from attacking Venice. Elliot and Mundy therefore arranged an unofficial meeting between themselves and Garibaldi in the cabin of H.M.S. *Hannibal.* It took place on September 10. Bertani, who followed the Dictator about like his evil genius, had to be asked twice to quit the cabin before he would leave his victim alone with the two Englishmen. His fears on this occasion were groundless, for Garibaldi, though cordial and patient, was impervious to all representations of the dangers into which his further advance would plunge Italy. He repeated in a tone of enthusiasm that he

---

[1] *Chiala's Pol. Seg.* 129-142.
[2] *Mem. Stor. Mil.* ii. 188. The letter (September 17) is there wrongly attributed to Lord ' Salisbury,' but the reference to ' my son Evelyn ' (Ashley) shows the writer was really ' Shaftesbury.'
[3] *Times,* September 18, p. 7, c. 3.
[4] See *Garibaldi and the Thousand,* pp. 290, 311, 317-320.

would first crown Victor Emmanuel in Rome, and that then the task of liberating Venice would devolve upon the King.[1]

The conduct of Bertani in Naples was unworthy of his former great services to Italy. He who had once done so much to bring together Garibaldi and Cavour now worked only too successfully to divide them. He became the mouthpiece of self-seeking politicians like Rattazzi and his friends, who, hoping to step into Cavour's ministerial shoes, were not ashamed to write that 'Garibaldi was the only person who could strike him down.'[2] Urged on by such counsellors, Bertani daily inflamed the Dictator's hatred against 'the man who had sold Nice,' regardless of the fact that the man was now, in consequence, liberating the Papal Marches.[3] Garibaldi published a letter stating that he could never again work with Cavour,[4] and then sent a note to Victor Emmanuel asking him to dismiss his great Minister.[5] Bertani indeed advised Garibaldi against this last step, not because he wished Cavour to remain in office, but because he rightly foresaw that the request would be refused, and Cavour's position strengthened.[6]

Unlike Rattazzi, Bertani was at least disinterested ; he was not seeking Cavour's place, but the union of Italy. He had impaired his health and his mental balance by working day and night on his sick-bed at Genoa, organ-

---

[1] *Mundy*, 238-244. *F. O. Sicily, Elliot*, September 8, Mundy's letter. *Elliot* 99-101. *Persano*, 240-241.

[2] Luzio's article in *Corriere della Sera*, March 1, 1910, on the *Archivio Bertani*.

[3] On September 11 the Piedmontese regular troops crossed the Papal frontier and Persano started with his fleet from Naples for the Adriatic to bombard the Pope's fortress of Ancona.

[4] *Ciàmpoli*, 181. *F. O. Sicily, Elliot*, No. 525, September 18.

[5] The note was delivered to the King by Trecchi late on September 23, having been taken to Turin by Pallavicino—see the narrative of Pallavicino's secretary, *Caranti*, 18-19. This must not be confused with the mission of Brambilla and Trecchi to the King ten days before ; it was not *then*, as was wrongly asserted, that the demand for Cavour's dismissal was made, see *Brambilla*, 42, *Bertani*, ii. 208-209. *F. O. Sicily, Elliot*, September 28, and above all *Bianchi, Polit. de Cavour*, p. 384 and note.

[6] *Bertani*, ii. 219.

ising half the forces by means of which Garibaldi had
reached Naples.   He had brought on Italian unity by
such giant strides that year, that he could not believe
it necessary to call a halt.   He had by his rival activities
compelled Cavour to invade the Papal States himself,
and he could not see that, although, thanks to Cavour's
manipulation of Napoleon, Umbria and the Marches were
fair game, France still threw her shield over the city of
Rome.   On September 19 he persuaded the Dictator to
send round 300 men under Cadolini to land at Terracina
in the Papal States in order to prepare the way for the
advance of the main Garibaldian army on Rome.   The
orders for this foolish expedition were actually given,
but were rescinded at the advice of Sirtori.[1]   Garibaldi's
military lieutenants, Sirtori, Cosenz, Türr, Medici, and
Bixio, were all opposed to the extravagant counsels of
the civilians Bertani, Crispi, and Mazzini.

For Mazzini, too, was in Naples.   He arrived on
September 17[2] and remained, not in hiding, but in obscurity.   A stranger, who met him one evening in a
private house without knowing at first who he was,
describes him as 'an old man with a sweet voice saying
wise and noble things' to a group of Garibaldian officers
who listened to his words with profound respect.[3]   When
he touched actual politics, he was less happily inspired.
He wrote on September 23 to Garibaldi, saying that he
preferred not to come to see him in the crowd at the
Palazzo d'Angri, but that he hoped the Dictator would
offer these terms to Victor Emmanuel—immediate annexation of Naples in return for the dismissal of Cavour
and war with the Austrians in Venetia.[4]   The Dictator
would probably have been better pleased if Mazzini had
stayed away, but since he had come, he would listen to
no suggestion for sending him back, and when the scum

[1] *Mem. Stor. Mil.* ii. 182 (Cadolini).   *Ire Pol.* 67-68 (Bertani).
[2] *Fam. Crauford*, 227.   [3] *Paolucci's Corrao*, 144.
[4] Letter published in *Giornale d'Italia*, June 6, 1907, from Achille Fazzari's
MSS.

of Naples shouted 'death to Mazzini' under his windows, Garibaldi protected him and rebuked the rioters.[1]

To the men who were making Italy, Mazzini's arrival in Naples was an exasperating addition to the dangers of the gamble on which their country's existence was staked; so long as he continued to play a part, and a mistaken part upon the whole, in political affairs, it was impossible for all men to give the father of Italian Unity his meed of thanks, and to be always remembering that but for his work in the 'thirties and 'forties there would have been no 1860. Throughout this year when his life's work was being brought to fruition by others, Mazzini was in a state of melancholy resignation, for although he felt confident that the union of Italy was at hand, it was not the idealist Italy which he had striven to evoke. He sought no thanks for himself from the country which he had made, and dreamt of no apotheosis, but only of a speedy end to life in his English land of exile, now grown dear to him. 'Unity,' he writes to Mrs. Taylor, 'you may consider as settled, and so far, so good. The rest is all wrong. And as for myself, don't talk of either prosperity or consciousness of having done, etc. All that is chaff. The only real good thing would be to have unity achieved quickly through Garibaldi, and one year, before dying, of Walham Green or Eastbourne, long silences, a few affectionate words to smooth the ways, plenty of seagulls, and sad dozing.'[2]

Except that there was less unanimity on behalf of the National cause, the attitude of the people of Naples after the entry of Garibaldi closely resembled that of the people of Palermo three months before. In Naples as in Palermo, devotion to the person of the Liberator was deep and genuine, and did not grow less on closer acquaintance. The southern populations found him far more *simpatico* than they found other Northerners, and

[1] *Mignona*, 229. *Mario's Mazzini*, 413.
[2] *King's Mazzini*, 359-360. *Fam. Crauford*, 217, 227-229.

when he retired in November and left them to the Piedmontese officials, they soon wished him back again.
But so long as he was with them, though they were never
tired of cheering him, they were annoyed by his policy
of postponing the annexation, in which alone they saw
a sure way of safety. The reason why the Neapolitans
shouted 'death' under the windows of Mazzini was that
he opposed immediate and unconditional annexation.
They wished Victor Emmanuel to come at once to
give them security and peace.

The impatience of the Neapolitans with the *interim*
government of the Dictator was increased by faults of
administration. Many common convicts were let out of
prison on the ground that they were political prisoners,
and stabbing and crime grew more rife than ever.[1] The
moderate Ministers whom Garibaldi had chosen on his
first entry found themselves overridden by the Dictator's
secretary, Bertani, who treated them as cyphers and
carried on the most important acts of government without consulting them. On September 22 the Ministry
sent in their resignation; five days later it was accepted,
and their places were taken by more passive tools of the
omnipotent 'Secretariat.'[2] The despotism of Bertani
and of Crispi, who succeeded him on September 30 as
secretary without altering the policy pursued,[3] would
have been endured gladly if it had meant order and a
peaceable transition towards the approaching regime of
Italian Unity. But it seemed rather to tend to anarchy
and maladministration. The hopes of the reactionaries
revived, and seditious correspondence was set on foot
between Naples and Gaeta.[4] Neither Garibaldi nor
Bertani had any conception of the proper limits to which
a Provisional Government should confine its work, and
many of their decrees made important changes in the

---

[1] *Russell MSS.* Elliot's letter of October 8.

[2] *Liborio Romano,* 84. *Ferrigni,* 66-70. *De Cesare's F. di P.* ccviii-ccxv.
Bertani, ii. 217. *F. O. Sicily, Elliot,* No. 540, September 29.

[3] *Crispi,* 1911, p. 313. *Bertani.* ii. 222-224.

[4] *D'Ayala,* 337-340.

principles of law, finance, and State machinery, which should have been left to the mature decision of the future Italian Parliament.[1]

Europe was justly shocked by a Dictatorial decree giving a pension to the mother of Agesilao Milano, the idealist fanatic who had attempted to assassinate *Bomba*,[2] though it is possible to plead, in mitigation of Garibaldi's offence, the flattery long bestowed on Milano's memory by eminently respectable persons in England as well as in Italy.

A more innocent act of patronage was more loudly blamed in Naples. The Dictator nominated Alexandre Dumas as honorary Director of the National Museum and excavations. Dumas, who really loved the Italian cause and had, in his swaggering way, done more for it than was pleasing to the Government and the fashionable classes of his own country, was ungratefully accused by the Neapolitans of dipping his fingers into their public purse. It was true that if he had not undertaken the duties of the Directorate for nothing, it might have been given as a paid post to some native. The appointment of a foreigner was unwise, apart from all question of the novelist's equipment as an archæologist. But Dumas was subjected to much undeserved abuse.[3]

All these political questions and quarrels revolving round the central problem whether or not annexation should be immediate and unconditional, found their solution in military events against which there was no appeal—the check of Garibaldi before Capua and the success of Victor Emmanuel's troops in the Papal States.

In return for the supreme sacrifice of his capital, King Francis had obtained a new position of strength, geographically and politically suited for a successful rally of the Royalist element in the army and the kingdom.

[1] *F. O. Sicily, Elliot*, No. 512, September 15.
[2] See *Garibaldi and the Thousand*, p. 67.
[3] *Berlani*, ii. 209. *Du Camp. Souvenirs*, ii. 246-258.

Gaeta afforded a secure base of operation, and in the event of defeat a last stronghold which could hold out for months even against a regular army with siege guns. But the front line of defence was the northern bank of the lower Volturno, a deep, muddy river, fordable at widely scattered points known as *scafe* or ' ferries.' The only bridge was that which led into Capua. The celebrated Monsieur Vauban, whose creations so often baffled William III and retarded Marlborough, had designed the defences of Capua, and they had been modernised and enlarged by a Russian military architect as late as 1855. The bastions, well furnished with cannon, proved strong enough to oppose a final limit to Garibaldi's career of victory. This impregnable *tête du pont* of Capua enabled the Bourbon troops to cross the river whenever they wished, and to debouch on the cultivated plain on the south bank, which was admirably suited for the operations of regular troops against ill-disciplined levies.

Behind these strong barriers raised by art and nature the Royalists rallied round their King. There were no longer any constitutional Ministers, any officers or privates of doubtful loyalty to create an atmosphere of division and distrust. The white flag of the Bourbons was again unfurled, the tricolour and the constitution were stowed away together and reactionary passions were no longer discouraged and concealed. In the course of September some 50,000 soldiers assembled in the lines, some of them from distant parts of the kingdom, all having come voluntarily and out of genuine devotion to a fallen cause. The privates were still the most enthusiastic grade in the service, but disloyal officers were no longer to be found in the camp.[1] The fighting spirit shown by the Bourbon troops in the battles of September and October, after the Capital had been surrendered without a blow, contrasts strangely with the manner in

[1] *Cava*, 13 note. *De Sivo*, iv. 106-110. *Maria Sophia*, 138-139. *Conv. Primerano.* For the numbers see Appendix J, below.

which they had fled and disbanded in August, when the
royal cause had been in a far less desperate condition.
The change was partly due to the presence of the King
in their midst, and to the fact that they no longer had
half-hearted friends within and a hostile population
around. But there always remains something inscrutable
to Northerners in the vagaries of the Southern tempera-
ment.

The Volturno region was not only militarily but politically well chosen. The peasants were the most reactionary in the kingdom, and the friendly border of the
Papal States was close in the rear. It was suggested in
high quarters that Lamoricière, who commanded the
Pope's army of foreign crusaders in Umbria, should make
a forced march southward, unite with King Francis'
troops and carry him back in triumph to Naples. On
the advice of Persigny, the French Ambassador in London,
King Francis telegraphed from Gaeta to ask for the
Pope's consent to this plan.[1] But the invasion of the
Papal States by the armies of Victor Emmanuel from the
north gave the Pope's generals plenty to do at home.

The Bourbon position on the Volturno was by no
means merely defensive. It threatened Naples, which
was divided from Capua by no more than eighteen miles
of flat ground, well supplied with country roads concen-
trating on the Capital. Garibaldi's nominal attack on
Capua soon became no better than a defence of Naples
conducted with great difficulty and peril before the gates
of Capua.

To the 50,000 Bourbon regulars gathered behind the
Volturno, Garibaldi by the end of September opposed
some 20,000 volunteers. Besides his own field army,
there were ' insurrectionary bands ' and private regiments
enlisted throughout all the provinces under his Dictatorship. When his forces were paid off in November it was

---

[1] *Persigny*, 276-277. Did Napoleon know of his Ambassador's advice ? I
doubt it. I suppose that as he did things behind the backs of his Ministers and
Ambassadors, they took similar liberties with him.

stated officially that as many as 50,000 names appeared
on the muster rolls, but Garibaldi himself declared that
only a third of those enrolled ever came near the scene
of actual conflict. Sicily held seven out of the fifty thousand, and besides those who were engaged in garrisoning
and patrolling the Capital, and the southern provinces,
thousands of ne'er-do-weels drew pay for trailing rifles
and sabres in the cafés of Naples and parading themselves along the streets in uniforms of many colours.[1]

The force actually at the front, varying during
September and October from 15,000 to 20,000 men, was
mainly composed of Northern volunteers. But there
were among them 3000 Calabrians and Lucanians and
about as many Sicilians; the city of Naples, so Türr
reported in the middle of October, had sent exactly eighty
of her half-million inhabitants to join the army protecting
her on the Volturno.[2]

Dispassionate observers of the Garibaldini in that
autumn agreed that they contained 'the cream and the
dregs' of the nation.[3] When the Thousand sailed for
Sicily in May there had been no dregs, but the process of adulteration had been continuous ever since, the
bad element increasing in exact proportion to the success
already achieved, until after the occupation of Naples
the red shirt covered as much heroism and baseness as
has ever been concealed by cloth of any colour. Garibaldi's lifelong dream of the *levée-en-masse* of regenerated
Italians, which was to sweep French and Austrian back
across the Alps, wrecked itself on the realities of human
nature and the stern requirements of effective military
organisation. Instead of the 150,000 men for whom he
had hoped, he got 50,000, out of whom perhaps not more
than half could look the enemy in the face. But of these
several thousands were of really heroic mould, and it was

[1] *Risorg.* anno iii. fasc. 1-2, pp. 87-88, and Appendix J, below. *Orero,* 106.
Revel's da Ancona, 114-117. *Zasio,* 104-105.
[2] *Russell MSS.* Appendix A, p. 313 below.
[3] ' *Fiore e feccia.*' *Corsi's Rimembranze,* 28.

these few who saved Italy on the Volturno.[1] The further supply of the best sort of fighters had been cut off by Cavour, who since the middle of August had stopped the exodus of volunteers from Genoa and the North.[2] By cutting off the supply of men, Cavour secured his object of rendering Garibaldi too weak to attack Rome, but in so doing he nearly caused him to lose Naples.

Garibaldi's head-quarters were established in the Palace at Caserta. This monotonous and gigantic edifice is at least more pleasing than Versailles, in imitation of which it was built by Vanvitelli, architect to Carlos III, *Bomba's* great-grandfather. It has been reared upon the plain, but a mile behind it, at the end of the long Palace garden, rises a steep mountain range of white limestone, on the top of which can be seen in the distance the ruined castle and hill-town of Old Caserta.[3] Out of the mountain-side spouts and tumbles a force of water conducted from twenty miles away into that arid region by the great aqueduct of Vanvitelli, which spans the Maddaloni valley with a structure worthy of Imperial

[1] Mr. W. G. Clark gives the following account of his twofold impression at Caserta (*Galton*, 62-63) :—

‘ When I reached the railway station, I found a train of empty trucks and cattle waggons just starting. A number of the red-shirted gentry demanded that a carriage should be attached to it for their use. The stationmaster declared that he had none, whereupon they threatened, hustled, and collared him, and finally carried him off to the Palace to answer to some one for his contumacy. . . . The train started without waiting for the issue of the dispute. I got upon a truck with a number of common soldiers (Garibaldians), whose behaviour presented a very favourable contrast to that of their officers. One provided me with an inverted basket to sit upon, another compelled me to accept a cigar, a third insisted upon my taking a cartridge as a keepsake. One of them had been an artist, he told me, and had abandoned his easel at Milan to carry a musket in Calabria. Never, surely, was there such a motley army as this. It contains men of all ranks, and of all characters. There are men of high birth and gentle breeding, there are also outcasts and vagabonds ; there are generous and chivalrous enthusiasts, there are also charlatans and impostors, and unhappily it is not always the former who fill the highest places.’ From the mass of other evidence which I have read, I should not say that the officers were badly selected in the better regiments. But see p. 246 below.

[2] See pp. 122-123 above. *Mario Supp.* 280.

[3] See Map III, B, at end of book.

Rome.   Below the cataract at Caserta the water glides more gently towards the Palace, from basin to basin, between groups of classical statues and dark groves of evergreen.   At such pains was this artificial river brought to the King's country seat by the first and most popular of the Neapolitan Bourbons, who realised the highest ideal of kingship as understood under the *ancien régime* : for he did not forget to send on the water to irrigate the plain and to supply the Capital.   Carlos III died the year before the French Revolution began, and his descendants failed to adapt themselves to the new era. And so now, among these groves so long reserved for princes, the Garibaldini were encamped, poaching the Royal pheasants much to the subsequent scandal of Victor Emmanuel's lackeys, who thought that the sacred birds ought to have been kept till their master arrived to shoot them.

While the advanced guard over against Capua held Santa Maria and Sant' Angelo in Formis, the reserve was bivouacked in the courtyards and gardens of Caserta Palace, and on the great parade ground that lies between it and the station.   As in the Palace at Palermo, Garibaldi and his staff occupied some of the smallest rooms they could find.   The Dictator enjoyed this much of kingly pomp, that wherever he appeared, in the field or in the street, any band that perceived him at once struck up 'Garibaldi's hymn.'[1]   And he was now attended by a body-guard of red-shirts, whom it amused him to arm with a set of pompous halberds from one of the State rooms of the Palace.   The principal duty of the body-guard was to save him from the hundreds of petitioners who besieged his door day and night, clamouring for offices and pensions and for revenge upon their private enemies.   Rival committees, mutually denouncing each other as Bourbonists with the envenomed sycophancy of the Levantine, revolted the soul of Garibaldi.   He passed them on as far as might be to Bertani in Naples, and was

[1] *Conv. Dolmage.*   For the music of the ' hymn ' see pp. 298-304 below.

glad to spend all the hours of daylight on horseback upon the mountains, whither they could not follow him. But when he returned to Caserta each night, he found them still at their posts before his door.

His habit of retiring at nightfall and rising before dawn saved him from prolonged contact with this human plague. At Caserta he was always up and about before his staff. Once, indeed, shortly after midnight, while Nullo and Zasio were still sitting on in the outer room, having held festival over some simple luxuries of the camp, their chief came out from his bedroom, fresh from sleep and booted for the day. He nodded and smiled to them as he passed out, and they could only look at each other foolishly enough and murmur, ' He gets up too soon.'

Thus abroad betimes, he proceeded every day to visit the outposts, travelling from Caserta to Santa Maria by train or by carriage, and thence riding along the lines to the village of Sant' Angelo, built at the foot of the mountain out of the ruins of Roman pleasure-villas. Thence he would climb on foot to the summit of Monte Tifata or to the ruined chapel of San Nicola a few yards below, where once a temple of Jupiter had overlooked the rich Capuan plain.[1] Monte Tifata, the most westerly spur of the mountains that lie between the Caudine Forks and Capua, is also one of the highest peaks of the group. It rises almost two thousand feet sheer out of the seaward level. Half its flanks are clothed with forest and half are naked limestone with shrubs and flowers breaking out between the white rocks. Arrived at its summit, Garibaldi felt safe from sycophants and political tormentors of every kind. Here he spent many happy hours in the September sunshine watching through his telescope the movements of his own and of

[1] On some days he took another route, riding up Monte Tifata direct from S. Leucio by the charcoal-burners' path through the woods which clothe the eastern slopes. It is possible to ride up this path, but on the steeper and barer western side towards Sant' Angelo the mountain can only be ascended on foot.

the enemy's columns. On clear days he had the view of every winding of the Volturno from the ferry of Cajazzo to the sea, and of each ribbon of road on the vast plain stretching on all sides of Capua. It was from Monte Tifata that Hannibal had watched, week after week, for the glint of sunshine upon armour which might betray to him some cautious move of Fabius in the plain below, when they two matched wits and Capua was the prize.[1] And now from the same rocks Garibaldi in his turn was watching the red and blue pieces in the game of chess to which he had challenged the Bourbon Generals.[2]

The proper strategy for the Royalists to adopt would have been the very opposite to the delay by which Fabius restored the fortunes of Rome. They should have attacked in the middle of September, while Garibaldi's position at Santa Maria and Sant' Angelo was still a skeleton line. Marshal Ritucci, the commander-in-chief at Capua, unlike the generals of Sicily and Calabria, was neither a coward nor a fool, but he failed to grasp the need for instantly taking the offensive. Overawed by Garibaldi's unbroken record of victory, he preferred Fabian tactics, being sure that he could hold Capua against him.[3] No doubt he calculated that when the Dictator's advance was shown to be permanently checked, his political hold on Naples and South Italy would relax and his volunteer forces melt away. And there was talk of help in a few months' time from Austria or the Pope. Ritucci's plan was well laid, but he had forgotten Cavour. It was the Piedmontese and not the Austrians, Victor Emmanuel and not Lamoricière, who arrived to decide the well-balanced struggle on the banks of the Volturno.

[1] Ancient Capua was on the site of modern Santa Maria, where the amphitheatre still remains. The inhabitants of Capua moved to the present city on the banks of the Volturno in the ninth century A.D.

[2] *Zasio*, 96-104. *Du Camp*, 264-267. *Arrivabene*, ii. 233-234. *Galton*, 52. *Colletta*, i. 85-86. *Forbes*, 278. *Sirtori*, 223. *Times*, October 6, p. 9, c. 3.

[3] *Franci*, ii. 216-217, 221-222.

CHAPTER X

CAVOUR INVADES THE PAPAL STATES WITH THE ARMY OF PIEDMONT

'Su le dentate scintillanti vette
Salta il camoscio, tuona la valanga
Da' ghiacci immani rotolando per le
Selve croscianti.

'Ma da i silenzi de l'effuso azzurro
Esce nel sole l'aquila, e distende
In tarde ruote digradanti il nero
Volo solenne.

'Salve, Piemonte! A te con melodia
Mesta da lungi risonante, come
Gli epici canti del tuo popol bravo
Scendono i fiumi.

'Scendono pieni, rapidi, gagliardi
Come i tuoi cento battaglioni e a valle
Cercan le deste a ragionar di gloria
Ville e cittadi.'

CARDUCCI. *Piemonte.*

'Over the glittering, jagged summit
Leaps the chamois, sounds the avalanche
Off the cruel ice-beds rolling
Through crashing forests.

'Out from the silence, out from the encircling blue,
Floats in the sun the eagle, and extends,
In circles slowly earthward borne, his dark
And solemn flight.

'Hail, Piedmont! hail! to thee with melody
Sad, from afar resounding, like the songs
The heroic songs of thine own mountaineers,
Thy rivers fall.

'Down fall thy rivers, rushing, rapid, full,
Like thy battalions, in the plain below
Seeking the hamlets and the towns astir
With thoughts of glory.'

THE States of the Church, stretching across the Peninsula from sea to sea, opposed a geographical veto to the Union of Italy which Garibaldi's successes in the south had brought into the region of practical politics. At the moment of his entry into Naples the whole of Central Italy from Ancona to Civita Vecchia, from Perugia to Terracina, was still in the most literal sense subject to priestly rule. In the Papal territories priests were the legislators and the administrators, not, like William of Wykeham or Wolsey, lending their abilities to the State at the invitation of the lay power, but acting in their own right divine. Both in theory and in practice priests were the sole judges of what might be published, said, or done by the millions of laymen who chanced to be subjects of the Pope. There was no longer, as in 1848, any attempt at reform from within or concession to the laity. ' We are advised to make reforms,' said Pio Nono (Pius IX) to Odo Russell, the British Resident at Rome ; ' it is not understood that those very reforms, which would consist in giving this country a Government of laymen, would make it cease to exist. It is called the " States of the Church " and that is what it must remain.'[1]

While many of the parish priests, as soon afterwards appeared, shared the desire of their flocks to be ruled by the King of Italy instead of by the Pope,[2] the Roman *curia* was implacable. At no period was the spirit of priestly intolerance and interference exercised with greater impolicy than in these years and months when the threatened theocracy had its last chance of making terms with the modern world. Up to the very day of reckoning the hierarchy seemed to find a pleasure in reminding every layman in Central Italy that he belonged to an enslaved class and must submit to any humiliation or injustice that the Church was pleased to impose. On August 22, 1860, Odo Russell sent home to

[1] *Queen's Letters*, ed. 1907, iii. p. 311, January 14, 1859.
[2] *Gregorovius*, 106. F. O. Rome, *Russell*, No. 170, November 11, 1860.

Lord John an official dispatch narrating a characteristic incident of Papal rule :—

'A respectable tradesman of Civita Vecchia died some days since, and five young men, friends of the deceased, wishing to show the respect and affection they bore towards him, applied to the Ecclesiastical Authority for permission to carry his coffin themselves instead of allowing it to be carried by the religious Confraternity on whom funeral functions usually devolve.

'The request was granted at Civita Vecchia but it appears not approved in Rome, for after four days the young men were arrested in the night at their houses by Papal Gendarmes and conveyed to prison, and the next day they were sent to the State Prisons of Soriano beyond Viterbo, where they will in all probability remain for some months and then be released without trial. The charge brought against them is interference with Ecclesiastical Customs and Privileges.[1]

This system of government was perpetuated no longer by the submissiveness of the Pope's subjects, but by the presence of foreign armies. The troops of Napoleon III held down Rome and the Patrimony of S. Peter. An army of Austrians in the pay of Pio Nono maintained order in Umbria and the Marches. In the summer of 1859 these Eastern Provinces had nominally been evacuated by Austria, but the very same officers and men who had composed the former garrison had been encouraged by the Government of Vienna to go back 6000 strong and enrol themselves in the Papal service.[2]

Thus the newly liberated Romagna was threatened from the south by the Papal forces, of which these Austrians were the main strength, and from the north by the official army of Austria in the Venetian territory. Cavour had no time to lose. He must overwhelm the Pope's army in Umbria and the Marches and make Italy one by joining hands with Garibaldi in Naples. If he delayed it was clear that Austria, as soon as she had recuperated her strength after her losses in the war of 1859, would reconquer North Italy in alliance with the

[1] *Br. Parl. Papers*, vii. p. 55.
[2] *Mérode*, 136, says the Austrians were 'upwards of 6000.' Odo Russell (*F. O. Rome, Russell*, August 31, 1860) puts them at 10,000, and adds: 'The men and officers thus sent by the Austrian Government to General Lamoricière are chiefly those who formed the Austrian garrisons of the Legations before the war in Lombardy and also men who had served in that Province and in Venetia. A *de facto* Austrian occupation is thereby gradually being re-established in the Adriatic Provinces of the Holy See.'

H

Pope. Cavour, well aware of the necessity for invading the Papal States, knew that the indispensable condition of success in an enterprise so repugnant to the interests of Austria was the passive consent of the ruler of France.

The French Emperor had no goodwill for the Austrians who were maintaining the Pope's temporal power on the eastern seaboard of Italy, although he still found himself compelled to do similar police work in the west. Napoleon's throne depended on the support of the Pope's followers in France, and the Pope's temporal power in Rome depended on Napoleon's bayonets, so each must perforce accommodate the other. But the chain of their mutual dependence was galling, and only made them hate one another the more. Napoleon, half a Liberal and wholly a man of the modern world, detested the obscurantist Government of which he was the unwilling protector; while the Pope and the *curia*, after the Franco-Austrian war of 1859, recollected that the Third Napoleon was the nephew of the First, and thenceforward chose to regard him as the embodiment of the European revolution. They entertained high hopes of a Bourbon restoration in France, and began to talk of the present occupant of the Tuileries in the language which Cardinals and Papal Secretaries now sleeping in silent Roman cloisters had used in their day about Queen Elizabeth and Henry of Navarre. The French Ambassador reported with amused indignation that, according to His Holiness' Irish Chamberlain, Napoleon III was in league with the Devil and often consulted Him on political affairs.[1]

Pio Nono considered that Napoleon had deprived him of the Romagna by the war of 1859, and that he was preparing at the earliest opportunity to rob him of Umbria and the Marches.

' *Caro mio Russell,*' he said in his ' mild and benevolent voice ' to the British Resident, ' you are mistaken if you take

[1] *Thouvenel,* i. 275-276.

the present crisis in Italy for a national one. What is being done now will be undone again in time. Piedmont is an instrument in the hands of the Emperor Napoleon, who thinks it is his duty to carry out the ideas of his uncle. What his ultimate objects are I know not, but whatever he establishes will end with him as the Kingdoms of his uncle ended with the Empire. The Italians are not a bad people, but they are easily led astray by foreign agents, who revolutionise the country for their own wicked purposes ; when they have suffered more they will repent and return to us.' [1]

Misled in this fashion by the false historical analogy of a bygone period, when France had imposed the revolutionary system on Italy from without, the Pope and his advisers persuaded themselves that no genuine national movement existed in the Peninsula, and looked forward to another 1815, another fall of Napoleon, and another restoration of the old Italian world. Even so shrewd a man as Cardinal Antonelli, who shared but few of the illusions of his rivals around the Papal throne, declared that he was waiting for 'the 1815 of the Second French Empire,' after which the Pope would enjoy his own again in the Romagna and elsewhere.[2] The second French Empire has indeed since then met with its Waterloo, but it is not the Pope or the *ancien régime* that has arisen on its ruins.

The Pope, having quarrelled with his bread and butter in the shape of Napoleon's protection, was easily persuaded in the early months of 1860 to entrust his fortunes to the Belgian fanatic De Mérode, whose grand design it was to enlist an army of crusaders gathered from all parts of Europe which should be strong enough to defend the Papal territories, and so enable the Holy Father to dispense with the degrading patronage of the French usurper. Cardinal Antonelli, indeed, who saw what was possible in this life as clearly as any other worldling in Europe, argued that a mistake was being made 'in trying to turn the Holy See into a military

---

[1] *F. O. Rome, Russell*, No. 103, July 12, 1860.
[2] *Ibid.* No. 145, September 29, 1860.

power.'[1] But his warnings were drowned in the clamorous joy of the Church militant over the energy and zeal of his Belgian rival. Antonelli was forced to bide his time and allow the fatal experiment to be tried. The hour belonged to Monsignor de Mérode, priest and War Minister. All through the spring and summer of 1860 the quiet *piazze* of old Papal Rome resounded with the clash and tramp of regiments under arms, and the cries of officers drilling recruits in all the languages of Catholic Europe, while the French garrison, no longer the heroes of the sacristy, stared at the ' crusaders ' with mingled envy and contempt.

By September De Mérode's new army numbered not less than 15,000 men.[2] Of these the weakest regiments, with the exception of one or two battalions, were the native subjects of the Pope, enlisted for the sake of the pay, without zeal for the cause, despised by their foreign companions in arms, and conscious that they were traitors to their own country.[3] The foreign troops were, on the average, superior in quality. Six thousand Austrian veterans and several hundreds of Irish recruits were landed, enrolled, and drilled at Ancona. In Rome there were more Irish, besides French, Belgians, and other nationals. They were essentially crusaders, not mercenaries. The Irish, as was justly observed, could have obtained far better terms in the Queen's service, and had come solely out of religious zeal. Peasants straight from the soil of Ireland, they were riotous and difficult to manage, but by the influence of their priests rather than by the enforcement of strict military discipline, they were at length reduced to order, and presented a soldierly appearance in their green uniforms.[4]

---

[1] *F. O. Rome, Russell*, No. 145, September 29.
[2] Appendix K, ii. (*a*), below.
[3] *Castelli*, 327. *Poli*, 116. *Rome MSS. Br. Cons. Letter Book*, p. 190.
[4] Much information about the Irish will be found in *Rome MSS. Br. Cons. Letter Book*, *sub* 1860 *passim*, and in *F. O. Rome, Consuls*, vol. 81, June-September, 1860, and *F. O. Rome, Russell*, No. 100, July 10, 1860, and in *O'Reilly*.

But the troops who attracted most attention in this strange army were the French and Belgians of good family, who assumed the title of ' Papal Zouaves.' They were the men of the *ancien régime*, strayed into the wrong century, who had at last found a cause for which they could fight. They involved the whole army in the atmosphere of their own extreme Legitimist principles. Napoleon III was to them a usurper and a Jacobin. They proclaimed a Royalist restoration as imminent, and cheered for ' Henry V ' of France under the windows of Napoleon's officers in Rome.[1] In all this they were encouraged by the party now supreme at the Vatican, who spared the Emperor no insult. De Mérode in March had visited France and returned with a kinsman of his own, the retired French General Lamoricière, once a Republican, now a Legitimist and Clerical, but always openly hostile to the Napoleonic Empire. This man was put in command of the army of crusaders, as if to show that the Pope no longer valued Napoleon's friendship, and had no more need for his protection. If Cavour had been dictating the Papal policy by telepathic suggestion he could not have wished for anything better. The defenders of the Temporal Power behaved with the light-hearted insolence of some king in ancient Greek tragedy whom God has maddened that He may destroy him.

The invasion of the Papal States in September, 1860, was the crowning act of Cavour's life, and the greatest example of his political genius. He was hemmed in on all sides, and he laid all his enemies at his feet by this one stroke. It destroyed the league of reactionary Italian powers that threatened the newly formed Kingdom in the North, it liberated the populations of the Centre, it garnered Garibaldi's harvest in the South, it decided the rivalry between himself and the Dictator before it could grow into a fatal quarrel, it restored the prestige of the

[1] *F O. Rome. Russell.* No. 82, June 8, 1860. *Gregorovius,* 83, 91.

Monarchy as at once leading and controlling the revolution, and it made a United Italy stretching without a break from the Alps to Palermo.   But proportionate to the possible advantages were the dangers of the course. It was a defiance of Austria, of the whole Catholic world, and of the whole diplomatic world except England.   At best Napoleon might be persuaded to wink at an invasion of Papal territory, but he could not fight against Austria in defence of the sacrilege, because his political supporters, his soldiers, his ministers, his ambassadors and his wife, would all be on the side of the Pope.   And if Austria chose to attack, Piedmont alone could not resist her armies on the Mincio.   Knowing all this, Cavour decided to take the risk.   Perhaps no other statesman fully alive to the facts would have dared a venture so hazardous, and certainly none could have carried it through with such perfect nerve and skill.

Two men may claim to have advised Cavour before the event, Prince Jerome Napoleon and Ricasoli.   As early as June 30, while Garibaldi was still in Palermo, Prince Jerome had written urging Cavour to break with Naples and the Pope, but to be careful first to take the Emperor into his confidence, and to explain to him without reserve the true necessities of the Italian situation. Cavour waited for two months, until Garibaldi was at the gates of Naples, before he followed the Prince's advice. But he spoke of the invasion of the Papal States, when it actually took place, as 'the plan of Prince Napoleon,' and he gratefully acknowledged Jerome's services in keeping his Imperial cousin friendly to the Italian cause, and neutralising the hostile influence of the Empress and the Ministers.[1]

The necessity for action was also impressed upon Cavour in a series of vigorous letters from Ricasoli, Tuscany's 'iron baron,' whose fortitude and patience had carried through the annexation of his province to the territories of Victor Emmanuel.   In July, 1860, Ricasoli

[1] See p. 25 above. *Principe Nap.* 54-58. *Chiala,* vi. 617.

wrote to Cavour again and again, pointing out in impassioned language that the popularity and the prestige of the Monarchy was passing over to Garibaldi and the advanced parties who stood behind him, and that nothing short of a war of liberation waged in Central Italy by the Piedmontese regular troops could recover for the King the moral leadership of the national movement.   Ricasoli never tired of repeating his formula, ' Our real Garibaldi should be Victor Emmanuel.'[1]

On the first of August, Cavour announced his decision to invade the Papal States, but only in the strictest secrecy, to his representatives at London and Paris.[2] During the whole month the world knew nothing of his intention.

At the end of August, Napoleon III was at Chambéry, enjoying the Alpine scenery of his new Province of Savoy, recently acquired by the bargain with Cavour, as the fruits of the Italian alliance.[3]   The place, the time, his holiday humour, the constant news from Rome of fresh insults cast upon him by the Pope and the ' crusaders,' all combined to induce this halter between two opinions to lean for one moment to the Liberal side. And that one moment in Cavour's hands sufficed.

On August 28 there arrived at Chambéry two Piedmontese emissaries—Farini, the second man in the Cabinet of Turin, and Cialdini, the brilliant officer known as 'the Garibaldi of the regular army.'   In a secret conference with Napoleon they informed him of Cavour's intention to invade Umbria and the Marches.   The Patrimony of St. Peter, containing the city of Rome, was to be left to the Pope and the French garrison, provided that Napoleon would confine his own troops to that province and leave Lamoricière with his Austrians and his Legitimist French crusaders to try conclusions in Umbria with Cialdini's Bersaglieri.   ' The Emperor,' wrote Cavour, ' approved of it all.   Indeed he seemed greatly to relish the idea of

---

[1] *Ricasoli*, v. 161, 173, 176 and *passim*.   [2] P. 117 above.
[3] *Garibaldi and the Thousand*, p. 169.

seeing Lamoricière sent to . . . ' The Piedmontese emissaries reported that Napoleon discussed the military
chances of the campaign in the most friendly manner,
' laying down the limits of the plan of operations for our
army,' and finally dismissed them with the words, ' *Faites
vite* '—what thou doest do quickly.[1]

The southward march of the Piedmontese battalions
could be truthfully represented in either of two aspects
—liberty or order. Cavour and his agents in explain-
ing matters to the Emperor were careful to lay most
stress on the restoration of ' order ' as against Garibaldi.[2]
When the interview took place at Chambéry the red-
shirts, still in the full career of victory in Calabria, had
not yet received their check₁ on the Volturno, and
Napoleon had grave reason to fear that they would soon
be knocking at the gates of Rome, unless Cavour inter-
posed the shield of the Piedmontese army. It was to
the interest alike of Napoleon and of Victor Emmanuel
that the Italian monarchy should ' absorb the revolution '
before it came up north and involved the whole politics
of Italy and France in complications that might end on
either side of the Alps in civil war, Republican uprising,
or Legitimist restoration.

' Not being able to forestall Garibaldi at Naples,'
wrote Cavour to his Minister at Paris, ' we must stop him
elsewhere, that is to say, in Umbria and the Marches.
An insurrection is on the point of breaking out there,
and as soon as this occurs, in the name of order and
humanity, Cialdini enters the Marches and Fanti enters
Umbria. They pitch Lamoricière into the sea, occupy
Ancona, but declare Rome inviolable.'[3]   The name of

---

[1] *Chiala*, iii. 353-354 ; iv. 3 ; vi. 582-583. Cialdini told the '*faites vite*' story to
at least three several persons that autumn, see *Revel's da Ancona* 23 ; *Thouvenel*, i.
237-238 and 252, and I see no more reason to doubt it than any other report of the
exact words used in a private conversation, which are always a doubtful matter
afterwards.   The evidence for the alleged '*faites vite*' letter mentioned by
Della Rocca (180) may be as bad as *De Cesare* (*Roma*, ii. 57) argues : but the
'*faites vite*' story rests not on the *letter* but on the evidence in Revel's and
Thouvenel's books, which De Cesare does not seem to have considered.

[2] *Chiala*, iv. 3, 12-13.   [3] *Ibid.* vi. 582-583.

'humanity' was invoked in reference to the brutal conduct of the Pope's foreign mercenaries, who had re-
pressed the insurrection of Perugia the year before with
unnecessary slaughter.   Cavour's emissaries represented
to Napoleon that it was obligatory to invade the Papal
States in order to prevent a repetition of such horrors
on a greater scale.   An insurrection, they declared, was
inevitable in Umbria and the Marches, — and truly
enough the inhabitants of Urbino rose and held their
hill city for three days before Victor Emmanuel's troops
crossed the frontier to their rescue.[1]   Napoleon, in his
official version of the Chambéry interview, declared that
he had only promised his acquiescence because Farini
had undertaken on his side that the Piedmontese 'would
only enter the Papal States after an insurrection and to
re-establish order.'[2]   Whatever Napoleon really said or
tried afterwards to unsay, he left no doubt in the mind
of the two Italians that he would not actively resist the
invasion.

Three days later, to make assurance doubly sure,
Cavour sent another emissary—Count Arese, the old
Italian friend of Napoleon, during the period of his
connection with the *carbonari* thirty years before.[3]   Another tried friend of the adventurer now safely seated
on the throne of France, was Dr. Conneau, who had
aided him in his romantic and perilous escape from the
castle of Ham in 1846.[4]   In the midst of priests and
reactionaries and courtiers, the Emperor never entirely
forgot Arese and Conneau or their liberal doctrines,
which had once been his own.   These two intimates
of Napoleon were, at this crisis of Italian history, working in league with Cavour.[5]   Arese's instructions were to
seek out Napoleon and repeat the arguments of Cialdini
and Farini, of which Cavour sent him the following notes
for his guidance :—

[1] *Cialdini Rap.* 1-2.   [2] *Thouvenel*, i. 192.
[3] *Simpson*, 131, 335, 362, and index.
[4] *Ibid.* 193-198, 241-254.   [5] *Chiala*, iii. 360-361, vi. 582.

'Describe to him the Italian situation after Villafranca and Nice. Underhand war continued after Villafranca by enlisting of Austrians at Rome and Naples. Alliance as good as formed between the Pope, Austria, and Bourbons. Feeling of danger of this league very strong in all Italy. After cession of Nice impossible to hold Garibaldi back. Confess that the Government has tolerated and even supported him. But it has energetically prevented Mazzinian expeditions. Impossible to allow ourselves to be distanced by the demagogues at Naples. Once annexation made we will try not to attack Rome or Austria. Emperor will save Italy if he prevents an attack on us before next spring. If necessary we will fight alone against Austria. Sure the Emperor will not allow the only ally of France (*viz.* Piedmont) to be destroyed by coalition. Explain that it is not at Turin but at Paris that we are blamed.'

These arguments prevailed once more, and the Emperor repeated to Arese his undertaking not to defend the Marches and Umbria with French troops.[1]

The history of these negotiations clearly proves that but for Garibaldi's successes in the South, Cavour would have had no chance of obtaining Napoleon's passive consent to the invasion of the Papal States. Garibaldi's part in the making of Italy was not confined to the geographical area of the regions which he liberated with his own sword, for the influence of his victories in 1860 was the ruling fact in the dealings of Cavour with Napoleon and with all Europe, to whom he was able to say, 'If you won't take Victor Emmanuel, you may get Garibaldi.' Hudson's comment when he heard that the Piedmontese were about to invade the Papal States was, 'We see now what the Garibaldi expedition has produced.'[2]

Thus reassured from the only quarter whence he could hope to obtain assurance—except from England, whose approval could be taken for granted without the asking—Cavour staked the fortunes of his country on the hazard. An ultimatum launched at the Pope's Ministers

---

[1] *Chiala*, iii. 360-361, iv. 3, 13.   [2] Appendix A, p. 312 below.

on September 7, requiring the disbandment of the foreign
mercenaries, 'who suffocate in Italian blood every ex-
pression of the national will,' was followed up on September 11 by the invasion of the Marches and of Umbria,
and the sailing of Persano's fleet from Naples for the
waters of Ancona.   Half the regular army was left on
the Mincio, to protect Milan and Turin against a blow
by the Austrians.   The guard left was all too feeble,
but Cavour trusted that the 'internal condition of the
Austrian Empire' would deter the statesmen of Vienna
from moving, or would ruin them if they moved.[1]   He
had already made arrangements with Kossuth and the
Magyar leaders for a Hungarian rising to be armed
and financed by Italy in case of war between her and
Austria.[2]   But his hope was that peace would be preserved with Austria until, early next year, he could face
Europe with the *fait-accompli* of United Italy.

The news that Victor Emmanuel's Bersaglieri were
marching gaily along the high-roads of Umbria and of the
Marches, hailed with ecstasies of joy by the inhabitants,
and taking in the Papal fortresses at the rate of one a day,
dispelled in an hour the foolish dreams of De Mérode and
his party.   Now was seen how little confidence they had at
heart in the 'crusaders' for whose sake they had thrown
away the friendship of Napoleon.   At once the whole
tribe turned to the man whom they had been insulting
for months past, and demanded as a matter of course that
he should send the armies of France to save them from the
Piedmontese.   The demand of the priests was supported
by Napoleon's own Ambassador at Rome, the Duc de
Gramont, and by his Foreign Minister, Thouvenel, both
of them strong reactionaries and neither of them as yet informed of the promise which he had given at Chambéry.[3]
He yielded to the clamours of the Catholic world so far
as to break off diplomatic relations with Turin, and to
protest that he 'opposed' Cavour's act of aggression.

[1] *Chiala*, iv. 5.   [2] *Chiala Pol. Seg.* 115-129.
[3] *Thouvenel*, i. 185-201, 209-217, 236-239.

But he refused to 'oppose *by force*,' although the Papal Ministers, in their agony, added those two little words to the obscure message which De Gramont had been authorised to give them from his master. The priests were accused of deliberate deceit in this matter by the French diplomats, but it must be admitted that De Gramont's over-sympathetic personal attitude at the time made it very natural to attach a war-like meaning to the message, which otherwise could have no purpose except to save the Emperor's face.[1]

---

[1] For the long and embittered controversy on this subject see *Giornale di Roma*, October 24, 31, 1860. *F. O. Rome, Russell*, 1860, Nos. 119, 126, 140, 145, 147, 156, and 161, especially the last, October 27 and enclosures. *Thouvenel*, i. 272-275. *La Gorce*, iii. 418-419.

CHAPTER XI

THE BATTLE OF CASTELFIDARDO AND THE FALL OF ANCONA

'Ho! maidens of Vienna; Ho! matrons of Lucerne;
Weep, weep, and rend your hair for those who never shall return;
Ho! Philip, send, for charity, thy Mexican pistoles,
That Antwerp monks may sing a mass for thy poor spearmen's souls.'
MACAULAY. *Ivry*.

THERE were 33,000 men in the Italian army that crossed the Papal border, vowed like the Frenchmen at Ivry to deliver their countrymen from foreigners brought in by priests. Lamoricière, who had only half his opponent's numbers, could not hope to win unaided, but he might prolong the defence until France or Austria came to the rescue of the Pope. He held all the fortresses in Umbria and the Marches, including the formidable defences of Ancona. The task imposed on the North Italian army by Cavour was to destroy Lamoricière, to take Ancona, and to reach Naples all within a few weeks, under penalty of an Austrian attack upon Italy's rear. It was a race against time.

General Fanti was the Italian commander-in-chief. One of his two corps, under Cialdini, crossed the 'Rubicon' whence Garibaldi had been recalled ten months before,[1] and made straight along the Adriatic coast towards Ancona, capturing on his way the Papal fortresses of Pesaro and Fano with their small garrisons.[2] The other corps under General Della Rocca, accompanied by Fanti himself, entered Umbria by the upper Tiber valley at the point where Garibaldi long ago had crossed

---

[1] *Garibaldi and the Thousand*, pp. 119-123.
[2] See henceforth Map IV at end of book.

it in his flight with Anita and the remains of the army of the Roman Republic.   From Borgo San Sepolcro the deliverers followed down the poplared banks of the river, amid the blessings of the Umbrian peasants, until they reached the foot of the hill on which Perugia stands. The slaughter perpetrated there in June, 1859, by the Papal troops under Schmidt, was now avenged by the liberation of the city and the capture of the foreign bully and his 1500 men, after a sharp fight at the Sant' Antonio gate.   Della Rocca sent Schmidt away by night under an escort, lest the Perugini should effect their purpose of tearing him to pieces.[1]

From Perugia a detachment under General Brignone was sent to capture the garrison of Spoleto.   The town was not defensible, but the *Rocca* or mediaeval castle on the hill above was in good repair.   It contained a Monsignore, the clerical governor of the district, and a garrison of 800, of whom 300 Irish and a few score Franco-Belgians were the fighting elements.   The castle could, however, be commanded by the artillery and riflemen whom Brignone sent to occupy the wooded mountain on the other side of the gorge, beyond the Lombard aqueduct.   For twelve hours of September 17 the North Italians bombarded the *Rocca* of Spoleto, and in the afternoon attempted to storm its gate.   Almost all the small column of assault were killed or wounded.   Both Irish and North Italians, here, as a few weeks later at Ancona, displayed the ferocious self-sacrifice of men fighting for ideas.   The assault was repulsed for that day, but when night fell the castle was crumbling beneath the bombardment, the ammunition was running out, and the Swiss and Italian Papalists compelled Major O'Reilly and the boys to open the gates.[2]

There is all history's profoundest irony and pathos in

---

[1] *Della Rocca*, 182-187.   *Fanti*, 338-342.

[2] *Corvetto*, 250-251 (Della Rocca's report).   *Fanti Campagna*, 9.   *Fanti*, 343-344.   *Lafond*, 38.   *O'Reilly, passim.   Rome MSS. Br. Cons. Book*, pp. 180-183, contains another report by O'Reilly.   French and Italian witnesses on both sides are unanimous as to the valour of the Irish.

this tussle for an old fort 'in a gash of the wind-grieved Apennine.' What quarrel lay between the Piedmontese and the men of Munster that they should have come together in this place of all others to slay each other and be slain? Or what did it profit the peasant of Connaught as he dug his potatoes and paid his rack-rent, that the vine-dressers of Umbria should remain enslaved and without fatherland? It is a strange thing, this crossing of sea and land by these Irish, to die for a Monsignor-Governor of Spoleto, bayed in the last lair of his tyranny. It was to this that generations of England's greatest warriors and statesmen had brought it in their Protestant zeal. Thus does religious bigotry everywhere defeat its own end: Cromwell had planted the Pope's power firm and broad in Ireland, but Gregory XVI and Pio Nono had destroyed it in Italy.

Meanwhile Lamoricière, knowing that his field-force could not give battle on equal terms either to Fanti in Umbria or to Cialdini in the Marches, had determined to shut himself up in Ancona. His arrival there with his whole army would strengthen and encourage the garrison to hold out until Austria or France should come to the rescue. This plan might well have succeeded had a less enterprising General been in command of the North Italian column on the Adriatic coast. But Cialdini was not called 'the Garibaldi of the regular army' for nothing. As soon as he heard that Lamoricière was moving eastwards by Tolentino and Macerata, he knew that the issue of the campaign lay no longer in Fanti's hands but in his own, and would depend on the rapidity with which he could throw himself across Lamoricière's path to Ancona. He did not proceed any further along the coast to Ancona, because he feared to be caught under its walls between the formidable garrison within and Lamoricière coming from without. He decided to go round inland by Jesi and Osimo and stop Lamoricière near Loreto, and he was therefore obliged to make great demands on the speed and endurance of his men.

Two battalions of the Bersaglieri, trained to the quick, springy step that distinguishes their corps, led the way in a forced march by Jesi to Osimo and thence on to Castelfidardo and Crocette, which the vanguard entered on September 16, prostrated with heat, hunger, and exhaustion. If the enemy had been able to attack them that evening, they would scarcely have had the physical strength to defend themselves. But Lamoricière was only beginning to arrive with half his force in Loreto, three miles away on the other side of the Musone valley His men, though they had not marched so fast as the Bersaglieri, were almost as much exhausted, and the other half of his army under Pimodan was not due until the next day. On the 17th Pimodan came up, but too late for any united movement before nightfall. Cialdini's troops had now all arrived upon the scene. And so on the morning of September 18 the two armies were still watching each other from the hills on either side of the Musone valley ; both had rested well and recovered from the exhaustion of their forced marches.

The best that Lamoricière could now aspire to do was to creep into Ancona by the track along the coast, at the expense of his baggage and probably of some part of his army. He no longer hoped to march in by the high-road through Camerano, for the North Italians were planted across it, 16,500 strong to his 6500.[1] Cialdini, who was holding the line of hills from Osimo to Crocette, had not continued his line across the low ground between Monte d'Oro and the sea, because he had been erroneously informed by his staff officers that the Musone was unfordable in its lower course near its junction with the Aspio.[2] This fault in Cialdini's dispositions, if such it was, though it seemed to give Lamoricière a chance of slipping past into Ancona, proved in effect the snare that lured him to destruction.

Early on the morning of September 18 Cialdini awoke in Castelfidardo, fully expecting to be attacked by way

---

[1] Appendix K, below.
[2] Henceforth see inset map of battle of Castelfidardo. Map IV, end of book.

of the bridge and the high-road.   At dawn he visited the
troops at Crocette and put all in preparation for defence.
With a beating heart he watched the sun suck up the
mists out of the Musone valley, hoping that when the
bottom was clear Lamoricière's columns would be revealed
in the act of crossing.   But the valley was empty.   The
enemy were still on the hills above.   After giving orders
for his men to pile arms and breakfast, he rode back to
Castelfidardo, saying to his staff that after all there would
be no battle that day.

But meanwhile in Loreto the crusaders, gathered together under the dome of the huge church of the pilgrims,
were kneeling round the famous shrine in the centre of
the building, the 'Virgin's house' which, as many of them
believed, had been carried in the hands of angels from
Palestine to Italy.   They were preparing in a very sober
mood for a desperate service.   Pimodan's force, 3000
strong, was to cross the ford which had escaped the
knowledge of Cialdini's staff, storm the Monte d'Oro and
hold Crocette for a few hours, so as to enable the rest of
the army to hurry along the coast into Ancona.

More than an hour after Cialdini had returned to
Castelfidardo, the first files of Pimodan's column were
seen emerging from the woodlands below Loreto, and
making for the banks of the Musone by way of Arenici.

The North Italian army was taken by surprise.
Various Austrian battalions, another small body of Irish,
and the Franco-Belgian Zouaves splashed through the
river and fell with all the fury of religious zeal upon two
companies of Bersaglieri, who had been stationed as outposts in two farms near the river, known as the Lower
and Upper House.   Some more lukewarm Swiss and
native troops followed up across the ford.   The Bersaglieri
held out in the farms, delaying the advance of the enemy
long enough to prevent them from reaching the top of
the Monte d'Oro before the troops at Crocette had been
brought up to its crest.   When the crusaders, having at
length stormed the two farms, began to push for the top

of the hill, they were met by rifle volleys from the wood above, while a battery of artillery unlimbered and opened fire on them down the slope.

When the first sounds of the distant battle were heard in the streets of Castelfidardo, Cialdini mounted and galloped back along the ridge. He found the Tenth Line drawn up on the top of the Monte d'Oro. 'Colonel,' he cried, so that all the ranks could hear him, 'pile knap-sacks and charge with the bayonet.' In another minute the regiment swept like a wave over the edge of the hill and flowed headlong down the side, bearing before it like foam the gilded youth of Royalist salons, mingled in the rout with the peasants of Bavaria and of Tyrol.

For the next half-hour the plain between the Upper House and the ford of the Musone swarmed with con-fused masses of Italians, French, Germans, and Irish, trampling hither and thither, bayoneting each other in the frenzy of rage and firing wildly in every direction. Lamoricière himself rode into the *mêlée*, now far beyond the control of a General Officer, only to find his gallant lieutenant, Pimodan, dying in one of the farm buildings. Some of the houses, defended to the last by the Papal Zouaves, were finally set on fire with lighted straw.

Meanwhile, the head of the second column of 3500 men was drawing near the ford. Cialdini's batteries on the hills above opened upon them, firing over the heads of the regiments engaged on the north of the river. This second column, though like Pimodan's it was composed partly of foreigners and partly of Italians, appears to have contained a smaller proportion of good troops.[1] They were first brought to a stand because their own artillery became entangled in the lane along which they were all

---

[1] There is clear evidence that not *all* the Italian Papalists behaved badly, and not *all* the German-speaking battalions well. The first battalion native *cacciatori* behaved well, and many of the Swiss badly. But *on the average* the Italians in the Papal army fought worst, the Germans better but not always well, and the few Irish and Franco-Belgians best. But the Irish and Franco-Belgians in the battle were only about 300 each; the latter lost two-thirds of their small number. See authorities cited in note p. 224 below.

advancing, and when the round shot came crashing in among them or flying over their heads, when the wounded and the fugitives from the north bank of the river began to stream back past them in terrified crowds, a panic seized the regiments of the rear-guard.   Before midday the Pope's army, half of which had never fired a shot, was running for dear life to the shelter of the wooded hills, whence they had so recently emerged.   Cialdini let loose his lancers upon them.   Four hundred were captured in the valley and the rest climbed back to S. Mary of Loreto, whose magnificent dome had been in sight of the combatants during all that disastrous morning.

Lamoricière, when he saw the army break up under his eyes, rode off with the staff to find his way into Ancona, taking the coast track by which he had hoped to lead 6000 men.   He was accompanied for two miles by a few hundred German-speaking infantry whose officers had had the presence of mind in the rout to make for the coast instead of retreating by the way they had come.   This remnant would have reached Ancona, had not Cialdini seen them from the heights of Crocette and sent off the Ninth Line at a double, to go round by the Concio hill and cut them near Umana.   As the Germans were struggling along ankle-deep in the sand beside the blue Adriatic, the Italians appeared over the rocks at a few paces distance and began to fire into their flank, literally driving them into the sea.   The infantry had no choice but to surrender.   Lamoricière and forty-five horsemen alone escaped to Ancona, and entered its gates between five and six in the evening.   The garrison, recognising the General for whom they had been waiting all day, broke out into shouts of joy, and the Governor, Quatrebarbes, came down to welcome him.   'Here I am,' he said, 'but I have lost the army.'   There was no more cheering heard that night in Ancona.[1]

[1] Part of the garrison had marched out earlier in the day to co-operate with Lamoricière, but being carefully watched by some of Cialdini's battalions, had returned to Ancona.

Meanwhile, Cialdini had crossed the valley of the Musone and accepted the surrender of some 3000 crusaders around the shrine of Loreto. Two or three thousand more flung away their arms and dispersed. Most of these latter were natives who now attempted to pass through the country-side, changing their clothes and resuming their real character of Italian peasants. But in the course of the next few days the greater part of them were captured by Cialdini's flying columns. Except the garrison of Ancona, and a few small bodies nearer Rome, the crusaders had been wiped off Italian soil.[1]

The utter catastrophe of Castelfidardo within a week after the opening of the campaign acted as a strong deterrent to Austrian designs of interference. But there were still grave reasons for the invaders to take Ancona with the least possible delay. The city was Austria's traditional port of entry into Central Italy : until the year before she had held it with her own troops, and even now it was garrisoned by her veterans, diplomatically disguised as Papal soldiers. Its fall would be felt at Vienna as a serious blow. It would be easy and it was tempting for Austria by use of her fleet to preserve the city from capture, as a preliminary to more active interference. Such, at least, were the fears entertained at Turin.[2] Napoleon's ' Faites vite ' must still be the motto of the campaign.

The siege was pushed with energy on the land side, batteries were placed scientifically in position and the

---

[1] For this account of the battle, see *Castelfidardo* (*passim*) which contains official reports of both parties and the clearest Piedmontese official account of the battle. Other Piedmontese accounts: *Cialdini Rap.* 6-19. *Orero*, 38-76. *Prampero*, 9-11. *Fanti*, 344-358. *Fanti Campagna*, 10-13. Other Papalist accounts: *Lamoricière*, 13-34. *Rome MSS. Br. Cons. Book*, pp. 189-203 (letters from Papalist officers). *Poli*, 115-130. *Lafond*, 338-344. *La Gorce*, iii. 422-429. *Veuillot* (*passim*) and *Castelfidardo* (*passim*), especially 64-75. The widely spread but untrue rumours of treason on the field on the part of some of the Papal troops are disposed of by *Lamoricière*, 26-27 ; *Poli*, 117 ; and *Sacchi Dom.* 6-7.

[2] *Conv. Venosta.*

bombardment began. At the storming of various outer works both sides showed great courage, and Quatrebarbes, the Governor of Ancona, was amazed by the zeal of a small body of Irish under his command.[1] But his most vulnerable side was towards the sea. After a week's delay, which the event seemed to prove unnecessary, Persano on September 28 ordered his fleet to steam in close to the fortifications of the harbour and blow them to pieces. The order was gallantly executed, and after a severe duel ending with the explosion of a powder-magazine in the fortifications of the lighthouse, the defence of Ancona collapsed. On September 29 the formal surrender took place of Lamoricière, Quatrebarbes, and the whole garrison of four to six thousand men. The Pope's Generals and soldiers were treated with scrupulous courtesy by their captors, who knew that all over the world jealous eyes were watching for a chance to censure the conduct of the new Italian State.[2]

Nothing now stood in the way of the entry of the North Italian army into the Neapolitan Kingdom. The Province of Abruzzi, contiguous to Umbria and the Marches, had already risen and established a Provisional Government in the name of 'Italy, Victor Emmanuel, and Garibaldi Dictator.' The leaders of this provincial rising showed both spirit and sense. Fearing a reactionary movement in the form of anarchy and brigandage, they petitioned Victor Emmanuel towards the end of September to cross the Tronto and annex the Neapolitan Kingdom without more delay. Similar addresses reached

[1] He seems to have been much interested by their eccentric conduct, set off by their valour. He says that when under fire they 'chantaient en choeur les vieilles ballades de leurs montagnes [sic : names of ballads not given], ou défiaient à grands cris les Piémontais,' and that their officers had great difficulty in restraining them from constantly leaping over the battlements to hurl defiance at the infidel or to applaud the work of the Papal artillery. Quatrebarbes, 196.

[2] Fanti, 363-379. Lamoricière, 51-52. Genio, 13-27. Quatrebarbes, 196-234, 276. Persano (diary, September 11-30). Orero, 77-103. Corsi's Rimembranze, 29-32. Corsi's Vent. Anni, passim. F. O. Turin, Hudson, No. 394, Oct. 5, 1806.

him from the inhabitants of Naples. These petitions aroused Garibaldi's indignation because they contained sharp criticism of his Dictatorship, and even spoke of his friends as 'a stupid and incorrigible faction.'[1] And besides, he still wished the annexation to be postponed, because he had not yet ceased to hope that the military situation on the Volturno would so far change for the better as to enable him to march on Rome. But he never for one moment entertained the idea of resisting the advance of the North Italian army, even if it were to come sooner than he wished. His horror of civil war between the patriotic parties was one of those simple, fixed ideas that guided his sometimes too impulsive conduct throughout the whole course of his life.

Garibaldi's loyalty was soon put to the proof. On September 23, Tripoti, who commanded the Garibaldian force at Teramo in Abruzzi, asked for instructions in case the North Italian vanguard appeared on the frontier. Bertani sent back word from Naples : 'If the Piedmontese wish to enter, say to them that before you permit it you must ask instructions from the Dictator.' Having dispatched this correct reply, the Secretary went up to the lines next day to consult Garibaldi, who immediately sent word to Tripoti : 'If the Piedmontese enter our territory, receive them like brothers.'[2]

On September 27, two days before the fall of Ancona and four days before the battle of the Volturno, Garibaldi issued the following proclamation, characteristically inaccurate, and characteristically loyal and generous :—

[1] *De Cesare*, ii. 435-450 ; *ditto*, *F. di P.* ccxii-ccxiii. *Spaventa*, 298-301. *L Cecilia*, ii. 12-13.
[2] *Bertani*, ii. 266-269. *Ire Pol.* 87. A disgraceful story was invented by som of Garibaldi's enemies to the effect that Bertani had wired to Tripoti, ' Receiv the Piedmontese with rifle bullets.' In a modified but still libellous form it wa repeated by *Nisco*, 139, whence it has unfortunately been transcribed into *Whit house's* generally excellent summary of these affairs. It is on a par for baseles ness with Bertani's own untruths about Cavour, see *Garibaldi and the Thousan* Appendix F, ii. Neither party among the patriots can clear itself of the char of calumny and injustice towards the other, and writers on this period would d well to admit this frankly, whatever their own views may be.

'Our brothers of the Italian army commanded by the brave General Cialdini are fighting the enemies of Italy and conquering. The army of Lamoricière has been defeated by these brave men. All[1] the provinces subject to the Pope are free. Ancona is ours.[2] Our brave soldiers of the Northern army have passed the frontier and are on Neapolitan territory.[3] We shall soon have the good fortune to press these victorious hands.'[4]

But the North Italian army had still to traverse some 200 miles of road before it could reach Capua. Nearly another month was to pass before they arrived on the scene, and during that month Francis II had still the time, if he had the strength, to cut his way back to Naples over the ruins of Garibaldi's army. If he had succeeded, the moral effect of such a reversal on the public mind in Italy, Austria, and France would have rendered it impossible for Victor Emmanuel to turn him out once more, and European interference would have supervened in one form or another on behalf of a King who had won his way back to the allegiance of his subjects. The fate of Italy still hung on the issue of Garibaldi's defence of his lines before Capua.

[1] But the Patrimony of S. Peter was not freed till 1870.
[2] Premature by two days.   [3] Premature.
[4] *Ciàmpoli*, 185.   *F. O. Sicily, Elliot*, No. 536, September 28, 1860.   *Times*, October 4, p. 7, c. 4, correspondent's letter of September 29.

CHAPTER XII

THE EVE OF THE VOLTURNO

'. . . Tifata, onde, aquila in agguato
spia presso e lungi tutto il fiume e il piano
di vastissima pugna incendiato.'
MARRADI. *Rapsodia Garibaldina.*

'. . . Tifata's summit, whence, an eagle in ambush, he watches near and far
all the river and the plain far around ablaze with the fires of war.'

THE military position on the Volturno was in itself an
additional inducement to Garibaldi to acquiesce in the
coming of Victor Emmanuel. By the middle of September
his observations from the summit of Monte Tifata [1] had
shown him not only the uselessness for the time being
of any attempt on his part to attack Capua, but the grave
danger in which his own army would stand if General
Ritucci ventured on a counter-attack. In order to distract the enemy's attention from any such design, he sent
a few hundred men under the Hungarian Csufady to the
north bank of the Volturno, with a roving commission to
join hands with Liberal insurgents anywhere between
Cajazzo and Rome. Some bands around Alife and
Piedimonte had been in arms for three weeks past. [2]
With their help Csufady was to threaten the line of
Ritucci's communications behind Capua, and so prevent
him from making a forward move. But Garibaldi had no
intention of attempting to hold Cajazzo or any other post
north of the river, still less of attacking the walls of
Capua. [3]

[1] See pp. 201-202 above. And see illustration, p. 241 below.
[2] For this chapter see Map III, at end of book.
[3] *Du Camp*, 263, 290. *I. Mille*, 278. *Leg. Matese*, 47-50, 85-89 and *passim.*
Castellini, 77-78. *Turiello*, 223-224. *Türr's Div.* 182-184, 435-439. Benevento

Such was the state of affairs when he was called away on September 16 to pay a political visit to Palermo. The pressing demand of the Sicilians, headed by his own pro-Dictator, Depretis, for immediate annexation to Piedmont, required his presence. Türr, whom he left in command on the Volturno, ought not to have taken any important new step in his absence, but Türr's fault as a soldier was rashness, as he had shown the year before at Treponti.[1]   Finding himself in command for three days, he formed the ambitious scheme of occupying and holding Cajazzo, a hill-town north of the Volturno—a far more serious undertaking than the irresponsible gyrations of Csufady's flying column. In order to distract Ritucci's attention from Cajazzo, Türr made a reconnaissance in force against Capua on September 19, the day after the battle of Castelfidardo.

The reconnaissance procured, indeed, the unopposed occupation of Cajazzo, but was itself ill-conducted and disastrous. At dawn Rüstow's Milanese drove the enemy's advance-guard into Capua, but then, instead of retiring from before the walls, remained for two hours round the railway station and on the open parade ground exposed to the fire of the cannon on the bastions. They retreated after severe losses, and the Bourbon troops sallied out after them from the gate, led on by old General Rossaroll who, though on the retired list, rode to the sound of the firing and headed the advance in gallant style, until he was carried off wounded.   Rüstow's men made a stand at the cemetery and Cappuccini Convent and drove the Royalists back to Capua.   But the events of September 19 had at least all the appearance of a repulse for the Garibaldini, who had fired at the walls as if they intended to take Capua by a *coup-de-main*. Indeed, some of the officers who served that day under Rüstow still believe that he was inspired by a secret

had thrown off the Papal yoke (it was an enclave of the Pope's territory) before Garibaldi entered Naples.
  [1] See *Garibaldi and the Thousand*, p. 105.

hope that the gates would be opened to him by treachery, though he never confessed as much.[1] The day cost the Garibaldini 130 in killed and wounded.[2]

Meanwhile, the Dictator had settled affairs in Sicily. The love the people bore to him overcame their strong desire for annexation and their indifference to his projects on Rome. He had another magnificent popular reception in Palermo on September 17. He replaced the pro-Dictator Depretis by Mordini who had hitherto been more opposed to Cavour. But Mordini was a man capable of learning by experience, and although Crispi tried to poison his mind with false rumours of treachery on the part of Cavour,[3] the new ruler of Sicily had by the middle of October discovered the absolute necessity for the immediate annexation of the island to Piedmont.[4]

Garibaldi returned to the banks of the Volturno on the afternoon of September 19, too late for the fighting under the walls of Capua, but in time to join Türr in a duel, which he was carrying on with the enemy's forces on the other side of the river, across the ferry of Formicola. There is no reliable evidence as to what he said to Türr that day, but he afterwards wrote in severe condemnation of his lieutenant for the attack on the walls of Capua and for the occupation of Cajazzo.[5]

The events of September 19, especially the sally of the Bourbon troops under old General Rossaroll, gave self-confidence to those forces, and suggested to them the

---

[1] *Conv. Pedotti. Türr's Div.* 438-449. *Rüstow's Brig. Mil.* 33-35. *Arrivabene*, ii. 236-241. *Forbes*, 271-272. *Cava*, 54. *Palmieri*, 98. *De Sivo*, iv. 165. *Gazzetta di Gaeta*, No. 5, p. 17. *Franci*, ii. 11-20, 212-213. *Times*, September 27, p. 4, cols. 5-6. *Türr, Ai Miei Comp.* 3.

[2] *Schwabe MS.* 3.

[3] On September 28 Crispi wrote to Mordini (*Rosi*, 212) : ' The cession of the islands of Sardinia and Elba is agreed on in favour of France. Sicily is said to be promised to a Prince of the House of Bourbon. Victor Emmanuel will have the mainland. As we cannot unseat Cavour we must organise our party to resist these acts of violence.' There was not a word of truth in these stories.

[4] *Crispi*, 1911, 292-304. *Rosi*, 199-248. *Nisco*, 136. *Nievo*, 373, 376-377. *Ire Pol.* 89-91. *V.M.* 17. *Bandi*, 291-292. *Amari*, ii. 133-135 ; iii. 209, 212.

[5] *Bandi*, 293-294. *Türr's Div.* 198-199. *Türr, Ai Miei Comp.* 3. *Mem.* 385. *I Mille*, 278.

idea that they might successfully take the offensive on a
great scale.   That evening the Minister of War at Gaeta
sent Ritucci the King's orders, 'to march forward, seeking
to find and destroy the enemy and at the same time advance on the Capital.'[1]   Ritucci thereupon set before the
King a plan for an advance on the Capital by the country
roads to the west of S. Tammaro, which passing through
Arnone and Vico, Foresta and Casal di Principe, unite at
Naples on the side of Capodimonte. Garibaldi in his
memoirs declares that the enemy would in this way have
succeeded in reaching Naples if his own force had meanwhile been held in check by false attacks.   But the plan
was rejected as too dangerous by its author Ritucci, who
opposed as still more rash the frontal attack on Santa
Maria and Sant' Angelo, recommended by the Royal
counsellors at Gaeta.[2]

All that Ritucci would as yet consent to do was to
recover Cajazzo.   The Dictator made his one military
mistake of this year in not withdrawing from Cajazzo the
300 Bolognese under Cattabeni whom Türr had without
his consent placed in that isolated position across the
river.   Matters were only made worse by the dispatch
of another 600 men under Vacchieri; there were now
900 men collected in the hill-town to hold it against any
force that might come along the high-road from Capua.
On September 21 the best regiments in Ritucci's army—
the native *cacciatori* with a battery of guns, and a reserve
of three fine Swiss and German regiments—some 7000
in all, came to retake Cajazzo.   After a gallant defence

[1] If this letter had been written on September 17 as Türr's friend Pecorini-
Manzoni erroneously states (*Una Pagina*, 6), it would go far to support his
suggestion that the Royalists intended to attack prior to the events of September
19, and that this attack, which would have been so dangerous to the unprepared
Garibaldians at that time, was postponed owing to Türr's occupation of Cajazzo
and his reconnaissance against Capua on September 19.   But the real date of
the letter is September 19, and it was written in consequence of the encouragement given to the Royalists by their success on the morning of that day.
Franci, ii. 20, 213-214.   The correction of date turns the whole argument
against Türr.
[2] *Franci*, ii. 20, 214-217.   *Mem.* 393.

of several hours conducted by Cattabeni, who fell into the enemy's hands severely wounded, the town was stormed, sacked, and burnt by the Bourbon troops. The victors confessed to a loss of over a hundred. About 250 of the Garibaldini were killed, wounded, or captured, and the Swiss, who took no part in the sack, observed with compassion that many of the wounded were mere boys. Two-thirds of the defenders under Vacchieri escaped with difficulty by fording the flooded ferry of Limatola.[1]

After the storming of Cajazzo, the Bourbon troops were prepared for any adventure; the spell that had so long bound them was wellnigh broken, for they had proved that they could defeat the red devils, at least where the magician himself was not present. The King's counsellors in Gaeta, who had learnt the disastrous news of Castelfidardo, perceived that unless they could at once cut their way back to Naples their position on the Volturno, however impregnable in front, would be taken in rear by the victorious armies of Piedmont. They therefore overruled Ritucci's objections, and compelled him against his will to lead his eager troops to the general attack on the enemy's lines. It was the one chance left for the house of Bourbon on this earth, and if the attack had been made within two or three days after the victory of Cajazzo, before Garibaldi had erected his batteries at Santa Maria and Sant' Angelo, and if Ritucci's whole striking force had been directed in one solid mass against those two villages, it is difficult to see how it could have failed to succeed.

But again there was the delay of a week, and again there was the division of forces. For both these errors the counsellors at Gaeta were responsible. For although they had done well in compelling Ritucci to fight, they spoilt all by dictating to him a plan of battle of which he rightly disapproved. They were unnecessarily alarmed

---

[1] *Schweizertruppen*, 537-539. *Castellini*, 66-78. *Campo*, 146-149. *Cattabeni*, 18-42. *Leg. Matese*, 82-104. *Gazzetta di Gaeta*, No. 4, p. 15; No. 5, p. 17. *Forbes*, 275-277. *Times*, October 2, p. 7.

for the safety of the rear and flank of Ritucci's position, conceiving it to be threatened by the really negligible activities of Csufady and the Liberal bands round Piedimonte and Roccaromana. The council at Gaeta therefore compelled the commander-in-chief to send great forces under Von Mechel to restore order in that district, and thence to push them on to Amorosi and Ducenta. This not only caused a week's delay but drew the Royalists on to adopt the false strategy of attacking Garibaldi on two sides—not only from Capua by way of Santa Maria and Sant' Angelo, but also from Ducenta by way of Maddaloni. It appears that after the storming of Cajazzo, some of the advisers at Gaeta felt so completely confident of victory and of a submissive reception in Naples, that they were planning rather to make victory complete than to make it secure.[1] Misled by the golden hope of surrounding the enemy's head-quarters at Caserta from east and west at once, they took the unnecessary risk of operating on an outer semicircle, of which the two ends were not in effective communication. They thus gave to Garibaldi with his smaller force the advantage of acting on the inner ring; or rather along the straight diameter, while their communications ran round the circumference of the semicircle.[2] This advantage he used to the utmost on the day of battle, with the help of the railway-line running from Maddaloni through Caserta to Santa Maria.

The effect of this plan was to divide the Bourbon army into two separate forces, one under Ritucci at Capua, and the other under Von Mechel operating round Ducenta. Von Mechel, the brave Swiss whose stupidity in May had been one of the chief causes of Garibaldi's capture of Palermo,[3] was nominally under the orders of

[1] See Antonio Ulloa's letter of September 27, in *Franci*, ii. 236-239.
[2] The Bourbon communications ran round from Capua through Cajazzo, Amorosi, and Ducenta to their point of attack at the Arches of the Valley near Maddaloni : Garibaldi's communications ran straight from Maddaloni through Caserta to Santa Maria and Sant' Angelo. See Map III below.
[3] *Garibaldi and the Thousand*, pp. 281-282.

Ritucci, but he chose to act as if he had an independent command and left the commander-in-chief without news of him for days together.   On the 28th Ritucci in despair rode out from Capua as far as Cajazzo in search of the missing Von Mechel, and finally discovered that he had on the 26th advanced southwards from Amorosi through Ducenta as far as the cross-roads at Cantinella, and thence had sent out cavalry who located Bixio's force covering Maddaloni near the Arches of the Valley.   Von Mechel had thereupon retired again as far as Amorosi on September 27.   If he had on that day made a determined assault on Maddaloni while Ritucci in concert sallied out in force from Capua against Santa Maria, they would have had a good chance of meeting at Caserta that evening.   But owing to their entire want of communication, the great effort was postponed until the first of October.   'This delay,' wrote Ritucci to Von Mechel, when at last he was able to renew correspondence with his lieutenant, 'may well be fatal to our cause.'[1]

Ritucci was sulky but prepared to carry out with vigour the orders which he disliked.[2]   His men were elated at the prospect of battle, and confident that they

[1] The foregoing paragraphs are based on the dispatches printed in *Franci*, ii. 220-248, which must be studied by every serious student of the campaign. See also *Ruiz*, 18-19. *Türr's Div.* 230-232. *Palmieri*, 100-101. *Marra Oss.* 58. *Ponti della Valle*, 7-8. The absurd excuse for defeat set up by some Bourbon writers after October 1, *viz.* that the attack of that day was only 'a reconnaissance' is disproved by these dispatches before the date, *e.g. Franci*, ii. 228, 248.

Garibaldi in his *Memorie* (387) writes " our line of battle was defective, because too far extended, from Maddaloni to Santa Maria ".   But if he had not occupied both Maddaloni and Santa Maria he must have been taken in rear from one direction or the other : and if he had not held Sant' Angelo and M. Tifata, he could not have held Santa Maria, which stands on the plain commanded by the Tifata range.   No one of his critics has ever yet pointed out which of his positions was superfluous, in view of the double attack from Capua and from Amorosi-Ducenta.

[2] Ritucci to the Minister of War.   Capua, September 29 : ' Then the attack will take place the day after to-morrow (October 1) at dawn.   I free myself from all responsibility as to the wisdom of this action, because it is not due to my conviction but to the King's command and disposition ; nor am I responsible for what disappointments may occur owing to Von Mechel not acting in unison with me, since he has been detached from my base of operation with a strong column on his own account.'   *Franci*, ii. 248.

would sleep in Caserta the first night and in Naples the next. Their prospects were indeed bright, but they would have been still brighter if the attack had not been deferred till the beginning of October. On September 27 Garibaldi had only half a dozen field-guns and no entrenched batteries in his lines against Capua, but in the last three days of the month he and his men laboured day and night at planting cannon that arrived from Naples, and throwing up defences in their front. In this they received skilled assistance from Dowling, a British ex-sergeant of artillery, who had seen service before Sebastopol,[1] two ex-captains of Bourbon artillery,[2] and twenty gunners of the Piedmontese regular army, sent up from Naples on the night of the 29th, at the request of Garibaldi to Villamarina, and followed on the next day by forty more of their number.[3]

One of the new batteries was on the road between Sant' Angelo and Capua; another was in the middle of the scattered village of Sant' Angelo itself; a third, intended to fire at the enemy's batteries across the river, was erected on the top of the precipitous ridge of San Jorio, whither the guns were dragged with great labour and considerable engineering skill. Finally a battery was placed at the entrance of Santa Maria, under the ancient Roman archway which spans the road leading from old to new Capua. There were other mobile trains of artillery on the road between Sant' Angelo and Santa Maria.[4]

[1] *Forbes*, 292. *Conv. Brown Young.* *Conv. Dolmage.* *A.Y.R.* 105-106.
[2] *Matarazzi*, 41.   [3] *Mem. Stor. Mil.* i. 52-53, doc. v.
[4] Captain Deane, R.N., who served on board H.M.S. *Agamemnon* in 1860, tells me that he and some middies on leave from that ship went too near the Bourbon lines at Capua, were fired at, and ran for shelter to the nearest of the Garibaldian earth-works. They were pulled up the mound of the battery by a rope flung over by friendly hands. When they were safely landed inside the battery a moment of embarrassment followed, for the faces of the Garibaldian gunners who had just helped them up were exceedingly familiar and indeed curiously similar to those of some seamen who had recently been missing from H.M.S. *Agamemnon*. It was a case for the old proverb, 'The least said the soonest mended.' Captain Deane tells me that the enthusiasm for Garibaldi was perfectly

For the last time in his life Garibaldi had all his ablest lieutenants with him : Avezzana, the former War Minister of the Roman Republic, arrived just in time to help his old friend to set his batteries round Sant' Angelo ; Cosenz was doing his best to make bricks without straw as War Minister in Naples ; Sirtori was at the front as Chief of the Staff ; Bixio was defending Maddaloni against Von Mechel ; Medici held Sant' Angelo and M. Tifata ; Milbitz held Santa Maria. Türr was stationed with the reserves at Caserta, ready to bring them up by rail, either to Maddaloni or to Santa Maria as need should require at the crisis of the battle. By this last simple device Garibaldi obtained the full advantage of being on the inside of the circle—of acting on the diameter while the enemy moved round by the circumference.

In spite of these preparations, which greatly strengthened his position in the last three days of September, his army was still in evil case. 'Twenty thousand men, the greater part of them ill-armed and worse drilled,' many scarcely knowing how to use their rifles, had to stand the shock of twenty-eight or thirty thousand regular troops, coming on in the full confidence of victory.[1] Exhausted with starvation, exposure, and overwork, many of the best men were physically prostrated, while the cowards were slinking back to Naples or preparing to fly at the first onset. There was none of that certain assurance of victory which had carried them through Sicily and Calabria. In the coming battle Garibaldi had to depend upon his own military genius, which was seldom seen to better advantage than on that desperate day, and on the resolve to die at their posts which his presence inspired into the few thousand men who were really doing the work of the whole army. The spirit in

universal in all ranks from Admiral Mundy downwards. (The desertions from *Agamemnon* are mentioned by *Elliot*, 133, 145.) On the making of the batteries see *Matarazzi*, 41-43. *Campo*, 153-155. *Mem.* 387. *J. des D.* October 7, 1860.

[1] *Guerzoni*, ii. 187. For the numbers of the two armies, see Appendix J, below.

the Garibaldian lines on the eve of the Volturno is illustrated by a story told by the English preacher Haweis, who a fortnight later met a young Milanese noble at the siege of Capua :—

'He was poorly equipped and almost in rags ; he had nothing but a sword and pistol. "What induced you," I said, "to give up ease and luxury for this life of a dog, in a camp without commissariat, pay, or rations." "You may well ask," he said. "I tell you a fortnight ago I was in despair myself, and thought of giving up the whole thing. I was sitting on a hillock, as might be here. Garibaldi came by. He stopped, I don't know why. I had never spoken to him. I am sure he did not know me, but he stopped. Perhaps I looked very dejected, and indeed I was. Well, he laid his hand on my shoulder and simply said, with that low, strange, smothered voice that seemed almost like a spirit speaking inside me, '*Courage ; courage ! We are going to fight for our country.*' Do you think I could ever turn back after that? The next day we fought the battle of the Volturno." ' [1]

[1] *Haweis.*

CHAPTER XIII

THE BATTLE OF THE VOLTURNO, OCTOBER 1-2

'Pure as the Archangel's cleaving Darkness thro',
The sword he sees, the keen unwearied sword,
A single blade against a circling horde,
And aye for Freedom and the trampled few.

'The cry of Liberty from dungeon cell
From exile, was his God's command to smite,
As for a swim in sea he joined the fight
With radiant face, full sure that he did well.

'Behold a warrior dealing mortal strokes,
Whose nature was a child's : amid his foes
A wary trickster : at the battle's close,
No gentler friend this leopard dashed with fox.

'Down the long roll of History will run
The story of these deeds, and speed his race
Beneath defeat more hotly to embrace
The noble cause and trust to another sun.'

GEORGE MEREDITH. *The Centenary of Garibaldi.*

ON the last day of September, by way of prelude to their coming attack, the Royalists kept up a heavy cannonade, and their infantry skirmished along the line of outposts in front of Capua ; the hottest firing was at the ferries below San Jorio ridge on which the Garibaldian batteries had been mounted only the day before. After sunset all again fell silent. A mile to the south of the ferries, on the lowest slopes of Monte Tifata, stands the village of Sant' Angelo ;[1] its church, built a dozen centuries ago out of the ruins of Roman villas and temples, was the centre of Medici's position, filled that night with sleeping soldiers and on the morrow with the wounded and the dead. On the embanked terrace in front of the

[1] It is important to use Map III, section B, for this chapter.

SANT' ANGELO CHURCH, FRONT VIEW FROM THE TERRACE

Upper part of church is tufa blocks; lower part is ancient Roman pillars and campanile is ancient Roman masonry.

SANT' ANGELO VILLAGE AND CHURCH AT FOOT OF MONTE TIFATA

CASERTA PALACE.

church stood Garibaldi, with his back to the darkened
mountain, and his eyes fixed on the distant lights of
Capua.   Suddenly, far away in the middle of the enemy's
lines, a tongue of flame leapt up and flared on the night
sky.   He watched it for some time in silence, and then
turned round with a laugh.   'Sirs,' he said, 'we must
not sleep too heavily to-night.'   Next moment he was
on his horse, riding back to Caserta to arrange the last
details with Bixio and with Türr.   'He laughed—the
old lion,' said one of the group left upon the terrace ;
'that flame must be the signal for their attack.''

After midnight a heavy fog crept over the Capuan
plain, and wrapped itself round the Bourbon regiments
as they issued one by one from the gate of the fortress.
In the Volturno region all the ground that does not rise
to a certain level above the sea is composed of dark,
volcanic tufa, soft and easy to cut.   All above that level
is hard, white limestone rock.   The village of Sant'
Angelo, on the lower slopes of the mountain, stands on
the junction of the two strata, and is built half of tufa
and half of limestone ; while Santa Maria and all the
villages of the plain are built, like Naples itself, of the
black, spungy tufa of which the soil is composed, archi-
tecturally a sordid stone of discouraging and criminal
appearance.   The highly cultivated plain between Capua
and Monte Tifata is traversed by the peasants and their
flocks by means of a network of lanes, sunk ten feet
deep in the soft tufa, and therefore invisible at more
than a few yards' distance.   The road that leads from
Santa Maria to Sant' Angelo crosses by bridges over
four or five of these hidden lanes, up some of which
Bourbon columns penetrated before dawn on October 1,
and thus obtained unobserved a footing inside Garibaldi's
line at its weakest point, the almost undefended space
between Sant' Angelo and Santa Maria.

Further to the south the fog served to hide the approach of other columns under Tabacchi, who surprised
and routed the defenders of the cemetery and of San

Tammaro. Many of these first runaways fled by the high-road to Naples, and arrived there before noon, spreading panic like the first-comers from Waterloo in the Belgian capital. D'Ayala, who commanded the National Guard, called out the whole force and patrolled Naples and the neighbouring villages to prevent a reactionary movement. Knowing the impressionable character of the Neapolitans, D'Ayala sent out premature and exaggerated reports of victory to counteract the tales of the runaways.[1]

Meanwhile, Tabacchi's men seized the railway embankment and a large group of buildings called Sant' Agostino, whence they enfiladed the trenches in front of Santa Maria with cannon and rifle fire. Fortunately, since Garibaldi had come out by an early train from Caserta and was already at Milbitz' side, Santa Maria itself was vigorously defended. Under the Roman archway at its entrance two cannon, destined to be worked that day by many successive relays of professional and volunteer gunners, began their ten hours' duel with the enemy's batteries and riflemen posted at Sant' Agostino. The Sicilians held the amphitheatre of ancient Capua, a fine defensive position in the plain just outside the town; while fifty Frenchmen, who still named their company after their slain leader, De Flotte,[2] held an isolated farm in front of the amphitheatre with splendid courage all day long. At Garibaldi's order Türr began thriftily to feed Milbitz with portions of his reserve, which he sent up from Caserta by rail and road. Assanti's regiment was the first to arrive; some of them deployed in the open to the north of the amphitheatre, while others restored the fight on the railway.[3]

Seeing that Santa Maria could hold out for awhile, and hearing the noise of battle in the north, the Dictator, with Canzio, Missori, and his staff, mounted into two carriages and drove off towards Sant' Angelo. As the

---

[1] *D'Ayala*, 351-356.   [2] See p. 132 above.
[3] For authorities for above, see Appendix L, 1 and 5, below.

mist rolled away they saw the road clear before them, and never suspected that the enemy had already crossed it by the sunk lanes and was lying in wait under the Ciccarelli bridge.   At Garibaldi's side sat a young officer of the Piedmontese regular artillery going to serve his guns at Sant' Angelo.   He was Emilio Savio, one of a noble pair of brothers who with their mother, the poetess, were soon to be made famous by Mrs. Browning in every household of Europe and America where English poetry was read.   Emilio as he sat by Garibaldi's side did not yet know that, three days before, his brother Alfredo had been 'shot by the sea in the east' in the trenches beneath Ancona; any more than that he himself was in a few weeks' time, beneath the walls of Gaeta, to be 'shot in the west by the sea.'[1]

As the carriages drew near the Ciccarelli bridge, the Bourbon infantry in the lane beneath came scrambling up as if out of the bowels of the earth, and emptied their rifles at the Dictator twenty yards away.   The horses dashed forward through the midst of them, and as they ran the gauntlet the coachman and Cereseto of the staff fell mortally wounded.   A few yards on the further side of the bridge one of the horses rolled over and the carriage was brought to a stand.   Garibaldi stepped out into the road and drew his sword.   A small group of Medici's infantry from Sant' Angelo, who were fortunately not far off, came running up, and led by the Dictator, they charged and repulsed the enemy.[2]

After this incident, which had so nearly secured the restoration of the Bourbon dynasty to Naples, Garibaldi made his way on foot to Sant' Angelo, and spent the whole of the morning and the early part of the afternoon in heading charge after charge on the slopes of Monte Tifata and in the streets of the village.   The enemy, in greatly superior force, had stormed the advanced battery on the road to Capua, where Dunne fell wounded at the

---

[1] Mrs. Browning's poems, *Mother and Poet*.
[2] Appendix L, 2, below; and Appendix J, ii. (*c*), for Piedmontese artillery.

head of his Sicilians, and had poured into the lower part of Sant' Angelo. At the top of the village Garibaldi's cannon were planted on the terrace in front of the church, and here the struggle raged hottest. Other Bourbon troops crossed from the north bank of the Volturno by the ferries and began to ascend Monte Tifata through the forest of S. Vito.

Garibaldi was here, there, and everywhere, now on horseback, now on foot, now at the church, now on the summit of Monte Tifata, whither he led the Genoese Carabineers of the Thousand. His criticism of the Bourbon method of attack was that though they advanced bravely, they advanced firing instead of charging with the cold steel. The chief feature of his own method of defence was a series of bayonet charges, each of which drove back the Royalists and relieved the pressure for awhile. Wherever one of these rushes was being made in defence of Medici's position, whether on the rocky mountain-side or on the plain below, there was Garibaldi organising and leading the charge. His presence put courage into the most faint-hearted of Medici's 4000 men and made heroes of the bravest. Soon after noonday he began to cry 'victory' wherever he went, and to send off messages to all parts of the field reporting 'victory all along the line.' The phrase kept up the spirits of his outnumbered force, though the veterans muttered under their breath, 'victory! What victory?'[1]

In the attack on Sant' Angelo the Bourbon General, Afan de Rivera, who was in command, incurred censure for not appearing near the front.[2] But in the attack on Santa Maria General Tabacchi did his duty, and the commander-in-chief, Ritucci, exposed himself all day in a manner more suitable to the part of a divisional commander. The knowledge that King Francis was in the field, with his brothers, the Counts Trani and Caserta,

[1] Appendix L, 3 and 6 below.   [2] *Franci*, ii. 256.

and his uncle of Trapani, greatly encouraged the assailants. Both sides, an observer noted, fought in silence, with the intensity of an Italian vendetta. The Bourbon cavalry made several charges on the plain to the north of the amphitheatre, and the infantry penetrated as far as San Prisco. Their guard regiments alone lost 400 killed and wounded, but the grenadiers of the guard sulked and refused to advance a second time against Santa Maria at a moment regarded by Ritucci as the crisis of the battle.[1]

The attack directed from Capua on Santa Maria and Sant' Angelo was not the only part of the Bourbon operations on October 1. It has already been explained[2] how Von Mechel with 8000 men, acting from the base of Amorosi, had orders to capture Maddaloni and thence advance on Caserta, where it was hoped that they would in the afternoon join hands with the victors of Santa Maria coming from the opposite direction. This wide division of the Royalist forces was a mistake in strategy dictated to Ritucci by the Council at Gaeta. Von Mechel now proceeded to make on his own account a further mistake of the same character in the manipulation of his 8000 men. Instead of attacking Bixio's position before Maddaloni with his whole force, he led only the 3000 German-speaking troops down the valley road from Ducenta, and detached the 5000 native troops under Ruiz to make a long circle through the mountains by Limatola, Castel Morrone, and Old Caserta. Von Mechel declares that he intended Ruiz and his 5000 to come over the top of Monte Caro and fall from above on to the left flank of Bixio's position near the Villa Gualtieri, at the moment when his own frontal attack was engaging the full attention of the Garibaldini at the Arches of the Valley. But it was an error to employ 5000 men for a flank attack which required speed and mobility rather

[1] See the Bourbon authorities (starred) in Appendix L, 5, below.
[2] See p. 233 above.

than numbers, and to keep only 3000 for the main operation.   Perhaps his Swiss pride inspired him to send
away all the Neapolitans and to fight a pan-German
battle in the valley.   Whether from pride or sheer
stupidity, he pushed on his own attack with such haste
that Ruiz would barely have had time to make his way
round over the rocky and trackless mountains, even if he
had met with no resistance from bands of Garibaldini at
Castel Morrone or elsewhere.

But Von Mechel's worst mistake was that he never
gave Ruiz clear orders to cross Monte Caro and appear on the scene of conflict.   He merely instructed
him to occupy Old Caserta and there to await develop-
ments.   'You must keep up communications,' so Von
Mechel wrote, 'between the column attacking Sant'
Angelo and my column attacking the Arches of the
Valley.'[1]   This cannot be read as constituting an order
to assist in the battle of the Arches of the Valley, and
yet Von Mechel conducted his whole operations there on
October 1 on the assumption that Ruiz would hasten to
his assistance, and after the event blamed him for 'ad-
hering too literally to his instructions,' instead of marching to the sound of the guns.[2]   It may be pleaded in
favour of Ruiz that he heard guns firing on both sides of
him, at Sant' Angelo and at the Arches of the Valley,
and that the instructions given him by Von Mechel
were to 'keep up communications' between these two
battles eight miles apart.   No doubt a Clive or a Blucher
would have marched off to decide one or other of the
two battles, or else would have seized the opportunity to
attack the enemy's head-quarters at New Caserta, but
Ruiz was an ordinary Neapolitan officer and was content
to carry out his actual instructions a few hours behind
time.

Von Mechel, therefore, at six in the morning of
October 1, with only 3000 infantry and six mountain

---

[1] *Ruiz*, 46.   [2] *Franci*, ii. 261-269 (Von Mechel's report).

SUMMIT OF MONTE TIFATA

Garibaldi's favourite station, Sept.-Oct., 1860

CICCARELLI BRIDGE FROM THE SUNK LAKE BELOW

The bridge carries the road along which Garibaldi's carriage passed; the Bourbon troops were concealed in the lane where the goats are.

THE ARCHES OF THE VALLEY

Taken from close under the Mills, Monte Lecrone. Looking at spurs of Monte Caro, part of Pizio's second position which the Swiss

guns, attempted to dislodge Bixio from a strong position which he held with an equal number of guns and 5600 volunteers. This was the only part of the battle of the Volturno in which the Royalists were inferior, not in quality, but in numbers. The first of Von Mechel's three battalions of foreign troops was composed of Austrians and Bavarians, brave but ill-disciplined, and inclined to be mutinous on questions of food and forced marches. The second battalion consisted chiefly, and the third entirely, of Swiss, many of whom had been in the Bourbon service for years in the old privileged Swiss regiments disbanded in 1859.[1] They had been accustomed, when in garrison at Maddaloni, to field days in these mountains, and knew every yard of the ground near the aqueduct. Better troops could not have been found in all Europe for the purpose Von Mechel had in hand.[2]

Bixio had chosen to defend Maddaloni at the point where the valley connecting it with Ducenta narrows to a gorge, spanned by 'the Arches of the Valley'—Vanvitelli's colossal aqueduct that carries the water to Caserta Palace. Along the top of the water-pipe runs a narrow viaduct, some 200 feet above the valley bottom, and by this aerial footpath Bixio was able to establish rapid communication between his left wing on the slopes of Monte Caro and his right wing on the slopes of Monte Longano. His reserve was behind the left wing, on Monte San Michele and at Villa Gualtieri.

The Swiss veterans of the third battalion, dragging up with them a mountain battery, ascended the wooded slopes of Monte Longano and stormed the Mills at the eastern end of the aqueduct, driving in flight Bixio's right wing, the 'brigade' Eberhardt. Von Mechel's son was killed at the head of the mountaineers of Uri and

---

[1] *Garibaldi and the Thousand*, pp. 137-138.

[2] Bixio was under the mistaken impression that he was attacked not only by the foreign troops but by two regiments of Neapolitan line also. This is clearly proved to be an error by the Bourbon authorities quoted below in Appendix L, 4. Bixio's officer, Sclavo, of the Thousand, said to me, 'there were no Italians against us' at the Arches of the Valley.

Unterwald. The attack at the bottom of the valley, directed against the base of the great arches, was successful in consequence of the victory on the hill-side above. Several Garibaldian officers at the aqueduct, apparently of Eberhardt's Genoese 'brigade,' led the flight to Maddaloni. A few days later, at Bixio's request, they were degraded in sight of the whole army, at a review held in front of Caserta Palace, with the advice from Garibaldi's own lips to beg for muskets and get themselves killed in the next action.

But the left wing under Dezza and Menotti Garibaldi, and the reserves under Fabrizi behaved so well that even Bixio praised their conduct, especially that of the Sicilians.[1] Bixio, after his right wing had disappeared, still held the western mountain wall of the valley, the lower slopes of Monte Caro and the pass crowned by the Villa Gualtieri, over which Von Mechel now attempted to cut his way to Caserta in the plain beyond. The Austrians and Bavarians tried to ascend Monte Caro through the wood from the north, while the victorious Swiss began to climb out of the valley-bottom up the precipitous slopes to Villa Gualtieri, and to pour across from Monte Longano along the top of the Arches of the Valley. But the artillery got encumbered in endeavouring to cross the narrow viaduct, and as the infantry struggled up-hill through the sparse vineyards and the limestone rocks, they were met by vigorous bayonet charges and hurled back again into the valley-bottom.

Now was the time that Ruiz should have appeared over the top of Monte Caro, but he was not in sight, and the messengers sent to find him had failed in their mission. At midday, therefore, after six hours' fighting, Von Mechel gave orders to retreat to Ducenta. He

---

[1] This praise is the more to be believed, because Bixio had been especially contemptuous of the conduct of the *squadre* in Sicily. On September 19 some of the Sicilians (the *Cacciatori d'Etna*) had behaved badly. But on October 1 the Sicilians behaved well, not only here under Bixio, but also at Sant' Angelo under Dunne, and at Santa Maria under the Sicilian officers, Corrao and La Porta. See Türr's and Avezzana's reports, *Menghini*, pp. 357, 373-374.

acknowledged a loss of ninety men and one gun captured, and over 100 men killed and wounded. Bixio lost no prisoners, but acknowledged a loss of over 200 killed and wounded.[1]

Meanwhile, Ruiz and his 5000 were wandering about useless between the two battles, either of which could have been decided by their presence. Their only orders were to occupy Old Caserta. Arriving at Limatola at dawn, they drove out a few hundred Garibaldian irregulars,[2] and followed the road southwards through the hills on to the cultivated tufa plain that lies in the lap of this group of mountains. On the plain stand half a dozen villages around the foot of a conical mountain crowned by the feudal ruin of Castel Morrone. In the castle were stationed Pilade Bronzetti and 280 men of Cosenz' brigade, and Ruiz turned aside to storm their position. Bronzetti had expected the villages of Sant' Andrea and l'Annunziata in the plain to be defended for awhile by the bands who had retired thither from Limatola, and by 150 of Sacchi's men who had come over from San Leucio. But these all decamped without waiting for the enemy, refusing even to retire up the hill so as to join Bronzetti in the defence of the ruined castle.[3]

Bronzetti and his 280 men were therefore left alone in Castel Morrone against Ruiz and his 5000. The attack was delivered, first from the north only, and finally from all sides at once. The Bourbon General himself has recorded that this handful of Garibaldini held out for 'four hours of fierce fighting.' Castel Morrone was a well-chosen position for a determined body of men to resist

---

[1] Appendix L, 4.

[2] *De Sivo*, iv. 201, confuses them with Bronzetti's men who never approached Limatola.

[3] Later on, another small body of Sacchi's troops came on the scene further to the west and skirmished with Ruiz' men in the villages of Grottole and Casali. But Sacchi himself and most of his 1800 men remained far away at San Leucio, in accordance with Garibaldi's orders, which were to guard the communications of Caserta with Sant' Angelo.

more than ten times their number. The lonely mediaeval keep, raised high above the modern life of the plain
below, has been inhabited for hundreds of years past
only by yellow hawks, darting in and out of the upper
windows, whence the robber Normans once watched the
traffic along the banks of the Volturno. The keep itself is
surrounded by a ruined parapet a few yards out, which
Bronzetti had caused his men to repair. From the foot of
this outer wall the mountain falls away on every side in
a smooth glacis for several hundred yards, and on the
south side the straight, bare slope continues for half a mile
as far as the villages of the plain. Only on the west is
there a neighbouring hill-top within long rifle range of
the castle.

Firing from behind the parapet the Garibaldini again
and again repulsed the enemy advancing up the glacis of
the mountain-side. At length their ammunition ran out,
but still they resisted, using the bayonet and hurling the
heavy blocks of limestone which lay everywhere to their
hands. When the Royalists at length burst over the
wall and into the chambers of the castle they found
Pilade Bronzetti sitting wounded on the ground, and
stabbed him to death while he was attempting to negotiate the surrender of his men. He left a name as
memorable in Garibaldian story as that of his brother,
Narciso, who had been killed the year before at the foot
of the Alps.[1] His men were all captured, but not before at least a third of them had been killed or
wounded.

In the latter stages of this four hours' siege, Ruiz
with a part of his force had been skirmishing at Casali
against a few of Sacchi's men, and had then begun to
push on towards Old Caserta. After the fall of Castel
Morrone his whole force proceeded southwards, ascended
the Lupara range over the western shoulder of Monte
Viro, and reached Old Caserta in the middle of the after-

[1] *Garibaldi and the Thousand*, pp. 103-106.

CASTLE MORRONE

From the glacis to N.W. ; the limestone blocks are characteristic of all the
mountains in the battle of Oct. 1 and 2.

AMPHITHEATRE OF ANCIENT CAPUA

Outside S. Maria, houses of which are seen in background.

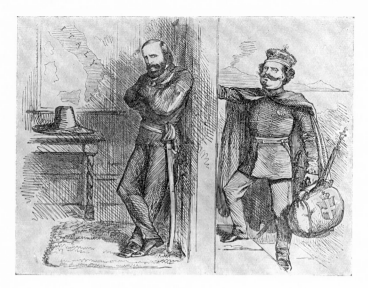

'THE MAN IN POSSESSION.' (*Punch*, Oct. 6, 1850)

'THE RIGHT LEG IN THE BOOT AT LAST.'
(*Punch*, Nov. 17, 1860)
GARIBALDI AND VICTOR EMMANUEL

noon, three and a half hours after Von Mechel had retreated from before Bixio at the Arches of the Valley.[1]

The appearance of Ruiz' blue-coats on the ridge overlooking the great plain and the sight of the Bourbon flag floating from the Castle of Old Caserta, were greeted with the ringing of joy bells in the reactionary villages of Casolla, Santa Barbara, and Tuoro at the foot of the mountain, and struck terror into the Liberal inhabitants of New Caserta. The head-quarters at the Palace were now practically destitute of troops, for Türr, though with some misgivings, had obeyed Garibaldi's orders and started for Santa Maria about an hour before with the last of the reserves.[2] Ruiz, however, having no orders to proceed farther than Old Caserta, remained on the top of the mountain all the rest of the day, looking down on the unprotected heart of the enemy's position, but never striking the blow that might so well have proved fatal if delivered in time.

The four hours' delay purchased by the heroism of Bronzetti and his handful of men at Castel Morrone, very probably saved Garibaldi from destruction. For if Ruiz had arrived at Old Caserta before noon, he would either have been in time to help Von Mechel to a victory over Bixio; or else he would, by threatening New Caserta in the plain, have prevented the departure thence of Türr's reserves for Santa Maria. In the latter case Santa Maria and Sant' Angelo would have been taken before nightfall.

At three in the afternoon, the last reserves from

[1] Appendix L, 7 and 9, below. Bronzetti's brave lieutenant, Giuseppe Mirri, thought that his commanding officer should have fallen back from Castel Morrone and resisted on the range of mountains running out of Monte Viro. Mirri, before he died, persuaded his friend, the fine old Garibaldian Senator Cadolini, of the justice of this criticism of Bronzetti's wisdom. Senator Cadolini has spoken to me about it, but I still venture to think that Bronzetti was right, for although the position he took up ensured the ultimate capture of all his small force, it also ensured a long delay to Ruiz, which was the all-important military object. Except on the top of a smooth, conical hill 280 men could not have held out for four hours against more than ten times their number.

[2] *Türr's Div.* 241.

Caserta,—the Hungarians,[1] Rüstow's Milanese and Eber's North Italians,—all picked troops, were brought up by Türr himself to Santa Maria. Almost at the same hour Garibaldi returned thither from Sant' Angelo. He had been forced to ride round by a long and dangerous circuit through Casapulla, for the whole plain, as far as San Prisco, was occupied by regiments of Royalist foot and horse. He found Santa Maria still holding out, but more like a besieged town than a point in the line of battle. The Frenchmen still held their farm-house, the Sicilians the amphitheatre, and men and guns were still lodged on part of the railway embankment. But every one else in that part of the field was packed into the streets of Santa Maria, which presented for hours together a scene of confused resistance and continual slaughter. All through the day fresh men were found ready to die beside the two cannon under the old Roman archway. The town band of Santa Maria, whose 20,000 inhabitants were devoted partisans of the new order, stood playing in the middle of the crowded street to hearten their defenders.

Arrived in the middle of this welter, which would have confused a less able soldier, Garibaldi took in the situation on the whole battlefield, and saw that the opportunity of the day had come. He at once determined to lead out northwards the last reserves whom Türr had just brought into the town. In this way alone could he relieve the pressure on Santa Maria and at the same time clear the enemy off the line of communications with Sant' Angelo. While he was giving his last orders in the street before riding out to try the final issue of

[1] The foreigners fighting for Garibaldi on October 1-2 were about 200 Hungarian cavalry; 200 Hungarian infantry; about 50 French of De Flotte's company; and 100 of Wolf's foreigners, deserters from the Neapolitan army. *Türr's Div.* 454. The British Legion had not yet arrived, but a few score English were fighting in various capacities. The foreigners in the Bourbon army on October 1-2 were six times as many, for besides Von Mechel's 3000 at the Arches of the Valley, a few companies of Swiss were fighting against Santa Maria. *Schweizertruppen.*

his own and his country's fortune, his old friend, Jessie White, Mario's English wife, came up to him with a glass of water and some figs. He had tasted nothing all day, and he gladly took food and drink from her hands. As he did so, he observed that she was being followed about by a group of British sailors on the spree, with no officer among them, on leave from H.M.S. *Hannibal*.[1] Being unskilled in Italian, they had fastened on their country-woman and were imploring her to have them supplied with muskets. 'What, Jessie! you are helping these sailors to desert their Queen?' said Garibaldi, good-naturedly, as he sat on his horse eating the figs she had brought him. 'They have only come to amuse them-selves,' she said. They were not supplied with arms, but stood by to bear a hand in some way more befitting their country's attitude of benevolent neutrality.[2]

The decisive movement now began. Garibaldi, fol-lowed by the Hungarians, by Eber's men and by the Milanese, issued from Santa Maria along the northern road and cleared the enemy off the communications with Sant' Angelo. Eber, continuing up the road towards the Ciccarelli lane and bridge where Garibaldi had fallen into the ambush in the morning, relieved the pressure on Medici. But the Dictator himself, followed by the Hungarians and Milanese, wheeled to the left not far outside Santa Maria, and swept the field in the direction of Capua. The onslaught with fixed bayonets of fresh and vigorous troops under such a leader could not be resisted by the masses of the enemy, who had been firing for hours past without making further head-

[1] Not to be confused with the *deserters* from the *Agamemnon*, who were helping to fight the guns at Sant' Angelo, see p. 235, note, above.

[2] After the charge of Hungarian horse that followed a few minutes later, the Royalist battery on the road near Sant' Agostino was seen lying dismounted and derelict. A handful of Garibaldini rushed out from under the Roman arch to drag off the enemy's guns, but they had not the skill to remount them. Then the sailors from H.M.S. *Hannibal*, seeing that their time had come, ran up to help, and the spectacle seen a few minutes later of sailors in British uniform dragging two captured guns into Santa Maria was reported far and wide, scandalised Royalist Europe, and became the subject of diplomatic correspondence.

way.   The 200 Hungarian cavaliers, Garibaldi's only
mounted force, were at length let loose.   They went
right over the batteries and on through regiment after
regiment.   Too few to rout the whole army, they were
too brave, and too skilled with horse and sword, to
be stopped anywhere on this side the walls of Capua.
Singly and in small groups, as evening fell, the survivors
rode back, well satisfied that they had honoured the
Magyar name before the eyes of Europe.

Behind the 200 horsemen followed the ranks of
levelled bayonets with Garibaldi in the midst of them.
Two hundred Hungarian infantry and 600 Milanese,
deploying to north and south of Parisi farm-house, with
their faces towards Capua station, drove the enemy's
tired regiments before them.   The Royalists, as they
retreated, turned round to fire, and still here and there
rallied for a stand under a covering charge of cavalry.
But Garibaldi still came on, and in the rear and on the
left of the men whom he was leading, came the defenders
pouring out from Santa Maria, men of Sicily, of Calabria,
of Tuscany, and of all the other provinces of United
Italy.   Sant' Agostino had been deserted by the enemy,
and now the cemetery and the Cappuccini Convent were
stormed, and De Angelis farm to the north of the road.
Medici, too, relieved by Eber's advance, sallied out from
Sant' Angelo and recaptured the battery where Dunne
had been wounded in the morning.   All the advanced
positions which had been lost at dawn when the Bourbon
army came out of Capua in the fog, were re-occupied
before sunset.   The masses of the beaten Royalists, converging from north and south upon the parade ground
before Capua, retreated sullenly through the gate whence
they had issued with such high hopes twelve hours before.   While Garibaldi rode back to Sant' Angelo through
the dusk, his men lay down exhausted and hungry on
the ground, each man where he stood, knowing that
they had saved Italy.[1]

[1] Appendix L, 5, below.

An epilogue to the decisive battle of the first of
October took place on the following day. Ruiz and his
five thousand on the hill-top of Old Caserta had spent
the afternoon and night in complete ignorance of the result of the fighting before Capua or at the Arches of the
Valley. Early on the morning of October 2 news reached
them of the double defeat of Ritucci and of Von Mechel.
Ruiz thereupon held a Council of War at which he decided to retreat at once to the north bank of the Volturno,
while the way was still open. Nearly three thousand of
his men obeyed the order to retreat and escaped through
Limatola, but more than two thousand, seized by a sudden
impulse for battle and plunder, refused to obey their
General, and descended off the mountain, officers and
men together, to attack Caserta in the plain below. Part
of them advanced through the park and by way of the
cascade, driving a company of Sacchi's men before them
down the wooded hill-side. Others made straight into
Caserta town through Casolla and Altifreda. A panic
seized the few troops defending Caserta, and the Royalists
entered in triumph and commenced sacking the houses.

But all this while Garibaldi was throwing his net
round them with equal energy and skill. He had already
caused orders to be conveyed to Bixio bidding him come
over Monte Viro and cut them off from the north-east.
He himself with such of the troops from Sant' Angelo as
were not completely prostrated by their efforts of the
day before, crossed the tracks over Monte Tifata and
arrived at San Leucio, a little after nine in the morning.
Here he effected a junction with Sacchi and with some
troops just arrived by train from Naples, who had taken
no part in the battle of October 1, namely, Stocco's Calabrians and a few companies of Piedmontese Bersaglieri and
other regulars. Led on by Garibaldi himself, the picked
troops of Victor Emmanuel's army in their round hats with
the cocks' feathers, climbed through the steep park in the
direction of Old Caserta, side by side with the red-shirts
and the gaitered Calabrians in their brigand costume.

Before he himself began to mount the hill from San Leucio, the Dictator had detached thence a few score of Genoese Carabineers of the Thousand by the lower road, to save the Palace and to clear the enemy out of Caserta in the plain.   The Genoese charged into the main street of Caserta, singing Mameli's hymn of '48, and after a sharp struggle in which a dozen fell on each side, drove the horde of plunderers back out of the town and up the hills towards Old Caserta.   Meanwhile, the larger force under the Dictator was shepherding the other flocks of Bourbon infantry out of the park, and up towards the same point on the hills above.   Before long the whole two thousand, emerging from brush-wood and the olive groves below, were to be seen flying for their lives along the stony flanks of the mountain towards Old Caserta. At this moment Bixio's force appeared over the top of Monte Viro, barring their flight northwards.   The net closed in upon them, and after another hour spent in hunting detachments of various sizes over the great bare plateau, 2012 men and 77 officers were secured as prisoners of war.[1]

Taking all parts of the battle of the Volturno together, the Garibaldini officially acknowledged a loss on the two days of 306 killed, 1328 wounded, and 389 missing.   Of these losses scarcely fifty can be attributed to the fighting on the second day ; at Castel Morrone there were under 300 lost, most of them prisoners ; and at the Arches of the Valley rather more than 200 killed and wounded. It follows that some 1400 must have been killed or wounded in the main battle of October 1, in defence of the line of Santa Maria and Sant' Angelo over against Capua.   The Bourbon Generals officially acknowledged a loss in that part of the field of 1065 men—260 killed, 731 wounded, and 74 prisoners ; besides 200 more lost at the Arches of the Valley on October the first, and

[1] Appendix L, 8.

2089 prisoners taken near Old Caserta on October the second.[1]

Garibaldi had now nearly 1500 wounded on his hands, besides large numbers of sick, disabled by constant exposure and under-feeding at the outposts. As the autumn drew on, long grey overcoats were served out, which gave the army a more uniform appearance, besides some chance of warmth at night. But the conditions of service before Capua continued to be very severe.

The Neapolitans did little or nothing to make life more comfortable for their deliverers. Those of the wounded who were sent back to the Capital fared worse than those left at the front, for the usual peculation and carelessness of the hospital officials and the consequent dirt and absence of necessaries were not remedied on behalf of the Garibaldini, except to some degree by British help in the form of materials and money from England and personal service by some of our countrywomen in Naples. The field hospitals at Caserta and Santa Maria, though far from perfect, were better, being under the control of the medical staff of Türr's division, and under the eye of Jessie White Mario herself. The English women in the hospitals of Naples were deeply affected by the patience and gentleness of the North Italian wounded, and by their complete unselfishness. Indeed their only anxiety seemed to be not to give trouble, by any complaints, however reasonable, to Garibaldi or to those who had volunteered to nurse them. In spite of the pain and squalor of their lot, the wounded were not unhappy, for there were days in October on which Garibaldi was in the Capital, when he never failed to visit them, stopping to speak to each one and to make the dying envied by some special mark of his gratitude and love.

'All the men,' writes an English lady, 'when they heard him coming, began to sit up in their beds and clap

[1] Appendix L, 9.

their hands and shout, *Papà nostro, papà nostro!* They long to be allowed coffee in the morning instead of grease and water, so my sister said to one of them, "Now ask the General to order that you have coffee." The young man answered, "O lady, how could I trouble him with that, when he has so much to see to, and when his very presence gives us new life." [1]

The battle of the Volturno, the last of Garibaldi's great feats of war, differs from Como, Calatafimi, Palermo, Milazzo, and the Crossing of the Straits, firstly, because it shows him acting on the defensive, and secondly, because it shows him handling some 20,000 men, a larger number than the handful of guerillas which according to his critics was all he could command with success. His defensive strategy on this occasion is excellent, and proves that he had learnt much about the conditions of European warfare since his defence of Rome in 1849, on his return from the South-American pampas. While the Bourbon generals on October 1 went out of their way to divide their army and attack him from east, north, and west at once, Garibaldi made full use of the central position in which they thus placed him. Communications between the various parts of the assailing force were therefore lost, with the result that Ruiz' division was of no practical use to Ritucci on the great day and was destroyed in detail on October 2. Garibaldi, on the other hand, took advantage of his central position, and of his short line of communication, strung together by the Maddaloni-Caserta-Santa Maria railway, to keep his reserve under Türr at the central point between the various battlefields until the very last moment. He could thus postpone the vital decision as to whether the reserve should be sent from Caserta to Santa Maria, or from Caserta to Maddaloni, until events showed where they were most needed. The arrival of this body of fresh troops at Santa Maria, half-way

[1] Appendix L, 10.

through the afternoon, and the vigorous use which he made of them to attack the enemy's tired regiments, decided the even balance of the day. The success of the National army in holding its own against greatly superior numbers is therefore to be attributed, apart from the valour of the volunteers, to three qualities shown on this occasion by Garibaldi : the personal inspiration of his presence at so many of the important points, the combined caution and vigour of his offensive-defensive tactics, and last, but not least, a sound strategy governing the disposition of his men over the whole region of conflict from the Arches of the Valley to the gate of Capua.

CHAPTER XIV

THE MEETING OF GARIBALDI AND VICTOR EMMANUEL

'To watch the new Kingdom of Italy rising as it were by magic is a marvellous sight. When time has veiled the events of the period and wiped away all that is perfidious and adventurous, Cavour, Victor Emmanuel, and Garibaldi will stand forth as heroes of this epoch. While I am writing of the struggles and sufferings of Rome in the Middle Ages, the observation of the present, which is realising the work of which centuries have despaired, is an experience of inestimable value to the historian.' *Gregorovius' Diary.* Rome, November 7, 1860.

THE battle of the Volturno saved Naples from the Bourbons, but it did not deliver Capua to Garibaldi. It redressed the balance of war which had begun to incline against him, but it did not weigh down the scales on his side. A condition of military stalemate continued for more than three weeks of October, until Victor Emmanuel's army arrived upon the scene.

During this period of waiting, the only military event of interest was the expedition to Isernia. That town, like most others in the Molise and in the neighbouring province of Abruzzi, had been seized by the citizens in the name of Garibaldi and Victor Emmanuel. But on the day before the battle of the Volturno it was invaded by peasants from the hills, authorised to act for the good cause by their Bishop and by the authorities at Gaeta, and led on by Royal gens-d'armes. During the following week pillage, massacre, torture, and mutilation were the lot of the inhabitants of Isernia and of other centres of Nationalism in the neighbourhood. This system of 'reaction' or 'brigandage,' accompanied by all the bestial cruelty of which the half-savage peasants of the South were still capable, afforded a last weapon for the

expiring system of Church and State. Francis II, when
finally driven from Gaeta by Victor Emmanuel's army,
took refuge in Rome in 1861, and thence, under the protection of the Pope, continued to foster this kind of
'brigandage' in his lost dominions in the Abruzzi for
nearly seven years to come. No such horrors were
committed on the other side by the Garibaldian peasantry
of Calabria, Basilicata, Abruzzi or any other province of
the mainland, and the difference may fairly be attributed
to the higher ethical standard of the local Nationalist
leaders—men like Stocco and Pace, touched by the idealism of the *risorgimento* movement—as compared with the
reactionary clergy and the Bourbon officials, who had
been brought up in an evil school on frankly mediaeval
ideas of religion and government.

Early in October, Nationalist refugees from the neighbourhood of Isernia arrived at Caserta, told the tale of
horror to Garibaldi, and assured him that if he would
send some of his officers into the Molise they would there
find 3000 peasants ready to place themselves under their
orders and suppress the reaction. The Dictator accordingly sent Nullo, Mario, and Zasio in command of a few
hundred Sicilians and irregulars from the Alife district,
and a few dozen North Italians. But when they arrived
in the Molise, there was no sign of the 3000 friendly
natives who were to have joined them. The reactionary
peasants, backed by several battalions of Bourbon regulars, fell upon them near Isernia on October 17, and
drove them out of the Molise with heavy loss.[1] In the
Abruzzi the Liberals held their own, but eagerly awaited
the crossing of the Tronto by Victor Emmanuel.

On October 15 the British Legion, otherwise called
the 'Garibaldi Excursionists,'[2] landed in Naples, over

[1] *Isernia*, 7-36. *Leg. Matese*, 108-111, 153-168. *Zasio*, 116-125. *Red Shirt*,
225-226, 234-264. *Castelli*, 331-332. *Türr's Div.* 282-286. *Arrivabene*, ii. 291.
[2] A thin pretence that such was their innocent character had been kept up
in England to save diplomatic appearances. The advertisement that enlisted
most of them ran as follows: '*Excursion to Sicily and Naples*. All persons

600 strong. They looked a fine body of men as they marched up the Toledo in their red tunics with green facings, the muzzles of their Enfield rifles stuffed with flowers by the admiring populace. Four days later they gave a good account of themselves in a skirmish in front of Sant' Angelo, conducted up to the walls of Capua, where they lost two killed and eight wounded.[1] But the warning that Dunne had uttered when Garibaldi consulted him at Milazzo as to the advisability of allowing such a Legion to be recruited,[2] was unfortunately borne out by events. One part of the Excursionists consisted of roughs principally from Glasgow and London, who considered that they were out for a holiday at other people's expense, and though they did not object to the fighting, expected a maximum of food and good quarters and a minimum of discipline. The other half, old soldiers, 'volunteers,' and generous enthusiasts of all classes from a Duke's son downwards, could not, by their own better conduct, save the Legion from acquiring a name for disorder similar to that which the Pope's Irish had acquired in Rome. 'You see,' said the Italians indulgently, 'these men are not accustomed to a country where wine is cheap.' Peard, whom the Dictator set over them as Colonel, was not so well qualified for this difficult command as for the individual knight-errantry which had made him a well-beloved figure in the Garibaldian field armies for eighteen months past. If the campaign had been prolonged and carried to the walls of Rome, as the Committee in London had expected when it raised the Legionaries, there is little doubt that they would have

(particularly Members of Volunteer Rifle Corps) desirous of visiting Southern Italy and of *aiding* by their presence and influence the *Cause* of *Garibaldi* and *Italy*, may learn how to proceed by applying to the Garibaldi Committee at the offices, No. 8 Salisbury Street, Strand, London.' *Holyoake*, i. 245.

[1] *St. Maur*, 227 (Peard's report). *Peard MS. Journal*, Oct. 19. *Arrivabene*, ii. 288-289. *Menghini*, 375-376. *Conv. Ellis.* Garibaldi wrote of 'the brilliant courage they displayed in the slight engagements they shared with us on the Volturno.' *Holyoake*, i. 255.

[2] See p. 98 above.

done us credit.   As things were, although the Legion came too late, the fame of our country had been upheld throughout the campaign, and yeomen's service rendered to the Italian cause by the English free lances, by Dunne and Wyndham, by Peard and Dowling, and by others who have survived them.

Garibaldi estimated accurately the limits of the degree to which he had improved his position by the recent victory on the Volturno.   One day soon after the battle he came to Mario with a letter from Mazzini in his hand.   'Read this,' he said.   'Mazzini urges me on to attack Rome.   You know that I have long been thinking of it.   On the first of October we defeated the enemy so that they cannot meet us again in the open field.   But I cannot advance on Rome leaving behind me 60,000 men intrenched in Capua and Gaeta, who can march into Naples the moment my back is turned.'[1]   He fully accepted the political consequences of the military situation.   He abandoned all idea of advancing on Rome, and prepared to welcome the immediate advent of Victor Emmanuel.

Cavour, gravely anxious that Italy should present a united front to the Monarchs of Austria, Prussia, and Russia, who were about to hold an ominous conference at Warsaw, desired above all else that the Dictator should go out to welcome the King in the face of Italy and Europe, and was much concerned lest he should sail home to Caprera in dudgeon before Victor Emmanuel's arrival.   This, rather than any fears of actual civil war, appears to have been the limit of Cavour's anxiety with regard to Garibaldi, from the first days of October onwards.[2]   The Minister wisely sought counsel with

---

[1] *Mario Vita*, ii. 3.   *Guerzoni*, ii. 205.

[2] On September 24 he had feared a collision with Garibaldi (*Chiala*, iv. 15), but this fear had been removed by Garibaldi's manifesto of welcome to the Royal troops a few days later, see pp. 226-227 above.   On October 4, Augusto Vecchi writes to Garibaldi: 'Cavour sent me word to call on him.   I will tell you about our two hours' conversation.   I laid bare to him all your noble heart.   He regretted

Garibaldi's oldest and best friend, Augusto Vecchi, who had worn the red shirt beside his chief in South America, who had fought shoulder to shoulder with him in the midnight *mêlée* when the French troops burst through the defences of the Janiculum, and from whose house at Quarto, Garibaldi had sailed with the Thousand for Sicily. On October 1 Vecchi wrote to Garibaldi to implore him to hasten the plebiscite for the annexation of Naples, and to send a message inviting Victor Emmanuel to march without delay into his new dominions. Three days later Vecchi wrote again : 'Invite the King personally by a telegram to come quickly to Naples. And go to meet him. I ask this of you in the name of Italy, our mother, for whose greatness we two swore many years ago to make every kind of sacrifice.' [1]

On the very day when Vecchi was writing in this strain, Garibaldi had already yielded the point and was inditing his famous letter to Victor Emmanuel, which, besides many expressions of goodwill and desire for unity, contained the following words :—

'CASERTA, *October* 4, 1860.

'SIRE,

'I congratulate Your Majesty on the brilliant victories won by your brave General Cialdini and on their happy results. . . . Since Your Majesty is at Ancona, you must make the journey to Naples by land or by sea. If by land, as would be best, Your Majesty ought to march with at least one division. If I were informed in time, I would move forward my right wing to meet you, and would come in person to present my homage and to receive your orders as to the final operations. . . .' [2]

---

that you had not answered a letter of his. At the end of our interview, he told me to accompany you to meet the King. And he ended by saying that Venice would be ours six months sooner, if you did not separate yourself from Victor Emmanuel,—to put it more clearly, if you did not obstinately retire to Caprera ' [*viz.* before welcoming Victor Emmanuel to Naples]. *Fazzari MSS.* If Cavour had still thought there was any chance of civil war, he would have been only too glad that Garibaldi should ' retire obstinately to Caprera.'

[1] *Fazzari MSS.* Vecchi's letters of Oct. 1 and 4, 1860.

[2] *Guerzoni*, ii. 208-209. *Ciàmpoli*, 186-187.

Cavour, therefore, as early as October 4 had gained his point that Garibaldi should invite the King and go out to meet him. But for another ten days there was trouble on the further question of the plebiscite, a controversy which became the storm-centre of the last political crisis of the Dictatorship. The question at issue was the proper method of obtaining the consent of the inhabitants of the Neapolitan Kingdom to their absorption in the Monarchy of Victor Emmanuel. Should they be consulted directly by plebiscite, by a simple referendum on the question of annexation, to which each elector could answer by his vote, 'yes' or 'no'? Or should they place their fate in the hands of an assembly of elected representatives, who might then propose conditions on which the South would come into the National union? Such were the two alternatives, and the choice between them was a question of more than mere form.

If Italy had had no armed enemies to fear either within or without the barrier of her guardian Alps, if she had been in safe possession of her own house, then indeed she ought to have gone about the difficult business of setting it in order with long and careful deliberation. If the union of North and South Italy, like the union of North and South Britain in 1707, had been proposed in a year when the two Kingdoms were immune from invasion and revolution, then indeed a Parliament at Naples and a Parliament at Palermo might reasonably have sat for many months bargaining with the Parliament at Turin. In such a case some of the evils that have actually resulted from a too close union might possibly have been avoided. Those who know South Italy of to-day deplore the rigid and mechanical application of the Piedmontese laws and administrative system to a state of society very different from that of the sub-Alpine populations; and they deplore no less the immense powers of self-government which under the constitution of 1860 have been committed to the backward communes of the South.[1] But this was the necessary price that Italy paid for her existence. In the crisis of that autumn, with war and revolution still in the bowels of the land, with an Austrian army eagerly awaiting the word to cross the Mincio and rush on Milan, with the French Minister already withdrawn from Turin, and every great European Power except England hostile to the unification of Italy, it would have been the height of unwisdom to waste two months in electing and calling together Neapolitan and Sicilian assemblies, and half a year more in bargainings and intrigues of every kind, public and personal, into which Southern Parliamentarians would instinctively plunge and revel, if they found that they had their country in their gift and Cavour on his knees to them to hand it over. If Italian unity were to be accomplished at all—and all were agreed that there was no other port of safety in sight—then it must be done at once by direct acceptance of Piedmontese law and custom for the whole Peninsula, not because that was best for all but because that alone could be established everywhere without delay. A plebiscite for unconditional annexation could be held in a fortnight, but an assembly might sit until it was dispersed by Austrian bayonets.

The men who in the second week of October besieged Garibaldi with petitions for an assembly instead of the plebiscite, were not, with the exception of the 'federalist' Cattaneo, primarily interested in obtaining a separate system of administration for the South. Their opposition to the plebiscite was essentially factious. Crispi and his friends desired an assembly where they might hope to dominate, and they objected to a plebiscite because it would in a fortnight's time bring to an end the Garibaldian Dictatorship which, so long as it lasted, left the executive power in their hands and kept out the hated Cavour. They played on the Dictator's distrust of the Minister. They cunningly reminded him that the plebiscite had been the device by which Napoleon III

[1] *De Cesare*, ii. 142-144.

had filched Nice and Savoy. There had arisen one of those complicated situations through which Garibaldi was least able to see his way in the light of the few simple rules by which he guided his conduct. His mind was darkened and he sat stupefied at the head of the council-board while the rival parties of plebiscite and assembly defied each other shrilly across the room.

Between October 11 and 13 a series of such councils were held at Caserta and in Naples. Old Giorgio Pallavicino, 'the martyr of the Spielberg,' the Austrian dungeon where he had sat for fourteen years in the early days of the *risorgimento* movement, was now Garibaldi's Pro-Dictator of the Neapolitan mainland. He it was who stood in the breach against Crispi and Cattaneo, on behalf of immediate Italian unity. On October 11, at Caserta, Garibaldi decided for Crispi and an assembly. Pallavicino at once gave in his resignation, and the city of Naples rose in a great demonstration of protest in his favour. On all doors, windows, carriages, coats, and hats appeared cards inscribed *sì* ('yes'),—the vote that all desired to be allowed to give in plebiscite. Garibaldi returned to the Capital to find the streets in an uproar. He heard Pallavicino's name coupled with his own for *vivas*, while *morte* was cried out against Mazzini, Crispi, and the others who had persuaded him to summon an assembly. All along the Toledo it 'snowed *sìs*' into the carriage. Garibaldi was much perturbed by this clear manifestation of the popular will, for obedience to the people was one of the formulæ of his creed, in accordance with which he had long ago abandoned his republicanism in order to be in touch with his fellow-citizens.

On the thirteenth another council was held in his rooms at the Palazzo d'Angri. Pallavicino refused to take back his resignation unless the plan for an assembly were cancelled. In the middle of an angry dispute between the Pro-Dictator and Crispi, Türr produced a petition signed by thousands of hands in favour of the plebiscite. Garibaldi bowed his head over it in melancholy silence, and for some minutes his face was hidden. When he looked up the clouds had cleared away, and he wore the 'serene gaiety' of his happiest and gentlest mood. 'If this is the desire of the Neapolitan people,' he said, 'it must be satisfied.' '*Caro Giorgio*,' he said to Pallavicino, 'we need you here still.' The same evening Crispi resigned the secretariate, and his part in the history of Italy came to an end for that year.[1]

The plebiscite was held on October 21. The electorate had no choice but to vote *yes* or *no* to the following proposition : 'The people wishes for Italy one and indivisible with Victor Emmanuel as Constitutional King, and his legitimate descendants after him.' The result was shortly afterwards declared as follows :—

Neapolitan mainland   1,302,064 yes ; 10,312 no.
Sicily   -   -   -   432,053 yes ;   667 no.[2]

The voting was open,[3] and every one who voted 'no' did so in the face of a disapproving world. No doubt, therefore, the real minority was a very much larger proportion of the citizens. But if the plebiscite exaggerated, it did not belie the opinion of the people. Whether the majority of the inhabitants of South Italy wished for Italian unity on its own merits is fairly open to question, but they had shown in more ways than one their earnest desire for immediate and unconditional annexation as the only security against the return of the House of Bourbon and the dreadful past from which Garibaldi had delivered them.

Meanwhile, Victor Emmanuel was coming to take possession of his new dominions. On the afternoon of September 29 he left Turin[4] on his triumphal progress

---

[1] *Caranti*, 29-42. *Crispi*, 1911, pp. 326-334, 360-362. *Türr's Div.* 277-281. F. O. *Sicily, Elliot*, 1860, Nos. 569, 585, 627.

[2] In the Papal dominions the vote, held a few days later, went as follows :—
    Marches 133,072 yes; 1,212 no.
    Umbria - 99,628 yes ; - 380 no.

[3] *Mundy*, 258.   [4] *F. O. Sard. Hudson*, No. 384, Sept. 29, 1860.

that was yet a most perilous adventure, hoping that when he wanted to return he would not find his northern capital occupied by Austrians or by French. Passing through Bologna to the Ravennese coast he embarked on October 3 for Ancona.[1] A storm arose, the frigate was in great danger, and the seamen declared that the safest course was to run across the Adriatic towards Pola in Austrian territory. But Victor Emmanuel, refusing to be put into the hands of his enemies at such a crisis of Italian affairs, came on deck to encourage the sailors, and remained there throughout the storm, while his staff officers were prostrated below. Towards evening the sea went down, and before midnight they entered the harbour of Ancona, where the King was welcomed ashore by Fanti, Cialdini, Della Rocca, and their victorious troops.

Some delay occurred in starting from Ancona, but on October 9 the great march began, the whole army moving, with the King in the midst, along the road to Naples. He passed near the battle-field of Castelfidardo, through Macerata and Loreto and thence along the Adriatic coast. He reached Grottammare, the last town in Papal territory, on October 11, and remained there four days inactive, probably from some cautionary reasons of diplomacy or politics. These were the days during which the political crisis on the question of the plebiscite was taking place in Naples. Only on October 15, after Pallavicino had triumphed over Crispi, did the King cross the Tronto and enter the Neapolitan Kingdom.

After following the coast-road as far as the fortress of Pescara, which had already come in to the national cause, they turned inland by way of Chieti and Popoli to Sulmona. Thus far, in Papal and in Neapolitan territory alike, the enthusiasm of the liberated people for their new King had been abundantly shown. All classes, including very many of the clergy, joined in the demon-

---

[1] See Map IV at end of book for the King's route from Ravenna southwards.

strations, and triumphal arches and addresses of welcome impeded the rate of military progress. It was felt that no offence must be given to the King's new subjects, and he showed as much rough graciousness as his impatient nature contained. Other causes of delay were the neglected state of the high-road, and the absence of bridges over the innumerable dry torrent beds through which the siege-guns and commissariat waggons had to pass. For this was not a Garibaldian army; it moved slowly, but it was bringing with it the means to take Capua and Gaeta.[1]

After they had passed Sulmona, the political sympathies of the inhabitants were less unanimous. There was still an enthusiastic 'Italian' party to welcome them, but at every turn of the road they saw fresh evidence of civil war and massacre. The 'good Italians' came in with stories, usually only too true, of massacre and mutilation which their relations and friends had suffered. Rough justice was administered on the road-side by Piedmontese court-martials assisted by firing parties, and a proclamation was issued that all peasants found with arms in their hands would be shot. Even in this district some of the parish priests showed themselves on the national side.[2]

Cialdini with the vanguard was now two days' march in front of the King. On October 20, near Isernia, where a handful of Garibaldini had been repulsed only three days before,[3] he fell in with 5000 Bourbon troops under General Scotti. Scotti neglected to send out scouts or advance-guard, and marched his men in column right up to Cialdini's hidden batteries. The Bersaglieri and line regiments were let loose upon the enemy's surprised and disordered mass, and the lancers of Novara charged through the whole length of their column. In a few minutes Scotti with nearly a thousand of his men had

[1] *Castelli*, 326-329. *De Cesare*, ii. 451-461. *Orero*, 113.
[2] *Castelli*, 330-331. *De Cesare*, ii. 462-463. *Orero*, 115-116
[3] See p. 259 above.

been captured, and the rest dispersed over the country-
side in hopeless disbandment.[1]

On October 25 Garibaldi crossed the Volturno by a
crazy bridge of planks a yard wide, supported on boats,
which had been flung across at the ferry of Formicola.
The Italians had failed to make any bridge at all with the
scant materials to hand, but the task had been accomplished by the British Legion with the expert assistance of
some 'handy men' who appeared to be their fellow-
countrymen and showed a suspicious readiness for any
service connected with ropes and water.[2]   The making of
the bridge had been conducted under fire, but the Bourbon
troops, who had already abandoned Cajazzo, withdrew
towards Capua and did not attempt to dispute the
passage of the river after the bridge had been completed.

Leaving Medici to protect the lines at Sant' Angelo,
Garibaldi with a few regiments of Italians and the
British Legion advanced northwards through Bellona
and Calvi to meet Victor Emmanuel.[3]   They bivouacked
on the night of October 25 to 26 in the broad valley
between the hills of Cajanello and Vajrano, where the
high-road then, as the railway now, debouches from the
gates of the wooded mountains into the flatter country
that soon broadens out into the great plains of Capua.
Most of the troops slept by the roadside below, but
some were stationed on the heights of Vajrano, whence
their watch-fires could be seen afar by three armies : for
below them lay the camp of their fellow-Garibaldini ;
close at hand to the south were Bourbon regiments ; and
a few miles to the north lay Victor Emmanuel's army,
the corps of Della Rocca and of Cialdini side by side
on two converging roads, with the King's quarters between them

[1] *Orero*, 122-124. *Revel's da Ancona*, 64-65. *Isernia*, 42.
[2] *Conv. Brown Young* (who with Dowling conducted the operation). *Mario
Vita*, ii. 17. *Red Shirt*, 273. *Adamoli*, 167. *Times*, Nov. 6, p. 9, c. 4.
[3] See henceforth Map III, A, at end of book.

On the morning of October 26 an Englishman among the Garibaldian outposts, who was sleeping in a dry ditch, was awakened by shouts of *Viva il Re!* Accustomed to hear 'Long live the King' as the Bourbon war-cry, he sprang up half-awake, thinking the enemy were upon them. Next moment he saw his mistake. Victor Emmanuel, King of Italy, was riding by.[1]

About the same hour the Garibaldini on the hills of Vajrano awoke to see the whole Italian army, in all the panoply of war, move swiftly along the valley below towards the camp of the red-shirts on the edge of the great plain.[2]

Garibaldi had overnight sent on Missori and Zasio to the Royal camp to announce his presence and offer his homage. At dawn he himself rode out with his staff to find the King, and stationed himself in front of the Toll-bar Tavern (*Taverna la catena*)—'a rustic cottage with a few poplars near it'—at the point of junction of the two roads along which the Royal army was coming.[3]

The Dictator and his staff, including Canzio and Mario, with Missori and Zasio who had now rejoined them, dismounted in front of the tavern and took their stand a little off the road along which the Northern regiments filed past. Battalion after battalion went by, gazing on Garibaldi, some with unmingled enthusiasm, gratitude, and love, others with a greater or less admixture of professional jealousy and political distrust. Generals Della Rocca and Cialdini both greeted him warmly that morning and were warmly welcomed in return, for neither of them was touched with that jealousy of the volunteers which embittered Fanti and many others among the regular officers. The victor of Castelfidardo and the Liberator of Sicily and Naples were

---

[1] *Conv. Dolmage.*

[2] *Bell MS.* (letter of Mr. Bell, who was among the Garibaldini on the hill).

[3] The modern railway-station of Cajanello-Vajrano is built within a few yards of the historic cross-roads.

divided by no cloud of petty rivalry, and if Cialdini instead of Fanti had been commander-in-chief of the Italian army, Cavour's instructions to show gratitude to the Garibaldini would have been heartily obeyed, much might have been forgotten and forgiven on both sides in the enthusiasm of the meeting, and the Serbonian bog of mutual reprisals and recrimination might have been shunned.

So the early morning wore on, while regiment after regiment of the Royal army marched past the Liberator. It was a damp autumn air, and Garibaldi was not only wearing his *poncho*, but had in homely fashion bound a coloured handkerchief over his head. His staff, in their war-stained red shirts, presented a curious contrast to the brilliant uniforms that were filing by them hour by hour. Suddenly the strains of the Royal march were heard, and the cry arose, 'The King! The King is coming!' Garibaldi and his staff mounted their horses and rode forward to the edge of the road. Victor Emmanuel, on a prancing Arab, dashed up to meet them. The Dictator, sweeping his hat off his kerchiefed head, cried aloud—'*Saluto il primo Re d'Italia*'—'I hail the first King of Italy.'[1] The King stretched out his hand and the two men clasped and held hands for more than a minute.

'*Come state, caro Garibaldi?*'

'*Bene, Maestà, e Lei?*'

'*Benone.*'[2]

Then they rode on together, and the two staffs behind them, red shirts side by side with resplendent uniforms, crosses, and cordons of honour. It was an epitome of the union of conservative and revolutionary forces that had crushed the obscurantists and expelled the foreigners. The constrained conversation between

---

[1] Missori was always very particular to say that the words he heard uttered by Garibaldi were '*primo* re,' not merely 're.' Missori told me that Garibaldi's idea was to make a kind of implied 'investiture' or at least 'ceremony.' *Conv. Missori*, and *Risorg.* anno. i. fasc. 4, p. 752. *Castellini*, 93-94 note.

[2] 'How are you, dear Garibaldi?' 'Well, your Majesty, and you?' 'First rate.' *Red Shirt*, 285. *Castelli* (Solaroli), 333.

the two groups betrayed the heart-burnings on either side and the grudging sacrifices that each was making to the other.   But although there was cold politeness where there should have been enthusiasm, none the less that ride together was the making of Italy, and seen down history's lengthening vista, remains evermore a goodly sight.

After a while Garibaldi and his men turned off the road to the left and made their way back by country lanes to Calvi, while the King held on to Teano.   'Garibaldi's countenance,' writes Mario, 'was full of melancholy sweetness.   Never did I feel drawn to him with such tenderness.'   He said little that evening to his friends.   Next morning they met Jessie Mario, who had crossed the Volturno to provide hospital arrangements north of the river.   'My wounded,' said Garibaldi to her somewhat sternly, 'are all on the south of the Volturno.'   And then, relapsing into his gentlest mood, he added, 'Jessie, they have sent us to the rear' ('*ci hanno messi alla coda*').   During their ride together Victor Emmanuel had told him in soft words the hard decree that the Royal army would take over all the operations of war and that the Garibaldini were no longer required.[1]

[1] No doubt whatever as to the place and circumstances of the meeting can remain in the minds of those who will study the following authorities, a collection of eye-witnesses outweighing tenfold the story told by Giuseppe Porta in the *Tribuna*, Aug. 14, 1907. *Mem. Stor. Mil.* i. 43-73 (alone sufficient to decide the matter).   *Risorg.* i. fasc. 4. pp. 751-752; fasc. 5-6, pp. 1109-1116.   *Castelli* (Solaroli), 333-334.   *Revel's da Ancona*, 67-69.   *Mario, Vita*, ii. 18-21, and *Red Shirt*, 273-290.   *Zasio*, 126.   *Castellini*, 93-94 note.   *Times*, Nov. 6, p. 10, c. 3.   *Canzio MS.* (a statement of Canzio's contradicting Porta and bearing out all the other evidence: in my possession).   *Della Rocca*, 193, and see *Guerzoni*, ii. 229 and note.

CHAPTER XV

'Semplice in atti e semplice in parole,
Chi della Patria cavalier si cinse
Dona tutto alla Patria, e nulla vuole.'
        MARRADI. *Rapsodie Garibaldine.*

' Simple in act and word, his country's knight,
He gives his country all and nothing takes.'

THAT part of the enemy's force which had been in the
neighbourhood of the two national armies at the moment
of their junction on October 26, retired in the afternoon
towards Gaeta and effaced themselves behind the line of
Garigliano.   On the morning of the 27th Victor Emmanuel rode from Teano to Calvi in search of Garibaldi.
Finding that he had returned to the south bank of the
Volturno, the King pushed on alone with his staff in the
same direction, crossed the rickety little bridge, and
entered the Garibaldian lines at Sant' Angelo.   The
volunteers came swarming out to welcome the unexpected visitor, with cries of devotion and enthusiasm
which showed how far a very little attention from the
official world would have gone to win the hearts of the
main body of Garibaldini.   Unfortunately this surprise
visit was the last effort which His Majesty was permitted to make by way of showing personal gratitude to
the rank and file of the volunteers.

Since Garibaldi was absent, not knowing of the King's
visit, Medici did the honours of the occasion, helped by
Nino Bixio's lieutenants.   Bixio himself was in hospital
at Naples.   At the crossing of the Volturno two days
before, whence he was to have accompanied the Dictator

to meet the King, Nino had headed a hue and cry after a priest suspected of acting as spy, and riding furiously after the man to arrest him had let his horse slip in a narrow lane, and fractured his leg against a wall.   He lay, however, quite happy in the hospital at Naples, for his wife came out from Genoa to nurse him, and since the volunteers' part in the fighting was over he was able to turn his mind to the docile family affections which shared dominion in his heart with the rage for his country's service.[1]

Victor Emmanuel, after having fraternised with Medici's men, and ridden close up to the walls of Capua at the greatest risk of being cut off by the enemy's outposts, recrossed the Volturno and returned to Teano. His army was there divided into two, one part going on towards the line of the Garigliano and Gaeta, and the other under General Della Rocca coming south to besiege Capua.   Della Rocca had to negotiate a delicate situation with Garibaldi.   Although the red-shirts were no longer to be allowed to take part in the serious operations of the campaign, yet on October 28 their services were still required for yet a few days longer to help guard the lines for the royal siege batteries.   Garibaldi, fearing that his men might be annoyed at receiving orders from Della Rocca if they considered that a slight was being put upon themselves or their chief, not only placed the whole of his army at the absolute disposal of the Piedmontese general, but was at pains to devise a plan whereby Della Rocca's orders were conveyed to the red-shirts through Sirtori, as though they still came from Garibaldi himself.   He strictly enjoined on his staff to prevent the men from knowing that the orders did not in reality emanate from him.   Shaking his supplanter warmly by the hand, he wished him luck, and rode off to Caserta.[2]

Two days later Della Rocca, who had been deeply

[1] *Menghini*, 388-390.   *Castelli*, 335-336.   *Red Shirt*, 275.
[2] *Della Rocca*, 194-195.   *Revel's da Ancona*, 69.

touched by Garibaldi's generous conduct, hearing that he was ill at Caserta, went there to pay him a visit. He found him in a little room over the guard-house of the Palace, exactly above a large store of gunpowder.

' I begged him,' writes Della Rocca, 'to move immediately, and smiling he promised to do so. Propped up with pillows, he was wrapped in a military cloak, a little cap on his head, and a silk handkerchief knotted round his neck. As I entered, he held out his hand, and seemed quite touched when I told him I had only come to ask how he was. He was still more pleased when I told him how well I got on with his generals, Cosenz and Sirtori, notable personages and most excellent men, and how I regretted the enforced absence of Bixio. . . . Mine were no idle compliments. I meant what I said, and I saw that Garibaldi was pleased that I appreciated his friends.'[1]

Meanwhile, Della Rocca's batteries were being scientifically erected by the engineers of the regular army, in front of the Garibaldian lines. On November 1, at four in the afternoon, all was ready, and a red flag run up on the summit of Monte Tifata gave the signal for the bombardment. The enemy replied and the duel lasted on through the night. Some of the houses in the town were set on fire, and the Capuans, many of whom secretly hated the falling dynasty, protested to the General of the garrison the necessity for instant surrender. At dawn of November 2 the officers on the terrace of Sant' Angelo Church eagerly turned their telescopes towards Capua, and saw the white flag hoisted on its walls. The garrison of 10,000 men became prisoners of war, and the fortress that had set a limit to Garibaldi's career at length surrendered to the Italian army.[2]

While Della Rocca was taking Capua, Fanti and Cialdini were drawing the net round Gaeta. On October 29 a reconnaissance against the enemy's strong posi-

[1] Della Rocca, 197-198.
[2] Franci, ii. 176-179, who estimates the Bourbon garrison at 'about 11,000.' Della Rocca, 194-200. Menghini, 464-465. Genio, 106. Times, November 6, p. 7, col. 3. Türr's Div. 297-298, 301, 304-306. Cava, 26-36.

tion on the hills behind the mouth of the Garigliano was pushed too far, partly by the carelessness of the generals, partly by the unwillingness of the Bersaglieri to obey the orders to retreat. The action cost the Italian army over fifty men and showed that their opponents could still fight. But a day or two later, when the Italian fleet opened fire on their flank and rear, the Bourbon forces abandoned the position on the Garigliano and fell back towards the great fortress. On November 2, the day of the fall of Capua, a successful action at Mola di Gaeta on the coast placed the Italian army in a situation to besiege Gaeta in form.[1]

During the first ten days of November some 17,000 Neapolitan soldiers, closely pursued by Victor Emmanuel's troops, escaped over the frontier into Papal territory at Terracina, and were disarmed and interned among the Alban hills by the Papal authorities and the French garrison of Rome.[2] The remainder of the Bourbon army that had not already disbanded or surrendered, was now shut up in the citadel of Messina, in one or two small forts in Sicily and the Abruzzi, or with the ex-King and Queen in Gaeta.

The siege of Gaeta was protracted all the winter, because Napoleon III kept the French fleet in those waters with orders to prevent the Italian fleet from bombarding the fortress. The siege operations had therefore to be conducted entirely from the land side, and were not brought to a successful issue until February, 1861. The long siege enabled Maria Sophia, Francis II's young Bavarian Queen, to display to Europe from the battlements of the bombarded fortress a heroine's courage, which illuminated with sunset glow the last vision of that inglorious dynasty which had known no rays at noontide.

---

[1] *Franci*, ii. 154-176. *Orero*, 127-143. *Castelli*, 337. *Della Rocca*, 195 note. *Corsi's Rimembranze*, 33-34. *Mezzacapo*, 134-135.

[2] *De Sivo*, iv. 314-317. *Franci*, ii. 195-200, 386. And see Appendix J, I. (*a*) below. *Persano*, 456-457. *Castelli*, 341.

Napoleon's action in stopping the war at sea while allowing it to be carried to its conclusion on land, had no permanent effect save to irritate Italians and to efface from their minds all claims of gratitude for his recent complaisance with regard to Umbria and the Marches. It is difficult, at first sight, to assign a reason for an interference at once so feeble and so exasperating. The Emperor's biographer, unable as ever to understand his sympathy with Italian freedom, supposes that he wished to 'clear his personal honour' by this tangible protest against Victor Emmanuel's piratical attack on the Kingdom of Naples.[1] Such may be the feelings of a French Clerical in face of the Liberation of Italy, but it is difficult to suppose that they were those of Napoleon III, only two months after he had given his consent to Cavour's invasion of the Papal Marches. The secret agreement which he had made at Chambéry was that the North Italian army should invade and traverse the Papal territory, so as to arrive at Naples in time to stop Garibaldi and 'absorb the revolution.' In making this arrangement Napoleon did not imagine that Victor Emmanuel had undertaken to put down Garibaldi merely in order to restore Francis II to the throne. The Emperor did not like the annexation of South Italy by Piedmont, but he had agreed to it as the least of many possible evils. Therefore his motive in sending the French fleet to Gaeta was probably not so much genuine indignation at the conduct of the King of Italy, as the perception that he must appear to be angry for the sake of the French Clericals, whose loyalty, so essential to his throne, he had strained almost to breaking-point.[2]

On the 8th of October, Cavour had written to Farini, the Minister in attendance on Victor Emmanuel :—

' If Garibaldi's army acclaims the King, it must be treated well. We have to contend against the requirements and

---

[1] *La Gorce*, iii. 448.   [2] This is the view of *Chiala (Stor. Contemp.* 12-13).

pedantries of the regular army.   Do not give in.   Reasons of
State of the first importance demand firmness.   Woe to us if
we show ourselves ungrateful to those who have shed their
blood for Italy!   Europe would condemn us.   In the country
there would be a great reaction in favour of the Garibaldini.
I have had a warm argument with Fanti on this point.   He
spoke of military requirements.   I replied that this was not
Spain, and that here the army had to obey.' [1]

It was a great misfortune that Cavour was unable to
secure the fulfilment, in spirit as well as in letter, of his
wise and benevolent intentions.   Victor Emmanuel, who
had hitherto been more enthusiastic for Garibaldi than
Cavour himself, fell at this critical moment under the
influence of Fanti and the military pedants.   Garibaldi
and his troops had welcomed the King and his army,
and had taken the place assigned them in the rear, in a
manner which no one had been able to criticise, and
which had elicited the gratitude and praise of Della Rocca,
the General most concerned.   There was therefore not
the smallest provocation for the official insult to which
the whole body of Garibaldini were subjected on November 6.   On that day they had been instructed that the
King would come to review them at Caserta.   The Dictator was to present his Generals and his favourite officers to
their Sovereign, and the red-shirts were to march past.
Such a day might well have been a turning-point in the
life of the new-born nation.   Old feuds, instead of taking
on fresh and more virulent forms, would have been
soothed or healed.   The Garibaldini assembled at Caserta
with feelings of loyalty and pride.   They were drawn
up in front of the Bourbon Palace in their picturesque
regiments—good, bad, and indifferent, Sicilian and Calabrian, Northerner and Tuscan.   They waited till after
the appointed hour and then learnt that the King had
determined not to come.

No apology or explanation was sent, or has ever since
been offered.   Further to point the moral, Victor Emman-

[1] *Chiala*, iv. 34.

uel did not even write an order-of-the-day thanking
the men who had won for him the crown of the Two
Sicilies.   Still less would Fanti, the commander-in-chief,
put his name to such a document.   It was signed by Della
Rocca.[1]

The man who suffered most from the consequences
of this ungracious conduct was the man who had vainly
striven to avert the folly.   It was against Cavour that
Garibaldi turned his wrath ; his personal devotion to
Victor Emmanuel stood the shock.   He persuaded himself that these acts of petty meanness had been specially
ordered by the Minister at Turin, though in fact they had
been suggested either directly by Fanti or indirectly by
the atmosphere of jealousy natural to a regular army in
the presence of volunteers.   This jealousy, common to
every professional service in the world, and aggravated
at Naples by the fact that these volunteers had really
won their laurels, Cavour was unable to control from his
cabinet in Turin.   Next spring, in the first session of the
first Parliament of United Italy, Garibaldi's pent-up wrath
boiled over in a misdirected and malicious attack on the
statesman who had been his guardian-angel throughout
the year of wonders.

Garibaldi was sometimes unjust, but he seldom missed
an occasion to be generous.   And on the very afternoon
of the thwarted review he had a magnificent opportunity.
General Cialdini arrived at Caserta, commissioned to
obtain his promise to enter Naples on the following day
in the same carriage with the King.   It was very desirable that the Dictator should appear at Victor Emmanuel's side, for if it became known that he had absented
himself with a grievance, it was doubtful what sort of
reception the Royal party would obtain.   There would
indeed have been a fair case for him to refuse to enter
Naples with the King who had failed his appointment at
the review.   But he liked Cialdini well, and after some

---

[1] *Corsi's Vent. Anni*, 507-509.   *Peard Journal*, *MS.* Nov. 6.   *Du Camp*,
349.   *Adamoli*, 171.   *Guerzoni*, ii. 231-232 note.

demur, and a good deal of strong language against Fanti and Cavour, he finally consented to go.[1]

On November 7 the first King of Italy entered his southern capital, with Garibaldi sitting beside him in the carriage. They were both out of temper, and it rained in torrents. But the Neapolitans were again in a state of frantic enthusiasm, which the rain could not damp, although it ruined the triumphal arches and caused the rows of paste-board allegorical figures to double up as if they had been shot.

If the King had been permitted to use common courtesy to the Garibaldian army in the matter of the review, and had shown more imaginative sympathy with men perhaps over-sensitive, little complaint could justly have been made of the treatment accorded to their material interests. In this matter Victor Emmanuel was firm to see the right thing done, saying, 'I cannot show less generosity than Garibaldi'.[2]

It had been Cavour's original intention to divide the Garibaldini into three sections: the first and far the largest to be disbanded at once with a gratuity for each man; the second to constitute a separate volunteer division of the army under the title of *Cacciatori delle Alpi;* the third to consist of a small number of officers to be given commissions in the regular army.[3] But this plan was not carried out. It was decided not to constitute a permanent force of volunteers attached to the army, partly for fear of professional quarrels and political complications that might arise out of the existence of such a force, and partly because nearly all the genuine volunteers who had done the fighting were anxious to return at once to their families and their work in life. The privates, therefore, were sent back each to his home with a gratuity. The Hungarians alone, who had no homes to which they could return, were taken into the Royal service, and were engaged for many years in the

[1] *Cialdini e Garibaldi*, 546-548.   *Castelli*, 340.
[2] *Della Rocca*, 198.   [3] *Chiala*, iv. 34-35.

inglorious but dangerous task of tracking down the reactionary brigands of Molise and Abruzzi.

There remained the question of the officers. Since Cavour's scheme of a permanent volunteer force had been abandoned, it was felt to be only just that a very large number of Garibaldi's officers should be given posts in the regular army. A military commission, on which Sirtori, Medici, and Cosenz had seats, chose out the officers most fit to be admitted into the King's service. It was a difficult task, for there were six or seven thousand so-called 'officers' of all sorts, drawing Garibaldi's pay in Sicily and on the mainland in the first days of November, about one 'officer' to every seven privates. Half or more of these must have been absolutely unworthy of permanent commissions. In the course of the next two years 1584 of the best men were picked out and admitted as officers to the regular army.[1] Medici, Bixio, Cosenz, and nine others were made Generals. These arrangements were regarded with intense indignation by Garibaldi and his intimates at Caprera, who had expected that the volunteers would be kept in being as a permanent force, to form a nucleus for the national *levée en masse* in the coming war for Venice and Rome. But the settlement cannot, in a fair review of all the circumstances, be called either impolitic or unjust, although there were many individual cases of harsh treatment of men who had deserved well of their country.[2]

Although Victor Emmanuel was now in full possession of Naples, the half-formed Kingdom of Italy was still

---

[1] *Türr's Div.* 327. It is only fair to point out that one excuse for the sour temper which Fanti showed to Garibaldi was his knowledge that Garibaldi claimed to have the rank of all his officers recognized. This claim, if conceded, would have rendered impossible Fanti's task,—sufficiently difficult already,—of creating a National army out of the different military elements of North, Centre, and South.

[2] *Fanti*, 433-439. *Fanti Apr.* 1861, pp. 4-17. *Corsi's Vent. Anni.* 511-515. *Türr's Div.* 321-329. *Revel's da Ancona*, 114-119.

in grave danger. On October 22 Cavour had felt 'the
certainty that Austria will attack us.'[1]   Every day that
passed in safety added to the chances of peace and to the
meagre possibilities of resistance in case of war.   But the
Emperors of Austria and Russia and the King of Prussia
had met in conference at Warsaw, an ill-omened gather-
ing of the murderers on the tomb of their victim, and
Europe looked on to see whether they would decide to
slay Italy as they had slain Poland.   At this crisis the
Italian position was strengthened by the pronouncement
of the British Foreign Minister in favour of the right
of the Italians to settle their own affairs.   Lord John's
famous dispatch was his own spontaneous act, a personal
proclamation of the principles of Charles James Fox,
the gospel by which Russell's life had been inspired
and guided.   England, who has often supported these
principles and often opposed them, was in one of her
generous moods, and applauded to the echo her cham-
pion's defiance of despotic Europe.   The first sentence
plunges *in medias res:* 'It appears that the late proceedings of the King of Sardinia [Piedmont] have been
strongly disapproved by several of the principal Courts
of Europe.'   After telling some home-truths about the
character of the Papal and Neapolitan Governments,
Lord John announces that—

'Her Majesty's Government must admit that the Italians
are the best judges of their own interests.' 'It is difficult,' he
proceeds, 'to believe, after the astonishing events that we
have seen, that the Pope and the King of the Two Sicilies
possessed the love of their people.' Therefore 'Her Majesty's
Government can see no sufficient ground for the severe censure
with which Austria, France, Prussia, and Russia have visited
the acts of the King of Sardinia. Her Majesty's Government
will turn their eyes rather to the gratifying prospect of a people
building up the edifice of their liberties, and consolidating the
work of their independence.'[2]

This dispatch, written on October 27 and made
public in the early days of November, was greeted with

---

[1] *Chiala,* iv. 61.   [2] *Br. Parl. Papers,* vii. pp. 125-127.

ecstasies of joy by the Italian people.[1] Cavour, who
had recently been somewhat annoyed by Lord John's
insistent warning that Italy must not go to war to liberate Venice, declared that he had now more than made
amends.[2] Lord John's dispatch has sometimes been de-
preciated as a mere blowing of trumpets over the *fait-
accompli* of United Italy.   But such was not the view of
the men who best understood Italy's needs.   Hudson
wrote to Russell that when Cavour first read it, 'he
shouted, rubbed his hands, jumped up, sat down again,
then began to think, and when he looked up tears were
standing in his eyes.   Behind your dispatch he saw the
Italy of his dreams, the Italy of his hopes, the Italy of
his policy.'   Cavour himself wrote to thank Russell in
the strongest language for 'the immense service he had
rendered Italy,' and his trusted agent Villamarina said
the dispatch was worth an army of 100,000 men.[3]

The feeling of Cavour's countrymen for Lord John
Russell, as one of the chief instruments in their liberation, was shown in many different ways during the remainder of his life.   Once, in 1869, when he and his
family were staying in a villa at San Remo, they found
the ceiling of the principal room frescoed with portraits
of four national heroes.   The four turned out to be
Mazzini, Garibaldi, Cavour, and, to their surprise and
delight, Lord John himself!   Neither had the house been
specially prepared for their reception.

It has of recent years been somewhat the fashion to
blame Lord John Russell for his failures, but never to
praise him for his triumphs.   Fashions in history come

---

[1] See Appendix A, p. 314 below.
[2] *Chiala*, iv. p. cccxiii; vi. pp. 634, 643. *Br. Parl. Papers*, vii. pp. 35-36, 50.
Lord John feared in 1860 that a war for Venice, under the existing conditions of
Europe, would mean a renewal of Italian dependence on France, more Napoleonic
aggrandisement, and a general European war.   He was not lukewarm in his
desire to see Austria quit Venetian territory, for when that happy event took
place in 1866 he went with his family to see and rejoice over the official act of the
liberation of Venice, and the entry of Victor Emmanuel up the Grand Canal.
[3] Appendix A, p. 314 below.

and go, more often the reflex of tendencies in the present than the result of new knowledge of the past. It is probable that very few British statesmen in the course of their lives did as much to reinvigorate and secure the institutions of our country as was done by Russell in 1830-1832, or won for her as much well-deserved gratitude and such enduring friendship abroad as was secured by his action in 1859-1860. On the Italian question England secured peace with true honour, and has never since, either in point of interest or of conscience, had reason to repent of her work.

On the day of their entrance into Naples and on the following day, Victor Emmanuel and Garibaldi held private colloquies. The out-going Dictator asked to be continued in power for another year as the King's Lieutenant, and to have the grade of all his officers recognised. Such requests showed how utterly incapable Garibaldi was of understanding the difficulties of administrative and military reorganization that confronted the new State.

On November 8 the throne-room in the Palace was the scene of an imposing ceremony, the official presentation of the result of the plebiscite, and the investiture of Victor Emmanuel with the Kingship of Sicily and Naples. The new Monarch was seated on his throne. Garibaldi and his friends stood in one group, the courtiers and army officers in another, and small cordiality was shown between them. But the act of annexation was duly signed by all parties, and Garibaldi, formally resigning the Dictatorship, left the room a private citizen once more. His first act in that capacity was to publish a letter calling on all Italians to rally round Victor Emmanuel, and to be prepared to follow him next spring, a million strong, against Rome or Venice. 'By the side of the *Re galantuomo*,' he wrote, 'every quarrel should disappear, every rancour be dissipated.' Garibaldi's public utterances during this period of strained relations were as loyal as if every demand he made had been conceded by the King.[1]

Before nightfall he sent Missori to tell the British Admiral that he would leave for Caprera early the next morning, November 9, and would come aboard the *Hannibal* to pay a farewell visit before he quitted the Bay.[2] He spent the night in the Hotel d'Angleterre (or *Isole Britanniche*) in the Chiaja, talking with Missori, Mario, Canzio, Zasio, and others of his intimate friends. As during all these last days, he was in a melancholy and gentle mood, moving his followers to tears when he spoke of their parting on the morrow. In spite of the brave words of the proclamation in which he thanked his soldiers, and called on them to be ready against the next spring, all felt in their hearts the presentiment that their day of glory was at an end. And so these men, who had seized occasion by the forelock and had performed at the appointed moment the miracle never to be repeated, sat up all night in the hotel and talked sadly of what they had done and left undone.[3]

Next morning, before dawn, they went down together to the port. The city was still asleep, and there was no one to witness the departure, which had been kept secret from every one except the British Admiral. They took a boat, rowed over to the *Hannibal*, and came up the side of the great three-decker, between the darkness and the first twilight. Admiral Mundy, still in his cot, was told that Garibaldi was in the cabin, and turned out with all haste to receive the strange man whom he had learnt to admire and love, while still keeping the open eye of common sense on his single-minded fanaticism. During a long talk in the cabin, Garibaldi invited Mundy to be his guest in his cottage at Caprera, 'and spoke much of

---

[1] *Castelli* (Solaroli), 345-346. *Bianchi, Polit. de Cavour*, 386. *Della Rocca*, 202. *Türr's Div.* 316. *Conv. Canzio. Cosenz Guardione*, 38. *Ciàmpoli*, 197-198.

[2] *Mundy*, 277. *Castellini*, 97 note (Missori's evidence).

[3] *Zasio*, 77, 130. *Türr's Div.* 317. *Red Shirt*, 291.

the beautiful harbour between the island and the main, where Nelson had once anchored for the protection of his fleet.' As they passed up from the cabin to the quarter-deck, Garibaldi saw the Admiral's visiting-book lying on the small table upon which, six months before, at Palermo, he and the Bourbon Generals had signed the armistice, the source of such mighty consequences.[1] He sat down and wrote in the book in French :—

'G. Garibaldi owes to Admiral Mundy the most lively gratitude, which will last all his life, on account of sincere proofs of friendship with which he has been loaded in all kinds of circumstances.'[2]

As he went down the ship's side many of the officers and crew of the *Hannibal* were deeply moved, and the expressions which some of them afterwards used about 'the look of intense love' upon his face testify to the unique effect of his presence upon men trained in no sentimental school of thought or character.[3]

From the *Hannibal* he rowed to the *Washington*, the steamer that was to take him home. On her deck he parted from Canzio, Missori, Mario, and his other friends, who returned to the quay. His last words to them were 'To meet again at Rome.' Only his son Menotti and one or two persons of less importance sailed with him to the island. He returned thither as poor a man as he had left it in the spring. In the last two days Victor Emmanuel had offered him an estate for Menotti, the title of King's aide-de-camp for his younger son, a dowry for his daughter, a royal castle and a steamer for himself. But he had refused them all.[4] His secretary, Basso, had borrowed a few hundred francs of paper-money from a friend, for necessary expenses. He himself had stowed on board the *Washington* a bag of seed-corn for his farm.

---

[1] See *Garibaldi and the Thousand*, p. 320.   [2] *Mundy*, 280-287.
[3] *Meuricoffre*, 82-83, Captain Farquhar's words.
[4] *Bianchi, Polit. de Cavour*, 385-386.

With these spoils the steamer, almost unobserved, left port at break of day.

He was soon back at his old daily occupations of man's primitive struggle with nature, at which, but for the call of a great epoch and a great cause, he would so readily have spent his whole life.   Again the dawn and the twilight on the Straits of Bonifacio saw him at work among the granite boulders, industriously putting seed into the scrapings of earth which he called his fields; sheltering a few sad vines from the sweeping winds of the Straits; calling up his cows by name from their pasturage among the wild, odorous brushwood; and seeking the strayed goats on the precipice-top.   Under these conditions the melancholy of his last days on the mainland soon left him.   When, a few weeks later, a visitor came on business from Genoa, he found Garibaldi 'robust in health, and radiant with a calm and serene joy.'[1]   For when once he had been left alone again with his mother Earth, between rock and sea and sky, no disappointment could prevent him from feeling in his heart the truth, that he had done a mighty labour, and taken his share in a task which the years would soon complete and the long generations ratify—the Making of Italy.

[1] *Brambilla.* 45.

EPILOGUE

I HAVE now told the story of Garibaldi for the two years 1849 and 1860 that give him his title to enduring fame. It is not my intention to carry any further the chronicle of his life; partly because the documents which alone could unfold the inner history of the affairs of Aspromonte and Mentana are not available; still more because Garibaldi's actions after 1860 are no longer the hinge on which the fortunes of Italy revolve, but are merely important episodes in the movement to liberate Venice and Rome, which was brought to fruition by very different forces. But I feel the need to add here a few pages of summary, unnecessary to the student, but perhaps useful to the reader unfamiliar with the bare outlines of Garibaldi's subsequent career.

In 1861 the spell of Italy's amazing good fortune was broken by the irreparable calamity of the death of Cavour. If he had died two years before, it is not improbable that Italy might still at this day be divided and enslaved; if he had lived ten years longer the young country would have escaped many falls in learning to walk.[1] Cavour was succeeded by smaller men, who made it their custom to court popularity one day by flattering Garibaldi's designs on Rome, and on the next to arrest his movement in panic, when faced at close quarters by the inevitable collision with the Pope's protector, Napoleon III.

In 1862, with a body of volunteers hastily got together in Sicily, he crossed the Straits of Messina and began

[1] There is an adequate biography of this great man available for the Anglo-Saxon public in Mr. W. R. Thayer's forthcoming *Life and Times of Cavour* (1911).

his march for Rome. But on the plateaus of Aspromonte he was stopped by Victor Emmanuel's troops,
who opened fire at sight. Obedient to his cardinal
principle that civil war between patriots must not take
place, he walked up and down in front of his men for-
bidding them to return the fire, and while so doing was
wounded in the foot by an 'Italian bullet.' He was
carried down, a prisoner and in great pain, from the
mountain where two years before he had triumphed
over the Bourbon armies.

He had not fully recovered from the wound of Aspromonte when in 1864 he paid his famous visit to England.
Never has any foreigner, hardly ever any native hero,
been received as Garibaldi was received by our fathers.
The quiet square in front of Stafford House, near St.
James's Palace, is one of the rare places in modern
London which is still 'a haunt of ancient peace,' and few
of those who hurry across it on their daily avocations
would guess what scenes it witnessed when Garibaldi
was lodged there. When the Duke of Sutherland's
four-horse carriage, containing the son of the skipper
of Nice in his red shirt and grey blanket, struggled
in the course of six hours through five miles of London
streets, amid half a million of our people who had turned
out to greet him, the wild procession made its way at
length into this little square, startling its Royal and
Ducal sanctities with democratic clangour. Then, amid
a noise of shouting like the noise of the sea in storm,
Garibaldi stepped out of the carriage, as calm as in the
day of battle, into a circle of fair ladies and great statesmen on the steps of Stafford House, while the Duke's
carriage, in which he had come, literally fell to pieces in
the stable, strained to breaking-point by the weight of
thousands of strong arms that had snatched at and clung
to its sides as it passed through a London gone mad
with joy.

After the long interval following the Chartist collapse,
the tide of British Democracy was just beginning to stir

again with that peaceful but irresistible ground-swell that resulted three years later, after the quietest of great crises, in the enfranchisement of the working men. The successful emancipation of Italy and the visit of Garibaldi had their part in stimulating this movement in England. To the common people it was an unexampled privilege to carry one of themselves in triumph through London streets, as if he had been Wellington or Cæsar. But he won, no less, the hearts of the English upper classes, at that time heartily antagonistic to continental clericalism and despotism. The Duchess of Sutherland drove him into School-yard at Eton, followed by boys and masters shouting after him as if he had just won them the match against Harrow.

While he was staying under Mr. Seely's roof in the Isle of Wight, he went to visit his brother poet, always an enthusiast for Italian freedom. They smoked and repeated Italian poetry to each other with great fervour. 'What a noble human being!' wrote Tennyson when he had parted from his guest. 'I expected to see a hero and I was not disappointed. One cannot exactly say of him what Chaucer says of the ideal Knight, "As meke he was of port as is a maid." He is more majestic than meek, and his manners have a certain divine simplicity in them, such as I have never witnessed in a native of these islands, among men at least, and they are gentler than those of most young maidens whom I know.' In worldly matters, Tennyson noted that he had 'the divine stupidity of a hero.'[1]

During the same month he saw much of Mr. Gladstone, his 'precursor,' as he called him, in the liberation of Naples. Mr. Gladstone, though pained by his 'attenu-

---

[1] *Tennyson, A Memoir*, ii. 1-4. It was on this visit that Garibaldi planted the tree which Tennyson long afterwards celebrated as—

· · · the waving pine which here
The warrior of Caprera set,
A name that earth will not forget
Till earth has roll'd her latest year'

GARIBALDI AND ENGLISH FRIENDS. ENGLAND, 1864

ated belief,' thus spoke of his visit in after years : 'We
who then saw Garibaldi for the first time can many of
us never forget the marvellous effect produced on our
minds by the simple nobility of his demeanour, by his
manners and his acts. . . . Besides his splendid integrity, and his wide and universal sympathies, besides
that seductive simplicity of manner which never de-
parted from him, and that inborn and native grace which
seemed to attend all his actions, I would almost select
from every other quality this, which was in apparent contrast but real harmony in Garibaldi—the union of the most
profound and tender humanity with his fiery valour.'[1]

In 1866 the quarrel of the two German powers enabled Italy to acquire her present North-Eastern frontier
without that barter of her independence to France which
Lord John Russell had always feared would be the price of
Venice.   While the Prussians defeated the main Austrian
army in the plains of Bohemia, their Italian allies un-
successfully attacked the Venetian quadrilateral.   The
regular army under La Marmora and Della Rocca was
repulsed by the Austrians at Custozza, owing to bad
generalship which failed to bring the great mass of the
troops into action.   The naval disaster at Lissa, under
Persano, was much worse.   The only glimmer of partial
success shone on the arms of Garibaldi and his volunteers
in the Trentine Alps, though Garibaldi scored no remarkable victories such as he had won over the Austrians
in his Alpine campaign of 1859.   His vigour was not what
it had once been.   The regular army was preparing to renew the attack on Venetia when the war came suddenly
to an end.   The complete Prussian victory at Königgrätz
had led to the surrender by Austria of her Venetian terri-

---

[1] *Morley*, ii. book v. chap. vii.   'The General's gestures,' wrote Bruzzesi,
one of Garibaldi's most discerning followers, 'are marvellous, and much more
perfect than his language.   In his language he sometimes repeats himself, in
his gestures never.   His language is not invariably good; but his gestures
are always dignified, perfect.   They are never comic, always dramatic.   I
believe if he were not Garibaldi, he would be the greatest tragic actor known.'

tory.   All Italy was now free, except Rome and the small
province in which it stood.

In the autumn of 1867 Garibaldi, now turned sixty,
headed another rush on Rome, with an ill-selected mob
of followers, very different from the thousand youth-
ful veterans who had been so carefully picked out to
follow him to Sicily seven years before.   At Mentana
the intervention of the French troops on behalf of the
Papalists turned the day against the Garibaldini, part of
whom stood their ground and were mowed down by the
chassepots, while part ran, as Garibaldi said, like ' cowardly
rabbits.'   Hedged by French bayonets, Rome remained
to the priests for three years more.   Aspromonte and
Mentana had at least kept the country's passion fixed
steadily on Rome, and prevented the Government from
acquiescing in a state of things that appeared only too
likely to become permanent, though it could never have
given peace.

But the end came at last.   The result of the first
battles in the Franco-Prussian war caused the withdrawal of the French garrison from Rome, and on September 20, 1870, less than three weeks after Sedan,
Victor Emmanuel's Bersaglieri entered by the breach near
the Porta Pia.   Garibaldi himself was kept away from
the scene till all was over, but his old friends Bixio and
Cosenz took part, as Royal Generals, in the final operations against Rome.   Bixio made a feint against the Porta
San Pancrazio, which he had once helped to defend for
the Roman Republic, while Cosenz led the storming
party up the breach on the other side of the city.   So fell
the Temporal Power, which Mazzini and Garibaldi had
defied on the Janiculum twenty-one years before.   Italy
had her capital, and the *risorgimento* epoch came to an
end.   Two years later Mazzini died.

In the winter of 1870, after the withdrawal of the
French from Rome, the deposition of Napoleon III, and
the proclamation of the Republic in Paris, Garibaldi's
sympathies went round to the side of France, whom he

regarded in the later stages of the struggle as a free country once more, despoiled and oppressed by a power representing the military and despotic principles of Eastern Europe. The old man summoned his followers and went off to defend the French Republic against the Prussians. Much controversy has raged as to the part played by the gallant Italians in that winter campaign. But whether it is true or false that Garibaldi's powers were atrophied by advancing years, at least he had not grown old in generosity to a sister nation or in his will to succour the oppressed.

After his return from France he lived on another dozen years, to the age of seventy-five. He was nearly always on Caprera, but occasionally he visited the mainland and Rome. It is entirely to the credit of his countrymen that they continued to regard him as a demi-god when his star had paled for the rest of Europe, and when it was only too apparent that this demi-god was no more exempt than Tithonus from the ravages of age, and from other weaknesses of mortal men.

The end came in his white house at Caprera, on a June evening in 1882. The old sailor, farmer, and fighter was propped up on the pillows to watch for the last time the sunlight gilding the waves and the granite rocks. While his life was slowly ebbing out, two little birds whom he had taught not to fear him fluttered in from the moor, and sat chirping on the window-sill. The attendants were about to drive them away lest they should disturb him, when that voice was heard once more by men, bidding them let the little birds come in, and always feed them after he was gone. And having given these orders, he went upon his last expedition.

This year (1911) Italy has been celebrating the fiftieth anniversary of her birth, which she dates from the official proclamation of the Italian Kingdom in 1861, the immediate outcome of the events narrated in this volume. After the lapse of half a century it is possible to see whether the men of the *risorgimento* were building on the sand or on the rock.

Nothing is more remarkable—though to believers in nationality and ordered liberty nothing is more natural—than the stability of the Italian Kingdom. The oscillations of the structure that Cavour reared in the earthquake of 1860 went on for some forty years; but the vibration has now ceased, and the building is as safe as any in Europe. To-day politics in Italy could be more easily criticised for their stagnation than for any dangerous tendency towards either revolution or reaction. The foundations of human liberty and the foundations of social order exist there on a firm basis. The growing difficulties of the social problem, common to all Europe, find at least mitigation in the free political institutions of a nation so recently created by the common efforts of all classes. In some European countries, freedom and order have not yet been secured, and until our fathers' times there was no reason to suppose that these benefits would accrue to Italy for many generations to come.

The power of this great national movement has fortunately been directed only to the securing of Italian liberty, and not to the oppression of others. No doubt the reason of this is the fortunate fact that no alien race dwells beside the Italian within the boundaries of the Peninsula. There is no one for the Italian to oppress. But the result has been the unstained purity and idealism of patriotic emotion there, from the time of Mazzini's Young Italy to our own.[1] While English, French, German, and Magyar freedom were all vindicated more or less at the expense of some other race or races, there is no one who can complain that he was enslaved in order that Italy might be free. No other Power—certainly not Austria or the Pope—is the worse off for having been forced to yield the Italian soil to the Italian State. All diplomats now recognise what our British statesmen foresaw, how great is Europe's gain in peace and security by the success of the *risorgimento*—in its own day the bugbear of diplomats In this way the 'Italian question,' for nearly four centuries the most frequent cause of international disturb-

[1] I leave this sentiment as I wrote it in the early summer of 1911 when it still appeared to be true. (*Note to Second Edition.*)

ance and war, has been laid to rest once for all. Italy,
which ever since the wars of Francis I and Charles V,
had been the arena wherein French and German ambition wrestled for supremacy, with England ever hover-
ing, an uneasy spectator, on the skirts of a conflict so
dangerous to the Balance of Power—Italy has now been
'neutralised' as securely as Switzerland, to the immense
benefit of the cause of peace and goodwill among men.

In Italy herself it is the traditions of the *risorgimento*
that unite and elevate her children. All classes from
king to workman, all provinces from Piedmont to Sicily
are bound together by these memories of a history so
recent yet so poetical and so profound.

Nor has material progress been wanting, especially
of late years and in the North. In the South and in
Sicily brigandage has been stamped out. Justice and
order are far better in Italy than they have ever been,—
except under the Roman Empire, and then there was no
liberty. In the Middle Ages the Italians could paint
and build, and trade and write, but they murdered and
tortured and slaughtered each other like fiends. The
change towards humanity and freedom has been immense. The evils of modern Italy are the result of two
thousand years' misgovernment and three hundred years
of foreign domination and national death. The good
is the revolt of the modern Italian against this ancient
heritage of evil, and the *risorgimento*, the 'resurrection'
as it is well called, was the symbol of that revolt.

The comparison by which modern Italy fails is the
comparison of her achievement with the ideals and the
character of the men of her own *risorgimento*. But if the
comparison be made, materially, morally, or intellectually with the Italy of the eighteenth century, or of the
restoration after Waterloo, the balance is so immensely
on the side of modern Italy that we feel that the men of
the *risorgimento* are justified and have essentially succeeded in their aim. Their sufferings and their deeds
are recorded, not only as a high example and inspiration

such as history too seldom affords, but because they have had practical consequences of great and beneficent import to succeeding generations.[1]

And what of Garibaldi himself? How will the Garibaldian legend—which turns out on examination to be true—live in the minds of succeeding generations?

Garibaldi is not to be judged as a professional soldier leading modern armies, but as the greatest master that the world has seen of that special department of human activity known as revolutionary war. He could never have commanded a regular force of 100,000 men, though in his day he managed to defeat one. Owing to the size and efficiency of modern conscript armies, there cannot be another revolutionary war precisely of the Garibaldian type in the Europe of the coming era. But history is concerned with the past and not with the present or future. In 1860 Garibaldi was the right man in the right time and place.

But Garibaldi's claim on the memory of men rests on more than his actual achievements. It rests on that which was one part of his professional equipment as a soldier of revolution, but which surpasses and transcends it—his appeal to the imagination. He was a poet, in all save literary power. He was guided in political, and somewhat even in military situations, by a poet's instincts and motives. He is perhaps the only case, except Byron for a few weeks in Greece, of the poet as man of action. For most poets, if they ever take part in action, cease to be poetical. While he was alive this quality was both his strength and his weakness — Samson's locks and Achilles' heel. But now that he is dead, the poetry in his character and career is all gain in his race for immortal laurels. The history of events is ephemeral and

[1] These half-dozen paragraphs, very slightly altered, are reprinted by kind permission from a longer article on *The Festival of Italian Unity*, 1861-1911, that appeared in *The Times*, March 27, 1911.

for the scholar; the poetry of events is eternal and for the multitude. It is the acted poem that lives in the hearts of millions to whom the written words of history and the written words of poetry are alike an unopened book. So Garibaldi becomes the symbol of Italia to her children in all ages to come and on either side of the Atlantic. As the centuries slip by, carrying into oblivion almost all that once was noble or renowned, Mazzini's soul and Cavour's wisdom will be forgotten by the Italian who tends the vine or sweats beside the furnace, sooner than the old grey cloak and the red shirt and that face of simple faith and love. And to us of other lands, and most of all to us Englishmen, Garibaldi will live as the incarnate symbol of two passions not likely soon to die out of the world, the love of country and the love of freedom, kept pure by the one thing that can tame and yet not weaken them, the tenderest humanity for all mankind.

GARIBALDI'S HYMN

INNO GARIBALDI

(INNO DI GUERRA DEI CACCIATORI DELLE ALPI)

(Reproduced by kind permission of G. Ricordi & Cia.)

Trascrizione di LUIGI TRUZZI

Tempo di marcia. *f*

Al - l'ar - - mi!
To arms! . . .

Al - l'ar - - mi! Si
To arms! . . . The

sco - pron le tom - be, si le - - va - no i
tombs are un - cov - ered, the dead come from

mor - ti, i mar - ti - ri no - stri son
far, . . . The ghosts of our mar - tyrs are

tut - ti ri - sor - ti! Le spa - de nel
ris - ing to war . . . With swords in their

pu - gno, gli al - lo - ri al - le chio - me, la
hands and with lau - rels of fame . . . And

fiam - ma ed il no - me d'I - ta - lia sul
dead hearts glow - ing with It - al - y's

cor ! Cor - ria - mo ! cor - ria - mo ! Su, o
name. Come join them, come fol - low O

gio - va - ni schie - re ! su al ven - to per
youth of our land . . . Come fling out our

tut - to le no - stre ban - die - re ! Su
ban - ner and mar - shal our band . . . Come

tut - ti col fer - ro, su tut - ti col
all with cold steel and come all with hot

L

ra, va fuor d'I - ta - - - - - - lia, va fuor d'I -
. . go from I - ta - - - - - - lia, go from I -
. . ra,

- - ta - - - - - - lia,   va fuo - - - - -
- - ta - - - - - lia!   O stran - - - - -

Fine.

- - ra, o stra - nier!
- - ger, be - gone.

GARIBALDI'S HYMN

Si scopron le tombe, si levano i morti,
I martiri nostri son tutti risorti !
Le spade nel pugno, gli allori alle chiome,
La fiamma ed il nome d' Italia sul cor !
Veniamo ! Veniamo ! su, o giovani schiere !
Su al vento per tutto le nostre bandiere !
Su tutti col ferro, su tutti col fuoco,
Su tutti col fuoco d' Italia nel cor.
     Va fuora d' Italia, va fuora ch'è l' ora,
     Va fuora d' Italia, va fuora, o stranier.

La terra dei fiori, dei suoni e dei carmi
Ritorni qual era la terra dell' armi !
Di cento catene ci avvinser la mano,
Ma ancor di Legnano sa i ferri brandir.
Bastone tedesco l' Italia non doma,
Non crescon al giogo le stirpi di Roma :
Più Italia non vuole stranieri e tiranni,
Già troppi son gli anni che dura il servir.
     Va fuora d' Italia, va fuora ch'è l' ora,
     Va fuora d' Italia, va fuora, o stranier.

(Verses added after 1860)

Se ancora dell' Alpi tentasser gli spaldi,
Il grido d' *all' armi* darà Garibaldi :
E s' arma allo squillo, che vien da Caprera,
Dei mille la schiera che l' Etna assaltò.
E dietro alla rossa vanguardia dei bravi
Si muovon d' Italia le tende e le navi :
Già ratto sull' orma del fido guerriero
L'ardente destriero Vittorio spronò.
     Va fuora d' Italia, va fuora ch'è l' ora,
     Va fuora d' Italia, va fuora, o stranier.

Per sempre è caduto degli empi l' orgoglio,
A dir-viva Italia-va il Re in Campidoglio :
La Senna e il Tamigi saluta ed onora
L' antica signora che torna a regnar.
Contenta del regno fra l' isole e i monti
Soltanto ai tiranni minaccia le fronti :
Dovunque le genti percuota un tiranno
Suoi figli usciranno per terra e per mar.
     Va fuora d' Italia, va fuora ch'è l'ora,
     Va fuora d' Italia, va fuora, o stranier.
               LUIGI MERCANTINI.

APPENDIX A

By the great kindness of Mr. Rollo Russell, to whom, as to his sister, Lady Agatha Russell, I am much indebted for materials for the history of 1859-60, I have been allowed to see the private correspondence with Italy of Lord John Russell while Secretary for Foreign Affairs. I have spoken on pp. 28-30 above of the very great importance of these private letters, more particularly those of Henry Elliot, the British Minister at Naples, and Sir James Hudson, the British Minister at Turin. We see in them the process by which British statesmen were induced during the course of Garibaldi's expedition of 1860 to accept the idea of Italian Unity contrary to their previous views and intentions. Russell, Palmerston, and Gladstone had long been friends of Italian liberty, but they did not see that unity was the condition of liberty until they were convinced by events and by the letters of Hudson and Elliot, who were themselves converted to the doctrine of Unity only by Garibaldi's success in Sicily. The following extracts and analyses will interest the student, and even, I think, the general reader.

1860, May 1. *Hudson to Russell*. From Turin. [Garibaldi still at Quarto, preparing to sail for Sicily.]

'I feel convinced that both France and Austria mean mischief, France will not tolerate the substantial aggrandisement of this country [Piedmont] and its institutions, and Austria yet dreams of reconquest. If you abstain in Sicily and at Naples, Italy, in my opinion, has not much chance of being left to the Italians.'

May 4. *Hudson to Russell*. [Two days before Garibaldi sailed.] Hudson encloses a letter of Mr. Fenton's from Florence dated May 2, narrating on fairly reliable evidence that Victor Emmanuel at Florence had 'said that he would be at Naples before the end of the year.' Hudson comments: 'I quite believe that he is capable of saying so, because when he received a sword of honour from the Romans, he said "*anderemo al fondo*," and because also he is in the habit of blurting out just what happens to be present to his mind at the moment.'

May 18. *Hudson to Russell.* [Garibaldi in Sicily, not yet in Palermo. Three days after Calatafimi.]

Hudson advises against the union of North and South Italy, because—'1. Naples cannot be ruled from Turin or Florence with the Papal States intervening.' [This objection of Hudson's was removed in September when the Piedmontese overran and annexed the Papal Marches and Umbria.]

2. 'The Neapolitans are too corrupt and the entire civil and military administration is so abominable that their junction with North Italy, where honesty is the rule in public affairs, would merely produce a social decomposition and then a political putrefaction.' We must therefore, argues Hudson, find a *mezzo-termine* in order to arrive at the end Russell desires, *viz.* to check the Murat party and the French designs on South Italy. The *mezzo-termine* recommended by Hudson is a Prince of the House of Savoy on the throne of Naples and Sicily, guaranteed by France and England. This is to be got by 'amicable representation' at Naples by France and England, which would result in either the grant of a constitution, or an abdication. Either would do, but the latter would be best, for then a Prince of the House of Savoy might be put into the vacant throne. 'I believe Cavour heartily desires an Anglo-French intervention at Naples. I cannot go and speak to him on the subject, but I have caused him to be sounded, and I have myself sounded some of the best and wisest heads on the matter;—the above is the result.' *Here we see that as late as May* 18, 1860, *Hudson himself was not in favour of Italian unity.*

May 27. *Hudson to Russell.* [Day Garibaldi entered Palermo.]

'I received your telegram this morning instructing me to ask Cavour to stop any more expeditions from Genoa and Tuscany. He told me some days ago he would not permit any repetition of the Garibaldi expedition, and I believe him.' [If so, Hudson was unusually credulous, for Cavour was at that moment helping his friends to fit out the expedition of Medici.]

May 31. *Hudson to Russell.* [First day of the armistice at Palermo.]

Hudson discusses whether there is truth in the rumours

that Italy will make ' further concessions ' of territory to France, in return for Venice or the South. Cavour denies it, and Hudson believes him. ' For my part my belief is based not upon Cavour but upon Cavour's necessities. . . . You speak of Cavour as though he were Dictator. But he depends on public opinion.' The deputies supported him in the cession of Savoy, because they knew they must pay France for Central Italy, and because the greater part of Nice is French in population, and Savoy ' is as reactionary as Ireland or the Vatican.' But he could not command fifty votes to give away Sardinia or Genoa. ' The King told me that he had made the sacrifice of Savoy and Nice with a heavy heart, but there was no means of avoiding it. He added that he had paid his shot to France and he would hang the first Minister who proposed to make another cession. Supposing the King's word is worth no more than Cavour's, why should Venice be worth Genoa ? In my opinion Genoa is the real *tête de pont* of the King of Sardinia's Dominions. To give Genoa means to give Spezia, in which case there is no Italy at all, and the Italians have no intention of changing an Austrian master for a French one.'

' Cavour and Farini were here with me for an hour last night. They went over the whole question of Italy and her independence. They came here with a telegram announcing the fall of Palermo. I did not detect a word which smacked of further concessions to France. But I perceive very clearly that the more you hang back, the more easy do you make the propagation of French notions in Italy. Upon whom can the constitutional party in Italy lean save upon us? And if we refuse to allow them to lean upon us, you force them to lean upon France. Consequently if you abstain from interference in some shape or other in these Sicilian movements you leave a free field to France.'

June 2. *Elliot to Russell.* From Naples [during armistice at Palermo].

' It is extremely fortunate that the protest of the Admiral [Mundy] against the bombardment ' [of Palermo, see *Garibaldi and the Thousand*, pp. 290, 311, 313] ' was not listened to, for if it had been abandoned on that account the success of the insurgents would indubitably have been put on our shoulders, but nevertheless, as it was not listened to, I am delighted that the protest should have been made. . . . I do not feel much fear that the bombardment will be renewed, but it was charming to see how its defence was taken up by the Nuncio who gesticulated in favour of shells and shrapnel, till his purple stockings got almost scarlet with excitement.'

July 10. *Elliot to Russell.* [More than a month after fall of Palermo].

Elliot says he is favourable to complete annexation by Piedmont, either by means of Garibaldi continuing his career of victory, as he will do if the Sicilian settlement is delayed till he has crossed the Straits : or else, as Elliot would prefer, by Piedmont declaring open war on the House of Bourbon. If Piedmont 'would come forward openly and say that she intends to take up arms for her Sicilian brothers, I think it would simplify matters much, for the whole concern would probably tumble down without much further trouble, and it would moreover be an infinitely more manly and creditable course.'

The treaty ceding Sardinia and Genoa to France is apocryphal, and comes from Vienna. But false rumours, adds Elliot, have often preceded such objectionable pretensions of France.

July 16. *Hudson to Russell.* From Turin. [Four days prior to the battle of Milazzo.]

'The Unionists of North and Central Italy hold that policy because they see in it their principal means of escape from all foreign influence, and for my part I cordially and entirely agree with them for the very same reason that heretofore I advocated the annexation of Tuscany. Because now that the notion of a Prince of the House of Savoy' [see his letter of May 18 above] 'has been set aside by the force of circumstances, I do see very great danger to the Balance of Power in the Mediterranean if France should in the midst of the Neapolitan confusion find means to place a creature of her own on that throne or on both of the Sicilies. As to further compensation to France in the event of annexation of one or both of the Sicilies,' . . . Cavour 'exclaimed vehemently only last night— "*I will guarantee that nothing of the sort shall happen. I want Italy for the Italians, not for the French.*" I replied, that you were of opinion that if he only *ran straight* all would yet be well, and to this he solemnly declared that he would *run straight.*'

July 22. *Farini to Russell.* From Turin.

Farini, Cavour's principal colleague, writes solemnly denying rumours circulating in Europe that Italy and France are negotiating for a cession of Sardinia and the Ligurian coast to France.

July 31. *Russell to Farini.* From Chesham Place. (Reply to last.)

'Sir,

'I beg to assure you that I entirely believe your denial of the sinister rumours which have been spread. But we know that Count Cavour thought himself compelled to yield contrary to his declarations on the subject at Savoy and Nice. So that many say what happened once may happen again. For the present I entirely disbelieve in any secret treaty.'

July 25. *Ricasoli to Russell.* From Florence.

Ricasoli writes to thank Lord John for his support of the Italian cause. 'La régéneration Italienne repose uniquement sur son unité. Veuillez bien en être persuadé, My Lord. Il n'y a de salut pour l'Europe que dans l'Italie-Nation, et il n'y a pas de Nation que dans l'unité.'

July 27. *Hudson to Russell.* [Garibaldi's army, victorious at Milazzo on the 20th, is arriving at Messina on the Straits.]

'To state what are the plans of Cavour would be to do that which he himself would not dare to attempt, for my belief is that he has no plan. He is a waiter upon Providence and the chapter of accidents.' . . . 'The general aspect of affairs is a complete imbroglio for which there would, as a choice of evils, appear to be no other remedy than annexation. If, therefore, I am an advocate of that principle, it is rather because it appears to me to be less prejudicial to *British interests* (of which you remind me) than the anarchy of Sicily and Naples, and the discontent of North Italy.'

July 28. *Elliot to Russell.* [Three or four days after Lacaita's visit to Russell's house, see pp. 105-108 above.]

'De Martino [Neapolitan Minister for Foreign Affairs] is evidently much vexed that you will not join in preventing Garibaldi from crossing the Straits, though I scarcely think he can have really expected that you would, as I have over and over again told him not to reckon on any such help.'

July 31. *Hudson to Russell.* [Garibaldi still at Messina.]

A long reasoned letter to prove that the Unity of Italy is in accordance with British interests. [For a synopsis of this letter and some further extracts, see p. 29 above.]

'To constitute Italy under Duality is not easy with public opinion opposed. I was then a Dualist. I continued to be so till the capture of Palermo. I then proposed a Prince of the House of Savoy. [See letter of May 18, above.] You received the notion coldly and did nothing to promote it. The tidal wave of unity which the victory of Palermo set in motion carried that idea to the frozen sea of diplomatic nostrums.'

The Neapolitans are turning to Victor Emmanuel as to the only man to save them from 'anarchy and civil war, plunder and massacre, a licentious foreign soldiery, and a degraded mob.'

After stating many suggested solutions and the objection to each, he writes, 'It is not then my *sympathies* with Italy, but my sympathy with British interests which leads me in the face of existing circumstances to advocate the least prejudicial of these various issues, the Unity of Italy.'

'The interests of Italy turn, naturally, rather towards Germany than France, provided Germany will allow her. There is no reason why Austria should not give a real, efficient protection to Italy; they have great interests in common, and they have a common danger, France. But then this protection should be a moral one, not such an interest as Rudolf of Hapsburg tried to create in Italy by a corrupt bargain with Rome. It should be a protection shared by England and Prussia, with no other guarantee, no other pact than that which springs from natural necessities shared in common and felt by all. . . . If Austria would consent to cede Venice she would find security, compensation, and safety. She would re-establish her finances and gain a barrier on her Western frontier which would be impregnable so long as England is mistress of the sea.'

Such a league of Austria, Prussia, Italy, and England, argues Hudson, would put an end to all our fears of French hegemony.

[In view of the arguments used by Hudson in this letter in favour of Italian Unity, compare the letter of Lord Palmerston on January 10, 1861 (*Queen's Letters*, vol. iii.). 'Upon the subject of Italy your Majesty reminds Viscount Palmerston that he stated last summer that it would be better for the interests of England that Southern Italy should be a separate Monarchy, rather than that it should form part of a United Italy. Viscount Palmerston still retains that opinion, because a separate Kingdom of the Two Sicilies would be more likely, in the event of war between England and France, to side, at least by its neutrality, with the strongest naval Power, and it is to be hoped that such Power would be England. But then it would be necessary that the Two Sicilies as an independent and separate State should be well governed, and should have an enlightened Sovereign. This unfortunately has become hopeless and impossible under the Bourbon Dynasty, and no Englishman could wish to see a Murat or a Prince Napoleon on the Throne of Naples. The course of events since last summer (1860) seems to have finally decided the fate of Sicily and Naples, and there can be no doubt that for the interest of the people of Italy, and with a view to the general balance of Power in Europe, a United Italy is the best arrangement. The Italian Kingdom will never side with France from partiality to France, and the stronger that Kingdom becomes the better able it will be to resist political coercion from France. The chief hold that France will have upon the policy of the Kingdom of Italy consists in the retention of Venetia by Austria.']

August 11. *Elliot to Russell.* [Garibaldi still on Sicilian side of Straits of Messina.]

'Villamarina told me this morning, but again swore me to secrecy, that Victor Emmanuel has just received a letter from Prince Napoleon saying that *the time has come for securing the independence of Italy : courage on your part is all that is now required.*' But Elliot adds that the Piedmontese Government, frightened of the men around Garibaldi, have instructed Villamarina 'to do all he can to prevent Garibaldi from coming over,' but without letting it appear as if Piedmont was doing so. The object in this is to get a revolution in Naples for annexation without a Garibaldian dictatorship. But Elliot prophesies [correctly] that the Neapolitans have so little pluck that the attempt to anticipate Garibaldi will fail.

August 20. *Elliot to Russell.* [Garibaldi just crossing the Straits.]

'The only tolerable solution which I see remaining is that there should be war between Naples and Sardinia. The former dare not quarrel, and I am afraid the latter may continue to think it more profitable to go on working underground. But open war would be infinitely more creditable, and it would avoid the dangers both of Mazzinism and reaction through which we shall otherwise have to pass. If this were to be done, Naples would be settled, but we should then have the affairs of Rome and Venetia which must arise out of the annexation of Naples. If the Neapolitans shook off their King for themselves it is perhaps possible that they might be induced to be satisfied with the second son of Victor Emmanuel ; but there is little chance of their doing their work for themselves, and those who do it will impose the new arrangement on them,' viz. annexation.

August 24. *Hudson to Russell.*

' The expeditions of Garibaldi have ceased, *bonâ fide*, and, as the fine weather has set in, the country people are thinking more of their harvest than of politics. Turin is deserted. The King is in the mountains shooting chamois, and nearly all the diplomats gone too.' [And Cavour was meanwhile making his final arrangements for the invasion of the Papal States : I wonder whether Hudson really knew this.]

September 1. *Elliot to Russell.* From Naples. [Six days before Garibaldi entered Naples.]

Narrates discovery of what is called Count Trapani's reactionary plot, which has led to the resignation of the constitutional Ministers. But their resignation is not yet accepted. The National Guards almost insist on the Ministry remaining in, and say that if it does so the tranquillity of the town will be guaranteed by them. But the Ministers, or rather De Martino, insist on going, and say that if the King becomes privy to plots for their arrest, which was part of the programme of Trapani's plot, they cannot remain in to please the National Guard, or to become the Government not of the King but of the people. In a few hours it must be settled one way or other.

' I cannot yet give any true details of this plot, but the French connection of the leaders both of it and of Count Aquila's [plot of August 11] is a remarkable feature. The most prominent man in the present one is Prince Castropiano, and Prince Ischitella is also said to be in it, and both of these men I pointed out to you as devoted to French interests. It was also a Frenchman in whose rooms the compromising papers were found, and I believe Brenier has called for his liberation. In fact on all sides there is an atmosphere of intrigue that bewilders me.'

September 7. *Hudson to Russell.* [Day of Garibaldi's entry into Naples ; a few days prior to Cavour's invasion of Papal States.]

'Cavour must choose between one of the horns of his dilemma. Either intervention with Victor Emmanuel, or anarchy with Garibaldi. Of course he chooses for the former, but we see now what the Garibaldi expedition has produced. Cavour told me this morning that he would willingly have avoided all this, but being determined not to let Garibaldi and the Mazzinians get the whip-hand, he is forced to resort to extreme measures in order to avoid the Venetia difficulty. When I read your dispatch to him this morning he said : *Believe me, Garibaldi shall not attack Venice ;—if Venice is ever attacked it will be by an Italian army. I have no intention of attacking Venice, and this Lord John may rely on.* This appears to mean he will attack Venice when he is strong enough to do so, but that day appears to me to be distant.'

October 16. *Elliot to Russell.* [A fortnight after the battle of the Volturno.]

'General Türr, who is Garibaldi's right hand, says that the town of Naples furnished eighty fighting men' [to Garibaldi's army of 20,000 Italian volunteers at the front, protecting Naples].

October 30. *Elliot to Russell.* [Last days of Garibaldi's Dictatorship.]

'No change of any kind has taken place here since I last wrote except that the necessity of having a Government becomes daily more and more apparent, and each day adds immensely to the difficulty that will be experienced in setting matters a little straight, after the universal and wholesale plunder and confusion, which is by degrees becoming a system.'

October 19. *Hudson to Russell.* [Victor Emmanuel advancing from Ancona to Naples.]

'The King has sent me through General Solaroli a message to the following effect. That considering the jealousy with which his constitutional system of government is regarded by most sovereigns, and especially by Austria, Russia, and France, and the lukewarm support of Prussia, he has no one to rely on for moral support save England, and he would esteem it as a favour if on his arrival at Naples he could be supported by a British representative.'

[The 'moral support' was forthcoming in Lord John Russell's famous dispatch of October 27 (No. 195 in the *F. O.* MSS. = No. 136, p. 125, in the *Br. Parl. Papers*, vii.). It contained the sentiment—'It appears that the late proceedings of the King of Sardinia have been strongly disapproved by several of the principal Courts of Europe.' But 'Her Majesty's Government must admit that the Italians themselves are the best judges of their own interests.' See p. 282 above. The publication of this dispatch produced in Italy the effect recorded in the following letters.]

November 2. *Hudson to Russell.*

'Cavour begs me to make to you his warmest acknowledgments for your dispatch No. 195. . . . Yesterday it would have done your heart good could you have seen him read your No. 195. He shouted, rubbed his hands, jumped up, sat down again, then he began to think, and when he looked up tears were standing in his eyes. Behind your dispatch he saw the Italy of his dreams, the Italy of his hopes, the Italy of his policy.'

November 12. *Elliot to Russell.*

'For the last week Naples, and I believe Italy, have been more occupied about your dispatch to Hudson than about anything else, and though you must have been in great measure prepared for it, you can hardly quite have expected the immense sensation it has made. Villamarina's first exclamation was that it was worth more than 100,000 men, and King Victor Emmanuel appears to have spoken to Admiral Mundy in terms almost as strong.'

November 16. *Cavour to Russell.* Thanking him for the dispatch.

'L'appui moral que vous nous prêtez dans cette circonstance suprême, nous permettra, j'espère, d'établir sur des bases larges et solides l'édifice de la nation Italienne. . . . Ma vive reconnaissance pour le service immense que vous venez de rendre à l'Italie.'

The following letter has already been printed in Spencer Walpole's *Russell*, ii. pp. 328-329.

'MR. ODO RUSSELL TO LORD JOHN RUSSELL.

'ROME, *December 1st*, 1860.

'MY DEAR UNCLE,

'Ever since your famous dispatch of the 27th you are blessed night and morning by twenty millions of Italians. I could not read it myself without deep emotion, and the moment it was published in Italian, thousands of people copied it from each other to carry it to their homes and weep over it for joy and gratitude in the bosom of their families, away from brutal mercenaries and greasy priests. Difficult as the task is the Italians have now before them, I cannot but think that they will accomplish it better than we any of us hope, for every day convinces me more and more that I am living in the midst of a *great* and *real* national movement, which will at last be crowned with perfect success, notwithstanding the legion of enemies Italy still counts in Europe.

'Your affectionate nephew,

'ODO RUSSELL.'

While this book is being printed (1911) an important document has come to hand, through the kindness of Mr. William Warren Vernon,[1] who finds in his diary under the date February 22, 1870, the following contemporary entry :—

'Reached the Hotel Vittoria at San Remo at 5.30. We dined with Lord and Lady Russell who live close by. Lord Russell is looking very well. Lacaita, he, and Lady Russell discussed how in July, 1860, when Persigny was trying to induce Lord John to stop Garibaldi's landing in Italy from Messina, he (Lacaita) being very ill at the time, managed to see Lady John who was ill in bed. She, however, received him and sent for Lord John, who was mightily surprised to find Lacaita there, who immediately attacked him on the treaty he was supposed to be arranging with Persigny, to have an Anglo-French fleet in the Straits of Messina to prevent Garibaldi from crossing to Italy.

'After a long discussion which nearly exhausted Tino, [Lacaita] who was very ill, Lord John said to him "go to bed, and don't be so sure that I am going to sign the treaty yet ". Tino went home to bed; and two hours after, George Elliot, then Lord John's secretary, came to him to tell him from Lord John to be of good cheer. Tino took the hint, sent for D'Azeglio and dictated a telegram to Cavour, implying that the intended treaty was at an end. Garibaldi was accordingly undisturbed. How few people knew that this was owing to Lacaita. I myself heard Lord Russell confirm this story.'

This passage from Mr. Vernon's diary puts the story (*q.v.*, pp. 103-109 above) beyond all possible doubt, by proving that Lord and Lady Russell bore out Lacaita's account of it. With the Hudson letter (see p. 105 above, note) the chain of evidence is now complete.

[1] It may be explained that Sir James Lacaita and Mr. Warren Vernon were intimate friends, and in 1870 were travelling together to Tuscany by the Riviera. Mr. Vernon was married to a first cousin of Lady Russell.

EXPEDITIONS OF VOLUNTEERS FROM NORTH ITALY WHO JOINED GARIBALDI AFTER THE FIRST SAILING OF THE THOUSAND IN MAY

Date of Leaving Genoa.	Name of Ship.	Approximate Number of Men on Board Notes.	Evidence of Statements as to Date and Numbers.
May 24	*Utile*	60, under Agnetta. Chiefly arms and ammunition	*Bertani*, ii. 73. *Bertani Comp.* p. 5. *La F.* (*Biundi*), ii. 528.
Night of June 8-9.	*Utile* (2nd voyage). *Charles and Jane* (American clipper)	900 or 1000, under Corte. Captured at sea and taken to Gaeta. Released and came out again in the *Amazon*, which left Genoa July 15. They were just in time for the battle of Milazzo	*Menghini*, 434–440. *Türr's Div.* 409. *Bertani Comp.* 22–23. *Medici* (*Pasini*), 11.
Night of June 9-10	*Washington* (formerly *Helvétie*), French steamer, belonging to the Messageries Impériales Cie. (*F. O. Sard. Hudson*, June 9-10, Nos. 271, 277)	1200 or 1400, with Medici in person. (Peard and the Marios on board)	*Peard*, 813–816. *Menghini*, 104, 433. *Türr's Div.* 409 (exaggerates numbers on *Washington* and *Oregon* by adding those who really went in the *Franklin*). *Bertani Comp.* 23.
Night of June 9-10	*Oregon* (formerly *Belzance*), etc., *see F. O. ibid.*	209, under Caldesi (some estimate a little higher)	*Medici* (*Pasini*), 11–13 (shows that, with the 900 or 1000 men under Corte captured at sea, the expedition *would* have numbered 3500). *Daily News*, June 26, 1860, p. 4, col. 5; letter by the Marios from on board the *Washington*, June 14.
June 10 (from Leghorn)	*Franklin* (formerly *Amsterdam*), French steamer, etc., *see F. O. ibid.*	800, under Malenchini	*F. O. Sard. Hudson*, June 10-11 and 15, Nos. 271, 273, 277, 281.

Medici's expedition close on 2500 men with 8000 firearms and much ammunition

Date	Ship	Number / commander		Notes
June 29	Medeah	365 or 650, under Fazioli		Türr's Div. 409 gives the higher number Bertani Comp. the lower.
July 2	Washington (2nd voyage)	1270, with Cosenz in person	⎱ Cosenz' expedition over 2000	Türr's Div. 409 and Bertani Comp.
July 2	Provence	770		Türr's Div. 409 and Bertani Comp.
July 7	Oregon (2nd voyage)	404, under Siccoli		Bertani Comp. p. 24 (mentioned in Menghini, p. 441).
July 9	Provence (2nd voyage)	765, under Curci		Türr's Div. 409, Bertani Comp. and Cremona MSS. Memorie del Carasi. F. O. Sard. Hudson, 1860, No. 307, enclosure of letter from Brown, British Consul at Genoa, July 20, which speaks of the Provence as the Durance. Brown's information is probably not quite as accurate as the official papers of Türr's Div. and Bertani Comp.
July 9	Saumon	526, under Vacchieri	⎱ Close under 1300	Türr's Div. 409 and Bertani Comp.
July 10	Isère	407, under Ciravegna		Türr's Div. 409 and Bertani Comp.
July 10 or 11	City of Aberdeen	900, under Strambio		Türr's Div. 409 says 900 and Bertani Comp. 890. F. O. Brown's letter, as above.
[July 15]	Amazon (British)	The men of Corte's 'Gaeta' battalion, see above sub Utile, 2nd voyage, June 8		Türr's Div. 409 and Bertani Comp.]
July 16	Provence (3rd voyage)	405, under Cesarò		Türr's Div. 409 and Bertani Comp. F. O. Brown's letter, as above.
July 18	Città di Torino (large steamer, formerly belonged to the Cia Transatlantica. F. O. Sard. Hudson, 1860, No. 307, enclosure of Brown's letter of July 20)	1535, under Sacchi		Türr's Div. 409 gives 3435 by a misprint I suspect for 1535, since Bertani Comp. gives 1535, and is confirmed by F. O. Brown's letter, see above, I think the lower number most probable.

Date of Leaving Genoa.	Name of Ship.	Approximate Number of Men on Board. Notes.	Evidence of Statements as to Date and Numbers.
July 21	Franklin (2nd voyage)	564, under Gobbi	Türr's Div. 409 and Bertani Comp.
July 21 or 22	Amazon (2nd voyage)	390, under Berti	Türr's Div. 409 and Bertani Comp.
July 23	Isère (2nd voyage)	413 (or 423)	Türr's Div. 409 and Bertani Comp.
Aug. 6 or 8	Provence (4th voyage)	211, under Pietro Cortes	Türr's Div. 409 and Bertani Comp. 24.
Aug. 10 to 15 (mostly by Aug. 11, according to Brown's reports)	Isère (3rd voyage) ?; Bizantine (French ship) 1800; Amazon (3rd voyage) ?; Citià di Torino (2nd voyage) ?	3708[1] (Pianciani's expedition), pp. 118-122 above	Türr's Div. 409 (F. O. Sard. Consul's Report, No. 19, Cagliari, Aug. 17, for Bizantine).
Started by Aug. 11 from Genoa, reached Cagliari by Aug. 15	Generale Garibaldi (Piedmontese) 680; R. D. Shepherd (American, U.S.) 1500	Over 2000 (Pianciani' expedition), pp. 118-122 above	These 2000 are not mentioned in Türr's Div. or Comp. Bertani, but are mentioned by British Consul at Cagliari in F. O. Sard. Consul's Report, No. 19, Cagliari, Aug. 17, and this is confirmed by Consul Brown's report from Genoa, Aug. 11, which speaks of 4000 men gone to join Garibaldi in last few days, and '2000 more' to 'embark to-night.' (F. O. Sard. Hudson, No. 317 enclosure.) So I believe nearly 6000 left Genoa between Aug. 9 and 11, as Brown states in his letter of Aug. 28.[1]
From Spezia, reached Cagliari by Aug. 15	Weasel (English)	32	
Aug. 16	Sidney Hall	542	Türr's Div. 409 and Comp. Bertani.
Aug. 20	Provence (5th voyage)	582	Türr's Div. 409 and Comp. Bertani, 24; the latter erroneously puts July 20 instead of Aug. 20.

| Sept. 1-3 (from Leghorn) | Febo . . . . .
Garibaldi . . . .
Veloce (Provence?) . .
S. Nicola . . . . | } 2000 Nicotera's 'Castel Pucci' Brigade, about which there was the quarrel with Ricasoli, p. 122, above | Türr's Div. 409.
Pianciani, doc. lett. N. 'Nicotera,'
Ricasoli, 213-223. | 'Protesta del Col. Gio. |

These various expeditions together make a total of about 21,000 men.

[1] *F. O. Sard. Consuls*, 260, Brown writes, from Genoa, Aug. 28: 'The main body of the expedition sent to the Golfo degli Aranci, in Sardinia, started on the 9th to 11th August, fully 6000 having started on those three days,' 'From 9th to 20th August 8000 Garibaldians sailed from this port and were collected in Sardinia, but these have all since arrived at Palermo and Messina. Since then only those by *Orwell* and 500 who being able to procure passports started night 26th for Palermo.' The *Orwell* was carried off piratically and had to be given back. In the latter part of August Cavour stopped further help from being sent to Garibaldi from the North, as he had determined himself to invade the Papal States and thence the Nea-politan territory. Thus Hudson writes privately to Russell (*Russell MSS.*) on Aug. 24: 'The expeditions to Garibaldi have ceased *bonâ fide.*'

Besides the ships in the above list which took the men south, there were many other ships engaged in carrying arms and stores, as the large *Queen of England* (also called the *Anita*, Durand Brager, 169) and the *Independence*, the small *Ferret* and *Badger* which, together with the *Weasel* in the list above, were the five steamers bought by Bertani's Central Committee (*Bertani's Reso.* pp. 17-18). We also find mention of the ships *Spedizione* and *Colonello Sacchi* taking out stores, in the *Milan MSS. Archivio Bertani*, Plichi li-lv.

Guerzoni, ii. 126 note, *Bertani Comp.*, *La F.* (*Biundi*), ii. 528, *Bertani Reso.* and *Bertani*, ii. chaps. xvi.-xvii., Luzio in *Giornale d'Italia*, May 5, 1907, and *Corr. della Sera*, August 23, 1907, prove that *the expeditions of June and July, especially those of Medici and Cosenz, were fitted out, paid for and sent mainly by the Cavourian National Society, and by the Million Rifles Fund, financed for the purpose by the Government itself. But the expeditions of August (of Pianciani and Nicotera) were fitted out, paid for and sent mainly by Bertani's Central Committee and the more advanced parties*, who also bought the *Queen of England*, the *Independence*, the *Ferret* and the *Badger*, steamers used only for carrying arms from Genoa, and therefore not mentioned in above list.

APPENDIX C

THE RIVAL ORGANISATIONS THAT HELPED GARIBALDI

I. THE list of seventeen cities where *Bertani's Committee* had local Committees (*Milan MSS. A. B.* Plico, lxxxix) runs as follows: Modena, Parma, Forlì, Bologna, Reggio, Ferrara, Piacenza, Florence, Leghorn, Faenza, Ravenna, Rimini, Cuneo, Brescia, Bergamo, Cremona, Milan. I do not think that the list is complete, but it seems to show that the Committee was active in Lombardy, Tuscany, and the Romagna, and to a less extent in Piedmont.

The Cavourian *National Society*, whose seat was Turin, was most active of all in the cities of Piedmont (*Bertani Comp.* 4), but it also had very active local Committees in the towns of the Romagna (see *Dallolio*, 97-145), not excluding those in which there were also local Committees of Bertani's. In Tuscany the Committee initiated in May by Amari and Malenchini worked hard in conjunction with La Farina and Medici, quarrelling with Bertani; see *Amari*, ii. 82-90, *Risorg.* anno i. fasc. 5-6, pp. 989-993 ; *Bertani Comp.* 8 (note).

II. The accounts of *Bertani's Committee* are given in *Bertani Reso.* They were most scrupulously kept and stood the audit, as Bertani's critics readily admit (*Luzio, Corr. della Sera,* March 1, 1910). The total sum received was 6,201,060 *lire* 13 *cent.* But of this sum five-sixths was sent to Bertani by Garibaldi—5,106,655 *lire* 45 *cent* from Sicily, and 201,632 *lire* 05 *cent* from Naples. In this way Sicily was made to pay for the liberation of Naples, as the price of its own liberation, for it was the 5,000,000 *lire* from Sicily that principally paid for Pianciani's great expeditions in August, equipped by Bertani. (See *Rendiconto* at end of *Bertani Reso.* ' *denari tratti dal governo di Sicilia,*' *Onze* 416,000 = 5,006,655 *lire*, and *Luzio, Corr. della Sera,* March 1, 1910.) Garibaldi had been lucky enough to capture from the Bourbon Government an immense quantity of treasure in the *zecca* (mint) of Palermo, when he took the town. They had, by great good luck for Garibaldi, been calling in old money to make a re-coinage. A large part of the five millions from Sicily came from this source. *Forbes*, 59. *Conv. Dolmage.*

The total of the private subscriptions received by *Bertani's Committee* amounts to 851,735 *lire* 28 *cent.* The subscription list, including sums from 1·50 upwards, is given in full in *Bertani Reso.* The Cavourian *National Society* and the *Million Rifles Fund* probably drew subscriptions from richer classes on the average, and were more patronised by the municipalities voting rates to help Garibaldi. The *National Society* received and spent over 1,000,000 *lire.* (See accounts given in *La F. (Biundi)*, ii. 527-529.) The *Million Rifles Fund*, besides many thousands of rifles and muskets, supplied more than 2,000,000 *lire (Bertani Comp.* p. 24). Of these two millions a large part was furnished by subscription or out of municipal rates, and another large part by the Royal Government (*Luzio, Giorn. d'It.* 5 May, 1907, Finzi's correspondence). The Royal Government, through the agency of the National Society, itself secretly paid for the arms brought to Garibaldi by Agnetta in the *Utile* on its first voyage : since the *Utile* left Genoa on May 24 (see Appendix B) before the taking of Palermo, we have here evidence that Cavour financially assisted Garibaldi's expedition before its initial success was assured; Mr. Nelson Gay has proved this from documents in his possession, in his article in the *Deutsche Revue*, December, 1910, p. 313.

APPENDIX D

THE STATE OF SICILY UNDER THE DICTATOR AND HIS PRO-DICTATORS

THIS is an obscure subject, and I am not aware of any work of careful historical research dealing with it. The noise that was made about the outbreak of social war at Bronte shows that these disturbances were local and exceptional; they were very promptly suppressed by Bixio. The history of the march of Eber's column through the heart of Sicily from June 20 to July 15, recorded in great detail in the *Times, Morning Post* (correspondents *passim*), *Adamoli*, *Türr's Div.*, *Abba Not.*, and elsewhere, shows on the whole a peaceable state of society in the villages considering that they were in process of revolution. Some banditti complained of by the villagers were arrested by the Garibaldini. But from Amari's letter of August 3, quoted below, one would gather that the country grew more disturbed near Palermo at the beginning of August.

La Farina himself admits that 'in spite of the disorder the taxes and duties are paid' (*La Farina*, ii. 340). But he is no doubt right in complaining that there was still considerable disorder and delay in the work of the magistracy, police, and judicature of the island within a month of the taking of Palermo (*La Farina*, ii. 350).

It will be well to record the impressions of several impartial and well-informed persons.

1. The British Consul, Goodwin, who had been many years in the island and was perhaps the man most generally trusted there, reported to his Government that peace and order in Palermo as early as June 11 were far better than the state of things after the revolution of 1848, which he had witnessed. In no subsequent passage in his Political Journal or official correspondence for the year does he complain of a lapse towards anarchy, either in Palermo or in the island. (Goodwin's Political Journal can be found both in the *F. O. Sard. Hudson, passim*, and in *Palermo MSS. Br. Consulate.*)

2. Michele Amari, a most impartial observer, a moderate Cavourian, who was in his native island from the beginning of July onwards, writes on July 3 : 'In Palermo nothing is heard of the thefts, homicides, and other violent acts of 1848. I can affirm this. They have, until a few days ago, continued to kill some of the ex-police agents, but the case is exceptional. It is bad certainly, but does not prove anarchy.'

On July 6 he writes : 'If I am not mistaken, the condition of the country is far from anarchy, as some cry out seeing there is neither the order of quiet times, nor authority in the proper hands. In Palermo, though the week before I came one of Maniscalco's ex-police agents was killed, there is complete security of person and property. Business is conducted as usual. People frequent the streets until late at night. Up country there are perhaps local parties with their quarrels and revenges, but I have not heard recently of any spilling of blood, and I hope that gradually order will recover its natural balance.'

A month later, on August 3, he writes less hopefully of 'every sort of disorder in the provinces, though in Palermo there is security and tranquillity as in time of peace. . . . In the provinces the stupid local parties tear each other to pieces, ambitious of power, vain and greedy. In some places they come to blows, and the robbers . . . let out from the prisons feast and riot in the country-side, particularly in the district of Palermo. There is ample provision under the laws, but who enforces them ? The Governors of the districts and provinces have done badly with a few exceptions. The National Guard, through fault of the Governors or owing to municipal quarrels, is powerless to combat the robberies and acts of violence.'

He very wisely says that nothing but a strong force of gens d'armes from the North, 'neither Sicilian nor Neapolitan,' can enforce order in the island ; this was one of the strongest arguments for an early annexation (*Amari*, ii. 97-98, 109-112).

3. Türr, though he served Garibaldi well, was almost as much of Cavour's as of Garibaldi's party, and was bitterly attacked by Bertani's friends. But in July he wrote to the papers to protest against La Farina's interference in Sicily ; 'La Farina,' Türr wrote, 'depicts Sicily in prey to anarchy and declares that the setting up of the National Guard was opposed in every way. This is false.' Türr says that there was no ill-feeling between parties in Palermo till La Farina came and stirred it up, and that it died down after his departure (*Bertani*, ii. 108 note).

4. Nievo, one of the Thousand, remained at Palermo from June to December as Military Intendant, supplying Garibaldi's armies. He saw the inside of Sicily all that year; he was an honourable and an intellectual man, though he cannot, like Amari and Türr, be called impartial as between Garibaldi and Cavour. For whatever his opinion was worth, he wrote on October 16 : ' Pay no attention to the talk about anarchy here. Order is perfect, as it never was before in Sicily.'

5. The *Times* special correspondent (Eber the Hungarian) writing from Castrogiovanni in the middle of the island on July 10, says (*Times*, July 26, p. 10, c. 2):—

' Garibaldi, from the first moment of his arrival in Sicily, has adopted the policy of leaving the internal administration of the country in the hands of Sicilians, and every day shows that he was right in this measure ; for in the general greediness of *employés* the nomination of any one but Sicilians would have been looked upon as intrusion. . . . It is only justice to say that in spite of this office-hunt public tranquillity has not suffered in more than three or four *communes* in the whole island, and even in these the disturbances happened before the regular Government was established. In all the rumours of disturbances which you hear there is not a word of foundation, and this is perhaps the greatest of all the wonders which Garibaldi has achieved since his arrival in Sicily, for to his *prestige* alone must this be attributed.'

6. See also *V. M.* 16, for a frankly Garibaldian account of the government of Sicily from June to November.

APPENDIX E

THE ARMS OF THE CAMPAIGN

THE following three statements can be made with confidence :—

1. That practically the whole of the Bourbon infantry were armed with rifles.

2. That the Thousand (except the Genoese Carabineers) had smooth-bore muskets of an obsolete pattern.

3. That, after the arrival of Medici at Palermo, one part of the Garibaldini had rifles and another part smooth-bore muskets.

The doubtful problem is whether among the Garibaldini the rifles were the general rule and the muskets the exception, or *vice-versâ*. I will place before the reader all the pieces of evidence which I have been able to collect on this point.

1. My friend, Mr. J. A. Dolmage, an officer in the British Army, both before and after 1860, was on leave from his regiment and travelling in Sicily in 1860. He joined Garibaldi's forces in June, was unofficially attached to Türr's Brigade, saw most of the fighting in the campaign, and was professionally well fit to speak on its technical side. He sends me the following notes :—

' *Smooth-bore.*—The Thousand were armed with military smooth-bore muskets. These had evidently been sold as obsolete by Piedmont and other European countries ; and could be purchased very cheaply, I should think. The Sicilian and Calabrian volunteers were armed with smooth-bore muskets, many of these being weapons which had been disposed of by our own Army and the East India Company. They were purchased for, probably, from ten to fourteen shillings a-piece.'

' The smooth-bore weapon was not at all an unsuitable fire-arm for the tactics of Garibaldi, which was to get as quickly as possible to close quarters with the enemy, when the bayonet became of use. These muskets were sighted up to 300 yards. But after the first 100 yards or so it was quite a matter of chance if men hit what they aimed at. On the other hand, the rifle was not of service to a soldier until he had been properly trained to use it.' [See Captain Forbes' remarks p. 329 below.]

'*The Squadre* (Sicilian irregular bands) had a very primitive and curious gun of their own. It could make noise and kill bird or man, but at no very great distance. It was not in any way suited for a bayonet and was fired by means of a percussion cap.'

'*Rifle.*—The men of Peard's Company were armed with revolving-rifles. Colt, an American, the inventor of this weapon, had presented 100 of these to Garibaldi.[1] Not only were they troublesome to load, but the user, in firing, would sometimes have his left wrist badly scorched from the breech.' [See p. 87 above. This explains why revolving-rifles have never come into general use.] 'The Colt's revolving-rifle was the only thing like a breech-loader in Garibaldi's army.'

'*Medici's Expedition brought the first Enfield Rifles.*—Major Wolf received 135 of these for his Foreign Company, and they were the only rifles of any kind with Eber's brigade in Sicily.' [Mr. Dolmage was with Eber's brigade in its march through Sicily, see p. 66 note 2 above.] 'Though it was of course a muzzle-loader, the Enfield was an excellent rifle and was sighted up to 900 yards. *The men of Cosenz' Brigade, whom I met at Milazzo, were in possession of Enfields.*' [Mr. Dolmage came to Milazzo bearing messages from Eber, a day or two after the battle.] 'The English Legion had them also' [*viz.* in October]. 'I should say too that others had been placed in the hands of the best Italian volunteers.'

'*Neapolitan Army.*—The Bourbon Forces were very well equipped and armed. They were strong in cavalry, and had excellent artillery also. At the operations before Capua they had several rifled field-pieces, very unusual at that time. The infantry soldiers were armed with a good serviceable minie rifle, with a large bore. This bore struck me as so large that I made inquiry on the subject, and was told that the weapons were muskets which had been sent to Austria to have the barrels grooved, and so converted into rifles. I do not, however, vouch for the truth of this story.'

[1] See *Ciàmpoli*, 126 (letter of January 19), and *Bertani*, ii. 13 (letter of March 15), on the expected arrival of these 100 Colt's revolving-rifles from America.

'The *Cacciatori*—light infantry, sharp-shooters in fact—had a shorter rifle, but with the same bore. There were several regiments of *Cacciatori* which were looked on as picked troops. It is possible that there may have been smooth-bore muskets in the Neapolitan army, but I never saw any.'

'In Sicily, on such occasions as the surrenders at Palermo and Milazzo, the Neapolitans marched out with their arms, which they retained by agreement. In Calabria, however, where many surrenders took place, the arms must have been handed over to our people ; but I do not know what became of them, nor whether any were given over for use to our volunteers.

'We took a large number of prisoners on the 1st and 2nd of October, and several thousand stand of arms thus came into the possession of Garibaldi's people ; but as Capua surrendered during the first days of November following, these came to us a little late for use.'

2. Mr. A. B. Patterson (*aet.* 17 in 1860, given a commission by Garibaldi on the field of Milazzo; since British I.C.S.) writes to me :—

'Dunne's men [see pp. 65, 85 above] were *certainly* armed with Enfield rifles, I remember my own perfectly. *I believe all the men in Medici's command were so armed.* It is improbable that Dunne's Sicilians (a regiment which of course had little training) should have been selected for arming with rifles in preference to the picked troops of which Medici's command was mainly composed. Most of these had seen service in 1859 either under Garibaldi or in the Sardinian army. My belief is that rifles were the *rule* at Milazzo. Probably only the newly raised *squadre*, who were not, I think, engaged at Milazzo, were armed with smooth-bores. I may add that Dunne's men had no target practice at Palermo. They had blank cartridge practice only. So they were not able to make the best use of their weapons. But it did not matter much ; everywhere the contest was decidedly at close quarters. The enemy was so sheltered by walls, trees, etc., that we did not see him till very near, and the firing was mainly at close quarters. Success was obtained by the constant, determined advance always under heavy fire and against a brave enemy in a strong position, superior in numbers and of course in training. Only the heroic leading of Garibaldi and his Lieutenants made the victory possible. I venture to claim Dunne and Wyndham among the best of these.'

3. In *Times*, August 4, p. 10, c. 2, the special correspondent, who took part in the battle of Milazzo, says that Medici's men were then armed with Enfield rifles.

4. Mariotti, a veteran of Malenchini's regiment, the Tuscan part of Medici's expedition which came out in the *Franklin*, in his detailed and generally accurate memoirs, says : 'Our fire-arms (*fucili*) were those of the Million Rifles Fund, rifles (*rigati*) come from America, small bore, with the barrels varnished black ; they were technical perfection for that period ' (*Mariotti*, 420).

[Mr. Dolmage says these are clearly the Enfields, and that Mariotti mistook in supposing they came from America ; they came from England.]

5. Captain C. S. Forbes, R.N., who arrived at Milazzo from Palermo within a few days of the battle, and was familiar with Garibaldi and many of his principal followers, writes of the victors in that battle :—

'Generally speaking the entire force was armed with Enfields, but few knew how to develop the use of those deadly weapons, the sights being deemed a superfluity.'   But he adds : ' *A musket or rifle*, sixty rounds of ammunition, a water-bottle, and for the most part an empty haversack, and you have the *impedimenta* of a Garibaldian '   (*Forbes*, 92).

6. *Guerzoni*, ii. 126, speaks of Medici as bringing with him to Palermo in June ' 8000 carabine rigate (*rifles* inglesi) '. But in a foot-note on the same page the list supplied by Guastalla, the secretary of the Million Rifles Fund, we read of 4850 *fucili francesi*, 200 *carabine enfield* (query 2000 ?), 200 *fucili di Liegi*.

Now the word *fucili* may mean either rifles or smoothbores.

7. Finzi, a Director of the Million Rifles Fund, in his letter of September 6, 1869 (printed in *Chiala*, iv. pp. cxxvii-cxxxi), says that the Directors ' had given the preference to French *fucili*, model of 1842, which that Government had abandoned, but which had done good service in the campaign of 1859—besides *fucili* of the Prussian army which had also been changed.   The Directors had also obtained a good number of *carabine* (*Stützen*) and Austrian rifles (*fucili rigati*), besides 2000 new Enfield *carabine*.'

[This leads me to suppose that the statement in Guerzoni's note about ' 200 ' Enfields is a misprint for 2000, especially as in that case the numbers, 4850 + 2000 + 200 would amount to something nearer the 8000 spoken of in Guerzoni's text.]

Later in his letter Finzi speaks of ' 200 excellent Austrian rifles,' and '3744 Prussian *fucili*,' as the property of the Fund.

8. Medici himself, in his letter to Garibaldi (*Persano*, 41) and *Medici* (*Pasini*), p. 13, uses the ambiguous term 8000 *fucili*. But on p. 11 of *Medici* (*Pasini*), he speaks of ' 10,000 fucili e molte munizioni, *oltre le carabine Enfie'd destinate ad armare la mia spedizione*,' ' over and above the Enfield rifles destined to arm my own expedition '—which consisted of 2500 men.

9. In the letters of the Ministers to D'Azeglio about the weapons in the Million Rifles Fund armoury at Milan, the ambiguous word *fucili* (or *fusils*) is employed (*Luzio Corr. della Sera*, Dec. 8, 1909).

10. After the battle of Milazzo, the British steamer *Queen of England* brought to Garibaldi's camp at Faro, on August 15, a few days before he crossed the Straits of Messina, 23,500 Enfield rifles from England in 1175 cases, and several rifled cannon (*Schwabe MS.*, *Manifest for Queen of England* (*Gibraltar, cleared* 31 *July*, 1860)). This bears out *Times*, August 25, p. 9, c. 4, and Forbes, 141. The rifled cannon were not used in Calabria, but there were rifled cannon at the Volturno on both sides.

Putting together these various pieces of evidence, I am inclined to believe that Medici's and Cosenz' men and Dunne's regiment were at the battle of Milazzo armed with good rifles, which they had not yet learned to use properly, but that most of Eber's column and a great many of the Sicilians and subsequently of the Calabrians were armed with smooth-bores.

APPENDIX F

BATTLE OF MILAZZO

I

I HERE give a list of the principal authorities which I have studied for this battle. In traversing this and all my other accounts of actions in the campaign, if critics find one or another of these authorities going counter to statements in the text, they must bear in mind that in points of military detail even first-hand authorities and eye-witnesses contradict each other, not infrequently, and that therefore I have been forced, in collating the different accounts, to come to a separate conclusion on each incident, deciding in each several case in favour of one authority and against another for reasons which it would take a separate volume to set out in full. In the general aspects of the strategy and tactics there is much less difficulty, especially when the ground has been visited.

A. Bourbon first-hand authorities.—The first of Bosco's long reports can be found in *Cronaca*, 207-209. A second, later one, originally printed in the Neapolitan *Rivista Militare*, August, 1860, can be found reprinted in three places—*Palmieri*, p. 30 text and 40-46 note ; *Nove Mesi*, 23-25 ; and *Gaz. di Milano*, August 20-21, 1860, translated back again from a French version. *Zirilli*, doc. 5, gives a letter from a Bourbon officer. *De Sivo*, iii. 313-317, and *Franci*, i. 73-76, are *second-hand*, drawn from Bosco's report.

B. Garibaldian first-hand authorities, *q.v. sub loc.* are *Mem.; Medici (Pasini)* ; *Times*, August 4, 1860 ; *Piaggia* (best authority of the topography) ; *Zirilli ; Milazzo* (G. B. Z.) ; *Mistrali's da N.; Castellini ; Mario Mac.* and *Red Shirt; Guerzoni; Morning Post*, August 9, 1860 ; *Milan MS. Cosenz and Bruzzesi*, and *Bronzetti*, i. 3 ; *Nelson MS.* (in my hands) ; *Rome MS. Savi ; Menghini ; Paolucci's*

Corrao ; Peard's Journal MS. and *Cornhill ; Brancaccio, Bandi, Uzielli, Mariotti,* and *Fonvielle* for Malenchini's defeat on left wing ; *Pozzi ; Durand-Brager ; Forbice ; Magni ; Forbes* (arrived just after battle, as did Mr. Dolmage, Mario and Piaggia) ; *Milazzo* (*G. B. Z.*), *Campo,* 136-137, and *Baroni* for Corte's ' Gaeta battalion '. I have also had the great advantage of *conversations* with *Missori, Canzio, Tedaldi,* and *Sclavo ;* and my own countrymen *Patterson* and *Dolmage.* See Appendix E above, on arms used in the battle.

Good *second-hand authorities* are *Villari, Cosp. ; Türr's Div. ; Rüstow.*

II

The Numbers on Both Sides.—In no case may the numbers be calculated from statements made by the opposite side. The Bourbon Generals officially state their force in Milazzo at 122 officers and 4514 men (*Nove Mesi,* 2 ; *Cronaca,* 178 ; *Palmieri,* 43-44). That was the total number of men against whom Garibaldi had to act. But of those about 1000 were the normal garrison of Milazzo Castle (*viz.* six companies of the first infantry of the line, and a number of artillery, *Palmieri,* 34 note). The infantry of this garrison did not take part in the fighting outside the walls of the fortress on July 20, but lent 100 men to help carry off the wounded (*Palmieri,* 45). Bosco's expeditionary force (making up the rest of the 4514 men and 122 officers, and therefore over rather than under 3000) consisted of three battalions of *cacciatori* (1st, 8th, and 9th regiments), the crack troops of the Neapolitan army, together with a mountain battery of eight pieces and a squadron of cavalry ; all arms were first-rate troops and behaved well on July 20 (Bosco's report ; *Palmieri,* 34 *et seq. ; Cronaca,* 190). If Bosco did not use all these troops of his own force (excluding the garrison) it was his own fault, and his statement (*Palmieri,* 45) that only 1600 of them took part in the battle is a quibble, for in the same sentence he admits that 900 more formed the reserve and that some of these did actually ' fire a few shots.' Also in both his reports (*Cronaca,* 208 ; *Palmieri,* 45) he complains that the reserve were sent into action too early by Lt.-Col. Marra, so that he had no reserve at the critical moment. Besides this reserve, he says that he also kept 400 men on the Peninsula behind the town (*Palmieri,* 43). To sum up, Bosco admits that 2500 men were under his orders in the plain in front of the castle, of which 1600 were in the front line and the remaining 900 the reserve, and that the reserve was all taken into action by Lt.-Col. Marra (*Palmieri*, 45 ; *Cronaca*, 208). Above in the castle was a garrison of 1000 infantry and gunners ; the latter fired effectively at the Garibaldini when they reached the bridge. And there were 400 more *cacciatori* in the Peninsula, not engaged.

The Garibaldini, whom Bosco reported sometimes at eight sometimes at twelve thousand, did not on July 20 reach more than 5700 at the highest serious estimate, and were probably nearer 4000 or 5000. The best Garibaldian writers (*e.g. Guerzoni*, ii. 143 ; *Rüstow*, 215) generally calculate the total as 4000, or (like *Piaggia*, 39, and *Paolucci's Corrao*, 136) as high as 5500 or 5700. It is impossible to tell which is nearest the truth, on account of the absence of any official statistics, and on account of variety in the estimates made of the various bodies of irregulars from North Italy and Sicily of which the army was composed. Each of these bodies was usually called a 'battalion,' but no 'battalion' contained over 900 men, and some were as low as 300 or less. The following table, which mentions, I believe, every one of these bodies present at the battle of Milazzo, will at least serve to show the difficulty of calculating the numbers of the Garibaldian army. From these lists I should be inclined to place it somewhere between the two estimates 4000 and 5500.

	Number of Men.		Authority for numbers given.
Medici's force, with which he left Palermo = *Malenchini's* and *Simonetta's* 'battalions'	1800	according to	*Medici (Pasini)*, 18.
Dunne's Sicilians - -	600	„	„ *Medici (Pasini)*, 21 ; *Piaggia*, 30 ; *Paol.'s Corrao*, 135 ; *Conv. Patterson.*
Specchi's so-called 'Bersaglieri[1] battalion'	400	„	„ *Medici Pasini*, 22 ; *Peard's Journal MS.*
Genoese Carabineers	- 82 or 85	„	„ *Forbes*, 100 ; *Rome MS. Savi*; *Times*, Aug. 4, p. 10, c. 4.
	or 150	„	„ *Medici (Pasini)*, 22; *Piaggia*, 39.

[1] Not of course related to the *Bersaglieri* of the regular army. Pilade Bronzetti was one of its principal officers. It was the only portion of Cosenz' expedition (Appendix B, above) which arrived in time for the battle. The remainder of the 1500 men of that expedition only reached Milazzo on July 21, see *Magni*, 6. Cosenz had large bodies of other men under his command during the battle, who had not formed part of his original expedition from Genoa.

	Number of Men.	Authority for numbers given.
Corte's 'Gaeta battalion	500 „	„ Campo, 136-7, who fought in the battalion; Milazzo (G. B. Z.) 13.
	or 600 „	„ Medici (Pasini), 22; Piaggia, 39.

(900 was the number of the original expedition from Genoa, captured at Gaeta, see Appendix B, above, but some remained at Genoa after the return from Gaeta. *Conv. Pedotti.*)

Peard's company (revolving-rifles; too small ever to be called a 'battalion')   30 according to *Nelson MS.*

Sprovieri's 'battalion' -	300 „	„ *Medici (Pasini)*, 22.
	or 400 „	„ *Piaggia*, 39.
Vacchieri's 'battalion' -	300 „	„ *Piaggia*, 39.

Borelli's and *Montovani's* 'half battalions' | *Corrao's* Sicilians | *Guerzoni's* Sicilians

} No estimate is anywhere given of the numbers of these four bodies, but they are spoken of as quite small. Corrao's men fought hard and had 20 casualties in the battle (*Paol.'s Corrao*, 140-141).

Besides these bodies, engaged in the battle, there were Fabrizi's 300 Sicilians who were not on the field at all, but were sent to guard the road from Messina against a possible attack by the 5th *cacciatori*, who were occupying Gesso and Rizzo (*Palmieri*, 36 note; *Piaggia*, 30; *Medici, Pasini*, 21).

Cavalry.—Garibaldi had none. Bosco had a squadron, who played an important part on both wings.

Artillery.—Against Bosco's mountain battery of eight pieces, all of which did great execution, and over forty pieces of different kinds mounted on the castle walls, Garibaldi had two ridiculous pieces, dragged by hand, which were brought into action late in the day on the bridge for a few minutes, and withdrawn as useless (*Forbes*, 89; *Bandi*, 238-239; *Paolucci's Corrao*, 134; *Baroni*, p. 2; *Peard*, 821; *Mistrali's da N.* 620-621; *Fonvielle*, 103, 145). But the cannon on the *Tüköry* assisted him towards the close of the day.

III

Losses.—There are no precise statistics, but the best-informed Garibaldian authorities estimated their loss in killed and wounded on July 20 at 750 or 800. *Medici (Pasini)*, 29; *Mistrali's da N.* 622; *Rüstow*, 219; *Piaggia*, 56, calculates 800, and gives an interesting list of those tended in Barcellona; *Times*, August 4, p. 10, col. 4; *Menghini*, 225; *Cremona MS. Carasi.*

The Neapolitan loss every one agreed to have been much less; Bosco placed it as low as 116 killed and wounded (*Palmieri*, 46 note), but in *Cronaca*, 208, he also mentions 31 missing, besides a dozen more killed and wounded.

It may be noted that the Genoese Carabineers had 44 men killed or wounded in the battle (names given, *Menghini*, 218) out of a total of 85 (or as some say 150, see above). Corte's 'Gaeta battalion' lost 14 or 17 out of 30 or 32 officers (*Menghini*, 215; *Campo*, 137), and 190 out of 500 or 600 men (*Campo*, 137; *Milazzo* (*G. B. Z.*), 13).

APPENDIX G

DATE OF LANDINGS IN CALABRIA

I. *Date of Garibaldi's Landing*

BIXIO'S dispatch (*Bixio*, 232-233), by a slip of the pen, gives the date of the crossing as the night of August 19-20, whereas it was really the night of August 18-19. This has misled many historians since, *e.g.* the author of *Türr's Div.* 132; *Castellini*, p. 52 note 2, and *De Cesare* himself.

Bixio, in fact, makes his own error patent to any one who reads his dispatch with special care, for the dispatch is not consistent with itself. He says (*Bixio*, 234), *that they entered Reggio before dawn on August* 21,[1] *after having passed in Calabria two full days with a night in between them.* Not only Bixio but Garibaldi (*Mem.* 375-376) and other members of the expedition (*Menghini*, 451-452) agree that after landing at dawn they spent first one whole day, then one whole night, and then another whole day before making the night attack on Reggio. That attack was made on the night of August 20-21, after midnight.[2] Therefore they must have landed at dawn on August 19, not at dawn on August 20. That they crossed in the night of August 18, landing at dawn on August 19, is expressly stated by the following first-hand authorities : *Menghini*, 451 ; *Peard MS. Journal*, August 18, 19 ; *Arrivabene*, ii. 100-101 ; *Durand Brager*, 171 ; *Times*, August 25, p. 9, c. 5, where the correspondent writing on August 19 describes the departure from Giardini on the previous evening (18th) ; *Castellini*, 52 (text, the modern note being in error) ;

---

[1] *Bixio*, p. 234. 'Alle 3 ant. del 21 si penetra in Reggio.' These words have in the later edition of the report printed in *Türr's Div.* p. 413, doc. 46, been most unjustifiably altered into 'alle 3 a.m. del 22 si penetra in Reggio.' Yet the same version of the report (p. 414) speaks of the *next* day as the 22nd! 'La mattina del 22 il generale marcia per Villa S. Giovanni.'

[2] This is proved by many authorities, especially by Neapolitan dispatches of that very day (August 21) in *Pianell*, 54-55.

and the Neapolitan dispatches of the date, *Pianell*, 45-46, which alone would be conclusive.   When once the inconsistency in Bixio's dispatch has been detected and the necessary emendation made it may be said that all the first-hand authorities who give any dates at all agree that the landing was at dawn of August 19.   The second-hand authorities are mostly wrong, having followed the error in Bixio's dispatch.

II. *Date of Cosenz' Landing*

Cosenz crossed from Faro to Favazzina at dawn—on August 22 according to *Orsini*, 53, on August 20 according to *Maison*, 44.   Both are wrong.   He landed on the morning of the 21st, while Garibaldi was taking Reggio.   This is proved by the date of the Neapolitan dispatches in *Pianell*, 52-56, by *Morisani*, 105 ; *Menghini*, 276, and *Times*, September 4, p. 7, c. 3. Some of these authorities describe the flotilla as starting overnight, others at dawn, others not till eight in the morning. The *Times* says that the boats left the Faro in two batches, which may partly account for this inconsistency.   What is certain is that Cosenz' force landed at Favazzina on the morning of August 21.

APPENDIX H

IMMEDIATE CAUSES OF THE EVACUATION OF SALERNO

THE decision to recall the troops from Salerno was taken, according to *De Sivo*, iv. 39, and *Franci*, i. 113, not earlier than the evening of September 5, and in consequence of the complaints of Marshal Rivera[1] at Salerno to the effect that Garibaldi 'would assail him the next day, and he was afraid of being captured in his bed.' This is valuable as indicating that Marshal Rivera's complaints of the situation at Salerno influenced the decision at Naples. But the hour is not perhaps quite accurate. The telegram (printed in *Monnier*, 272) from the commander-in-chief in Naples to Marshal Rivera, ordering him to retreat from Salerno, is dated ' Naples, 2 a.m.' (presumably September 5) ; whether the hour of this important telegram is correctly printed or not, it is certain the actual retreat was begun in time for the Garibaldini to hear news of it 'whilst at dinner at Auletta on the 5th' (*Forbes*, 227, and *Peard's Journal sub* September 5 and 6).

It appears therefore that the final decision to abandon Naples and to withdraw Rivera from Salerno was taken in the *morning of September* 5, as a result of the telegrams, alarums, and excursions of the night of September 4-5, *during which night a ' last reunion of Ministers' was held all night ' until dawn'* (*Pianell*, 194-195, his wife's journal), and *during which Forbes and Gallenga were pouring their false telegrams into Naples and Salerno.* One of these is printed in *Monnier*, 273 :—

' Gallenga to [name of recipient not given]: Eboli, 1.30 a.m. September 5. Caldarelli's brigade has passed over to Garibaldi : 4000 men commanded by Türr have landed at Sapri. Other landings will be effected nearer to us.'

In *Forbes*, 225, and *Arrivabene*, ii. 168, Gallenga's other telegram (to Ulloa in Naples) is given thus :—

' Eboli, 11.30 p.m. Garibaldi has arrived with 5000 of his

---

[1] The officer commanding at Salerno was really Marshal Afan de Rivera, as the dispatches (*Monnier*) show, though *Peard* and others sometimes speak of him as Scotti, and *Franci* as Bosco.

own men and 5000 Calabrese are momentarily expected. Disembarkations are expected in the Bay of Naples and Gulf of Salerno to-night. I strongly advise you to withdraw the garrison from the latter place without delay or they will be cut off. And let me beg of you as a personal friend but a political enemy to abandon a sinking cause which must be your ruin.'

Forbes, 226, writes:—

' On my subsequent arrival at Naples I learnt from one of the ex-Ministers that the fact of the telegram being addressed to Ulloa by a private friend (Gallenga) was what gave colour to the whole proceeding.'

Peard's telegrams sent the same night (September 4-5) to Salerno are also said to have caused Marshal Rivera to wire to Naples demanding his own withdrawal from a position which he regarded as untenable. De Martino, then Minister of Francis II, told Arrivabene that such was the effect produced by Peard's telegrams (*Arrivabene*, ii. 169).

Also in *Revel's da Ancona*, 65, we read a letter of Revel's dated *October* 23, 1860, *Isernia*, setting down what a Bourbon officer just captured there had told him. The evidence seems first-hand and quite unprejudiced, as Revel knows nothing about Peard or his adventures. The Bourbon officer, so Revel writes, related to him that ' in the first days of September he was with General Scotti at Salerno to resist the advance of Garibaldi, when he received a telegram from the head of the gendarmerie at Eboli which announced the imminent arrival of Garibaldi with 3000 troops and 4000 insurgents, and the defection of Caldarelli's brigade which had joined the Garibaldini. Scotti, fearing the attack of such superior forces and still more the contact of Caldarelli's men with his own as the harbinger of further defection, sent the news to the Ministers, proposing to retire on Nocera or Nola, if there were enough men in Naples. The Ministry sent him orders to retire to Nola and thence to Capua. Later on he learnt that the telegram had been sent by a staff officer of Garibaldi's under the false signature of the gendarme, as a stratagem of war, but he was so preoccupied that he had not thought of verifying it. This explains how Garibaldi came to enter Salerno and then Naples.'

As a matter of fact it was not Scotti but Rivera who was in command at Salerno, though oddly enough Peard at the time thought that he was telegraphing to Scotti (see *Peard's Journal*).

In *Monnier* (273) the following telegram of Rivera is printed :—

'Salerno. September 4, 11 in the evening. The electric wire between Eboli and Salerno is broken. Two non-commissioned officers, returning from Calabria, have brought the news that the main body of Garibaldian revolutionists and the Caldarelli brigade have reached Auletta. . . . I am sending by rail the two non-commissioned officers, Neamburgo of the fifteenth line and Guida of the fourth, to see Colonel Anzani.'

This telegram is at first sight puzzling ; it shows indeed that the exaggerated rumours about the defection of Caldarelli's Brigade, and the false rumours of the close propinquity of Garibaldi and his men (due to Peard's game at Auletta and Eboli) reached Marshal Rivera and deeply affected him. But it says nothing about any telegrams from Eboli as the source of this information (which is attributed to two Bourbon sergeants), and the wire from Eboli is said to be broken an hour before midnight. But the explanation is clear : Rivera at Salerno wrongly thought that the wire was broken, because after Peard's entry into Eboli the telegraph official was being brought before Peard, and the Eboli office was no longer being served. Peard's telegrams began to pour into Salerno half an hour later, for the date of Gallenga's telegram to Ulloa (*Forbes*, 225) is 11.30 *that night*, and his telegram to the other friend in Naples (*Monnier*, 273) is as late as 1.30 *the next morning*. Peard's and Gallenga's telegrams were therefore sent off shortly before and shortly after midnight ; this is quite consistent with Peard's and Forbes' account of the matter, as they say that they did not enter Eboli till after dark, nine o'clock according to Peard, eleven o'clock according to Forbes. In short, Rivera at Salerno, soon after the time (eleven o'clock) when he had declared the wire from Eboli to be broken, found the communication restored and received the telegrams dictated by Peard.

NUMBERS OF THE ARMIES ON THE VOLTURNO

I. THE BOURBON FORCES

(a) *Total Bourbon Force North of the Volturno*

THE late Senator General Primerano, who in 1860 was an officer in the Bourbon army, told me that there must have been 50,000 behind the Volturno, including the garrisons of Gaeta and Capua. After the reorganisation behind the Volturno, the regiments, he said, were very full, often amounting to 3000 each, *viz.* three battalions of 1000 each.

This impression is fully borne out by the following calculation, based on Bourbon authorities only :—

Losses on Oct. 1 and 2, killed and prisoners only (not wounded) -	2500	*Franci*, ii. 260, 271.
Taken in Capua Nov. 2 -	11,000 or 8000	*Franci*, ii. 177, says 11,000 ; *Cava*, 27, says 9000.
Interned in Papal States, Nov. 8	[1] 17,000	*De Sivo*, iv. 314, 317.
Took part in subsequent defence of Gaeta - - - -	21,000	*De Sivo*, iv. 323.

These four categories are mutually exclusive, and added together give a total of 50,000. If we consider that nearly 1000 more were captured with Scotti near Isernia on October 20 (see p. 268 above), and that at least some others must have disbanded, unaccounted for under any of these categories, it will seem rather an under-estimate to place the total force north of the Volturno at 50,000.

The names of a large number of the regiments of which this force was composed will be found in *Franci*, ii. 260-261, 271-276, 328-329.

(b) *Total Bourbon Force Engaged in the Battle of October* 1-2

Here there is perhaps more uncertainty. We can, however, calculate Von Mechel's force, the Bourbon left wing,

---

[1] Lowest estimate : the British Consul at Rome reported the interning of 30,000 ; see *Br. Cons. Rome, Letter Book MS.* p. 219.

accurately. The Swiss who attacked Bixio at Maddaloni numbered 3000 (*Schweizertruppen*, 544 ; *Ruiz*, 19) ; and Ruiz' men who took Castel Morrone and Caserta Vecchia on October 1, and lost 2000 prisoners on October 2, numbered 5000, enumerated by Ruiz himself (*Ruiz*, 19). This brings Von Mechel's force, *the Bourbon left wing*, to 8000, as Ruiz (19) himself tells us.

It is far more difficult to estimate the Bourbon right wing under Tabacchi and Afan de Rivera (and Ritucci himself) which attacked S. Angelo, S. Maria, and S. Tammaro. There is no authoritative statement like that of Ruiz for the other wing. *De Sivo*, iv. 184, 189, puts it at 4500 against S. Maria + 4500 against S. Angelo, + 1500 cavalry reserve, + two squadrons of cavalry and cannon against S. Tammaro, = about 11,000 in all. But this is likely to be an under-estimate, just as the Garibaldian calculations (not quoted here) are likely to be over-estimates. Some attempt at real calculation can be made from the official figures given by Franci. We there find that this wing acknowledged a loss in killed and wounded of about 1000 (*Franci*, ii. 260), and beyond all doubt it consisted of five regiments and eight battalions of infantry, eight regiments of cavalry and dragoons, and seven batteries of artillery ; *for every one of these made a return of losses under fire on October* 1, see *Franci*, ii. 260. In view of General Primerano's statement as to the fullness of the regiments and battalions, it is difficult to see how five regiments + eight battalions of infantry + eight regiments of cavalry could be much below 20,000, and indeed it would be over 30,000 if every battalion and regiment of infantry was really up to strength.

But if we put the Bourbon right wing tentatively at 20,000 and the left confidently at 8000, we get 28,000 in all for the battle of October 1-2. [Another Bourbon authority, *Cava* (57), seeking to minimise, puts it at 18,000 or possibly 24,000.] In view of the official document printed in *Franci*, ii. 260, and Ruiz' statements, I think 28,000 a fair estimate.

II. The Garibaldian Forces

(a) *Total of Garibaldian Forces in Sicily and the Mainland*

We have official evidence that at the time of the disbanding of Garibaldi's forces in November, 50,000 were paid off, *viz.* 7000 in Sicily and 43,000 on the mainland (*Risorg.* ann. iii.

fasc. 1-2, Nievo's accounts ; *Revel's da An.* 117, puts it at 1400 more). But of these 43,000 on the mainland, only a third, so Garibaldi declared (*Orero*, 106) were ever under fire. For with regard to the 43,000 we must remember that—

1. Many were enrolled during October after the battle had been fought.

2. Many regiments, even at the time of the break-up of the forces in November, were only in process of formation, and had never been actually under arms (*Risorg.* ann. iii. fasc. 1-2, p. 87).

3. These new enrolments in the autumn were going on principally in Calabria, Apulia, and Basilicata, far from the scene of action (*Risorg.* ditto).

4. The grand total includes everyone in Garibaldi's pay, *viz.* all the troops doing garrison and patrol work in Naples and the provinces.

5. The grand total was composed at least half of irregular bands, forces raised by private persons, local militia, etc. (*Revel's da Ancona,* 114.)

6. A large part of the nominal force was fraudulent ; men put down their names merely to draw food and pay, or to be able to swagger about in uniform. Garibaldi's own words were, 'one-third were present in the hour of battle, and the other two-thirds only at pay-day and the dinner-hour' (*Orero*, 106 ; *Revel's da Ancona,* 114-117).

There is therefore no reason to suppose, on account of the grand total 43,000 on the mainland and 7000 in Sicily, that more than 20,000 men were ever at the front on the Volturno Of the 20,000 volunteers from North Italy (Appendix B), the backbone of the force, many were in hospital and more in garrison or patrol work in the provinces, but it is reasonable to suppose that well over 10,000 Northerners were on the Volturno, and the names of the regiments engaged on October 1 confirm this view.

(*b*) *Total Force of Garibaldini Engaged on October* 1

This is almost as difficult to calculate as the number of their opponents. I think it is agreed on all hands that, except at the Arches of the Valley, where Bixio had 5653 men against the 3000 Swiss, the Garibaldini were outnumbered at all points. In the mountains north of Caserta, Sacchi had 1800 men (very slightly engaged) and Bronzetti at Castel Morrone had 283, who managed to delay for four hours the advance of Ruiz' 5000.

S. Maria, S. Angelo, and all those regions on the Garibaldian left were defended against an attack of five regiments
and eight battalions of infantry and several thousand cavalry
—probably not less than 20,000 of all arms, and possibly far
more. The Garibaldian force in this part of the field, which
was, all agree, outnumbered, consisted of the men under Medici
defending S. Angelo ; the men under Milbitz defending S. Maria
and at first S. Tammaro ; and the reserves under Türr, brought
up from Caserta to S. Maria as the day went on. (Corte, in
command of some Lucanians at Aversa, took no more part in
the battle and is not therefore to be counted.)

The most probable enumeration of the Garibaldian forces
in the battle of October 1 seems to me as follows :—

Under Bixio	at Maddaloni	5653	(Bixio's report : *Türr's Div.* 474.)
„ Bronzetti	at Castel Morrone	283	(G. Mirri's report: *Castel Morrone*, 23.)
„ Sacchi (Took little part in battle.)	at S. Leucio	1800	(Sacchi's report : *Türr's Div.* 469.)
„ Medici (Medici's own division, Spangaro's and Dunne's regiments.)	at S. Angelo	4000 (?)	(*Castellini*, 83, 88 ; *Türr's Div.* 234.)
„ Milbitz (Malenchini's Tuscans and small bodies of men like the French company, Pace's Calabrians, Corrao's Sicilians, etc.)	at S. Maria and S. Tammaro	3000 (?)	(There is no estimate of their number by Türr or any other good authority. The original forces under Milbitz were fewer than Medici's men at S. Angelo, and he required the assistance of nearly all Türr's reserve.)
„ Türr (Reserve brought up mainly to S. Maria. Contained Assanti's, Eber's, and the Milano ' brigades,' the Hungarians, and part of La Masa's Sicilians and Pace's Calabrians.)	at Caserta	5600	(*Türr's Div.* 230. This is no doubt right, as Türr was himself in command.)

20,336

Therefore, if I had to *guess* at the numbers engaged
on October 1, I should say 20,000 Garibaldini and 28,000
Royalists.

(*N.B.*—Guerzoni, ii. 186-187, counts another 1000 men for
Milbitz at S. Maria, and 1000 less for Türr at Caserta. But as
Türr was gradually sending up men to Milbitz all day long,

this apparent difference of calculation is easily accounted for and has no significance.)

(c) Garibaldian Force on October 2, and Piedmontese Assistance

In the fighting on October 2 Stocco's Calabrians and the Piedmontese Bersaglieri also took part, having arrived at Caserta from Naples after the end of the fighting on October 1 (*D'Ayala*, 354; *Laracca Ronghi*, 19; *Conv. Fazzari*; *Leg. Mat.* 145-146). There had been several score of Piedmontese gunners helping to serve the guns at S. Maria and S. Angelo on October 1, but *no infantry*, as has been sometimes erroneously alleged. The regular *infantry* only came up for the fighting of October 2, near Caserta; (they consisted of two companies of Bersaglieri and two companies of the first regiment of the Brigata del Re). This is proved not only by all Garibaldian sources but by the only official Piedmontese source, the reports printed in *Mem. Stor. Mil.* i. 52-55. These troops had been sent to the Bay of Naples on board Persano's ships as early as August, when Cavour hoped they might be useful if a spontaneous revolution took place in Naples before Garibaldi's arrival: see p. 168 above.

APPENDIX K

I. NORTH ITALIAN ARMY

(a) Total Force

GENERAL FANTI says that his army consisted of 33,000 men all told. This was the total expeditionary force that liberated the Marches and Umbria, and includes Della Rocca's and Cialdini's corps (*Fanti, Campagna,* 6; *Della Rocca,* 181).

(b) Present at Battle of Castelfidardo

The official return, with full details of every regiment, etc., given in *Castelfidardo,* pp. 34, 68-71, is as follows:—

	Officers and Men.	Cannon.
Present on the field	16,449	+ 42
Effectively engaged	4,880	+ 14

viz. 9th and 10th line, 11th, 12th, and 26th Bersaglieri, regiment of lancers of Novara and artillery.

Losses, 62 killed, 140 wounded. The 10th line bore about three-quarters of these losses.

II. Papal Army

The exact enumeration of Lamoricière's army is more difficult, because there is discrepancy between the statements of the Papal Generals as to the numbers they commanded, and the statements of the Piedmontese Generals as to the number of prisoners whom they took.

(a) Total of Lamoricière's Force

This may be calculated in three sections, the field army the small garrisons, and the garrison of Ancona.

1. *Field Army.*—8000 'bayonets' and 300 artillery, says *Lamoricière* (5-6) himself.

2. *Small Garrisons* (Pesaro, Fano, Perugia, Spoleto, Orvieto, Viterbo, San Leo, Paliano, Civita Castellana).—*Lamoricière* (5) says ' 20 companies '—say 3000 men, certainly not an over-estimate, seeing that 1500 were taken in Perugia alone (*Della Rocca*, 184 ; *Fanti*, 342), and 800 in Spoleto (*Corvetto*, 250 ; *Fanti, Campagna*, 9).

3. *Garrison of Ancona.*—*Lamoricière* (5) puts it at ' 2 battalions,' but Quatrebarbes, the Governor of the place during the siege, tells us he had, towards the end of the siege, 600 sick or wounded and 3500 combatants. This official estimate of 4100 for the garrison of Ancona is the lowest possible. [Of these less than fifty were refugees from the field army, brought in by Lamoricière after the battle of Castelfidardo, see *Lamoricière*, 33.] The Piedmontese assert that they counted 6000 men and 348 officers as prisoners when the place surrendered (*Fanti*, 378).

Accepting these *data* we arrive at a total of 15,000 or 17,000 men for the whole force commanded by Lamoricière. This is, I think, a more exact estimate than that of *De Cesare* (*Roma*, ii. 66), who makes the total only 11,000, accepting Lamoricière's under-estimate of the garrison of Ancona, and not noticing Quatrebarbes' admission that he had 4100 soldiers in Ancona. In the clerical life of *De Mérode* (138) the total is put at 18,000 ; and *Fanti* (*Campagna*, 23) says, possibly with exaggeration, that he took 17,000 to 18,000 prisoners. It is admitted that he took all Lamoricière's army in the field and in fortresses, except two or three thousand men.

(b) Present at Battle of Castelfidardo

Of the field army of ' 8000 bayonets ' and 300 artillery (*Lamoricière*, 6), the very great majority were present at the decisive battle, though not nearly all were effectively engaged. The ' bulletin of the Pontifical army,' published in *Castelfidardo*, 85-87, estimates those present at 6550, Lamoricière's own division being 3500 and Pimodan's 3050. *Lamoricière* (20) reduces each of these totals and makes the whole force present 4600, but the bulletin is most likely to be right. It is quite certain that 3094 prisoners (mostly foreigners) had been taken by September 20 (*Castelfidardo*, 38, 67, detailed list), and the statement of *Orero* (68-69) and *Fanti* (*Campagna*, 13) that 3000 more, chiefly native Italians, disbanded after the battle, of whom 2000 more were captured piecemeal in the following week, is probably not far from the truth.

APPENDIX L

(The Bourbon Authorities are Starred)

(TWO important authorities are the maps at the end of *Ansiglioni* for the topography of 1860, and the map at the end of *Türr's Div.* for the position of the various Garibaldian regiments.)

1. *Eve of the Battle and First Attack at Dawn*

J. des D. October 7. *Matarazzi,* 42-43. *Du Camp,* 300-307 (Garibaldi at the Church of S. Angelo). *Guerzoni,* ii. 189. *Veritas,* 47-53. *Mariotti N. A.* 433. *Ciàmpoli,* 192. ** Franci,* ii. 50-56. *Mem.* 388-389. *Türr's Div.* 235-236, 457 (*Assanti's* report).

2. *Attack on Garibaldi's Carriage on Road to S. Angelo*

Matarazzi, 48, defines the exact spot 'ponte Ciccarelli.' *Savio,* ii. 1-17. *Conv. Canzio. Arrivabene,* ii. 253, 264, and in *D. News,* October 23. *Bandi,* 303, 305, 311. *M. Post,* October 12. *Menghini,* 339-340. *Veterano. Ciàmpoli,* 192-193.

3. *S. Angelo and M. Tifata.*

Türr's Div. 236-240, 247-250, 460-467 (officers' reports). *Menghini,* 329, 342, 373-374. ** Franci,* ii. 54-64, 256. *Campo,* 153-154. *Castellini,* 84-88 (unofficial report by some officer under Medici, not by Medici himself, Cadolini tells me). ** Gazzetta di Gaeta,* No. 6, p. 23. *Zasio,* 109-110. *Pungolo Milano,* October 13. *Du Camp,* 309-322. *Forbes,* 291-293. *Mario, Vita,* i. 273-275. *Mem. Stor. Mil.* i. 53. *Conv. Pedotti. Matarazzi,* 47-48, 51-55, 60. *Conv. Cadolini. Times,* October 9, p. 7 ; October 11, p. 7 ; cols. 3-4 (October 25, p. 7, c. 5, on Dunne, good but for great exaggeration of numbers). *Ciàmpoli,* 193. *Ansiglioni,* 40. *Pozzi,* 41-43. *Savio,* ii. 11-12.

4. *Maddaloni and Arches of Valley.*

* *Franci*, ii. 72-75, 261-271 (Von Mechel's report), * *Sch-weizertruppen*, 530, 541-552, and * *Ruiz*, 18-22, 46-53, are indis-pensable. *Türr's Div.* 472-475. Bixio's report, 475-480, his officers' reports. *Ponti della Valle*, pp. 15-16, Ghersi's letter. *Conv. Sclavo. Abba. Not.* 246-250. *Menghini*, 347-348, 367. *Red Shirt*, 267-268. *Times*, October 19, p. 7, c. 4.

5. *S. Maria.*

Türr's Div. 235-236, 241-246, 457-459, 467-469 (reports). * *Franci*, ii. 65-72, 260. * *De Sivo*, iv. 195-198. * *Marra, Oss.* 55, 60. * *Butta*, ii. 111-113, quoting from * *Palmieri*, 99-117 (*q.v.*). * *Cava*, 55. *Bandi*, 308-312. *Rüstow*, 377-380. *Rüstow's Brig. Mil.* 37-41. *Matarazzi*, 44-51, 55-59. *Adamoli*, 159-163. *Magni*, 10-11. *Forbes*, 298-301, 313-314. *Conv. Dol-mage. Mariotti* (*N. A.*), 433-434. *Veritas*, 53-56. *Times*, October 9, p. 7 ; October 11, p. 7. *Mem. Stor. Mil.* i. 51-53. *Ciàmpoli*, 192-195. *Fazio*, 90-100. * *Gazzetta di Gaeta*, No. 6, p. 23. *Mem.* 388, 391-393. *J. des D.* October 7. *Volturno. Uzielli* (*Risorg.*). *Castellini*, 88.

'La Flotte's' French company : *Elia*, ii. 96. *Una Pagina*, 16-17. *Arrivabene*, ii. 256. *Caraguel*, 193-206. *Matarazzi*, 45.

Sicilians under La Porta, Corrao, La Masa : *Forbice*, October 11. *Paolucci's Corrao*, 144. *Caraguel*, 200-206. *La Masa* (*Sic.*) xci-xcv, 200-206. *Türr's Div.* 234-236.

British sailors' incident : *Mario, Vita*, i. 278. *Forbes*, 313-314. *Mundy*, 300-301. *Elliot*, 133. *Br. Parl. Papers*, viii. 8-12.

End of battle : *Una Pagina*, 20. *Rüstow*, 380. *Maison*, 109. *M. Post*, October 9.

6. *Garibaldi Encourages his Men by Spreading the Message, ' Victory along all the Line' early in the Afternoon, while Victory was still in doubt.*

Türr's Div. 463-464 (Spangaro's report). *Castellini*, 87. *Fazio*, 98-99. *Zasio*, 110. *Tosi*, 103. *Conv. Cadolini.*

7. *Castel Morrone, Defence of ; Ruiz' and Sacchi's Movements*

* *Franci*, ii. 75-76, 271, but see note, sec. 9, below, *sub* ' Losses.' * *De Sivo*, iv. 201 (inaccurate). * *Marra, Oss.* 57. *Türr's Div.* 241, 250-254, 469-471. *Conv. Cadolini. Mem.* 394-395. *Laracca Ronghi*, 18. *Castel Morrone*, 10-30.

Ruiz, 19-23. *Milan MSS. Bronzetti*, 2. The three last are the real authorities, together with *Türr's Div.* 470, for Sacchi's men. It was not 'Perrone,' as Garibaldian authorities state, but Ruiz who commanded this part of the Bourbon army.

8. *Battle of October 2 round Old and New Caserta*

Türr's Div. 465, 471-472, 474-475. *Ruiz*, 23-27. *Franci*, ii. 76-78, 271. *Rome MS. Savi* (for Genoese Carabineers). *Leg. Matese*, 134-136, 144-148. *Ciàmpoli*, 195-196. *Ansiglioni*, 45-47. *Mem. Stor. Mil.* i. 54-55 (for the Bersaglieri). *M. Post*, October 12. *Times*, October 11, p. 7, c. 2. *Laracca Ronghi*, 18-20. *Conv. Fazzari. Menghini*, 344, 364. *D'Ayala*, 354 (departure of Bersaglieri from Naples). *Forbes*, 303-309. *Mem.* 395-397. *Conv. Dolmage. Red Shirt*, 269. *De Sivo*, iv. 201-205. *Türr's Div.* 251-254. And see above Appendix J. ii. (*c*) on Piedmontese assistance.

9. *Losses*

Türr's Div. 256, 465, 474. *Franci*, ii. 260, 271.

Franci, ii. 76 and 271, reports a loss of only about 10 killed and wounded at Castel Morrone and practically none on October 2, while acknowledging the loss of 2089 prisoners on October 2. The accounts we have of both these actions show that more must have been killed and wounded; the capture on October 2 of 2000 out of the 5000 men under Ruiz is enough to account for this mistake in the returns of killed and wounded, for no doubt a good many of the killed and wounded were put down as prisoners, since they were all missing together *en bloc*.

10. *Garibaldian Hospitals and Conduct of Wounded*

Schwabe MS. 3 (Madame Mario's letter about the S. Maria hospital). *Meuricoffre*, 61-72, and *ditto*, *Macmillan's Mag.* iii. 152-160. *Colet*, iii. 16, 21, 34-35. *Conv. Dolmage. Times*, October 18, p. 11, cols. 1, 2; November 6, p. 9, c. 3; November 9, p. 8, c. 3. *Elliot*, 124. *Nelson MSS.* (letters).

BIBLIOGRAPHY

LIST OF PRINTED MATTER AND MSS.
CONSULTED BY THE AUTHOR

Abbreviations in the notes explained

[The mark * means that the book or document so marked gives information from Bourbon or Papal sources, and narrates events from the point of view of defenders of the old monarchies. It will be seen by those who consult these works, some of them now rather rare, that the official and other documents at the disposal of the historian for the movements of the armies destroyed by the national forces in 1860 are plentiful and detailed, especially as regards the dispatches of the defeated generals.]

N.B.—The Bibliography in this volume is meant to refer only to events beginning after the fall of Palermo (early June, 1860) and ending with the return of Garibaldi to Caprera early in November.

I have not repeated in many cases my remarks on books commented on in the bibliography of *Garibaldi and the Thousand*, though I have in all cases given the title and its abbreviation if the book has been used again as an authority for this volume.

I. BOOKS, PAMPHLETS, AND MODERN JOURNALS

Abba's Bixio = Abba (G. C.). *La Vita di Nino Bixio.*
Abba's 'Cose' = Abba (G. C.). *Cose Garibaldine.* 1907.
Abba's Not. = Abba (G. C.). *Da Quarto al Volturno, Noterelle d'uno dei Mille,* ed. 5.
About = About (Edmondo). *Roma Contemporanea.* 1861.
    (A social study of Rome and the Papal States, shortly before 1860.)
Adamoli = Adamoli (Giulio). *Da San Martino a Mentana.* 1892.
    (Valuable narrative of personal experiences, and veracious portraits of his companions in arms which I have heard praised by other survivors.)
Albo Com. = *Albo Commemorativo del gran re Vitt. Em. II.* Bologna. 1884.
    (Contains, pp. 75-83, Lacaita's story as in *Villari Pasq. q.v.* below.)
Amari = *Amari (Michele) Carteggio di.* By A. d'Ancona. 1896 and 1907. 3 vols.
    Cf. also Amari's important letter of 1862 printed in *R. S. Del R.* 1897, ii. p. 136, giving an account of his opinions and actions in 1860.
    [This Michele Amari, Sicilian leader of 1848-1849, and exile since then, the famous historian of the *Vespro Siciliano,* may easily be confused with his namesake *Count* Michele Amari, with whom he corresponded and worked in the crisis of 1860, and whose political views he shared.]

Ansiglioni = Ansiglioni (Giuseppe). *Memoria della batt. del Volturno.* Torino. 1861. (With valuable map.)

Arese = Bonfadini (R.). *Vita di Francesco Arese.* 1894. (Roux e C. Rome.)

Arrivabene = Arrivabene (Carlo). *Italy under Victor Emmanuel.* 1862. (Vol. ii. contains personal reminiscences of Garibaldi's campaign : author was *Daily News* correspondent.)

Artom = Artom (Ernesto). *Cavour e la questione Napoletana.* N. A. Nov. 1, 1901.

Ashley Nat. Rev. = *National Review,* 1899. *A Garibaldi Reminiscence.* By the Rt. Hon. Evelyn Ashley. (Lord Palmerston's private secretary describes how he accompanied Garibaldi into Naples.)

A. S. Sic. = *Archivio Storico Siciliano.* Palermo. 1899-1904. *Vid. Paolucci.*

A. Y. R. = *All the Year Round, a weekly journal conducted by Charles Dickens.* 1860-1. Vol. iv.

P. 101 (Nov. 10, 1860) and p. 199 (Dec. 8, 1860), articles describing service before Capua, British Legion, Dowling, etc. (by Henry Spicer, says Mr. Dolmage).

Bandi = Bandi (Giuseppe). *I Mille.* Ed. 1906.

Baroni = Baroni (Primo). *Da Genova a Gaeta e Milazzo.* Published in the *Gazzetta del Popolo della Domenica.* Torino. 1894, Dec. 9, 16, 30, and 1895, Jan. 6. (Personal narrative for the capture of the *Utile,* etc., and for battle of Milazzo, where author was wounded.)

Bersezio's V. E. = Bersezio (Vittorio). *Il regno di Vitt. Em.* 1878-1893. (Careful, but nothing very new.)

Bertani = Mario (J. W.). *Agostino Bertani e i suoi tempi.* 1888. (The best book written by the authoress. Especially important for Bertani's correspondence with Garibaldi and other chief actors in 1860, copiously selected from the Archivio Bertani, Milan.)

Bertani, Comp. = *Le spedizioni di volontari per Garibaldi. Cifre e documenti complementari al resoconto Bertani.* Genova. 1861. (Written in reply to *Bertani's Reso.* (*q.v.*) to show what was done by the National Society, the Million Rifles Fund, and Military Office respectively and in common, apart from the work of Bertani's Central Committee in Aid of Garibaldi, whose operations were described in *Bertani's Reso.* (*q.v.*). These two pamphlets together give a fair notion of the amount of help received by Garibaldi from Cavour's friends and Cavour's enemies respectively.)

Bertani's Reso. = Bertani (A.). *Resoconto di.* Genova. 1860. (Report of administration and accounts of the *Cassa Centrale,* of the Central Committee in Aid of Garibaldi. May to Dec. 1860.)

Bianchi = Bianchi (Nicomede). *Storia Documentata della diplomazia Europea in Italia.* 1814-1861. (A most important source of information.)

Bianchi's Cavour = Bianchi (Nicomede). *Il Conte Camillo Cavour. Documenti editi e inediti.* Torino. 1863.

Bianchi, Polit. de Cavour = Bianchi (Nicomede). *Politique du comte Cavour.* Turin. 1885. (Contains important letters of Cavour to Em. D'Azeglio.)

BIBLIOGRAPHY 353

Bixio = Guerzoni (G.). *La Vita di Nino Bixio.* 1875.

Bixio, Sclavo = Col. Sclavo. *Commemorazione: ai mani illustri di Nino ed Alessandro Bixio.* (Fratelli Pozzo. Torino.) 1907.

(Letters of Bixio, 1859-1860.)

* *Bosco* = Bosco's report of the battle of Milazzo. Printed in various places; *e.g. Gazzetta di Milano,* Aug. 20, 1860, see p. 331 above.

Bourgeois = Bourgeois (E.) and Clermont (E.). *Rome et Napoléon III.* 1907.

(Deals with 1849, 1864, and 1870, not with 1860 in particular. But this valuable work should be studied by all wishing to understand the true bearing of the French occupation of Rome.)

Brambilla = Brambilla (G.). *Ricordi,* 1848-1870. Como. 1884.

(Agent of Bertani and the *Comitato Centrale* in 1860.)

Brancaccio = Brancaccio (di F., di Carpino). *Tre mesi nella Vicaria di Palermo nel* 1860. *Le Barricate. Milazzo.* 2nd ed. 1901.

Br. Parl. Papers = British Parliamentary Papers (Blue Books).

Br. Parl. Papers VII. = *Further correspondence relating to the affairs of Italy, No. VII.* (c. 2757). 1861. (Refers to May to Dec. 1860.)

Br. Parl. Papers VIII. = *ditto* VIII. (Refers to June, 1860, to March, 1861.)

Br. Parl. Papers IX. = *ditto* IX. (Refers to Jan. to March 1861.)

(For the papers not printed and laid before Parliament see *F. O. MSS.*)

Bruzzesi Mem. = *Memorie del Colonello Giacinto Bruzzesi.* Milano.

(For 1862 only. But his diary gives a living portrait of Garibaldi.)

Busetto = Busetto (Girolamo). *Il Generale Nino Bixio.* Fano. 1876.

* *Buttà* = Buttà (Giuseppe). *Un viaggio da Boccadifalco a Gaeta.* Napoli. 1882. 2nd ed.

(A reactionary history compiled partly from the primary authorities of his side, partly from the author's imagination. Where he deserts such well-known Bourbon authorities as *De Sivo, Cava, Nove Mesi, Palmieri, Franci, Marra Oss.* (*q.v.*) he is nearly always misleading. He is the worst tempered writer of any party. He boasts of having been the chaplain in the *ergastolo* on S. Stefano island, where Settembrini and Spaventa were confined, and approves of their treatment there (ii. 19). By inventing a notorious untruth about the attack on Palermo, he is able to achieve the quite singular feat of accusing Garibaldi of cowardice (i. 57). In short, he stands by himself among the authorities of the period, and must not be confused with the really valuable Bourbon writers like *Franci, Nove Mesi,* and *Palmieri.*)

Cadolini = *vid. sub Mem. Stor. Mil.*

Cairoli = Rosi (M.). *I Cairoli.* 1908. (*Bib. di Storia Contemp.* No 1.)

Campo = Campo (Marietta). *Vita politica della famiglia Campo.* Palermo. 1884.

(Last part of the book relates to the Battaglione Gaeta and Vacchieri regiment at Milazzo, Cajazzo, and battle of Oct. 1.)

Cappelletti's V. E. = Cappelletti (Licurgo). *Storia di Vitt. Em.* 3 vols. 1892-3.

Caraguel = Caraguel (Clément). *Souvenirs et aventures d'un volontaire garibaldien.* (Paris. 1861.)

(Personal reminiscences of French volunteer of Medici's expedition. Good for De Flotte's French company at Solano, through Calabria, and at the Volturno.)

Caranti = Caranti (Biagio). *Alcune notizie sul plebiscito nelle provincie napolitane.* Torino. 1864.
(Caranti was secretary to Pallavicino. Important for Neapolitan affairs Sep. to Oct.)

Carosi = Carosi (Salvatore). *La Battaglia del Volturno.* 1905, tip. Francesco Cavatta. S. Maria, Capua.
(Second-hand but well-informed.)

Castelfidardo = *La Battaglia di Castelfidardo. Pubblicazione dell' ufficio storico del Corpo di Stato Maggiore. Narrazione documentata.* Roma. 1903.
(The best authority on the battle. The narrative is based on all the known official documents of both sides, including those preserved in the *Archivio storico del Corpo di Stato Maggiore* which are printed in full at the end of the volume. These documents include the reports of officers engaged in the battle, both National and Papal.)

* *Castelfidardo (Narr.)* = *Narrazione della Battaglia di Castelfidardo scritta da un Romano.* Italia. 1862.
(By a Papalist. Translated from the French, with some good critical notes by the translator of the same party.)

Castelli = Chiala (L.). *Ricordi di M. A. Castelli.* 1888.
(Pp. 325-346 contain the very important diary of campaign of 1860, by Major-General Cav. Paolo Solaroli, as aide-de-camp at Victor Emmanuel's side: see *De Cesare*, ii. 459 note.)

Castelli, Cavour = Castelli (M. A.). *Ricordi. Il Conte de Cavour.* Editi da Chiala.

Castelli, Cart. = Chiala (L.). *Carteggio politico di M. A. Castelli.*

Castellini = Castellini (Gualtiero). *Pagine Garibaldine, dalle Memorie del. Magg. Nicostrato Castellini, con lettere inedite di Mazzini, Garibaldi, Medici e con carteggio di L. S. Mantegazza.* 1909.
(Contains much valuable material for the campaign of 1860.)

Castel Morrone = *Ai Caduti di Castel Morrone, il 1. Ott. 1860.* Tip. Vesuviana. Portici. 1887.
(Contains Major Mirri's official report of the action and narrative of ' G. M.,' a survivor, who is clearly Giuseppe Mirri himself; it is an unofficial and much more detailed narrative than his official report. Mirri afterwards became Italian Minister for War.)

Cattabeni = Spadoni (Dott. Domenico). *I Cairoli delle Marche. La Famiglia Cattabeni.* Macerata. 1906.
(For Cajazzo.)

Cattaneo = Mario (Alberto e Jessie). *Carlo Cattaneo.* 1884.

* *Cava* = Cava (Tommaso, Capitano dello stato maggiore dell' esercito delle due Sicilie). *Difesa nazionale Napoletana.* Napoli. 1863. *Parte Seconda Difesa Militare.*
(Neapolitan officer's complaints of his commanders' conduct. Valuable documents, some of which are also in *Marra Oss., Morisani, Nove Mesi, etc.*)

Chiala = Chiala (Luigi). *Lettere edite ed inedite di Camillo Cavour.* 6 vols.

Chiala's Dina = Chiala (L.). *Giacomo Dina.* 1896.

Chiala's Pol. Seg. = Chiala (L.). *Politica segreta di Napoleone III e di Cavour.* 1895.
(For relations of Kossuth and his agents to Cavour and Napoleon.)

Chiala's Storia Contemp. = Chiala (L.). *Pagine di storia contemporanea.* 1892.

Cialdini e Gar. = R. S. *Del R.* (*q.v.*). 1896. Vol. i. Fasc. 5-6, pp. 546-548. *Mutue relazioni dei Generali Cialdini e Garibaldi.*

Cialdini Rap. = Cialdini (Gen. Enrico). *Rapporto a S. E. il gen. in capo sulle operazioni del quarto Corpo di Armata dell' 11 Sett. al 29*, 1860. 1860. (Very important for Castelfidardo campaign.)

Ciàmpoli = Ciàmpoli (Domenico). *Scritti politici e militari di G. Garibaldi.*

* *Cognetti* = Cognetti (Biagio). *Sui fatti politico-militari della riv. Siculo-Nap. nel* 1860. Napoli, Androsio. 1869.

Colet = Colet (Mme. Louise). *L'Italie des Italiens.*

(Memoirs of an impressionable literary lady, most sympathetic with Italy, who was in the Peninsula, 1859-1860, and finally at Naples during the Garibaldian occupation. Gives the rumours, talk, and atmosphere of the time excellently, but is as often as not wrong as to facts.)

Colletta = Colletta (Gen. Pietro). *History of the Kingdom of Naples*, 1734-1856. Translated by S. Horner. 1858.

Cornhill = *Cornhill Magazine.* See *Red Shirt, Peard, etc.*

Corr. Sera = *Corriere della Sera.*

(Contains important articles by Luzio and Mirabelli on Cavour's relations to the expedition ; see below *Luzio* and *Mirabelli.* For the most important article by Luzio on the Archivio Bertani, see March 1, 1910.)

Corsi's Rimembranze = Corsi (Carlo). *Rimembranze di guerra*, 1848-1870. 1896.

(All given in much greater detail in his *Vent. Anni.*)

Corsi's Vent. Anni = Corsi (Carlo). *Venticinque anni in Italia.* 1870.

(II. p. 391 *et seq.* for Castelfidardo campaign and junction with Garibaldi.)

Corvetto = Magg. G. Corvetto. *La campagna di guerra nell' Umbria e nelle Marche.* Torino. 1861.

(Important account reprinted from *Rivista Mil.* Contains most of the important reports and documents, including Della Rocca's report *re* Spoleto, and *Fanti Campagna, q.v.*, and *Cialdini Rap. q.v.*)

Cosenz = De Cesare (R.). *Commemorazione di Enrico Cosenz.* 1902.

Cosenz (*Guardione*) = Guardione (F.). *Enrico Cosenz.* Palermo. Reber, 1900.

Courier = Courier (Paul Louis). *Œuvres*, 1828, vol. iv. *Lettres de France et d'Italie.*

(For the Calabrian guerilla war of 1806 as described by that philosophical observer and brilliant writer.)

Cremona = *Il comitato di soccorso alla Sicilia costituto in Cremona. Frammenti inediti pubblicati dal Prof. Gennaro Buonanno in occasione delle Nozze Cottarelli-Mauri.* 1890.

(Acts of the Committee at Cremona, 1860, and private letters from the front.)

Crispi = Crispi (Francesco). *Scritti e Discorsi Politici.* 1890.

Crispi, 1911 = Crispi (Francesco). *I Mille*, da documenti dell' archivio Crispi. Treves. 1911.

(Contains his diary, letters, and other documents for 1860.)

* *Cronaca* = *Cronaca degli avvenimenti di Sicilia da Aprile*, 1860, *a Marzo*, 1861. *Estratta da documenti.* Italia. 1863.

Cuniberti = Cuniberti (Capitano, F.). *La spedizione dei Mille. Studio Militare.* Palermo. 1880.

Also a second edition, Roux e C., Roma, 1893, with slight alterations. (Military criticism of strategy and tactics of both sides.)

Da Forio = Forio (G. da). *La Vita di G. Garibaldi.* Napoli (Perrotti). 1862.

Dallolio = Dallolio (Alberto). *La sped. dei Mille nelle memorie Bolognesi.* Zanichelli. 1910.
(From the papers of the Museo del Risorgimento, Bologna, many of which are printed here in full. A scholarly work, and full of political wisdom. Gives facts about the relations of La Farina and Bertani to each other and to the Committees organising the later expeditions.)

D'Ayala = *Memorie di Mariano D'Ayala.* Scritte dal figlio Michelangelo. Torino. 1886.
(Important for annexationist intrigues in Naples, August-Sept. 1860.)

D'Azeglio = *Lettere inedite di Massimo D'Azeglio al nipote Emanuele.* Torino. 1883.

De Benedictis = De Benedictis (Biagio). *Difesa della sua diserzione.* Palermo. June 16, 1860.

De Cesare = De Cesare (R.). *La Fine di un regno.* 3 vols. new ed. 1909.
(The new edition in three volumes of this well-known work contains much additional matter on September and October, 1860. I have been therefore obliged to use it for references in the foot-notes to this volume of mine, although the pagination is different from that of the earlier two-volumed edition of *De Cesare* to which the foot-notes of my *Garibaldi and the Thousand* referred.)

De Cesare's F. di P. = De Cesare (R.). *Una famiglia di patriotti.* 1889.
(Contains the best narrative from local sources of Garibaldi's march from Reggio to Naples, and of the rising in Calabria.)

De Cesare's Roma = De Cesare (R.). *Roma e lo stato del Papa.* 1907.
(History of Papal dominions from 1850-1870.)

De la Rive = De la Rive (W.). *Le Comte de Cavour, récits et souvenirs.* 1862.

Della Rocca = Generale Della Rocca. *Autobiografia di un veterano.* 1897.
(References above are to the English translation, 1899.)

Depretis, Lettera A. = *Sulla presente condizione della Sicilia. Lettera al deputato Depretis.* Torino. 1860. Signed Palermo, 2 Ott. 1860, by *compilatori del giornale 'Il Regno d'Italia,'* Morello, Abbate, Nicolao, Mirone, Virzi.
(Complains of one-man rule of Garibaldi, or rather of rule of faction that rules him, of disorder in Sicily, and begs for instant annexation. Testimony to Depretis' excellence while he was Prodictator.)

* *De Sivo* = De Sivo (Giacinto). *Storia delle due Sicilia dal 1847 al 1861.* Vols. iii. iv. 1864-1867.
(An ill-natured and credulous author, but based upon the primary authorities, and therefore useful for the movements of the Bourbon armies for those unacquainted with those primary sources, which should be studied preferably. *Franci* (*q.v.*) is a much better book, written from the same sources, many of which are printed in *Franci's* appendices.)

Du Camp = Du Camp (Maxime). *Expédition des deux Siciles.* 1861.
(For the march through the Calabrias and the battle of the Volturno. The best of all the books of purely personal reminiscences, and good reading too.)

Du Camp Souv. Lit. = Du Camp (Maxime). *Souvenirs Littéraires.* 1883.
(Vol. ii. chap. xxii, 'En guerre' is excellent on Dumas at Naples in 1860, when Du Camp was much in his company. Du Camp writes not only well but justly of the men and things of 1860.)

Dumas = Dumas (Elder). *Les Garibaldiens.* 1861.

(The latter half of the book relates the experiences and intrigues of the author in Sicily and at Naples, June to October, 1860.)

Durand-Brager = Durand-Brager (H.). *Quatre mois de l'expédition de Garibaldi.* Paris. Dentu. 1861.

(One of the best of the French books on the subject. Well written, sensible, and first-hand. For Palermo, Milazzo, and Messina.)

Elia = Elia (A.). *Ricordi di un Garibaldino.* Ed. 1904.

Elliot = Elliot (Henry). *Diplomatic Recollections.* Printed for private circulation.

Epistolario = Ximenes (E. E.). *Epistolario di Giuseppe Garibaldi.* 2 vols. Milano. 1885.

Fabrizi = Mirone (S.). *Cenni storici sul Gen. N. Fabrizi.* 1886. Catania.

Fam. Crauford = *Lettere di G. Mazzini a Aurelio Saffi e alla famiglia Crauford. Bib. Stor. del Ris. It.* Serie IV. N. 7. 1905. Città di Castello.

Fanti = Carandini (Federico). *M. Fanti generale d'armata.* 1872.

Fanti, Apr. 1861 = Generale Fanti. *Discorso del* 18 *Aprile,* 1861, *alla Camera dei Deputati.*

(Defence of Government action towards the Garibaldian volunteers and the ex-Neapolitan army.)

Fanti, Campagna = General Fanti. *Campagna di guerra nell' Umbria e nelle Marche.* Torino.

(Fanti's report to the King, dated Ancona, Oct. 1, 1860, with maps.)

Fazio = Fazio. *Memorie giovanili.* 1901.

(Autobiography of a Sicilian volunteer, from Palermo to the Volturno. Good on battle of Oct. 1.)

* *Ferrari* = Ferrari (Joseph). *L'annexion des deux Siciles.* Paris. 1860.

(French pamphlet, not valuable.)

Ferrigni = Villari (Luigi A.). *Cenni e ricordi di G. Ferrigni.* Napoli, tip. Priore. 1895.

(Not important.)

Filangieri = Teresa Filangieri Ravaschieri. *Il Generale Carlo Filangieri.* Milano. Treves, 1902.

(By his daughter, from the family archives. Important.)

Finali = Finali (Gaspare). *Le Marche: Ricordanze.* Ancona. 1897.

(For the Castelfidardo campaign. The author was attached to the Royal Commissioner accompanying the army. Better on political than on military affairs.)

Fonvielle = Fonvielle (Ulrich). *Souvenirs d'une chemise rouge.* Paris. Dentu, 1861.

(Interesting personal narrative, very good for Milazzo. Author, a French artist, was in Malenchini's regiment. In many details and stories agrees with other independent authorities. The book is to be trusted.)

Forbes = Forbes (Commander Charles Stuart, R.N.). *The Campaign of Garibaldi in the Two Sicilies.* 1861.

(Excellent on this latter part of the campaign of 1860, of which he was an eye-witness, familiar with Garibaldi and his principal followers. He is not always exactly informed about things which he did not see himself, but he saw a great deal.)

* *Franci* = Franci (Giovanni delli, Uffiziale superiore dello stato maggiore dell' esercito Napolitano). *Campagna d'autunno del* 1860. 2 vols. Napoli. 1870.

(The best account on the Bourbon side, both for fairness of mind and fullness of information. The documents, especially at the end of vol. ii for September and October, render this work the equal of *Türr's Div.* (*q.v.*) in importance as a source of accurate knowledge. Here we have the more important dispatches of the Neapolitan head-quarters leading up to the battles of Oct. 1-2, and the correspondence of Von Mechel, Ritucci, Ulloa, and the King. The documents which it gives ought to be more largely used by Italian writers, *e.g.* Von Mechel's report of Oct. 1, pp. 261-271.)

Galton = Galton (Francis). *Vacation tourists in* 1860. Macmillan. 1861.
    (Pp. 1-75 contain important narrative by W. G. Clark, Tutor of Trinity College, and Public Orator, Cambridge, describing what he saw of Naples and Garibaldi in 1860.)

Garibaldi's Defence of Rome = Trevelyan, G. M. *Garibaldi's Defence of the Roman Republic.* Longmans. 1907.

Garibaldi and the Thousand = Trevelyan, G. M. *Garibaldi and the Thousand.* Longmans. 1909.

Gar. Num. Un. = *Garibaldi. Numero Unico.* 1907.
    (Prints the Dunne-Scelsi correspondence, see p. 65, above.)

Garibaldi Poema = Garibaldi (G.). *Poema Autobiografico e altri canti.* Zanichelli. 1911.
    (The part about 1860 is disappointing.)

* *Garnier* = Garnier (Charles). *Journal du siège de Gaëte,* 1861. Bruxelles.
    (Diary, Nov. 1860 to Feb. 1861, kept inside walls of Gaeta.)

Gay (*Deut. Rev.*) = Gay (Nelson). *Deutsche Revue.* Dec. 1910. *Cavour und die Tausend.* (See Appendix C, above, last sentence.)

Genio = *Il Genio nella campagna d'Ancona e della Bassa Italia;* 1860-1. Pubblicazione autorizzata dal Ministero della Guerra. Torino. 1864.

Giorn. d'It. = *Giornale d'Italia.* (See *sub Luzio* and *Mirabelli.*)
    (Important letters to Mazzini of Sept. 1860 to Jan. 1861, printed in issue of June 6, 1907.)

Giorn. di Sic = *Giornale di Sicilia,* see *Guarneri.*

* *Goumoens* = Goumoens (Emmanuel de). *La Campagne de l'armée Napolitaine du Volturne à Gaète.* (Bibliothèque Universelle de Genève. Vol. xi. 1861.)
    (Goumoens declares he was on the staff attached to Ritucci's person. But his book is great nonsense, *e.g.* he makes Cajazzo recaptured by Borboni on Sept. 14, prior to its loss on Sept. 19. And he declares that Garibaldi and his men on Sept. 19 arrived by train at Capua station expecting to enter town, and were fired on *as they sat in the carriages!*)

Gregorovius = Gregorovius (Ferdinand). *The Roman Journals of,* 1852-1874. Translated by Mrs. Hamilton. 1907.

Griscelli = Colocci (Adriano). *Griscelli e le sue Memorie.* Roma. 1909.
    (Relating to the incident recorded p. 57 note, above.)

Guarneri = Article signed L. F. in the *Giornale di Sicilia,* Feb. 28-29, 1908, giving Senator Guarneri's recollections of the Ministry of June, 1860, at Palermo, in which he held a portfolio.

Guerzoni = Guerzoni (Giuseppe). *Garibaldi* Firenze. 1882. 2 vols.
    (Standard life of Garibaldi.)

Haweis = Newspaper cutting (anno 1888, name of journal not given) in family papers of the late Rev. H. R. Haweis, giving his personal reminiscences of Garibaldi and the Garibaldians in and near Naples, 1860.

Holyoake = Holyoake (George Jacob). *Bygones Worth Remembering.* 1905.

I Mille = Garibaldi (Giuseppe). *I Mille.* 1874. 2nd ed.

Ire Pol. = Bertani (Agostino). *Ire politiche d'oltre tomba.* 1869. (Part of a famous controversy. Reply to *La Farina, q.v.* and see *Türr's Risposta.*)

Isernia = *La reazione avvenuta nel distretto d'Isernia,* 30 *Sett. al* 20 *Ott.* 1860. Napoli. 1861.

Italia Marinara = Naples maritime weekly paper. (Contains interesting historical articles with a rather unusual standpoint.)

J. des D. = *Journals des Débats.* 1860.

Johnston = Johnston (R. M.). *The Napoleonic Empire in Southern Italy.* 1904.

King = Bolton King. *A History of Italian Unity,* 1814-1871. 1898. 2 vols. (Standard general history for the English reader.)

King's Mazzini = Bolton King. *Mazzini.* Dent. 1902.

Lacava = Lacava (Michele). *Cronistoria della Rivoluzione in Basilicata.* Napoli. Morano, 1895. (Many documents and much information about the local risings.)

La Farina = La Farina. *Epistolario.* 2 vols. 1869. (The unexpurgated publication of these vigorous and venomous letters after the death of their writer called out in reply Bertani's no less characteristic *Ire Politiche, q.v.*)

La F. (Biundi) = Biundi (Giuseppe). *Di Giuseppe La Farina e del Risorgimento Italiano.* 1893. Palermo. 2 vols. (Vol. ii. pp. 527-529, reprint of the summary of accounts of the National Society, showing what it did for the help of Garibaldi in June, July, and August, bears out *Bertani Comp. q.v.*)

* *Lafond* = Lafond (Edmond). *Lorette et Castelfidardo.* Paris. 1862. (A chatty clerical account of the Castelfidardo campaign. Gives curious details, illustrative of character of Papal army, as also does *Poli, q.v.*)

La Gorce = La Gorce (Pierre de). *Histoire du second empire.*

La Masa (Mem.) = *Memoria documentata del Deputato Generale Giuseppe La Masa sulla quistione che lo riguarda.* (Torino. 1862.) (Documents and defence of his conduct and that of the Cacciatori dell' Etna, on the Volturno, Oct. 1860. Contains little of value that is not also in *La Masa (Sic.).*

La Masa (Sic.) = *Alcuni fatti e documenti della Riv. dell' Italia Merid. riguardanti i Siciliani e La Masa.* Torino. 1861. (The documents here collected together with some others in *La Masa* and *O. B.'s La Masa (q.v.)* prove the courageous conduct of part of the Sicilian forces at Reggio, and on Oct. 1. See also *Paolucci's Corrao.*)

* *La Moricière* = *Rapport du Général de La Moricière à Monseigneur de Mérode.* Paris. 1860. (Official report by the Papal General of the campaign of Castelfidardo.)

Laracca-Ronghi = Laracca-Ronghi (E.). *Caserta e le sue Reali delizie [con cenni sulla campagna del Volturno.* 3rd ed. Caserta, tip. Marino. 1898.] Caserta. 1888. (Contains local information about the attack on Caserta by Ruiz' column at end of battle of Volturno.)

Lega Del Bene = Neapolitan Review. (Nos. for Dec. 1888 to Jan. 1889 contain a narrative of Garibaldi's entry into Naples, Sep. 7, 1860, by L. Rendina, who accompanied him. It is the fullest account of it, and is the basis of De Cesare's narrative.)

Leggi della Dittatura = *Collezione delle leggi, decreti e disposizioni governative, compilate dall avvocato Nicolò Porcelli.* Palermo. 1860.

Leggi (Napoli) = *Collezione delle leggi e de' decreti emanati nelle provincie continentali durante la dittatura da 7 Sett. a' 6 Nov.* 1860. Napoli. 1860.

Leg. Mat. = Petella, Dott. Giovanni. *La Legione del Matese.* Città di Castello. 1910.

(Careful study from local and other sources of the Liberal movement and local military aid given to Garibaldi in autumn and winter 1860 north of the Volturno. It is in fact the best authority on all military and political events north of the Volturno, as for instance for Csudafy's expedition, for Cajazzo, etc., as it puts them in relation with the other proceedings in that district.)

L'Estrange = L'Estrange (W. D.). *Under Fourteen Flags.* 1884.

(Adventures of Henry MacIver, one of which was with British Legion in Naples. Not very interesting and of questionable exactness.)

Liborio Romano. = Liborio Romano. *Memorie Politiche.* Napoli. 1873.

(His defence of his conduct. A very human document. Contains much important information, though not entirely reliable.)

Litta, Risorg. = *Risorgimento Italiano (Rivista Storica).* Anno ii. fasc. i. pp. 1-48. Count Litta's diary, etc., see pp. 101-103, above.

Lochroy = Lochroy (Édouard). *L'île révoltée.* 1877.

(Pleasant gossip by a French writer who was in Sicily during the revolution. Not authoritative.)

Luzio, Corr. Sera = Luzio's important article on Cavour's relations to the expedition; in the *Corriere della sera* of Aug. 23, 1907.

Another, *ditto,* Dec. 8, 1909.

Luzio, Giorn. D'It. = *ditto* in the *Giornale d'Italia* of May 5, 1907.

Luzio, Risorg. = *ditto* in *Risorg.* (*q.v.*) anno iii. Nos. 1-2, pp. 81-108, *Due relazioni di Ip. Nievo e di G. Acerbi sulla gestione dell' Intendenza generale dell esercito Meridionale nel 1860,* for the accounts of Garibaldi's army.

Luzio, Mazzini = Luzio (A.). *G. Mazzini.* Milano. 1905.

Luzio's Profili = Luzio (Alessandro). *Profili Biografici.* 1906.

(Contains a sketch of Bixio, pp. 303-316.)

Luzio's Studi = Luzio (Alessandro). *Studi e bozzetti di Storia letteraria e politica.* 2 vols. Milano. 1910.

Magni = Magni (Alessandro). *La 16a div. Cosenz nella campagna del 1860.* Roma. 1902.

(By a survivor. For voyage, Milazzo, crossing of Straits, and Volturno. Reliable.)

Maison = Maison (Émile). *Journal d'un volontaire de Garibaldi.* 1861. Paris.

(First-hand personal reminiscences.)

Malmesbury = Malmesbury, third Earl of. *Memoirs of an ex-Minister.* 1884.

Mancini = Mancini (Grazia). *Impressioni e ricordi.* 1908.

Maria Sophia = Tschudi (Clara). *Maria Sophia, Queen of Naples.* Translated from the Norwegian by Ethel Hearn. Sonnenschein. 1905.

Mario = Mario (Jessie White). *Garibaldi e i suoi tempi.* Milano. ed. 1905.

Mario, Mac. = *Macmillan's Magazine,* vol. 46, July, 1882. Alberto Mario's *Personal Reminiscences of General Garibaldi.*

Mario's Mazzini = Mario (J. W.).   *Vita di Mazzini* (Milano.   Sonzogno, 1896.)

Mario's Red Shirt = (*vid. sub Red Shirt*).

Mario, Supp. = Mario (J. W.).   *Supplement to English translation of Garibaldi's Memoirs.*

(Contains stray pieces of information not found elsewhere.)

Mario, Vita = Mario (J. W.).   *Vita di Giuseppe Garibaldi.*   Milano.   Ed. 1882.

Mariotti = *La seconda sped. Gar. del* 1860.   Temistocle Mariotti *N. A.* 1 Aug. 1909.

(Memoirs of veteran of Malenchini's regiment for Milazzo, Volturno, etc.)

* *Marra Oss.* = *Osservazioni del Generale Bartolo Marra sulla storia di A. B. Cognetti.*   Napoli.   1868.

(Answer to Cognetti's *Pio IX e il suo secolo ;* defence of Marra's conduct. Gives important first-hand evidence and documents as to his own conduct in Reggio, and that of Melendez and Ruiz at Piale ; his own conduct when left by King in charge of forts of Naples Sept. 6 ; and the battle of Oct.1-2 about which he quotes General Ritucci's narrative.)

Martinengo Cesaresco = Martinengo Cesaresco (Contessa).   *Patriotti Italiani.* Milano.   1890.

Latest English edition of this work (1901), *Italian Characters* contains sketches of Bixio, Poerio, and others.

Martinengo Cesaresco's Cavour = Martinengo Cesaresco (Countess).   *Cavour.* (In the Foreign Statesmen Series.)

See also *The Liberation of Italy,* 1814-1870, by the same authoress, 1895. An excellent brief history.   English readers desiring to know the history of the Risorgimento should begin with this book and then go on to Bolton King's *History of Italian Unity.*

Marzo-Ferro = Marzo-Ferro (Girolamo di).   *Un periodo di storia di Sicilia.* Palermo.   1863.

Massari's V. E. = Massari (Giuseppe).   *La vita di Vitt. Em.*   1878.   2 vols.

Matarazzi = Matarazzi.   *Avvenimenti politico-militari dal sett. al nov.* 1860. Napoli.   1861.

(Important.   Full of detail, especially for battle of Oct. 1.)

Mattigana = Mattigana (Piero).   *Risorgimento d'Italia.*   Milano.

(Pp. 328-393 contain an account by a volunteer at Milazzo of the fighting on July 17 and 20.)

Mazzini = Mazzini (G.).   *Scritti editi e inediti.*   17 vols.

(Vols. ix.-xi. covering this period, are rendered of special value by *Saffi's Proemio* (*q.v.*))

Medici = Medici (Gen. G.).   *Una pagina di storia del* 1860.   Palermo.   1869.

Medici (Pasini) = Pasini (Giovanni).   *La battaglia di Milazzo narrata dal Generale Giacomo Medici al Capitano Pasini (Giovanni).*   Cremona.   1883.

(A copy of this rare but important pamphlet is preserved in the Museum at Cremona.   Professor Manacorda kindly called my attention to it.   Medici's letter of June 8, 1881, and Pasini's preface, show that it was seen and corrected by Medici, and its matter bears the stamp of authenticity.   It is therefore of great importance, since Medici has nowhere else left a detailed account of his operations before Milazzo.)

Mem. = Garibaldi (Giuseppe).   *Memorie autobiografiche.*   Firenze.   1902. 11th ed.

Mem. Stor. Mil. = *Memorie Storiche Militari.* (Comando del corpo di Stato Maggiore. Ufficio Storico Roma.)

    I. = fascicolo I. Gennaio, 1909. *L'Incontro del re V. E. col Gen. Garibaldi il 26 Ott.* 1860. Generale Del Bono. (Docs. 5-7 are official Piedmontese reports of part taken by the regular artillery in Oct. 1 and by the companies of Bersaglieri and regular infantry of the line on Oct. 2.)

    II. = fascicolo II. Maggio, 1909. *Intorno alla ' Diversione.'* Giovanni Cadolini.

    (Important).

Menghini = Menghini (Mario). *La spedizione Garibaldina di Sicilia e di Napoli, nei proclami, nelle corrispondenze, nei diarii e nelle illustrazioni del tempo.* 1907.

Mérimée = Mérimée (Prosper). *Lettres d M. Panizzi.* 1881.

* *Mérode* = Monseigneur Besson. *Frederick Francis Xavier de Mérode. His Life and Works.* Translated into English by Lady Herbert. 1887.

Meuricoffre = Josephine Butler, sister of Me. Meuricoffre. *In Memoriam Harriet Meuricoffre*, no date.

    (Parts of these interesting memoirs were printed in *Macmillan's Magazine* for 1860-1861, vol. iii. 152-160, *q.v.*, which contains some incidents not reproduced in the book. The memoirs, from letters of the date, treat of the entry of Garibaldi, Sep. 7, and of the hospitals where Me. Meuricoffre worked among the Garibaldian wounded.)

Mezzacapo = Pesci (Ugo). *Il Generale Carlo Mezzacapo.* Zanichelli. 1908.

    (Acted as one of Cavour's agents in Naples in August.)

Mignona = Carbonelli (G. Pupino). *Nicola Mignona.* Napoli. 1889.

    (Patriot and exile of Basilicata and friend of Mazzini. Useful for Mazzini's action and for the Basilicata rising.)

Milazzo (G. B. Z.) = *Reminiscenze della Battaglia di Milazzo, fatti narrati da un combattente.* Milano. 1862. The Introduction is signed by author ' G. B. Z.' = Capt. G. B. Zaffaroni, see *Castel Morrone*, p. 22.

    (On Clemente Corte and the work of the *battaglione Gaeta* in the battle.)

Mirabelli = (1) Mirabelli (R.). *Giornale d'Italia*, May 14, 1907, and *Corriere della Sera*, July 29.

    (Answers to Luzio on Cavour and the expedition.)

    (2) By same author—*Per la storia rivoluzionaria del Sessanta.* Bologna. 1886.

Mirabelli Trev. = Mirabelli (R.). *Cavour, I Mille e lo Storico Inglese Macaulay-Trevelyan.* Biblioteca della Rivista Popolare, xxxv. Roma. 1910.

    (Anti-Cavourian.)

Mistrali = Mistrali (Fr.). *Le guerre d'Italia da Villafranca ad Aspromonte.* Milano. 1863.

    (Second-hand; not much use.)

Mistrali's Da N. = Mistrali (Fr.). *Da Novara a Roma.* Istoria della Riv. It. Vol. iv. 1862 *et seq.*

    (Good on Milazzo, memoirs of one of Medici's men.)

Monnier = Monnier (Marco). *Garibaldi. Rivoluzione delle due Sicilie.* Translated from French by Rocco Escalona, who adds notes. Napoli. 1861.

    (Diary of author, chiefly at Naples. Also many documents.)

Monteleone = *Numero Unico. A Garibaldi, La massoneria di Monteleone.* Oct. 1908.

    Interesting details about flight of Neapolitan and passage of Garibaldian army through Monteleone, and part played by the townspeople in Aug. 1860.)

* *Morisani* = Morisani (Cesare). *Ricordi storici. I fatti delle Calabrie nel luglio ed agosto* 1860. Reggio-Calabria, stamp. di Luigi Ceruso. 1872. (Very important for Reggio and Briganti's surrender. From Bourbon documents and local sources. Impartial, but inclined to attribute too much to definite treachery, especially in the case of Pianell, *cf.* to *Pianell* and *Marra Oss.* and *Ruiz.*)

Morley = Morley (John). *Life of Gladstone,* 1903.

Mundy = Mundy (Rear-Admiral Sir Rodney). *H.M.S. ' Hannibal' at Palermo and Naples, during the Italian Revolution,* 1859-1861.

Murray, 1858 = *Murray's Guide to South Italy,* edition of 1858.

Murray, 1862 = *ditto* of 1862.

N. A. = *Nuova Antologia.* See *Artom, Mariotti, Orsini, Trecchi.*

Nicotera = Mauro (M.). *Biografia di Giovanni Nicotera.*

Nievo = Mantovani (Dino). *Il poeta soldato : Ippolito Nievo.*

(Life of the poet Nievo, one of the Thousand. Contains his delightful letters to his family from Palermo. From June to November he remained in Palermo as sub-intendant, organising the revolutionary armies that conquered Naples.)

Nisco = Nisco (Niccola). *Gli ultimi Trentasei anni del Reame di Napoli,* vol. iii. *Francesco II.* Ed. 1894.

(Nisco was one of *Bomba's* ' Neapolitan prisoners '; an agent of Cavour in Naples, August and September, 1860 ; after the revolution he had access to part of the Bourbon archives for the purposes of his history.)

* *Noé* = Noé. *Trente jours à Messine.* 1861.

* *Nove Mesi* = [Gaeta (Luigi) dello Stato Maggiore dell' esercito Napolitano]. *Nove mesi in Messina e la sua Cittadella,* per ' G. L. ' Napoli. 1862.

(Contains very important dispatches of Bosco and Clary, and other officers' diaries, especially useful for Milazzo. The same important documents are mostly printed in *Palmieri* also.)

Nuvolari = Nuvolari (Giuseppe). *Come la penso.* Milano. 1881.

O. B.'s La Masa = Bonafede (Oddo). *Cenno Storico sul Generale G. La Masa.* Verona. 1879.

(Defence of La Masa's conduct, with documents, by *Oddo,* author of *I Mille di Marsala,* who later took name of Bonafede. Most of the documents are also in *La Masa (Sic.) q.v.*)

Oddo = Oddo (Giacomo). *I Mille di Marsala.* 1863.

Oddo's Brig. = Oddo (Giacomo). *Il Brigantaggio. L'Italia dopo la ditt. di Garibaldi.* 3 vols. 1867.

Olivieri = Olivieri (F.). *Errori e rimedi nell' Italia meridionale.* Pinerolo. 1861.

Ollivier = Ollivier (Emile). *L'Empire Libéral.*

* *O'Reilly* = O'Reilly (Major). *The Irish Papal Brigade Vindicated.* Dublin. 1861.

(For defence of Spoleto.)

Orero = Orero (Gen.). *Da Pesaro a Ancona.* Straglio. 1905.

(Important for Castelfidardo campaign and operations of regular army in Neapolitan Kingdom.)

Orsini = *Documenti inediti del Gen. Giordano Orsini,* by Francesco Guardione. *N. A.* July 1, 1907.

(For the passage of the Straits.)

* *Palmieri* = Palmieri (G., Brigadiere di Cav.). *Cenno storico del* 1859-1861.
(Neapolitan General. Like Luigi Gaeta in his *Nove Mesi* (*q.v.*) he prints
two documents of the first importance for the campaign and battle of
Milazzo, *viz.* (1) on pp. 47-50, the written instructions given by Clary to
Bosco on July 13, and (2) on pp. 30-46, Bosco's account of the campaign
and battle of Milazzo, published originally in the Neapolitan *Rivista
Militare* of Aug. 1860, Nos. 5 and 6. See also for cavalry in battle of
Volturno.) The book was written in 1861, and probably printed then, but
there is no date or place of printing on my copy.

Panizzi = *Lettere ad Antonio Panizzi di uomini illustri e di amici italiani*
1823-1870: pubblicate da Luigi Fagan. Firenze. 1880.

Panizzi's Life = L. Fagan. *Life of Sir A. Panizzi.* 1880.

Pantaleoni = Pantaleoni (Diomede). *L'idea italiana nella soppressione del
potere temporale dei Papi.* 1884.
(Cavour's confidential agent in Rome. Important for Cavour's attempted
negotiations with Pope and his ideas on Rome, 1860-1861.)

Paolucci Corrao = Paolucci (G.). *Giovanni Corrao.* In *A. S. Sic.* 1900, and
reprinted separately.

Peard = Trevelyan (G. M.). *War-journals of Garibaldi's Englishman.* Publi-
cation of parts of J. W. Peard's journal of 1860 in the *Cornhill Magazine*,
June, 1908.
(See also an article in same magazine, Aug. 1903, by Miss Frances M.
Peard, called *Garibaldi's Englishman.*)

Pecorini-Manzoni Pagina = Pecorini-Manzoni (Emilio). *Una pagina di storia.
In omaggio alla memoria dei prodi militi di Gar. morti nella batt. del Volturno il* 1 *Ott.* 1860. Santa Maria. 1905.

Perini = Perini (O.). *La spedizione dei Mille.* Milano. 1861.

Persano = Persano (Ammiraglio C. di). *Diario privato, politico, Militare.* 1880.
(Most important on Cavour's secret orders to the fleet. Persano was
necessarily one of Cavour's most confidential agents throughout 1860.)

Persigny = *Mémoires du Duc de Persigny.* Paris. 1896.

Piaggia = Piaggia (G.). *Dei fatti d'armi di Milazzo.* Palermo. 1876. 2nd ed.
(First edition was published in 1860 a few days after the battle. Piaggia
had intimate local knowledge of Milazzo and he was on the spot in the
hospitals a few days after the battle. It is a most important authority, and
as trustworthy as an account of a battle can be.)

Pianciani = Pianciani (Luigi). *Dell' andamento delle cose in Italia.* 1860.
(Important for the acts and intentions of Garibaldi, Bertani, and Pianciani
severally in August and for the history of the Tuscan volunteers and the idea
of invading the Roman States.)

* *Pianell* = Pianell (Generale). *Memorie.* Firenze. Barbèra. 1902.
(Very important for Aug. 1860.)

* *Pianell, Confutazioni* = Cav. Carlo Corsi, Maggiore delle artigliere Napolitane
Capitolato di Gaeta [not to be confused with *Corsi (Carlo)*, see above in this
bibliography]. *Difesa dei Soldati Napolitani : Confutazioni alle Lettere del
Generale Pianell e ricordi familiari ecc.* Napoli. 1903.
(Fierce attack on Pianell from reactionary point of view. Second-hand,
no new documents.)

Pianell, Vita = Félissent (G. de). *Il Generale Pianell e il suo tempo.* Verona.
1902.
(Less important than his own *Memorie.*)

Pittaluga = Pittaluga (Gen. Giovanni). *La Diversione.* 1904.

* *Poli* = Poli (Oscar de). *Souvenirs du bataillon des Zouaves Pontificaux (franco-belges).* Paris. 1861.

(For Castelfidardo campaign. Throws interesting lights on the motives and character of the Papal Zouave Crusaders, of whom the truly ingenuous author was one.)

Ponti Della Valle = *Ai Ponti della Valle.* 1 *Ott.* 1860. Numero unico. Maddaloni. 1899. (Portici.)

(Mostly reprinting of well-known documents, but has a new article by General Pittaluga on the general strategical aspects of the battle of Oct. 1. Also recollections of the battle by Ghersi, Bixio's chief of staff, and others.)

Pozzi = *In Memoria dell' Avv. Cav. Francesco Pozzi, morto il 25 maggio, 1907. La Famiglia riconoscente.*

(Contains Pozzi's own 'reminiscenze sulla campagna delle due Sicilie 1860.' For Medici's division at Milazzo, march through Calabria, and battle of Volturno.)

Prampero = Prampero (Senatore A. di). *La Battaglia di Castelfidardo.* Udine. 1896.

(Author present at battle, during which he received orders from Cialdini in person. Shows Finali to be wrong in saying that the battle took place in Cialdini's absence.)

Preda = Preda (P.). *Le sommeil interrompu ou sans brûler une cartouche. Souvenir de la Campagne de Sicile en* 1860. Novare, Miglio frères. 1885.

(For the operations of the *Veloce* as a Garibaldian vessel prior to the battle of Milazzo, by one who was on board her during some of the captures she made in Straits of Messina.)

Principe Nap. = Vayra (Pietro). *Il Principe Napoleone e l'Italia.* Torino. 1891.

Pungolo = *Il Pungolo.* (Modern Neapolitan paper, not to be confused with the Milanese *Pungolo* of 1860.)

1. *Sept.* 8, 1904, contains recollections of Lacava, Col. Visani, and other veterans, of Garibaldi's entry into Naples, Sept. 7, 1860.

2. *July* 5, 1907, contains letter of Medici to Cosenz, May 10, 1860.

* *Quandel-Vial* = Quandel-Vial (Ludovico, ex-Capitano di Artiglieria Nap.). *Annotazioni al libro 'Lettere del Gen. Pianell e ricordi familiari.'* Napoli, tip. degli Artigianelli. 1901.

(An attack on Pianell and a defence of Vial for the affairs of Calabria in August: the former more successful than the latter.)

* *Quatrebarbes* = Le comte de Quatrebarbes. *Souvenirs d'Ancone, siège de* 1860.

(Quatrebarbes was governor of Ancona during the siege. Important.)

Queen's Letters = *The Letters of Queen Victoria.* 3 vols. 1907.

Racioppi = Racioppi (Giacomo). *Moti di Basilicata.* Napoli. 1867.

Raffaele = Raffaele (G.). *Rivelazioni storiche della riv. dal 1848 al 1860.* Palermo. 1883.

Rampone = Rampone (S.). *Mem. Pol. di Benevento dalla riv. del 1799 alla riv. del 1860.* Benevento, tip. D'Alessandro.

Rass. Con. = *Rassegna Contemporanea*, ann. ii. fasc. ii. Feb. 1909. *Lettere inedite di Stefano Canzio.*

(Not important.)

Red Shirt = Mario (Alberto). *The Red Shirt.* 1865. (Smith, Elder & Co.)
(Important personal reminiscences of the campaign of 1860. A part had been published in *Cornhill Magazine*, June, 1864.)

Reggio = *Su i prodi Italiani caduti martiri in Reggio il 21 Agosto*, 1860. *Parole di Basilio Lofaro.* Reggio. 1860.
(Not important.)

Revel's da Ancona = Revel (Genova di). *Da Ancona a Napoli. Miei Ricordi.* Milano. 1892.
(Revel came south with the Piedmontese army.)

Ricasoli = Ricasoli (Baron). *Lettere e documenti pubb. per cura di M. Tabarrini e A. Gotti.* Firenze. 1887-1895.

Risorg. = Il Risorgimento Italiano.
(The Historical Review of Risorgimento History. First number, March, 1908. To be distinguished from the *Rivista Storica del Risorgimento Italiano* of 1895 and subsequent years (*vid. sub R. S. del R.*), a similar periodical of anterior date. *Risorg.* contains *Uzielli* (*q.v.*) and much other very valuable matter.)

R. S. del R. = *Rivista Storica del Risorgimento Italiano.* 1895 *et seq.*
(See *sub Amari, Cialdini e Gar., Turiello.*)

Rosi = Rosi (M.). *Il risorgimento italiano e l'azione d'un patriota cospiratore e soldato.* 1906.
(A life of Mordini. Well documented.)

* Ruiz = *L'autodifesa del generale Ruiz de Ballesteros.* First published in Naples in 1868, republished by his son, Col. Gaetano R. di B. Milano. 1910.
(For Lower Calabria in August, and the Volturno in October. A useful corrective of *De Sivo's* wholesale charges of treachery, etc. Most important as the Neapolitan general's own account of Castel Morrone, and battle of Oct. 2.)

Rusconi = Rusconi (Ferdinando). *19 anni di vita di un Garibaldino.* 1870.

Russell = Spencer Walpole. *Life of Lord John Russell.* 1889.

Russell (Lady) = Desmond MacCarthy and Lady Agatha Russell. *Lady John Russell. A Memoir.* Methuen. 1910.

Rüstow = Rüstow (W.). *La Guerra italiana del* 1860 *descritta politicamente e militarmente con 8 carte e piani.* Versione dott. G. Bizzozzero. Milano, tip. G. Civelli. 1862.
(Is a translation of Rüstow's *Erinnerung aus dem italienischen Feldzuge von* 1860. First-hand for latter part of campaign.)

Rüstow's Brig. Mil. = Rüstow (Wilhelm). *La Brigata Milano nella campagna dell' Italia merid. del* 1860. Versione dal tedesco. Eliseo Porro. Milano, tip. D. Salvi. 1861.
(Italian translation of *Die Brigade Milano*, 1860. Rüstow, a German Liberal exile, commanded the Milan 'Brigade,' or rather small battalion, originally of Pianciani's force, subsequently under Türr at Sapri and the Volturno. Important.)

Sacchi Dom. = Sacchi (Prof. Domenico). *Traduzione e Confutazione dell' opuscolo intitolato 'La Vérité sur les choses du Royaume d'Italie,' par J. A. ancien agent secret du comte de Cavour.* Torino. 1862.

Saffi's Proemio = Saffi (Aurelio). Preface to the *Scritti editi e inediti* of Mazzini (*q.v.*)
Reprinted also in Saffi, *Ricordi e Scritti.*

BIBLIOGRAPHY 367

Salazaro = Salazaro (Demetrio). *Cenni sulla Riv. It. del* 1860. Napoli. 1866.

Savio = Ricci (R.). *Memorie della Baronessa Olimpia Savio.* 1911.
(Mother of the Savio brothers: their letters from the front.)

* *Schweizertruppen* = Dr. Albert Maag. *Geschichte der Schweizertruppen in Neapolitanischen Diensten,* 1825-1861. Zürich. 1909.
(From Swiss sources. One of the most trustworthy books about the Bourbon side of the war, though unfortunately limited to the action of the Foreign Brigade. Important for Cajazzo and Arches of the Valley.)

Scrittori Manduriani = Gigli (Giuseppe). *Scrittori Manduriani.* 1896.
(Contains a short biography of Lacaita, including the story of the visit to Lord John Russell's house as told by Pasquale Villari on Lacaita's authority; see *sub Villari Pasq.* below.)

Simpson = Simpson (Rev. F. A.). *The Rise of Louis Napoleon.* 1909.
(The early life of Napoleon III must be known before his Liberal action with regard to Italy in 1859-1860 is understood. Mr. Simpson's fascinating volume is the best record of the important and neglected facts of the pretender's youth.)

Siracusa = De Benedictis (Em.). *Siracusa sotto la mala signoria degli ultimi Borboni.* Torino. 1861.
(Local account of events in Syracuse.)

Sirtori = De Castro (G.). *Giuseppe Sirtori.* Milano. Dumolard, 1892.

Solaroli = *vid. Castelli* above.

Spaventa = Spaventa (*Silvio*). *Dal* 1848 *al* 1861. Napoli. 1898.

Stamp. Off. = *Stampati in fogli volanti editi negli anni* 1860-1861. *Parte officiale.*
(A fine collection of the official proclamations of the successive Governments of 1860-1861. Collection Lodi, Arch. Stor. Patria, Palermo.)

Stiavelli = Stiavelli (G.). *Garibaldi nella letteratura italiana.*

Stillman's Crispi = Stillman (W. J.). *Francesco Crispi.* 1899.
(Not documented.)

St. Maur Letters = *Letters of Lord St. Maur and Lord Edward St. Maur.* Privately printed. 1888.
(Of the British Legion: kindly lent me by Mr. H. St. Maur.)

Stocco = number of *La Nuova Stampa* of Nicastro, 12 Feb. 1910, devoted to memory of Antonio Stocco, just deceased. He was nephew of Francesco Stocco, under whom he served in Calabria, 1860.

Strutt = Strutt (Arthur J.). *A Pedestrian Tour in Calabria and Sicily.* 1842.

Thayer = Thayer (W. Roscoe). *Throne-makers.* 1899.
(Contains an excellent appreciation of Garibaldi.)

Thouvenel = Thouvenel (L.). *Le secret de l'Empereur.* 1889. Lévy ed.
(Contains important private correspondence of Thouvenel, French Foreign Minister, with Gramont, French Ambassador at Rome, 1860.)

Tivaroni It. = Tivaroni (Carlo). *L'Italia degli Italiani.*

Tosi = Tosi (Raffaele). *Cenni autob. di un Garibaldino.* Rimini. 1889.

Tosi, 1910 = Tosi (Raffaele). *Da Venezia a Mentana.* Ricordi pubblicati del figlio.
(A later and slightly different edition of *Tosi.*)

Trecchi = *Nuova Antologia.* June 1, 1910. The letters of the marchese Gaspare Trecchi for 1860, published and commented on by Giuseppe Manacorda.

(Of the first importance, especially the King's secret message to Garibaldi, Aug. 5 (?) printed p. 426.)

Treitschke = Treitschke. *Il Conte di Cavour.* Translated from the German. Firenze. 1873.

(Excellent.)

Tribuna = Journal, No. 225 *et seq.* 1907, for controversy on the meeting of Garibaldi and Victor Emmanuel at Teano.

Trinity = *The Trinity of Italy, by an English Civilian for eight years in official connexion with the Court of Naples.* 1867. Edward Moxon & Co.

Trollope = Trollope (T. A.). *What I Remember.* 1887-1889.

(II. pp. 222-231 about Peard, Mario, and Garibaldi.)

Turiello = Turiello (P.). *Ricordi. Dal* 1847 *al '67. R. S. del R.* Anno i. vol. i. fasc. ii. e iii.

Türr ai miei Comp. = Türr (Stefano). *Ai miei compagni d'armi.* Maggio. 1903. Roma.

(Answer to *Bandi*, pp. 293-295, *re* events of Sept. 19 and Cajazzo.)

Türr's Div. = Pecorini-Manzoni (Carlo). *Storia della* 15*a Divisione Türr.* 1876.

Türr's Risposta = Türr (Gen.). *Risposta all' opuscolo Bertani.* Milano. 1869.

Una Pagina = Pecorini-Manzoni (Emilio). *Una pagina di storia. In omaggio alla memoria dei prodi morti alla battaglia del Volturno.* 1 *Ott.* 1860. Portici. 1905.

(Does not contain much that is not in his *Türr's Div.* or elsewhere.)

Uzielli = Uzielli (Gustavo). *Dai ricordi di uno studente Garibaldino* printed in *Risorg.* anno ii. fasc. 5-6, pp. 913-952.

(Letters, memoirs, and other documents. Important for Malenchini's regiment at Milazzo, and for the fight at the Porta Capua, S. Maria, Oct. 1.)

Venosta = Venosta (G. Visconti). *Ricordi di Gioventù.* Milano. 1906. 3rd ed.

V. M. = *Ventisette maggio* 1860; numero unico. Palermo. 27 maggio. 1885.

Veritas = Veritas (*nom de plume* of Doctor Giovanni Del Greco of Florence, see *Stiavelli*, 198). *Ricordi di un Garibaldino.* 1888.

(Personal reminiscences of fighting on July 17, before Milazzo, and of battle of Volturno, Oct. 1.)

Veterano = *Il Veterano* periodical. 1908.

(April 1908, contains two accounts of the fighting on road to S. Angelo when Garibaldi in his carriage was endangered; one by F. Bassani, then sergeant in Cadolini's regiment, and another by Emilio Caivano, both of whom took part in the affair.

* *Veuillot* = Veuillot (Eugène). *Le Piémont dans lès États de l'Église.* Paris. 1861.

(Clerical work on the Castelfidardo campaign.)

Villari Cosp. = Villari (Raffaele). *Cospirazione e rivolta.* 1881.

Villari Pasq. = *IX Gennaio, pubblicazione commemorativa per cura del circolo universitario Vitt. Em. II.* Bologna. 1882.

(Contains Pasquale Villari's narrative of the Lacaita-Russell interview as told to him by Lacaita, see p. 107 above. Told also in *Albo Com.* and *Scrittori Manduriani, q.v.*)

Vismara = Vismara (Antonio). *Bibliografia di Garibaldi.* Como, tip. C. Franchi. 1891.

(Part of E. Motta's *Collezione storica bibliografica.*)

Vitzthum = Graf Vitzthum von Eckstädt.   (Saxon Minister in Great Britain.)
    St. Petersburg und London, 1852-1864.   Stuttgart.   1886.
Volturno = *Pei Caduti al Volturno.*   Numero Unico.   S. Maria.   1905.
Walpole's Twenty-five Years = Walpole (Sir Spencer).   *History of Twenty-five years.*
Whitaker = Whitaker (Tina, née Scalia).   *Sicily and England,* 1848-1870.
    Constable.   1907.
Whitehouse = Whitehouse (H. K.).   *Collapse of the Kingdom of Naples.*   New
    York.   Bonnel Silver & Co.   1899.
Winnington-Ingram = Winnington-Ingram (Rear Admiral H. F.).   *Hearts of Oak.*   1889.
Zasio = *Da Marsala al Volturno. Ricordi di E. Z.*   Padova.   1868.
    (E. Z. = Emilio Zasio, one of the Thousand.   A fine fellow, of good
    judgment and modesty as I have been told by his fellow-soldiers, and as his
    book shows.   He was at Garibaldi's side at the entry into Naples, the
    meeting with the King, and on many other occasions.)
Zirilli = Zirilli (S.).   *Sulla conquista Garibaldina di Milazzo.*   Palermo.
    1882.   (*Note e schiarimenti al manuale di storia contemp. di G. Weber.*)
    (Zirilli was leading citizen of Milazzo, an active Liberal, and was one of
    the few Milazzesi who remained in the town during the battle.   His work is
    valuable for what he saw himself, and for doc. 5, the letter of a Bourbon
    officer.)

II. NEWSPAPERS AND PERIODICALS OF 1860

Arlecchino = *L'Arlecchino.*   Sicilian newspaper, June 11, 1860, *et seq.*
* *Civ. catt.* = *Civiltà cattolica.*   Clerical organ.
Corr. Merc. = *Corriere Mercantile,* 1860.   Genova.
    (Cavourian.   Contained article reprinted in 1861 as *Bertani Comp. q.v.*)
D. News = *Daily News.*
    (Special correspondents' and private persons' letters on all the important
    events.   But not generally so good as *Times* and *Morning Post.*   Arrivabene
    was their principal correspondent: see his book, *Arrivabene.*)
Diritto = Italian democratic journal.
Forbice = *Forbice, la.*   Palermitan newspaper for 1860.
    (Contains some letters from Milazzo, etc., of interest.)
* *Gazzetta di Gaeta* = Francis II's official newspaper after his leaving Naples.
    First number, Sept. 4, 1860.   Last, Feb. 8, 1861.
    (Contains official Bourbon accounts of Sept. 19, Cajazzo, and a very
    inadequate account of battle of Oct. 1-2, which is described as a successful
    'reconnaissance.')
Gazz. di Mil. = *Gazzetta di Milano.*   May to Sept. 1860.   Ten supplements,
    giving list of '*offerte per soccorsi nella Sicilia versate all' Associazione
    Italiana.*'   The ten sheets are subscription lists of several hundred in-
    dividuals, each sending between one and a hundred *lire.*
    (Moderate—for Garibaldi and Cavour both.)
Giorn. Off. di Napoli = *Giornale Officiale di Napoli,* for 1860.
Giorn. Off. Sic. = *Giornale Officiale di Sicilia,* 1857-1860.
    (The paper begins again under the new *régime* at Palermo on June 7.
I. L. N. = *Illustrated London News* for 1860.
    (Pictures and reports of Garibaldi's campaign from the entrance into

Palermo onwards. Their principal artist and war correspondent was Vize-telly, who lived on intimate terms with many of the Garibaldini, from whose narratives he made up his reports.)

J. des D. = Journal des débats.

(Sept. 15 for account of Garibaldi's entry into Naples, dated Sept. 7. Oct. 7 for account of Volturno, dated Oct. 2.)

L'Illustration. = L'Illustration. Paris. 1860.

(The French *Illustrated London News.* Accurate war-sketches from the front, nearly all reproduced in *Menghini, q.v.*)

Mondo Illustrato = Il Mondo Illustrato for 1860.

(Italian paper on lines of our *Illustrated London News.* First two years of it were 1847-1848, third year began July 7, 1860. Its pictures are not very good, but are fairly accurate.)

M. Post = Morning Post.

(Special correspondents' letters on march of Eber's column, Milazzo, Faro, San Giovanni, Volturno. The principal correspondent, an excellent one, was a Tuscan, as I have been told by those who went with him through Sicily.)

Opinione = Opinione.

(Cavourian: see *Chiala's Dina* for a reprint of many of its most important articles.)

Precursore = Il Precursore.

(Sicilian newspaper from July, 1860, onwards.)

Pungolo Milano = Il Pungolo, journal of Milan. 1860.

(The *Nostre corrispondenze* from officers with Garibaldi are often good.)

Times = The Times.

(Eber, the Hungarian, continued to send excellent letters as 'special correspondent' even while in command of the column that passed through the middle of Sicily to Catania. There were various correspondents during the campaign, among others Gallenga. The account of the battle of Milazzo, by a combatant [*Times*, Aug. 4, p. 10] is of great historical value. Other communications of historical importance are to be found in the *Times* of Aug. 20, 25, 31, Sept. 4, on Faro and crossing the Straits; Sept. 15 on the march through Calabria and Basilicata; Sept. 13, 18, on Garibaldi's entry into Naples; Sept. 27, on action of Sept. 19; Oct. 9 and 11, on battle of Volturno. And there is much else of interest.)

Un. It. = Unità Italiana, Democratic.

III. MANUSCRIPTS

1. MSS. BELONGING TO PRIVATE PERSONS

Bell MSS. = Letter of W. Walpole Bell, of British Legion.

Canzio MS. = Typewritten account of meeting of Victor Emmanuel and Gari-baldi by General Canzio, Garibaldi's son-in-law, who was present at the scene. He gave me this document in Jan. 1908, as being his own authorized account.

Dunne MSS. = Letters of Dunne to Countess Martinengo Cesaresco, and her notes of his conversations. Collection of cuttings from English and Italian newspapers about him at Milazzo and Volturno. Letter of Giacinto Scelzi to Dunne, recalling their actions in Sicily, which has also been printed in *Gar. Num. Un.*

Fazzari MSS. = Original MS. letters to Garibaldi of Admiral Persano, Türr, and Augusto Vecchi, summer and autumn of 1860, kindly lent me by the late Achille Fazzari of Staletti, Golfo di Squillace.

Forbes MSS. = Papers of Hugh Forbes, lent me by his daughter.

Lacaita MSS. = Papers of Mr. Chas. Lacaita referring to his father's interview with Lord John Russell, July, 1860. Letter of Hudson, 1885, and Lacaita's journal for 1860. See p. 105 above.

Miller MSS. = Narrative communicated to me by the Rev. Donald Miller, for forty-one years Minister of the Scotch congregation in Genoa. In 1860 he was still in trade (*aet.* 22) in the firm of Henderson Bros., his uncles, of Leghorn, and had important dealings with Garibaldi, relative to the *City of Aberdeen* steamer, and also sold him military stores at cost price out of sympathy with the movement. He became one of Garibaldi's friends.

Morgan MSS. = Letters of Charlton H. Morgan to author. (Mr. Morgan was United States Consul at Messina in 1860. He assisted Garibaldi at Faro and fought for him on the Volturno.)

Nelson MSS. = Letters of and about 1860, kindly lent me by the late Dr. Joseph Nelson of Belfast, formerly of Dunne's regiment at Milazzo. They contain letters of 1860 from the camps of Sicily and Naples by Mr. Walker, of Dunne's regiment and the British Legion.

Peard's Journal MS. = MS. journal for 1859, 1860 of J. W. Peard, 'Garibaldi's Englishman.' Kindly lent me by Miss Peard. Important.

Russell MSS. = For these very important papers see Appendix A.

Russell (Lady) MSS. = Letters of Poerio, Sir James Hudson, and others to Lady John Russell, 1860. In possession of Lady Agatha Russell, who kindly allowed me to consult them.

Schwabe MSS. = Papers of late Mrs. Schwabe, kindly lent me by her daughter, Lady Lockwood.

1. Medici's list of arms brought by *Queen of England* to Messina.
2. De Rohan's letter *re* formation of British Legion.
3. Madame Mario's account of hospitals at Caserta.
4. Garibaldi's letter to Bixio from Caprera, Nov. 10, 1860.

Taylor MSS. = Mazzini's letters to his English friends the Taylors.
(In possession of Mrs. Osler, Birmingham, and her uncle, Mr. Malleson, who kindly lent me copies.)

2. MSS. IN PUBLIC LIBRARIES, ETC.

I. BOLOGNA MSS. (MUSEO RISORGIMENTO).

Comitato di provvedimento in Bologna per soccorsi a Garibaldi.
(Lists, accounts, and correspondence, showing great activity and large number of volunteers raised in Bologna.)

Bixio MS. = Letter to his wife from Villa San Giovanni. 24 agosto, 1860.

II. CREMONA MSS.

Cremona MSS. = MSS. in the Museum of Cremona, which Prof. Manacorda kindly had copied for me.
(Memoirs and letters from the front, by Cremonese volunteers with Garibaldi, 1860; business letters of Cosenz and Bertani about enlistments at Cremona.)

III. GENOA MSS.

Bibl. Civ. = *Biblioteca Civica.*

MSS. Socc. Gar. = *Soccorso a Garibaldi. Genova. Bibl. civ. D bis.* 4. 4. 14.

Türr MS. = Letters of Türr to his friend Gen. Baja, written in last ten years of his life, about Cajazzo and other affairs of 1860. University Library, Genoa. [The original of the *Bixio MS.* are also kept here: but in these volumes I have referred to the MS. copies of the *Bixio MS.* at Bologna.]

IV. LONDON MS.

F. O. = Foreign Office Papers (MS.) in Record Office.

(The parts of the correspondence for Sardinia, Rome, and Sicily (= Naples) which were not printed and published in *Br. Parl. Papers* (*q.v.*), 1860-1861, I have been allowed to study by the kind permission of the Foreign Office.)

V. MILAN MSS.

The following important MSS. are kept in the Museo del Risorgimento, in the Castello, in the famous Archivio Bertani, on which see Luzio's article, *Corr. Sera.* March 1, 1910.

A. B. = *Archivio Bertani* (*secondo elenco*).

A. B., Plichi A. B. C. D. E. = *Autografi. Celebrità.*

Plico B. sec. C.　Dolfi's Letters.

Plico B. sec. G.　Reports from conspirators in the Marches.

Plico B. sec. H.　*No.* 1, Buschi's letter.

A. B., Plico XII. No. 13.　Dossier of offers of service, and replies, May, 1860.

Nos. 24, 29, 31, 41, 42, 44 are interesting.

No. 38.　Preparations for insurrection on mainland of Naples, June, 1860.

A. B., Plico XIII. May, 1860.　133 letters, mostly of application to join Garibaldi.

A. B., Plico XIV. June, 1860.　Over 300 letters, *ditto.*

A. B., Plico XV. July, 1860.　Numerous letters, *ditto.*

(The subsequent innumerable *plichi* are chiefly the accounts, receipts, orders, and all the business papers of Bertani's *Cassa Centrale* of 1860.

Cosenz MS. = Dossier of letters by General Cosenz. Letters of 1860 to Eleuterio Pagliano, about preparations for the expeditions.

Bronzetti MS. = Dossier of Narciso and Pilade Bronzetti, 1859-1860.

　　1. Letter of Giovanni Veneziani to Eleuterio Pagliano about Milazzo, 27 Luglio, 1860.

　　2. Letter (1905) and Discorso (1885) on Castel Morrone by G. C. Ferrario, one of the survivors.

　　3. Letter of Cosenz to Oreste Bronzetti, the third brother, about his good conduct at Milazzo.

Bruzzesi MS.　1. *Notebook.*　Giacinto Bruzzeti's notebook of 1860. Diary in ink, from Quarto to crossing of straits (May to Aug.), filled in only occasionally and slightly except after arrival at Faro, when it is fuller. Contains also a more detailed account of voyage of Thousand and landing at Marsala, in pencil, but done, as stated, some time after the event.

　　2. *Pencil and pen jottings* on little slips of paper of the voyage and Marsala, evidently done on spot. Accurate sketch-map of hills round Calatafimi and battle. Jottings about surrender of Milazzo.

BIBLIOGRAPHY

3. *Elenco dei Morti nella battaglia di Milazzo.*

4. *Maps* of Milazzo and Volturno battle-fields, latter on a large scale and showing batteries.

5. *Col. Giacinto Bruzzesi's military correspondence* for Sept. to Dec. 1860.

VI. PALERMO MSS.

Br. Cons. MS. = Papers of the British Consulate, Palermo, 1860. Official letters of Mr. Goodwin to the British Minister at Naples, including his '*Political Journal*' from May 19, 1860, onwards. Another copy of Mr. Goodwin's political journal will be found *sub loc.* in the F. O. Papers, Record Office, London, as Elliot forwarded copies to Russell.

VII. ROME MSS.

Savi MS. = Manuscript diary of Savi, a Genovese of the Thousand, kept on the spot during the campaign, on separate sheets of paper of different colours and sizes. Signor Menghini kindly allowed me to use this important authority. For Genoese Carabineers at Milazzo and Volturno.

Br. Cons. Rome = British Consulate Rome, *Letter Book* of 1860-1872.

(Letters of the Consul Newton to Lord John Russell, 1860, which I was kindly invited to consult by Sir Rennell Rodd, with the permission of the Foreign Office. Contains a good deal of value about the Castelfidardo campaign, including in a letter of Oct. 16 two enclosures), *viz.* :—

* 1. Letter from a German officer in the Papal service describing Castelfidardo, in which he took part.

* 2. Letter from a person resident near Ancona who was present at the siege and collected many facts about the battle of Castelfidardo from Papal officers and others present.

MS. Mazz. Letters, V. E. = Unpublished letters of Mazzini, 1859-1860, in the Vitt. Em. Rome.

IV. NOTES OF CONVERSATIONS

In studying the history of fifty years ago, an important source ot evidence besides books and MSS. is the oral testimony of survivors and of those who knew the actors well. I have not neglected this source, and have made it a practice to take down notes on the spot during the conversation, and if necessary to write the notes out again carefully within twenty-four hours afterwards.

In the following list of 'Conversations' (*Conv.*), this practice has in each case been adhered to, and I have notes taken at the time to show for every conversation used as evidence. In this list I have not put down my conversations with modern historians, such as Signori Luzio, De Cesare, and Paolucci, useful as those have been to me, but have confined the list to actors in or witnesses of the events related.

Conv. Brown Young = Notes from conversation with (Capt.) Brown Young, English officer of Garibaldi's army in the campaign on the Volturno.

Con. Cadolini = Notes of conversation with Senator G. Cadolini (veteran of 1849, '59, '60, and '66).

Conv. Canzio = Notes of conversations with the late General Canzio, one of the Thousand, Garibaldi's son-in-law (see also *Canzio MS.* above).

Conv. Capurro = Notes of conversation with Gio. Batt. Capurro of Genoa, one of the Thousand.

Conv. Deane = Notes of conversation with Capt. Deane, R.N. (retired Commander, 1894), was serving on board H.M.S. *Agamemnon* in 1860.

Conv. Dolmage = Notes of conversations with Mr. J. A. Dolmage, an officer of the British Army who was on leave from his regiment and travelling in Sicily in 1860. He joined Garibaldi's forces at Palermo in June and was, at first, attached unofficially to Türr's brigade. He was present at nearly all the actions fought during the campaign, and since he enjoyed the personal friendship of Garibaldi and of many of his officers, his information is interesting and important.

Conv. Ellis = Notes of conversation with Mr. H. Ellis of British Legion.

Conv. Fazzari = Notes of conversations with the late Achille Fazzari of Staletti, Calabrian leader of 1860 and friend of Garibaldi.

Conv. Goodall = Notes of conversation with Mr. G. Goodall.

(Valuable for crossing of Straits by Cosenz' expedition and action in Solano village in which Mr. Goodall took part.)

Conv. Mainoni = Notes of conversation with General Mainoni d'Intignano of the regular Piedmontese army, 1860.

Conv. Missori = Notes of conversation with Giuseppe Missori, a year before he died.

Conv. Patterson = Notes of conversations with Mr. A. B. Patterson of Dunne's regiment at Milazzo, and subsequently of the British I.C.S.

Conv. Pedotti = Notes of conversation with Senator General Pedotti, formerly of Pianciani's expedition, Türr's Division. Took prominent part on Sept. 19 before Capua, and fought on Oct. 1. Long afterwards became Italian Minister of War.

Conv. Primerano = Notes of conversation with the late Senator General Primerano (Captain in the Neapolitan army, 1860).

Conv. Sclavo = Notes of conversation with Col. Sclavo (Francesco), veteran of Milazzo, S. Giovanni, Arches of the Valley, etc.

Conv. Sivelli = Notes of conversation with Signor Egisto Sivelli, one of Thousand; after Palermo, fought in Dunne's regiment at Milazzo.

Conv. Tedaldi = Notes of conversation with Col. Cav. Fr. Tedaldi, Sicilian who went through the whole campaign.

Conv. Visconti Venosta = Notes of conversation with Marchese Emilio Visconti Venosta, sent by Cavour on unofficial mission to Naples, July to Sept. 1860.

V. ITALIAN AND ENGLISH POETRY

Garibaldi (Versi e prose). Giosuè Carducci.
Rapsodie Garibaldina. II. Giovanni Marradi.
La Notte di Caprera. Gabriele D'Annunzio.
Poems before Congress. Last Poems (1862). Mrs. Browning.
Aspromonte and other Poems. Mrs. Hamilton King.
Songs before Sunrise. Algernon Swinburne.

ADDENDA TO THE BIBLIOGRAPHY

Cadolini Mem. = Cadolini (Senatore G.).
Memorie del risorgimento. 1911.
Curàtolo = Curàtolo (G. E.) *Garibaldi, Vittorio Emanuele, Cavour.* 1911.

MAP II.

INDEX

380 GARIBALDI AND THE MAKING OF ITALY

Naples, 165; rally of reactionaries to, 196; in Volturno battle, 242; takes refuge in Rome, 259; fosters "brigandage" in the Abruzzi, 259

Franklin, 48, 126-7

GAETA:
Advantages of, as base of operation, 172, 196
Siege of, 276-7 *and notes*
Gaeta battalion, 78, 82
Gagliardi, Marquis, 143
Gallenga, —, 160, 163, 338-40
Gallotti, Gen., 128-9, 131
Garibaldi, Gen. Giuseppe:
Career, chronological sequence of— attacked by La Farina, 50; deports La Farina, 57-8; refuses to surrender Mazzini, 51; opposes premature annexation of Sicily, 53, 55-6; life in the Observatory, 60; civil policy in Sicily, 62; military disposition of columns, 65, 67; sets out for Milazzo, 78; battle of Milazzo, 83-8; afterwards, 90; accepts Bosco's capitulation, 94; disgraces him for treachery, 95-6; at Milazzo Castle, 96; Count Litta's mission to, 101-3; at the Straits, 109-11, 119; guides force for attack of Altifiumara, 112; receives secret message through Trecchi, 116 *and note* [2]; accompanies Bertani to Golfo degli Aranci, 120; at Caprera, 121; masking movements, 125; repairs to the *Franklin*, 126; the crossing, 127; taking of Reggio, 129-31; joins Cosenz, 133; at Campo Calabrese, 133; occupies Cannitello, 136; addresses surrendered Neapolitan troops, 137; starts for Naples, 138; advances against Vial, 141; at Nicotera, 142; demands Ghio's unconditional surrender, 142 *and note*, 144 *and note* [2]; at Mileto, 142-3; reception at Monteleone, 143; in pursuit of Ghio, 144-8; hurries on towards Naples, 150 ff.; sends Türr to command Bertani's 1500, 153; turns off towards Sapri, 156; decision at Il Fortino, 158-9; approves Peard's proceedings, 163; met by Ashley, 164; arrival at Salerno, 164-5; exchange of telegrams with Don Liborio, 177; entrains at Vietri, 178; the journey, 179-80 *and note* [2]; arrival at Naples, 181-5 *and note*;

bluffs commandant of S. Elmo, 186; hands over fleet to Victor Emmanuel, 188; moderate policy in Naples, 188; letters to, advising against attack on Rome, 190; interview with Mundy and Elliot, 190; requests dismissal of Cavour, 191 *and note* [5]; administrative blunders in Naples, 194-5; at Caserta, 200-1; sends Csufady to divert Bourbon attention, 228; visit to Palermo (Sept. 16), 229, 230; censures Türr, 230; dispositions for battle of the Volturno, 234 *note* [1], 235-6; eve of the battle, 239; in the battle—at Santa Maria, 240; ambushed, 241; at Sant' Angelo, 241-2; on Monte Tifata, 242; cries "Victory!" 242; back at Santa Maria, 250; leads final onslaught, 251-2; surrounds Ruiz' 2,000, 253-4; degrades Milanese officers, 246; despatches Isernia expedition, 259; letter to Victor Emmanuel (Oct. 4), 262; the plebiscite controversy, 265-6; sets out to meet Victor Emmanuel, 269; the meeting, 271, 272 *note*; tells Jessie Mario of the Royal decree, 272; generous arrangements with Della Rocca, 274; visited by Della Rocca when ill at Caserta, 275; claims as to officers' rank, 281 *note* [1], 284; resigns dictatorship, 284; publishes a royalist rallying call, 284; farewell visit to Adm. Mundy, 285-6; returns to Caprera, 286-7; attempted march on Rome (1862), 288-9; visit to England, 289-90; Trentine Alps campaign, 291; defeated at Mentana, 292; aids France in war of 1870, 292-3; death of, 293-4
Characteristics of:
Care for his wounded, 255
Frugality, 62-3
Generosity, 274, 279
Humanity, 297
Loyalty, 51, 226, 284-5
Military genius, 236
Patriotism, 188-9, 226, 297
Personal magnetism, 83, 85, 237, 242, 257
Simplicity, 57, 60
Enthusiasm for, 79, 235 *note* [4], 255-6
Estimate of, 296-7; by Neapolitan troops, 135; by Gladstone, 290-1; by Bruzzesi, 291 *note*; by Tennyson, 290 *and note*

388   GARIBALDI AND THE MAKING OF ITALY

Sapri (*continued*) :
  Pisacane's expedition to, survivors of, 61-2
  Site and scenery of, 156-7
  Türr's arrival at, 153
Sardinia :
  Cession of, to France, fears regarding, 30
  Golfo degli Aranci, 119-21
Savi, 45 *note* [1]
Savio, Alfredo, 241
Savio, Emilio, 241
Savoy, tricolour flag of, 15 *note* [1]
Scelzi, —, 65
Schmidt, —,218
Scilla, surrender of castle on rock of, 138
Sclavo quoted, 245 *note* [2]
Scotti, Gen., 268, 338 *note*, 339
Settembrini, Raffaele, 21
Settimo, Ruggiero, 59
Shaftesbury, Lord, letter of, to Garibaldi, 190 *and note* [2]
Sicilians :
  Annexation by Piedmont, attitude towards, *see under* Sicily
  Characteristics of, 63
  Italian unity, attitude towards, 115
  Place-hunting by, 62
  Troops, estimate of, 63-4. (*See also* Cacciatori d'Etna *and* Dunne's "English regiment")
Sicily :
  Annexation of, by Piedmont, suggested :
    Elliot and Hudson finally in favour of, 308-9
    Garibaldi's decision against, at Il Fortino, 158-9
    Mordini's advocacy of, 230
    Plebiscite or assembly controversy, 263-6
    Premature efforts for, 52-6
    Sicilians' attitude towards, 54-5 ; their demand for, 229
  Brigandage stamped out in, 295
  Church in, attitude of, to Garibaldi, 58-9
  Condition of, under Garibaldi's dictatorship, 323-5
  Conscription in, Garibaldi's edict for, 63
  Funds contributed by, towards liberation of Naples, 321
  Garibaldini garrison in, 198
  Home rule proposed for, 13 ; granted, 15
  Recruits from, 67 *note*, 68
  Savoyard Prince for, suggestion as to, 28-9, 306, 308, 309-11

Sicily (*continued*) :
  Squadre :
    Arms of, 327
    Disbandment of, 63, 65
Simonetta's Lombards :
  Medici's column including, 74
  Milazzo, at, 82, 84
Sirtori, —, against attack on Rome, 192 ; Chief of the Staff, 236 ; assists Della Rocca, 274-5 ; on military commission for selecting Garibaldini officers for royal service, 281 ; mentioned, 102, 144
Solano, 113, 132
Solaroli, Gen., 313
Soveria-Mannelli, Ghio's capitulation at, 147-9
Spaventa, Silvio, 22
Specchi, —, 84
Spezzano Albanese, 154
Spinelli, —, ministry formed by, 16
Stagnetti, —, 181 *note* [2]
Stocco, Francesco, feudal devotion to, 140 ; strength of forces with, 141 *and note* [2]; allows Ghio's men to pass, 144 ; at Soveria, 148 ; otherwise mentioned, 115, 253, 259
Styles, —, 98
Sutherland, Duchess of, 290
Swiss mercenaries in Neapolitan army, 245-6, 250 *note*
Sybaris, plain of, 154
Syracuse, strength of Bourbon troops in, 69
Syracuse, Count of, relations of, with Don Liborio, 167 ; public letter from, to King Francis, 171
Syracuse, Duke of (Philippe Egalité), 14

Tabacchi, —, 239, 242
Talleyrand, M. de, 26
Taormina rock, passage from, 126-7
Taylor, Mrs., Mazzini's letter to, quoted, 193
Tennyson's estimate of Garibaldi, 290 *and note*
Thayer's *Life of Cavour*, 288 *note*
Thouvenel, L., 11, 215 ; cited, 206 *and note*, 212 *note* [1]
Times—extract reprinted from, 296 *note* ; cited, 329
Tiriolo, 146
Torino, 126-7
Torre Cavallo fort, 111 ; surrender of, to Garibaldi, 138
Totti, —, 57
Trani, Count, 242
Trapani, Count, 243 ; plot of, 173, 312
Trecchi, —, 102, 191 *note* [5]; secret message conveyed by, 116 *and note* [2]

PRINTED BY J. AND J. GRAY, EDINBURGH

171 D